W9-CJF-918

Religion and Human Rights
Conflict or Convergence

∼

Interreligious Center on Public Life

Edited with an Introduction by
Adam B. Seligman

Religion and Human Rights
Conflict or Convergence

~

Interreligious Center on Public Life

Edited with an Introduction by
Adam B. Seligman

~

Foreword by
Sanford Seltzer

Preface by
David M. Gordis

Analysis and Comments by

Shlomo Fischer

Suzanne Last Stone

Riffat Hassan

Khaleel Mohammed

Max L. Stackhouse

John Clayton

ISBN 1-884186-29-7

 Hollis Publishing Company
95 Runnells Bridge Road, Hollis, NH 03049
(t) 603.889.4500 (f) 603.889.6551
books@hollispublishing.com

Printed in the United States of America.

Contents

Notes on Contributors

John Clayton, who passed away in September 2003, was Professor and Chair of Religion at Boston University. Before coming to Boston he was Professor and Chair at the University of Lancaster in the United Kingdom. He was a world-respected philosopher of religion with publications in most European languages.

Shlomo Fischer is Founder and Director of Yesodot Center for Torah and Democracy in Jerusalem. He has published numerous textbooks in Jewish history and articles on historical and contemporary aspects of Zionism and Jewish thought. He teaches at the Hebrew University and Beit Morasha.

David M. Gordis is President of Hebrew College and Founding Director of the National Center for Jewish Policy Studies. His articles and essays have appeared in numerous publications.

Riffat Hassan is Professor of Islamic Thought at the University of Kentucky, Louisville. She has written widely on issues of women and Islam and participated in many religious and inter-religious dialogues.

Khaleel Mohammed is Assistant Professor of Religion at San Diego State University and of its University Center for Arabic and Islamic Studies. He has published widely in the fields of Islamic law and culture.

Adam B. Seligman is Professor of Religion at Boston University and Senior Scholar for Human Rights at the InterReligious Center on Human Rights. He has published widely in the fields of political and sociological theory.

Sanford Seltzer is Director of the Interreligious Center on Public Life and Rabbi of Congregation Ohabei Sholom, Brookline, Massachusetts.

Max L. Stackhouse is Stephen Colwell Professor of Christian Ethics at Princeton Theological Seminary. He has published many books and articles in this and cognate fields.

Suzanne Last Stone is Professor of Law at Cardozo School of Law of the Yeshiva University, where she directs the Program in Jewish Law and Interdisciplinary Studies. She has published widely in the fields of Jewish religious thought and contemporary legal theories.

Foreword

The Interreligious Center on Public Life is pleased to present this volume of selected papers by distinguished scholars who participated in the Center's Conference on Sources of Human Rights: Religion's Role in Defining Human Dignity, which was held in October 2002. The Center is most appreciative of the support of its partners in this venture, The Pew Forum on Religion and Public Life and The Toleration Project at Boston University, without whose cooperation the conference would not have been possible.

It is our hope that these essays will deepen the reader's awareness of the complexities inherent in the ongoing struggle for human rights even as they provide insights into the perspectives of the three Abrahamic faith traditions and their historic pursuit of this ideal. Human dignity is a pervasive theme throughout the sacred literature of all faiths as reflected in the Decalogue, the Holiness Code of Leviticus, the works of the Literary Prophets of Israel, the demands of the Social Gospels, the Sermon on the Mount and the teachings of Mohammed.

Indisputably much of the progress achieved over the centuries leading to the betterment of the human condition has resulted from the inspiration and guidance drawn from these sources. Few if any of formal religion's most ardent critics would contest that reality or deny that the roots of secular aspirations in this regard are based upon religious antecedents. Yet despite these accomplishments, the record of organized religion in furthering understanding and acceptance among peoples has been less than exemplary. All too often religious doctrines have been the incentive rather than the antidote for hatred, persecution and the slaughter of innocents.

Much of this is a consequence of those strands within Judaism, Christianity and Islam, either taken directly from scriptural passages or interpreted accordingly, which have characterized nonbelievers and dissidents as the "other" and subjected them to all manner of disenfranchisement. Pejorative references in the

Hebrew Bible to the Canaanites and Moabites and in the New Testament to Jews, the zeal of the Crusades and the Inquisition, the excesses of the Protestant Reformation and Counter Reformation, and the classification and maltreatment of non-Muslims as infidels on the part of Islamic exegetes are all cases on point.

Such mixed and conflicting messages have made the struggle for human rights no less a daunting challenge for contemporary advocates, secular and religious alike, than it was in previous generations. Events that have ensued in the two years since the conference have dramatically illustrated the interplay of religious and cultural forces in undermining human rights. The war in Iraq with its revelations of the shameful abuse of Iraqi men and women held in the notorious Abu Ghraib prison, where deliberate violations of Islamic custom and practice were coerced among those incarcerated through threats and torture and justified in the name of both democracy and Christian ideals, is an egregious example. No less appalling have been the pronouncements of certain Imams declaring that Americans and other Westerners on Arab soil could be murdered and their bodies mutilated with impunity in the name of Allah.

The parameters of what once were considered to be acceptable norms for the conduct of war no longer apply. Ironically, even as the former leaders of Serbia are being tried for crimes against humanity perpetrated during the recent conflict in the Balkans and calls resound for Saddam Hussein to be prosecuted as a war criminal, jurists and ethicists are now debating what constitutes torture and what forms of physical and psychological pressure are morally justified for the greater good of humanity.

As the dimensions of war assume configurations heretofore unimagined, the role and treatment of civilian populations have come under renewed scrutiny as the old strictures imposed by the Geneva Convention and other international covenants are deemed to be anachronistic. In a world in which the use of weapons of mass destruction is no longer theoretical, the very concept of innocence is now under siege. The need to respond to Cain's outraged retort in the Book of Genesis, "Am I my brother's keeper?", has taken on new urgency.

In 1993, Samuel P. Huntington wrote a controversial article in *Foreign Affairs*, which later was expanded into book form. In contrast to the euphoria engendered in many quarters by what was seen as the imminent advent of a new world order prompted by the demise of the Soviet Empire and the manifold benefits of globalization, his was a far less optimistic prognosis. Huntington foresaw what he termed a forthcoming "clash of civilizations." "The people of different civilizations," he stated, "have different views on the relation between God and man, the individual and the group, the citizen and the state, parents and children, husbands and wives as well as differences over the relative importance of rights and responsibilities, belief and authority."[1]

The impact of globalization, the technological revolution and the miracles of mass and instant communication upon the intersection of diverse cultures is incontrovertible. All have led to the penetration of what were once thought to be impermeable barriers between populations and ideologies. The world has become a far smaller place. But rather than surmounting national, ethnic and sectarian biases, these advances have brought with them an unexpected and jarring reminder of the dissimilarity between the core values of specific societies.

Whatever the linkages forged by the internet and the computer, there are profound conceptual distances between nations, cultures and religions regarding many subjects, not least among them that of human rights, distances which may have well been exacerbated rather than narrowed in the first decade of the 21st century. The awareness that globalization was neither a panacea for solving the social and economic ills of the less fortunate nor an opportunity for the imposition of what some condescendingly believed to be superior American values upon so-called less civilized communities has been a painful discovery. It is one that has yet to be fully comprehended.

One wonders how solid was the common ground enabling the signatories to the UN Declaration on Human Rights to initially ratify that document in 1947, given the diversity of cultural orientations and political allegiances of the delegates. Since that time the ranks of the United Nations have been swelled with a multitude of new nation states, carved from the former empires of Britain, France and other countries of Europe and often born out of revolution and bloodshed.

In no small measure these burgeoning nationalisms were abetted by a long simmering rejection of Western values which, regardless of how beneficial those who introduced said values thought them to be, were often experienced by their

---

1. Samuel P. Huntington, 2003. The Clash Of Civilizations, *Foreign Affairs*, p. 26.

recipients as forms of oppression, as simply another extension of the "white man's burden." Now that these new nations have become part of the world order, renewed commitments to the ideal of human rights are again imperative. The Rwandan genocide, racial discord in Zimbabwe, ethnic conflict in Congo and Sierra Leone—these are clear indications of how desperate is that need.

Over the years it has been fashionable to focus upon the inconsistencies and contradictions of the great religions in their defense of human rights. But that burden of failure is hardly theirs alone to shoulder. The Enlightenment has been hailed as that illustrious period of history in which the basic philosophical foundations for human rights were established. The term itself is noteworthy for what it denotes. It was apparently coined by Immanuel Kant in tribute to the outspoken efforts of the 18th-century French *philosophes*, most notably Voltaire, in behalf of freedom and equality.[2]

Still, Voltaire and numerous other advocates of human rights in the 18th century and later were unanimous in their rejection of the Jews as deserving recipients of these prerogatives. "This nation," wrote Voltaire in words that were destined to become part of the legacy of Nazism, "is in many respects the most detestable ever to have sullied the earth."[3] They were doomed to remain beyond the pale of redemption unless they voluntarily abandoned their faith, surrendered their identities and embraced Christianity. Even Spinoza's writings were not to escape the taint of his Jewish ancestry, which made them suspect despite his atheism.

Those espousing such views were unmoved by the obvious dissonance of their positions. One might have even thought that the implications of such documented hypocrisy would have had a sobering effect upon the attitudes and policies of subsequent generations of churchmen, monarchs or legislative bodies as they determined the fates of various minorities and certainly of Jews within their borders. But it was not to be. More often than not, the Jew remained a marginal figure until at last the world stood by mutely as millions went to their deaths in Auschwitz and Buchenwald.

---

2. Harold J. Berman, 2003. *Law And Revolution II*, Belknap Press, Cambridge, p 11.

3. Adam Sutcliffe, 2003. *Judaism And Enlightenment*, Cambridge University Press, p. 23.

There exists a fascinating symmetry that is frequently overlooked when invidious comparisons are made, as they often are, between the status of non-Muslims, Christians and Jews as Dhimmi in Islamic States and the manner in which the rights of citizenship were accorded in Western countries. It was standard practice in pre-Enlightenment Europe and even for lengthy periods thereafter for civil liberties to be determined by one's correct religious identity as specified by the ruling monarch and the established church. Such restrictions—which depending upon the circumstances were not only endured by Jews but by Protestants and Catholics as well—are not all that dissimilar from those imposed in the Islamic world, our predilection to ignore those parallels notwithstanding.

The deprivation of the rights of French Huguenots by Louis XIV's revocation of the Edict of Nantes is one of many instances. Nor are the repeated claims of those voices who throughout American history including the present have declared that America is a Christian country wholly without foundation. Issues affecting the separation of church and state, the secular and the religious in the United States, are rooted in many rancorous debates in Colonial America. They remain far more complex than what is generally presumed and are still not fully resolved.[4]

In publishing this volume, the Interreligious Center on Public Life affirms its commitment to the furtherance of human rights and its unfaltering faith in the perseverance of the human spirit. It reasserts its belief in the positive role that religious doctrines and institutions can and must play in the enhancement of human dignity and the building of a world in which peace, justice and prosperity will be the inalienable inheritance of everyone.

Sanford Seltzer
Director
Interreligious Center on Public Life

---

[4]. For a through analysis see Philip Hamburger, 2002. *Separation of Church and State*, Harvard University Press, Cambridge.

Preface

This small volume represents the first book-sized contribution to public discourse by the Interreligious Center on Public Life, a joint project of the Andover Newton Theological School and Hebrew College, contiguous neighbors in Newton Centre, Massachusetts.

Predictions to the contrary notwithstanding, national, religious and ethnic diversity appear to be here to stay. Whether viewed as utopian or dystopian, expectations of the withering away of cultural and religious differences in an "enlightened" world have proved to be totally unfulfilled. In our contemporary world, we are witness to the calamitous results of intergroup strife, national, religious and ethnic. Whatever their contributions in providing a foundation for human rights and respect for the "other," religious traditions both historically and in our contemporary world certainly contribute to those calamitous results. In its modest way, the ICPL hopes to contribute to intergroup healing and to participate in shaping new intergroup relationships, drawing on the sources of our major religious traditions, so often guilty of contributing to that strife rather than helping to alleviate it.

Underlying the papers in this collection—and, in fact, the Center's work and mission—are a series of questions and principles:

1. Must diversity be a challenge and a generator of tension and bloodshed, or can it become a source of blessing and "repair"?

2. Can human rights discourse reach across particular religious and national boundaries, enriching the conversation without requiring a homogenization and leading to the abandonment of particularistic traditions?

3. How does one uncover sources for positive intergroup relations in our traditions and find ways of dealing with "difficult" or troubling sources, to be found in each of our religious traditions?

4. In the face of egregious violations of human rights and generally accepted principles of human dignity by those who passionately profess their religious commitment, how does one bridge the textual and theoretical on the one hand, and catastrophic reality on the other, canonical versus phenomenological?

The Interreligious Center does not presume to have answers to these questions, but was founded on the assertion that diversity of religious tradition, culture and nationality can enrich the experience of being human. We can learn from difference and be enhanced by it. We can find ways of talking to one another in which a process of teaching and learning goes on, the product of which is richer and more powerful discourse and commitment to those things which we share as well as that which characterizes our difference. To accomplish this, we need to speak openly and honestly with one another and develop strategies for circumventing the authority of texts which have been used to undermine the possibilities of relating to each other positively and to assert the authority of those texts which contribute to the building of positive discourse and a better world. And, together, the Center represents a call to brothers and sisters in all our religious communities to realize a vision of human relationships which draws on the best of our traditions by formulating an alternative to that put forward by those who seek to preempt religious traditions to destroy a sense of respect and common purpose among all people.

This book, whose origin was a conference on Religion and Human Dignity held on the campuses of Andover Newton and Hebrew College, seeks to contribute to advancing those purposes of the ICPL. The program of the ICPL is relatively modest in extent but it is broad in its ambition and scope. As co-sponsor of the International Summer School on Religion and Public Policy, the Center seeks to share its vision and leverage its resources. The Center aspires to expand its program of research, deliberation, public conferences and publications in the months and years ahead. We hope that you will find the present volume interesting and stimulating, and that it will lead you to take a further interest in our work and join us in our efforts.

David M. Gordis
President, Hebrew College
Founding Director, National Center for Jewish Policy Studies

Introduction

Adam B. Seligman

More and more policy makers, religious leaders and concerned citizens are coming to realize that the challenge of tolerance, mutual recognition and human rights, especially at the point of its intersection with religious beliefs and practices, is one of the critical issues of our times. Globalization has meant a higher degree of interaction with people and civilizations who are different, who are "other." Many of the burning political issues of our time, from the Balkan Wars of 1992–1995 to the continuing crises in the Middle East and the tensions on the Indian subcontinent, to the role of Muslim immigrants in Western Europe, all turn on issues of religion and rights.

Indeed, in some areas, religion has emerged as a new and potent element in long-standing ethnic and national conflicts. This has been the case in Indonesia, in parts of Africa, in the Balkans and of course in many parts of the Middle East. A particularly troublesome case of this is in the conflict between the State of Israel and the Palestinian people. Over the course of its many decades, the conflict between Israel and the Palestinians has taken many forms: from inter-ethnic, to inter-state to again, inter-ethnic conflicts. On the whole and until relatively recently it has not taken an explicit or unambiguous religious dimension, though such dimensions were of course present and for some, on both sides, do in fact define the terms of conflict. The rise of Gush Emunim in Israel after the 1973 War and the more recent increase in the strength of Hamas within the Muslim population are of course indications of such religious framing of the conflict—but also reminders of how circumscribed that idiom has been, and how strongly the conflict has remained rooted in a politics of simple interests and conflicts of interests rather than of ultimate religious truth claims—between which, we should recall, little compromise is possible. It is therefore both tragic and ironic that at the very historical juncture when some form of settlement appears on the horizon, religious arguments are gaining currency making compromise and understanding ever so much more difficult and ever perhaps unattainable.

An awareness of the importance of these issues can be ascertained in a grow ing allocation of funds and programs dealing with the topics of religion and o: tolerance. A few examples will suffice to illustrate this trend: The Unite Nations organized a conference of world religious leaders for a millennial sum mit in the summer of the year 2000 on the role that religions could play i peacekeeping worldwide. The Ford Foundation has recently added religion t its portfolio of programs. Pew Charitable Trust is funding the establishment o centers dedicated to excellence in the study of religion. The United Nations ha established programs dedicated to "Tolerance in Education" and the Deutsch Bank is exploring these themes in its fund-giving programs. Even the Unite States military is contracting out for programs to teach tolerance between dif ferent religious communities. There is thus a wide appreciation among polic makers, religious leaders and concerned congregants in the multiple and divers religious communities of this country and worldwide, of the need to addres these issues from a new perspective. Pope John Paul II's visit to Jerusalem an such statements as *Dabru Emet: A Jewish Statement of Christians and Chris tianity* are but small illustrations of this trend. There is—not to put too fine point on it—a growing awareness that one cannot argue Thomas Jefferson wit either the Muslim *ulema* or the Orthodox Rabbinate in Israel. Other bases an arguments for pluralism and mutual recognition must be found. The search fo these alternative arguments or resources can be found today within almost a Christian Churches and as well as within synagogues and mosques in man parts of the globe.

Human Rights and Religion

This is a significant change in perception, for modern polities have more or les defined social life in terms of a rights-based discourse of autonomous, indivi ual selves, bearers of certain inalienable rights, acting out their interests in neutral public square. However, it is precisely such a rights-based foundatio for society that has met with opposition in many parts of the world where ide of selfhood do not correspond to Western models and democratic imperative Indeed, the challenge of squaring a global rights-based civilizational discour:

with local cultural reasoning, whether predicated on the law of the Shariah or on Jewish halacha, is proving a formidable challenge to those involved.[1] As the Foreign Minister of the Taliban in Afghanistan reportedly said: "We believe we are actually here to serve human rights, but there is a slight difference on the definition of these rights. We believe in rights according to Islam, and if anybody is trying to impose their definition of the human rights on us, they will be badly mistaken because this world is not a world of one culture or one religion."[2] One of the greatest challenges facing those concerned with human rights in today's world is thus of articulating a position of universal and absolute human rights and, at the same time, of respect and positive valuation of local cultures, mores and religious identities.

To many, arguments on the universal and absolute nature of human rights are an almost religious idea. For precisely what makes human rights inviolable and sacrosanct, what removes them from the contingencies of political calculation and decisions based on expediency or conflicts between incommensurate goods should be their religious basis or foundation. What is absolute must be that which is, or linked to that which is, incontrovertibly Other. If not, the absoluteness will always be mediated only in nature, always contingent only on the play of forces, passions or calculations that make up our lot as human beings. To make an argument for the absoluteness of human rights, as for their universal applicability, beyond the play of ethnic, national and cultural boundaries and preferences, is to make a claim to a universal truth (akin to those of geometry) whose veracity is independent of any context and material condition. Such claims, in the ethical realm, are seen by many to be religious in nature.

However, making absolute and universal religious claims does often involve us in a stance of intolerance toward local cultures and particular identities that do not necessarily adhere to our universal and absolute beliefs. The history of many religions, not least being Christianity, is replete with examples of this intolerance to those others not willing to recognize its own universal truth claims. Such a stance of intolerance is, however, unacceptable in today's pluralistic and diverse world.

Lindholm, Tore, and Kari Vogt. 1993. *Islamic Law Reform and Human Rights*. Copenhagen: Nordic Human Rights Publication.

2001. *New York Times*, Friday September 7, A9.

This is a contradiction to which all those concerned with both issues of human rights as well as a valuation of diverse religious identities, commitments and desiderata must recognize. All too often Western ideas of the universality of human rights have run aground on the particularity of local practices and prohibitions. The debates in France over the wearing of the *foulard* in state schools, or in Milton-Keynes England on separate schools for boys and girls in all-Muslim communities, bear eloquent witness to the complexities of some of these issues.

Moreover, it must be acknowledged that certain actions that many in the West see as discriminatory and oppressive are viewed in a very different light by their practitioners. Thus, for example, the case of veiling: in many countries in the Middle East, as in Turkey, it is a practice sometimes willingly embraced by women (often daughters of an earlier generation of secularizing elites) as protest against the homogenization of culture and life-world represented by Western ideas and norms.

Issues revolving around the status of women are, however, only the most visible of an array of problems in this area. The very definition of the public square, or public realm, as a neutral arena with open access to all is a similarly contested issue. We may recall the acts of ultra-Orthodox Jews in Jerusalem some years ago who undertook a campaign of fire-bombing bus stations where advertisements offensive to their religious sensibilities were displayed. Indeed, it is not all that clear that the idea of the public arena or public sphere has the same resonances and meanings, let alone legal status, in other cultures as it does in the West (and generally in societies drawing on the Roman legal tradition).

What is true for the public sphere is true for the community and for the individual social actor. The problems arising from the differing definitions of these core coordinates of social life are, moreover, far from academic. How, for example, does one mediate between the rights of individuals and the rights of groups?[4] This is an issue much debated in Canada, in respect not only of French

---

3. Interesting comparisons can be drawn for example between the definition of res publica in the Western legal tradition and, in the Jewish tradition, the idea of reshut ha'rabim (public sphere) on the one hand and that of parhesia on the other. See Fischer, Shlomo. 1992. Reshut Ha Rasim Parhenia V'Shuk. *Studio* 37:50–51, 60.

4. For further perspectives on this, see Kymlicka, Will. 2000. *Politics in the Vernacular: Nationalism Multiculturalism, and Citizenship*. Oxford: Oxford University Press.

peakers (and English speakers) in Province Quebec, but of indigenous cultures
nd their protection. It is, similarly, a central issue in the politics of India where
engalis and Gujaratis ethnicities and Sikh, Khasmiris and Hindu nations strug-
le for primacy in the public sphere. Or, to take another example, what are the
ights and obligations of the family vis-à-vis the individual and of the individ-
al to the family? Indeed, the very legal status of the family is a much contested
nd differentially defined entity across different cultures and religious tradi-
ons.[5] And while it is not difficult to condemn "shame killings" out of hand,
s a violation of universal human rights, issues of divorce, education and the
gal status of the extended family are much more complex.

These are but a few examples where contradictory injunctions may be ascer-
ained between a purported standard of universal human rights and the very
iversity of human communities. It would be salutary indeed if all contradic-
ons could be written off as either negligible in nature or resultant from a mis-
ading, mis-interpretation or willful mis-representation (by state elites say) of
cal traditions. Though sometimes this is in fact the case, it is not by any means
ways so, though Western human rights activists often present it in such terms.
eal contradictions and tensions remain that are not always reconcilable.
ometimes, making universal claims does indeed denigrate particular beliefs
d local practices.

With the spread of globalization and the increasing interconnected nature of
e world's population the saliency of these issues only grows from day to day.
o longer are our identities, commitments and responsibilities bounded by the
orders of the nation-state. Global communication and global commerce impli-
te us in the social relations of some of the most far-flung corners of the world.

In many ways and as intimated above, a religious discourse is a uniquely
ivileged site upon which to work through these issues. Religion is after all,
storically, the language of universality par excellence. It was first and fore-
ost within religion where arguments for human dignity and worth were artic-
ated. Paradoxically perhaps, it is also from within religion and religious tra-
tions that many of the contemporary claims for a more relativistic and locally
nsitive approach to human rights are made.

Wikan, Unni. 2000. Citizenship on Trial: Nadia's Case. *Daedalus* 29 (4):55–76.

Moreover, the very paradox within which we all are caught when we argue for the universality of human rights—that we do so, necessarily from within the particularity of a specific language, culture and ethical idiom (indeed as expressed in the very idea of rights)—is one long recognized within religious traditions. Each has, after all, in its own manner had to unite the contradictory injunctions to universalism and particularism which define its very existence. The implications of ethical absoluteness and the dynamics of (local) heterodoxies are thus nothing new to religious thought. From both the universal as well as particularist perspectives then, religion provides a useful language with which to discuss the claims and counterclaims of universal rights (replete with their Western origins) and the way these are refracted in different civilizational contexts. What is, and is not, as it were, translatable and what is lost in translation.

One way to begin such a discussion of the different readings of rights in different traditions as well as of the universal applicability of Western definitions of rights may well be to inquire into the domain assumptions of the religious and rights-based political discourse. For they are not the same. The rights-based discourse is not a religious one, though the ethical claims it makes are universal in nature. Indeed, the modern, secular and democratic idea of rights sits in a very complicated and contradictory relation to its own religious heritage. While rooted, on the one hand, in the traditions of sectarian Protestantism (that is of a very particular Christian tradition defined by beliefs in the inner-light and the privatization of grace), is equally rooted in modern natural law tradition (of Pufendorf, Vattel and Grotius and, most importantly, in the overcoming of religious identities, commitments and desiderata as expressed in such documents as *La declaration du droit de l'homme et du citoyen* and the American Bills of Rights of the different states.

The process and progress of secularization is critical here, for to a great extent most Western ideas of universal human rights rest on a secular view of the individual and of the relations between such individuals in a secularized public sphere. Nineteenth century debates over "the Jewish Question" revolved precisely around this issue.

Moreover, the political and social order in which rights is an organizing category of behavior, reciprocity and action, in which it organizes the standing of social actors to one another and regulates the rules of distributive justice and the provision (even definition) of public goods, is not a religious one. The idea of individuals as bearers of something called *rights* presupposes a very particar understanding and reading of the self essentially as a self-regulating agent. t is a world that values autonomy over heteronomy and envisions social actors s self-contained matrixes of desires who direct their own appetites, desires, assions and interests. This is a vision of an instrumental self acting in the social phere as a utility maximizer.

This view of the autonomous individual as a self-regulating agent, makes for certain politics, or even for a certain philosophical anthropology. The politics calls forth is, in the final analysis, the politics of liberalism—of a principled rticulation of rights over any shared definition of the social good, of the awlesian original position, and the public sphere as a more or less neutral genda where individual interests can be maximized without impinging on the ghts (interests) of others.

In this regard the United Nations Universal Declaration of Human Rights of 948 and the international human rights covenants adopted by the United lations in 1966 as well as subsequent Bills of Rights and Covenants (granting eedom of thought and expression, freedom from arbitrary arrest and torture, eedom of movement and assembly, rights to work at fair wages, protection of e family, adequate standards of living, education and health care) may be seen an extension to the world stage of those three sets of citizenship rights xtended at different times and to different extent to members of European ttional states over the course of the nineteenth and twentieth centuries. As fined by T.H. Marshall these represented the political, civil, and social aspects citizenship: "the civil element is composed of the rights necessary for individ- l freedom—liberty of person, freedom of speech, thought and faith, the right own property and to conclude valid contract, and the right to justice [that is] e right to defend and assert all one's rights on terms of equality with others d by due process of law". The political element comprises "the right to par- ipate in the exercise of political power as a member of the body invested with olitical authority or as an elector of the members of such body". And the cial component includes "the right to a modicum of economic welfare and curity [and the] right to share to the full in the social heritage, and to live the e of a civilized being according to the standards prevailing in society."[6]

Marshall, T.H. 1973. *Class, Citizenship and Social Development*. Westport CT: Greenwood Press. p. 71–72.

Whether the concrete rights of citizenship which are the products of positiv
law can in fact be extrapolated onto the international arenas in such a manne
is of course a critical issue in advocating a position of universal human rights

And it is here that the religious perspective becomes most important–
though ambiguous and complex as well. For while religion does present a uni
versal language, or at least purports to, within which to express fundamenta
idea of human worth (from Israelite lessons on the stranger and fellowmar
through the Sermon on the Mount to Islamic injunctions on the *zakat*) it is
language in which (for all the differences between religions) the individua
appears very differently than in the modern secular language of the rights c
citizen.

For religion is not oriented around the autonomous dictates of a sel
regarding and rights-bearing conscience. Rather, it seeks to define the self a
constituted by heteronymous dictates—as the experience of transcendenc
constitutes an authority quite different from that of the State in whose orb
the individual is seen to exist. The world of the sacred and of religious autho
ity is, by definition, a world marked off from the play of negotiation an
exchange within which social order is defined. The sacred is that which
ineluctably Other, that which cannot be grasped, bartered or exchanged. I
dictates impose obligations that are simply of a different order of experienc
that involve totally different domain assumptions than those encompassed l
the play of reciprocity and autonomy upon which a regime of rights is base
The binding of Isaac is arguably a religious moment of paradigmatic impor
One may look to Kierkegaard for its continuing resonances through the ag
and across religious sensibilities.[7] Yet it sits poorly with any conception c
human or individual rights.

That a contradiction in sensibilities exists here is self-evident. The definitic
of the individual as rights-bearing citizen (on the national or internation
stage) is of a very different nature than the definition of the self within a re
gious idiom. Not however that one position necessarily trumps the other. O
need not draw the conclusion that religious obligations necessarily invalida

---

7. Kierkegaard, Soren. 1954. *Fear and Trembling*. Princeton: Princeton University Press. p. 26–3

individual rights or that human rights necessarily invalidate religious dicta and obligations. As Isaiah Berlin noted long ago, the human condition is one of plural and often irreconcilable goods making equally legitimate demands on us.[8]

Indeed, this plurality exists not only when comparing secular to religious ideas of personhood and community, but among and within the different religious and secular traditions themselves. It is for this very reason that it may prove useful to inquire into the religious idiom for a new or different way of framing the terms of human valuation and worth, one that may well allow a mediation between universal and particular desiderata not always given to the nomenclature of rights.

Thus, for example, the privatization of religious beliefs which provided the basis for that paradigmatic of all modern rights, the "right of conscience" is, itself, very much rooted in the institutionalization of Protestant religiosity. The very circumscription of religious truth claims to the realm of the private rather than of shared, public culture has much to do with the way sectarian Protestantism developed in England and New England in the seventeenth and early eighteenth centuries. The epistemological foundations of this orientation were, in part, laid by John Locke who claimed that since religion was a matter of belief, any coercion of the will would simply not work in enforcing religious conformity—for the structures of belief were not subject to the workings of the will.

While true, such an approach does also indicate its own particular religious assumptions, in its stress on belief as standing at the center of religious concerns, reflecting that is, a very particular type of Protestant religiosity. For while belief cannot be coerced, practice and most especially public practice certainly can. And there are religions where the public practices are a good deal more central than the structures of individual belief systems. If we look to Hinduism, Islam or Judaism we immediately see this to be so. No small number of people continues to be engaged in violent, illegal and often repressive behavior in many parts of the world over issues of religious practice: if coffeehouses can be opened in Jerusalem on the Sabbath, if women must go veiled in public, if they can attend university and so on.

Berlin, Isaiah. 1969. *Four Essays on Liberty*. Oxford: Oxford University Press.

Belief in the unmediated access of the believer to the Deity, the importance of faith and the freedom of conscience all contributed to the growth of toleration in early modern Europe. Eventually, these beliefs led to the secularization of the ideas of inner light or Holy Spirit, the internalization of the idea of grace and, by the eighteenth century, its secularization into more contemporary notions of morality and civic virtue and often romantic nationality as well. Critical here were developments in the thirteen colonies of what became the United States of America. The unique notion of individual rights as expressed in the Bills of Rights of different states was the perceived sources of these rights in Godly dictates rather than in any traditional or customary ideas of inherited privileges. Individual rights and the tolerance that accompanied them were deemed sacred and rooted in the words of the Gospel rather than in the positive law of the State.[9] A direct inheritance of the Puritan migration of the 1630s it is not clear that such an attitude can be generalized to other religious traditions and cultures.

A case in point would be Judaism which while it recognizes individual responsibility and agency does not privilege the type of modern, post-Hobbesian vision of the individual upon which a politics of rights and of liberal tolerance tends to rest. Nor does it share, for obvious historical reasons, the Christian privileging of intentionality and *Innerlischkeit* which provided important foundations for the modern doctrine of rights. Again, then, the presuppositions of individual rights as a precondition for a principled position of pluralism and tolerance may be a difficult position to sustain from a traditional Jewish conception.

More precisely, the philosophical problem of pluralism rests on the analytically prior problem of ethics, that is, on the acceptance of a realm of normative desirable behavior that is independent of the realm of legal injunctions. The separation of ethics from law, of conscience from obligation is central to Christian and most especially to Protestant consciousness and the modes of tolerance predicated on these assumptions. As noted, pluralism is a most American value reflecting this society's roots in seventeenth century sectarian Protestantism and

---

9. This has been the subject of Jellinek's classic analysis: Jellinek, Georg. 1979. *The Declaration the Rights of Man and Citizen: A Contribution to Modern Constitutional History*. Westport Hyperion Press.

the illuminism of the "inner light." From the apostle Paul's rejection of the law as the necessary vehicle of salvation for gentiles to Moses Mendelssohn's exposition on the centrality of law to Judaism, it has always been recognized that what distinguishes Jewish civilization from Christian civilization is precisely this matter of the relation of legal obligations to ethical ones.[10]

All of which brings us back, again and again, to the need to derive arguments for pluralism and recognition of difference on principles independent of a purely rights-based discourse whose preconditions are not shared by all. While sectarian Protestantism may well have shared an "elective affinity" with the idea of individual rights as a component of the autonomous conscience other civilizations developed differently and other arguments must thus be found.

It may indeed prove possible to articulate a position of human rights on assumptions of humankind and of the cosmos other than those of Western liberal civilization. Whether such is possible and what result would indeed be congruent with Western assumptions on rights remains to be seen. The quote quoted above by Taliban Foreign Minister Muttawakil in the matter of human rights shows that this may be a much more difficult task to accomplish than some would suggest.

This of course is not to say that a protection of the individual and of the individual's most elementary political freedoms and social entitlements is impossible from any perspective other than that of a rights based political discourse. The purpose of the present volume is indeed to demonstrate that it is possible to, at the very least, begin such a project of staking out such a claim and defending individual political and social liberties without necessarily (and I stress necessarily) invoking a universal doctrine of rights replete with its very particular philosophical presuppositions and historical trajectory.

What is at stake here is not the possibility of some collective or communal good, some organicist whole that would mediate the individual freedom of the social actor from a communal or communitarian perspective. It is not therefore the response of tradition as a perspective from which to judge and critique the

---

. Mendelssohn, Moses. 1983. *Jerusalem or on Religious Power and Judaism.* Translated by A. Arkush. Hanover, NH: University Press of New England.

modern world (which is what is involved in the "fundamentalist project") that is needed. Rather, what is called for is a whole new approach to the realm of inter-subjective action and interaction. Whether such a project, predicated on religious assumptions, is possible we cannot in fact know. The present volume however seeks to open up this possibility and in so doing to expose a language within which we can speak of tolerance and toleration in an idiom that has thus far remained mute.

To pursue this goal we have brought together half a dozen papers from leading scholars in the realm of ethics, law, and religious thought within the three monotheistic religions. The papers range from those focused more narrowly on the idea of human rights as they appear in the different Abrahamic traditions to disquisitions on alternative principles of mutuality and respect.

Human rights are, after all, a means, or more properly a meta-foundational theory upon which certain derivative principles of selfhood, community, interaction and mutual respect are based. Though often treated as sacrosanct they are but means to the further end of human mutuality, respect and recognition of difference; in the end, a way to live together based on some shared principles of fairness and justice. The following papers explore if indeed they are the only way to organize such shared principles of fairness. Ideas of a universal human dignity and respect, of recognition of difference and of acceptance of the "Other" do not depend solely on secular traditions of human rights. As we learn from the following papers, these ideas are deeply rooted in all of the monotheistic traditions which present their own, independent, particular and unique arguments for human worth and non-coercive relations to the stranger and those others beyond the boundaries of the normative community.

It is very much along such a course of engaging with such "local reasonings" to quote our last contributor, the late John Clayton, that we must pursue that search for a common ground which, while recognizing substantive difference, does not shy away from normative judgments.

Each of the contributions deals with a somewhat different aspect of the above noted themes. Fischer and Stone both engage the Jewish tradition, but from somewhat different perspectives. Fischer's piece analyzes the Biblical and legal concepts of *Kevod Ha'adam, Tzelem Elohim and Kevod Habriot* (that is The Dignity of Man, The Image of God and the Honor of the Fellow-Creature

His paper adumbrates the different implications of these different concepts and relates them to more contemporary notions of human dignity and rights and points out their importance as alternative sources of such ideas not, in themselves, predicated on those ideas of individual autonomy that we so easily assimilate with notions of rights and dignity.

Stone's paper is more concerned with the problems and perspectives Jewish particularism opens up in terms of relations with the other, whether that other be the stranger, the Noahide or the Jewish heretic and sinner. Her paper goes a long way in showing how a substantive communal notion, predicated on the "thick" bonds of God-given commandments, can, nevertheless, accommodate that which is beyond its own normative boundaries and organizing assumptions. While not shying away from the problems that a principled acceptance of modern pluralism does present to the Jewish halachic tradition her argument is central in providing the foundations for an idea of tolerance and mutuality predicated on communal belonging rather than autonomous individualism. Given the resurgence of such communal identities worldwide, her arguments are of great topical importance.

Khaleel Mohammed's paper on Islam and Human Rights provides an important starting place for many of us whose understandings of Islam are limited and unduly influenced by current political events and conflicts. Too often it is the media version of Islam, the CNN sound-bite, that becomes, for most, the normative understanding of what Islam professes and there is little understanding of even the fundamental building blocks of Islamic religion and civilization. Our two contributions on Qur'anic understandings of human rights attempt to address this. And while clearly written in the shadow of recent events and with the sense of foreboding with which so many Muslims in the USA and Europe are currently living Mohammed does not refrain from pointing out the continuing serious challenges that face the Islamic world in terms of properly institutionalizing its own religious edicts and assumptions. Following his contribution and in order to clarify somewhat more the most fundamental principles of Islamic belief in terms of human rights, mutuality, freedom of worship and tolerance of difference we have included a brief excursus by Riffat Hassan on selected Qur'anic readings on issues related to human rights.

The final papers, by Max Stackhouse and the late John Clayton, deal with the universality of human rights and the nature of their embeddedness within different traditions—religious or otherwise. Both authors would seem to be making their arguments from some in-between cultural space, the first more embedded within the Christian discourse, the second more disembedded. They provide us with that precisely calibrated distance from which that purposeful engagement—which is so called for today—is possible. ◁▷

Kevod Ha'adam, Tzelem Elohim and Kevod Habriot

(The Dignity of Man, the Image of God and the Honor of the Fellow-Creature)[1]

Shlomo Fischer

In this paper, I would like to discuss three concepts of Jewish thought and law—*Kevod Ha'adam,* the dignity of man, *Tzelem Elohim,* the image of God, and *Kevod Habriot,* the honor of the fellow-man or fellow-woman. I would like to argue that despite attempts to conflate these concepts and to regard them all as equivalents or even synonyms for the modern concepts of human dignity, they in fact ought to be distinguished as separate concepts and intuitions. Such recognition of their separate character and the initiation of a dialogue between these separate concepts, I suggest, could significantly contribute to the enrichment of the current discussion of human dignity and rights.

Kevod Ha'adam is a linguistic coinage of modern vintage; in this form it does not appear in the Bible or the Talmud and their Medieval or post-Medieval commentaries. It was coined in order to translate the modern concept of human dignity. This concept itself, I believe, only entered European discourse with Immanuel Kant's *Foundations of the Metaphysics of Morals. Kevod Ha'adam* entered modern Hebrew legal and philosophical usage in Israel in order to translate this concept which denotes that the human being has the right to have rights. The Israeli basic law guaranteeing human rights on the constitutional level is termed in Hebrew, *Chok Yesod: Kevod Ha'adam V'Heruto,* that is "Basic Law: The Dignity and Freedom of Man."

Originally delivered at Interreligious Center on Public Life conference in Newton, MA, in October 2002.

Yair Lorberbaum[2] has recently shown that the concept of *Tzelem Elohim*—the Image of God—had been a wide-ranging concept in rabbinic thinking an that it has informed fundamental concepts about man and God as well as crim inal law and law and norms concerning family and personal relations. Lorber baum concentrated his research on the Tannaitic layer of rabbinic literature that is, he located the central focus of interest upon the notion of *Tzelem Elo him* in those rabbis who were active between the start of the common era an around 200 C.E. Lorberbaum's research poses the question not only of the rela tionship between *Tzelem Elohim* and the modern concept of human dignity bu also to what extent can ancient philosophical and ethical concepts inform ou own modern ethical sensibility and how they can do so.

The heart of Lorberbaum's analysis is the insight that the rabbis understoo the notion of *Tzelem* as an *iconic* relationship between man and God. B "iconic" Lorberbaum understands that a figurative similarity between tw objects indicates an ontological relationship between them. Thus, if object A in the image of object B, then in some sense object B is "present" in object A object A is an "extension" of object B. This is especially the case if object B in some sense more primal than object A, if it serves as a "prototype" for it i the platonic sense. Lorberbaum argues further that this ontological connectio is conceived by the rabbis to be a basis for "theurgy." Because of the ontolog cal connection between the two entities, affecting the image or the *icon* (in ou terms object A) affects also the prototype (object B).

Lorberbaum applies this iconic relation to the relationship between man an God. Man is the *icon* of God, he is an image (*dyokan* in Greek) in which Go is *present*. Man is thus an ontological "extension" of God. This iconic relatio ship implies a "theurgic" one. What one does to man affects God. Thus by mu dering man or causing him pain or humiliation, one diminishes God, humiliat him or causes him pain. Conversely, by procreating, multiplying and augmen ing man one augments God.

The support that Lorberbaum adduces for this interpetation includes t very terms that the rabbis use to explain the biblical terms *Tzelem* and *Dmut* They interpret *tzelem* as *ikonin (icon)* and *dmuth* as *dyokan*. Lorberbau

---

2. Lorberbaum, Yair. 2004. *The Image of God: Halacha and Aggada*. Jerusalem: Schoken.

shows that this logical/ontological conception was extremely common in the late antique Greco-Roman world. It was widespread in Neo-Platonism and in the various Platonic schools with Plotinus and Iamblichus devoting extensive passages to it. It also informed various spiritual and religious practices of the various philosophical schools and mystery religions which involved images and icons (that is, idols in one form or another). Its assumptions also underlay the widespread political practice of worship of the Emperor's insignia. Thus, Lorberbaum claims, the adoption by the rabbis of the school of Hillel's perspective (especially Hillel the Elder and R. Akiva) was of a piece with philosophical and ethical notions common at that time.

Lorberbaum shows that especially in the school of Hillel the assumption of an iconic relationship between man and God underlay attitudes toward the body and the self and constituted a pervasive cultural theme. Beyond this, however, Lorberbaum wishes to show that the assumption of an iconic relationship between man and God shapes rabbinic norms concerning murder and capital punishment:

> Rabbi Akiva said: he who sheds blood negates the Image for it says: 'Whoso sheddeth man's blood, by man shall his blood be shed; for in the image of God made he man.' (Genesis 9:6) (Tosefta, Yevamoth 8:4)

> ר' עקיבא אומר כל השופך דמים מבטל את הדמות, שנאמר "שופך דם האדם דמו ישפך
> כי בצלם אלוהים עשה את האדם." (בראשית ט' ו') תוספתא יבמות ח', ד'

In this saying, the term, "image" refers to both the image of God and man's image which is in the image of God. By diminishing man's image through bloodshed one negates God's image which is present in man.

The rabbis did not restrict the ethical/legal consequences of the iconic relation of man and God only to criminal acts. It informed also the response of the criminal justice system to those very acts. One of the *locii classii* of the rabbinic conception of man as the *ikon* of God is in the following parable of R. Meir:

> Rabbi Meir would say: What does "He that is hanged is a reproach unto God" (Deut. 21, 23) come to teach us?

> Two identical twins, one the ruler of the whole world and the second became a bandit. After a period of time, the bandit was caught and he was crucified upon a cross. Every passer-by would say—"it seems that the king has been crucified." Therefore it says "He that is hanged is a reproach unto God." (Tosefta, Sandhedrin 9:7)

This parable refers to the relation between man and God. The King is transparently God (Ruler of the whole world) and the bandit is man who has transgressed a capital offense. As Lorberbaum emphasizes, the passers-by do not make a mistake. They identify the King in the crucified bandit, because of the very real connection between them.

This parable explains the symbolic nature of one of the central procedures of rabbinic capital punishment. The Torah (Deuteronomy 21:23) mandates that one who was judicially executed be "hung." The rabbis turned this into a symbolic procedure. "As one binds him, the other looses his binds." Lorberbaum argues that because God is present in man, insofar as man is the *ikon* of God, the rabbinic conception of criminal punishment tended to obliquely criticize the biblical procedures of execution and even nullify the biblically proscribed capital punishments. Thus Lorberbaum ascribes to the iconic relation of man and God the well-known Mishna restricting the application of capital punishment.

> A Sandhedrin (High Rabbinical Court) that executes one [guilty criminal] in seven years is considered "destructive." R. Elazar b. Azaria says, one in seventy years. R. Akiva and R. Tarfon say, were we in the Sanhedrin, no one would ever be executed in it. (Makot 1:10)

The major ramifications that we have seen thus far of the notion of *Tzelem Elohim* have been mainly in reference to life or death—either the criminal or the judicial taking of life. Those references in rabbinical literature to the prevention of pain and humiliation because man contains the presence of God, are generally also found in the context of the procedures for capital punishment. This is not terribly surprising because the verse that indicates the normative implications of *Tzelem Elohim* indeed deals with the shedding of blood (Genesis 9:6).

One important tradition, however, expands the implications of *Tzelem Elohim*. I would maintain that due to this expansion, in this tradition, *Tzelem Elohim* provides a concept that is close to the modern notion of human dignity and its ramifications not only in reference to life itself, but also in regard to the prohibitions against violating one's body, honor and property that are held to grow out of it.

As do many rabbinic traditions, the tradition in question has two "stories" or "floors." The first is a dialogue between two 2nd-century *Tannaim*, Be

Azzai and R. Akiva. The second is a constructed expansion of the dialogue, which appears only in one later text, Breshit (Genesis) Rabba, which was edited some time around the 4th century. This expansion constitutes an interpretation of what seems to have been original dialogue.

The dialogue seems to have been as follows: Regarding the quotation: "Love thy neighbor as thyself," R. Akiva commented, "This is a grand principle of the Torah." Ben Azzai replied that the verse "This is the book of the generations of man, in the day that the Lord created man in the image of God he made him" (Genesis 5:1) is a greater principle. This dialogue appears three times: in Torat Kohanim, the legal midrash on Leviticus, in the Palestinian Talmud and in Breshit (Genesis) Rabba, the aggadic midrash on Genesis. In the report in Breshit (Genesis) Rabba, we find a meaningful addition: "Said Ben Azzai: according to your principle one could say I am willing to be cursed, I am willing to be shamed,' perhaps the other fellow could be cursed and shamed. Look and see whom you are cursing and shaming? The image of God."[3]

In other words, Ben Azzai replaced the formal ethical criterion with a substantive one. In this rabbinic tradition the notion that man was created in the image of God is not only conceived of as a principle that informs judicial practice, it is placed upon the same plane as the ethical injunction of "Love thy neighbor as thyself" (Leviticus 19:18). Both are considered to be meta-halachic principles, that is, principles that inform many laws: "Grand principles of the Torah" (Breshit Rabba, Sifrei 7). The laws that both of these principles inform, as Maimonides pointed out, are the ethical laws, the laws that govern the relations between man and man. These are the laws that prohibit murder and theft and prohibit violence against the person, body, property of another. In other words they generally prohibit violations of the humanity of another, treating him as if he were an animal or a thing. These grand principles also include laws that affirm and enhance the humanity of the other—enjoining visiting the sick and acts of loving kindness.

As his other dicta indicate, R. Akiva strongly endorsed the notion of man as the *ikon* of God. Apparently in this dialogue, because of the similarity between the "images" all of whom reflect the same prototype (God), R. Akiva would like to form a formal ethical principle. Ben Azzai objects, pointing out the advantages of a substantive principle. For a different view see Lorberbaum pp. 397–405.

I would like to engage this rabbinical concept of *Tzelem Elohim* on two levels. The first is that of the validity or credibility of the concept itself. The second is that of its relation to our modern concepts of human dignity and rights.

As I have indicated the first issue is that of the validity of the iconic concept itself, as Lorberbaum presents it. Is this a concept that conforms to our intuitions about the Divine and its relations to man? As Lorberbaum explains, man as the *ikon* of God not only refers to his physical configuration, but also, perhaps primarily, to man's total psycho-intellectual being—his intellect, emotions, will, etc., which in the monistic rabbinic anthropology are all unified with his body. Nevertheless, *Tzelem Elohim* as an iconic concept implies an anthropomorphism which, I submit, is difficult for modern-day Jews (of whatever denomination) to accept. Second, I don't think that most people would accept the Platonic or iconic metaphysics that underlies the rabbinic concept of *Tzelem Elohim*. Since the 17th century, the main current in modern thought would hold that just because one object is the image of another, one is not "present" in the other, and there is no intrinsic ontological connection between them. Modern metaphysics holds that there is a great gulf fixed between extensive, material matter and intensive, mental, matter. Two objects are merely that—two separate objects which happen to look alike.

Nevertheless, the concept is highly suggestive. Both the biblical verses and the rabbinic parables and metaphors point to something which I think we feel has a truth to it. Yet, the conceptual and metaphysical garb that the rabbis have provided is not entirely acceptable. I think that in this situation, the model of interpretation that was suggested by Rudolph Bultmann for the study of the Gospels is appropriate.[4] Bultmann, it will be recalled, suggested separating the existential "Good News" from the "mythological" story of Christ, which he claimed was appropriate for its time and place, but incredible for modern readers. The "Good News"—of God's salvational activity—on the other hand, because of its deemed existential truth, is relevant for all readers at all times.

In a similar fashion, many writers such as Michael Perry, Robert Dahl and Max Stackhouse have pointed to the ineluctably sacred nature of human life—that human beings posses a "divinely endowed core that is the ultimate basis

---

4. Bultmann, Rudolph. 1969. *Faith and Understanding*. London: S.C.M. Press.

for the right to have rights."[5] These writers, I think, point to the widely held intuition that at the base of our concepts of human equality and human rights is this intuition of human sacredness. Yet what exactly this sacredness consists of is extremely hard to formulate; it tends to bring us to the limit of our conceptual abilities and moral reason. In this situation the rabbinic, iconic concept of *Tzelem Elohim* can stand a dual reading. In one sense it does give us a language in which to talk about human sacredness—God is "present" ontologically in human beings; when we hurt, humiliate or kill human beings we diminish God. Yet at the same time, without diminishing the force of this rabbinic language, we can perform, if we wish, a Bultmannian operation: we can identify with the phenomenology of human sacredness that is present in the concept of *Tzelem Elohim* without necessarily committing ourselves to the metaphysics of the rabbinic concept. We can treat it as a myth or metaphor which helps us formulate our thoughts, but we need not necessarily commit ourselves to its literal truth value.

The rabbinic concept need not function only as a vehicle for our pre-existent intuitions. Its very foreignness can help to critically challenge our received notion of human rights. This is the second issue that I have alluded to above. The concept of the image of God emphasizes the external source of the sacred value of human beings. The concern in rabbinic iconic concept is for God who is "present" in the human being, who is diminished, if His *ikon* is harmed. According to this religiously based concept human beings have value because they "participate" in the Platonic sense in something that is radically other to what otherwise would be human ontology. The basis for human value is a Being that is totally outside the immanent human world. This state of affairs *ipso facto* creates ethical standards which are heteronomous vis-à-vis the human world. This perspective on human value is in contrast to the accepted perspective, which might be termed modern or "secular", which, I think, anchors absolute human value in the immanent human being herself, or in some characteristic of hers such as autonomy or the ability to legislate one's moral laws for oneself.[6]

See Stackhouse, this volume.

A more "moderate" interpretation of *Tzelem Elohim*, one in which human beings "reflect" somehow the Divine being, would also, I think lead to a similar result. However, the rabbinic iconic approach to *Tzelem Elohim* with its emphasis upon Divine Presence and theurgy underlines the theo-centric nature of the ethics based upon it.

This contrast has immediate practical ethical implications. There are and will be some areas and situations that an approach to human dignity based upon the "image of God" will judge very differently than the secular discourse of rights. Three such limit areas immediately come to mind—suicide, abortion and responsibility for the life of the other. In regard to the first two, the religious image of God approach takes the general position that the continuation or extinction of human life cannot be the object merely of autonomous human decision making even if another autonomous human being is not harmed. The sacredness of human life comes from "outside," and does not fully belong to human beings, even to oneself, to dispose of as one sees fit. Thus human beings do not automatically have the right to conduct hunger strikes unto the death in order to make a political point, nor even to kill themselves if they decide that their lives contain too much pain and indignity. The very verse that prohibits murder because man is created in the image of God (Genesis 9:6), is understood by Jewish commentators to explicitly prohibit suicide. The ethic of *Tzelem Elohim*, if it permits suicide and abortion at all, will be very cautious and reluctant in doing so. This is in contrast with current liberal rights–oriented thinking which tends to affirm both assisted suicide and abortion.

Similarly, Jewish religious law based upon the ethic of *Tzelem Elohim* obligates one to actively intervene to prevent the death of another. Indeed, in contemporary Israeli law, simply being a passive bystander in the face of an accident without offering aid and assistance is a legal offense. This too, contrasts with at least some forms of the liberal sensibility, in which each individual lives within his own zone of privacy and self-reliance and one does not cross the boundaries of such zones without invitation.

Our third term, *Kevod Habriot*, which I have translated as the honor of one's fellow-man or -woman, is of early Talmudic origin and has served as a principle of Jewish religious jurisprudence until recent times. That is, it has figured in the literature of Jewish law as a consideration of some weight which can overcome injunctions and prescriptions of various sorts. Apparently because of the linguistic similarity between the two terms *Kevod Ha'adam*, which denotes the modern concept of human dignity and rights, and *Kevod Habriot* there has been a tendency among legal and talmudic scholars, looking for traditional Jewish roots for modern notion of the right to have rights, to conflate the two terms and concepts and to anchor the modern concept of *Kevod Ha'adam* in the Ta mudic concept of *Kevod Habriot*. In contrast to this approach, which was initiated, above all, by Professor Nahum Rackover, the distinguished former Deputy-Attorney General for Jewish Law, I would like to argue that the usage that the rabbis in the Talmud and the Halachic commentators and decisors make of this concept indicates a totally different intuition and principle; one in fact which exists in a certain tension with the modern concept of human rights.

I would like to argue that *Kevod Habriot* refers to the respect due to woman and man without reference to their special ontological positions as *ikons* of God. In order to amplify this and make clear the difference between it and *Tzelem Elohim,* I would like to make brief reference to the work of Louis Dumont on Early Christianity.[7] Dumont argued that in the era of late antiquity almost everyone existed within the framework of organic kinship communities of production and reproduction. It was only by developing an out-worldly relationship with Christ based upon contemplation that an individual in the Western sense was able to develop.

I would like to point to a similar relation in regard to *Tzelem Elohim* and *Kevod Habriot. Tzelem Elohim*, by focusing upon the iconic relationship with God, is able to "extract," as it were, the individual from his organic setting. It makes categorical normative claims vis-à-vis every individual which relate to his person, body or property. *Kevod Habriot*, in contrast, does not relate to these issues. It relates to the standing of a human being without reference to her special iconic status. Since the human being's special iconic status is disregarded, the human being that it relates to is the human being in society—the human being embedded in her organic community.

Since *Kevod Habriot* is concerned with standing, it is concerned with the "externalities" of human existence. Thus it addresses itself not to the sacred core of one's humanity, where God's presence is to be found, but to the penumbra, as it were, of that core—the necessary material layers in which that core is embodied. To use a Kabbalistic terminology, one could say that man is "clothed" in two garments; the "garment" of the physical body and the "garment" of the social body. *Kevod Habriot* does not relate to negations or affir-

---

Dumont, Louis. 1986. *Essays on Individualism*. Chicago: University of Chicago.

mations of man's essential humanity and its divine core, but to the "garments" of human existence—the body as a garment—when it is merely a corpse, devoid of the live human being that formerly gave it form and life and the garment of social existence. It is concerned with shame—you can commit an indignity upon a corpse and you can vaporize a man's standing in society by shaming him. Thus the basic commandments of *Kevod Habriot* are protecting the dignity of the corpse by burying it and protecting the standing of men and women in society by preventing their shame.

Of course, as we have seen, *Tzelem Elohim* is also concerned with the dignity of the corpse. One of the central prohibitions associated with man as the *ikon* of God, is to leave the executed man "hanging." Yet as all the commentators have pointed out, there is a fundamental difference between the two commandments. The prohibition against leaving the executed man hanging is categorical. Under no circumstances is one to leave the corpse on the cross, even if it cannot be buried. This reflects the iconic relationship. By leaving the corpse hanging one is harming and diminishing God. The obligation to bury in contrast is flexible and negotiable. It refers to the general honor accorded to the dead. One need not bury immediately if one needs to build a coffin or even wait for relatives to arrive at a funeral. Thus it belongs to the general obligations of *Kevod Habriot*, not to the peremptory and categorical injunctions (such as the prohibition on murder) of *Tzelem Elohim*.

What is especially interesting about the rabbinic concept of *Kevod Habriot* is that it extends to the social body as well. Thus in the rabbinic understanding *Kevod Habriot* also encompasses not obligating or forcing one to undertake actions or to suffer situations not in keeping with one's social standing. Thus an elderly gentleman is not required to chase, capture or return a lost ewe, and a king or even a prominent family is exempt from certain requirements.

I would suggest that the contribution that the concept that *Kevod Habriot* gives to current political and ethical discussion has to do with its universal aspect. When we think of the concept of a person's standing in society, we generally think of it in terms of hierarchy and stratification. Indeed, the laws of *Kevod Habriot* have a hierarchical aspect—priests, elders and kings are exempt from this or that obligation because of their standing. However the point of *Kevod Habriot* is that *everybody* has a body and a social existence. Thus the paradigmatic injunctions of *Kevod Habriot* are the *met mitzvah*—the overri ing obligation to bury the anonymous corpse found upon the field, and the prohibition against stripping any man naked in the marketplace (e.g., if he wears prohibited clothing) because of the social shame involved. In other words, having a social existence and the honor affiliated with it are part of the universal human condition. Along with the divine core and the human rights that it generates we must also, in any situation, consider the social being that women and men necessarily have, and the honor that goes along with it.

Conclusion

There has been some discussion of late concerning the religious origins and nature of human rights. Writers such as Max Stackhouse, Michael Perry and Louis Henkin have debated whether we ought to consider the three monotheistic faiths or the Enlightenment as the source of our concept of human rights. I would like to suggest that we consider the notions of human dignity and human rights not as single monolithic concepts which have a single exclusive source but as a field in which various related concepts of various origins co-exist and carry on a dialogue with each other. Thus, undoubtedly secular notions of rights that have their origin in Hobbes and the Enlightenment have enriched religious conceptions of the sacredness of human life by adding that human autonomy in one fashion or another is an essential component of that sacredness. On the other side the contemporary emphasis on autonomy may bring us into the danger of the fundamental violations of taboos, that not only fetuses but other helpless forms of human life may be extinguished due to the autonomous will of human beings. We have already seen the first stirrings of such a danger in those manifestations of child pornography that contain a component of sadism and murder. The notion of *Tzelem Elohim*, that man was created in the image of God, by reminding us of the external source of human sacredness could perhaps counteract such developments.

Another dilemma which faces us is that between the rights of victims and the rights of the public to know and issues of shame and confidentiality both in relation to victims and even perpetrators of crimes and violations of human rights. I would suggest that adopting the concept of *Kevod Habriot*, of the honor of our fellow-creatures, would at least give us a language to discuss the many sidedness of such ethical problems. In line with my explication, this concept states that aside from possessing a divine core on the individual plane, human beings necessarily have an existence in society that generates a modicum of social honor which too must be taken into ethical consideration.

As Aristotle pointed out many centuries ago, ethics and politics are practical sciences. Trying to solve ethical dilemmas involves weighing and deliberating among varied considerations, some of which are incommensurable with each other. The more refined and rich is our conceptual apparatus and the more we can define our considerations, the better chance we have of successful resolution. By introducing the concepts of *Tzelem Elohim* and *Kevod Habriot*, I have made an attempt to advance such refinement and enrichment. ⌇

Jews and Their Others: The Boundaries of Community

Suzanne Last Stone

In this paper I shall discuss three characteristics of Judaism that support plural-ism and acceptance of diversity, each instantiated in different social settings: first, the internal structure of Judaism—its limitation to one nation—which has led to a positive valuation of the role of other collectivities in the divine plan; second, the tradition of intellectual pluralism within the normative halakhic community fostered by its skeptical approach to truth-claims; third, the rab-binic appreciation that Judaism is a historico-national community as well as a religious community, which has led to increasing efforts to retain apostates within the boundaries of the community. I stress that these are tendencies within the tradition, potentialities that are both under-elaborated at present, and subject to competing claims. But it is our task today to read the tradition in its "best light."

Judaism and the Other Without

The particularism of Judaism (the fact that its injunctions are limited to the Jewish people) inevitably raises the question of the role of other collectivities in the divine plan and the relationship of Judaism to these other collectivities. Additional models of social solidarity overlapping the covenantal are provided by the biblical portrayal of the associational life that Israelites share with non-Israelites residing in the polity. The biblical concept of social solidarity among diverse ethnic members of the polity bears a resemblance to the fellowship of citizens in the modern nation.

The Bible speaks of three types potentially within the polity: the heathen, the stranger, and the resident stranger. The heathen is an idolater who is not per-mitted to associate with Israelites. Idolatry is not only an absolute falsehood; it is associated with moral corruption. The Bible repeatedly commands the community to purge the territory of idolatry and idolaters—pagan and Israel alike. Thus, idolatry marks the outer and inviolate boundaries of the Jewish polity as well as the community. In contrast to the heathen, Israelites are enjoined in the Bible to love the stranger as oneself, to provide one law for the stranger and the Israelite alike, and to provide the stranger with food, clothing and agricultural charity. In several biblical passages, the social solidarity that Israelites owe to the stranger is ascribed to the stranger's political and material dependency on Israelites. Not only is the stranger subject to Jewish authority, he does not have an allotted portion of the land and therefore is like the Levite, the widow and the orphan, to whom special consideration must be shown. In others, the duty to love the stranger is elevated to an absolute ethical plane. The stranger is no different from the Israelite in two essential respects: Israelites, too, were once strangers in Egypt; moreover, everyone is a stranger in the world in relation to God.

In its original biblical setting, the stranger is an individual of non-Jewish birth living in the land who accepts Jewish political authority and obeys some though not all, of the covenantal law. Indeed, by the Second Temple period, the distinctiveness of Jewish identity was blurred not only by the proliferation of Jewish sects but also by the existence of a variety of non-Jewish groups that adopted some though not all Jewish practices. Part of the early rabbinic project was to delineate between Jew and non-Jew, given the increased presence of hyphenated identities such as Jewish-Christians and of groups practicing some but not all of Jewish law. Strangers were gradually assimilated into the covenantal community and reconceived as converts, who became full members of the covenant once they assumed all the obligations of the law.

This process, however, left dangling the question of who occupies the category of biblical stranger to whom special obligations of social solidarity are owed. While the rabbinic strategy may be viewed as an attempt to maintain strict boundaries for the Jewish community, at the same time, the rabbis identified and recognized intermediate categories between idolatrous paganism and Judaism. The rabbinic tradition equated the biblical stranger with the resident stranger, which it identifies as a non-Jew who does not obey Jewish law, but rather, formally accepts the Noahide laws. The Noahide laws are the rabbinic codification of the moral order given by God to humanity, according to the bib lical account, prior to the Sinaitic election. The tendency to identify such inter-mediate models, as Jacob Katz has shown, is already evident in early rabbinic sources.[1] According to the rabbinic tradition, God stipulated the terms of a moral order to Adam and the children of Noah prior to the election of Israel at Sinai. This order consists of seven basic human obligations, the Noahide laws, consisting of prohibitions against idolatry, bloodshed, robbery, incest, blas-phemy, eating a limb torn from a live animal, and the positive command to establish systems of justice.[2] In Talmudic sources, the concept of Noahides is linked to the status of resident strangers in the Jewish polity, who must accept these minimal universalist principles as conditions for living in the land. Thus, the alien need not assimilate; he may retain his ancestral identity so long as he abides by a minimal set of obligations that are the marks of a civilized person. In return, Maimonides holds, the resident stranger is owed full ethical and char-table reciprocity. He portrays the duty to love the stranger as a pure moral law, one that is counter-instinctual, because the stranger shares no thick, primordial tie, no common ethnic bond, no religious tradition, with the Israelite. The obli-gation of Israelites to engage in concrete acts of solidarity with the stranger is based, instead, on allegiance to universal criteria of morality.

Genuine acceptance of other religions and forms of life requires more than toleration of their presence within Jewish society or even social solidarity and legal reciprocity, however. The critical question is whether Judaism is willing to ascribe independent, intrinsic value to other collectivities. Does rabbinic Judaism recognize that other groups share certain religious truths or moral cri-teria with Judaism, which are then properly instantiated in different religious, political or legal settings? A significant step in this direction was the early rab-binic association of observance of the Noahide laws with the condition for reli-gious perfection or salvation. One who obeys these laws is righteous and all the righteous of the nations have a share in the world to come.[3] It may be argued that inclusion of the righteous of the nations in the world to come is in spite of

See Katz, Jacob. 1961. *Exclusiveness and Tolerance*. New York: Schocken Books.

For a fuller account of the role of Noahide law in Jewish thought, see Stone, Suzanne Last. 1991. Sinaitic and Noahide Law: Legal Pluralism in Jewish Law. *Cardozo Law Review* 12:1157–1214.

Babylonian Talmud, Sanhedrin 105a.

the fact that they belong to other collectivities, not because of it.[4] Their inclusion rests on the fact that these individuals obey the Jewish law for non-Jews, hinted at in Maimonides's requirement that resident strangers formally accept the Noahide laws before the Jewish court. Yet, the Talmud itself seems to view the Noahide laws as the product of a revelation to humanity prior to Sinai, re-ratified at Sinai. Moreover, rabbinic literature describes even the Sinai revelation as conveyed to all nations in four or seventy languages, implying that redemption follows adherence to the obligations addressed by God directly to other nations. Thus, the rabbinic tradition can be understood as embracing a concept of divine religious pluralism. Each person or nation attains independent moral significance and is justified through adherence to the different obligations addressed to them by God.

In the medieval period, the idea of intermediate categories between Judaism and paganism was applied to legitimate not just individuals, but whole political and religious entities. The rabbinic legitimation of other collectivities laid the basis for legal and social interaction between Judaism and other political orders or social groups. Two examples of this process are particularly noteworthy. The Talmud rules that Jews must formally recognize certain laws of foreign rulers as legitimate. As the Talmud puts it, "the law of the kingdom is the law (dina de-malkhuta dina)."[5] The Talmud offers no substantive legal or moral grounds for this principle, however. The eleventh-century exegete Rashi offers a particularly suggestive rationale for this principle. Rashi links the principle to the Noahide obligation incumbent on the nations of the world to establish just systems of law. Because the creation of non-Jewish systems of law fulfills a divine command, Rashi comments, these systems are vested with divine legitimacy and their civil laws may serve as a residual source of law even for Jews. Thus, non-Jewish collectivities share with Judaism the divine goal of establishing a just social order. In the modern period, especially among halakhic decisors living under Western democratic rule, there has been increased recognition that

---

4. See Margalit, Avishai. 1996. On Religious Pluralism. In *Toleration: An Elusive Value*, edited by D. Heyd. Princeton: Princeton University Press. pp. 147–157.

5. Babylonian Talmud, Bava Kamma 113a–b.

6. Rashi, Babylonian Talmud, Gittin 9b. For further elaboration of Rashi's view, see Stone, Sinaitic and Noahide Law, pp. 1208–1212.

non-Jewish civil law often provides equitable rules missing from the corpus of Jewish law and an increased tendency to incorporate such laws into the Jewish legal system.[7]

A second example of the positing of a common interreligious project shared by Jews and non-Jews, instantiated in diverse and plural forms, is offered by Menahem Ha-Me'iri, a thirteenth-century French decisor. Ha-Me'iri ruled that all nations who are disciplined by enlightened religion are entitled to juridical equality and ethical reciprocity under Jewish law. Ha-Me'iri presented an original synthesis of the entire Talmudic system of discriminatory rules and exceptions, essentially rendering them obsolete. He held that juridical discrimination against non-Jews in the Talmud refers to non-Jewish idolaters who lived in the culture of the ancient world, who "were not bound by proper customs" and not to the people of the medieval era, who are "constrained by the ways of religion."[8] Indeed, in some rulings, as Moshe Halbertal shows, Ha-Me'iri forthrightly includes contemporary non-Jews in the category of one's "brother" delineated in Scripture, to whom full legal and ethical reciprocity is owed.[9]

As Halbertal details, Ha-Me'iri's principle of positive valuation of other faiths is deeply rooted in the rationalist school of the post-Maimonidean period, which viewed the role of religion not only in terms of doctrinal insight into the essence of God but also in terms of its functional aspect, the establishment of a well-ordered society.[10] Ha-Me'iri's formulation ascribes positive value to Christianity and Islam, not just as private religions that uphold basic tenets of belief, but as practical systems of governance, whose adherents are impelled by their faith to maintain legal institutions and establish moral standards in society. Ha-Me'iri's formulation is noteworthy for two reasons. Although other jurists often reached similar legal conclusions, they did so through the traditional Talmudic, casuistic method and confined their rulings to the practical needs of the com-

. See Shilo, Shmuel. 1991. Equity as a Bridge Between Jewish and Secular Law. *Cardozo Law Review* 12:737–752.

. Menahem Ha-Me'iri, Beit Ha-Behira, on Babylonian Talmud, Avodah Zarah 22a.

. See Halbertal, Moshe. 2000. *Bein Hokhmah Le-Torah* [Between Torah and Wisdom] (Heb.). Jerusalem: Hebrew University Magnes Press. p. 84.

0. See Halbertal, pp. 102–103.

munity. Ha-Me'iri, as Jacob Katz points out, formulated his distinction between the idolaters of old and contemporary nations as a "principle," and thus "transcended the conventional methods of halakhic thinking."[11] Moreover, although Ha-Me'iri compares religiously enlightened non-Jews to resident strangers who observe Noahide law, he does not equate them. Rather, Ha-Me'iri creates a new intermediate category between paganism and Judaism consisting of the "nations restricted by the ways of religion."

Ha-Me'iri's functional understanding of religion raises the question whether his views may be extended to encompass all civilized societies that maintain legal institutions and thus enforce moral standards in society. Ha-Me'iri's work was lost to the tradition until the last century but there are intimations that his view is slowly re-entering the tradition, stimulating debate whether the Talmudic patterns of juridical discrimination are inapplicable in empirically observed social and legal systems that view themselves as constrained by the rule of law.

In addition to detailing strategies of tolerance within the Jewish tradition, it is important to pursue the question of what thought patterns or historical experiences may have contributed to a move away from a model of Judaism that posits an elect group, on the one hand, and a moral abyss, on the other. I shall speculate about three. First, the tendency to posit intermediate categories between Judaism and paganism reflects a form of thinking that Patrick Glenn has recently ascribed to all complex legal traditions: the pursuit of "multivalent" as opposed to "bivalent" logic.[12] Bivalent thought implies clear boundaries between distinct and separate concepts and prevents boundaries from merging, once they are created. By contrast, multivalent thought, as Pierce anticipated, recognizes the once-excluded middle ground between truth and falsity. The middle ground emerges with more information, which the hasty drawing of boundaries excludes. Multivalent logic is highly precise and particular. It is essentially casuistic (the quintessential Talmudic form of reasoning) in its methodological insistence on detail, qualification and limitation. Thus, complex, casuistic legal traditions have the potential to multiply categories and recognize partial memberships in more than one set at the same time.

---

11. See Katz, p. 118.

12. See Glenn, H. Patrick. 2000. *Legal Traditions of the World*. New York: Oxford University Press, pp. 323–329.

Second, the rabbinic experience of living under other forms of government led to a view in the medieval period, and accentuated in the modern period, that the halakha is not, in its exilic form, all-encompassing or self-sufficient. In the first place, some accommodation with other systems of governance had to be reached to legitimate Jewish obedience to foreign rule and laws. Moreover, Jewish medieval speculation about the differences between Torah law and conventional forms of governance led to the view that the halakha, in its ideal form, has strengths and weaknesses, lacunae and gaps, and its most notable gap is its failure to provide for social order, the function of the biblical institution of kingship. The halakha began to see itself as dependent on other systems, such as non-Jewish systems of governance, to complete it. Such systems provided mechanisms for order, such as a realistic system of punishment and criminal enforcement jurisdiction, which the halakha in its ideal form lacked.[13] The halakha was forced to grant genuine legitimacy to these other systems in order to justify their utilization in the service of Jewish aims.

Third, there exists a deep structure in Jewish thought that is predisposed to value pluralism, diversity and difference over singularity and sameness and therefore to honor the uniqueness of distinctive collectivities. This pattern of thought is reflected in the biblical concept of creation as a process of distinction, difference and diversity. The uniqueness of divine creation of humans is that no two people are alike, whether in their character, views, beliefs or physical characteristics, despite the fact that each is in the image of God.[14] The idea that each individual is precious in his or her diversity is translated into the idea that unique human collectivities are also precious. Each collectivity has its own language and laws, commanded by the one God.

In sum, other collectivities are not just proper objects of toleration. They have a special role to play in the divine plan: establishing a just social order. Each community does not simply go its own way, however, in pursuing the divine plan. The model of pluralism that Judaism endorses is interactive. The positive valuation of other societies paves the way, in the halakha, for legal, social and cultural interchange between Judaism and other societies. Indeed,

---

3. For a fuller treatment of this issue, see Stone, Noahide and Sinaitic Law, pp. 1197–1212.
4. Mishnah, Sanhedrin 8:4.

Maimonides's view that Jews are obligated to enforce Noahide law—to aid all social and political collectivities in establishing a just social order—is often cited to ground a Jewish religio-legal obligation to engage the other in collaborative projects designed to improve the ethical, moral, spiritual and material condition of general society.[15] The intuition that such an obligation exists sustains those who interpret Judaism nontraditionally in terms of a Jewish mission to pursue justice in the social sphere. It is true that the more traditional segments of religious Judaism have not yet turned their energies in this direction in a significant way, favoring projects that advance the interests of Jews to the exclusion of those involving humanity. This tendency is in large part due to the historical experience of Judaism. As a result of persecution and exile, Judaism did not enter the marketplace of world religions until its emancipation on the heels of the Enlightenment. The potential for engagement with the world introduced by the Enlightenment was punctuated by the Holocaust, inaugurating a sense of despair about the possibility of cultural and social collaboration as well as an outpouring of energy into the reconstruction of Jewry. Given time and stable political conditions, this potential in the tradition may emerge.

Although the Jewish tradition does conceive of itself as part of other, overlapping communities, the boundary of the Jewish community remains distinct and the claims of its members take priority over others. Thus, Judaism's intricate system of associational duties presents, as Gordon Lafer points out, a "hierarchy of obligations," privileging community members over resident strangers, resident strangers over members of "civilized" societies, and "civilized" societies over those who disregard the moral law. Communal bonds, dependence and moral character determine the level of obligation owed rather than an abstract commitment to universal criteria, which assumes that "the proper subject of politics must be the human species."[16]

The rabbinic worldview does present a serious obstacle, however, to achieving a genuine Jewish vision of civil society, a pressing issue in Israel which must

---

15. See generally Shatz, David, Chaim I. Waxman, and Nathan Diament, eds. 1997. *Tikkun Olam: Social Responsibility in Jewish Thought and Law*. Mountvale, NJ: Aronson.

16. Lafer, Gordon. 1993. Universalism and Particularism in Jewish Law: Making Sense of Political Loyalties. In *Jewish Identity*, ed. David Theo Goldberg and Michael Krausz, Philadelphia: Temple University Press. p. 199.

deal with the place of the non-Jew within the state. Does the halakha provide an adequate "model of mutuality as a basis for stable group relations"?[17] Social reciprocity does not present a serious legal issue, given the norms of mutuality stipulated by Me'iri and achieved even in the earlier Talmudic model, through invocation of the principle of pursuing paths of peace. (Political reality is a far greater impediment.) The more critical issue is the extension of full citizenship rights. According to Maimonides, non-Jews (and Jewish women) are forbidden to hold positions of political authority in the Jewish polity.[18] The exilic models of reciprocity do not resolve this issue because they address only the sharing of acts of benevolence.

The admission of non-Jews (and Jewish women) as equal partners in the polity would seem to require a bolder theory, one that affirms the equality of all persons under the law. The Jewish philosopher Hermann Cohen claimed that the biblical injunction to provide one law for the citizen and the stranger (who obeys Noahide law) was, in fact, the precursor of this emancipation ideal. "The Noahide," he writes, "is a citizen," a person whose equal moral worth is recognized, triggering full equality under the law.[19] Cohen seems to have no followers within the halakhic community, however.

The more common rabbinic strategy is to retain the differential rules in theory but to make them inapplicable to the issue at hand. Thus, Chief Rabbi Isaac Herzog argued that the ban on non-Jews holding political authority refers to the exercise of non-elective, life-tenure powers because it had in mind the office of the Jewish king.[20] Rabbi Shaul Yisraeli proposes to circumvent the ban by conceiving of the state itself as no more than a partnership, modeled on the Talmudic partnership of the "townspeople." He analogizes the holding of office in the state to holding office in a business, which a non-Jew may head.[21] The difficulty with these opinions is not their result but their rationales, which high-

---

17. Blidstein, Gerald J. 1997. Halakha and Democracy. *Tradition* 32 (1). p. 28.

18. Mainomides, Mishneh Torah, Hilkhot Melakhim 1:4–5.

19. Quoted in Novak, David. 1981. Universal Moral Law in the Theology of Hermann Cohen. *Modern Judaism* 1 p. 105.

20. The opinion is discussed in Blidstein, pp. 25–27.

21. Rabbi Shaul Yisraeli, Ha-Torah ve-haMedina, again discussed in Blidstein.

light the paucity of resources in the tradition for the development of a genuine theory of equal citizenship based on principle.

Resort to casuistic reasoning and other technical means of problem-solving is, of course, the traditional rabbinic method. Such methods also often reflect a genuine shift in consciousness about the justness of an institution. The abolition of slavery, for example, was accomplished through a series of technical restrictions, clearly motivated by a deep abhorrence of the institution. There is an increased call, however, to attempt a new position based, as Gerald Blidstein writes, on the candid acknowledgment that Jews relate to non-Jews as "fully human possessors of the divine image." Blidstein asks whether the "divine image of man" can "become a more powerful halakhic concept than it seems to be at present or than it has been historically."[22] To draw the question out, can the idea that man is created in the image of God provide a new universal category of membership in the Jewish polity and a new universal category for the creation of social bonds with all members of society by virtue of their humanity alone? This is no easy task in a tradition that has as its centerpiece the idea of the distinctiveness of human collectivities and that values the particular over the general. Judaism's particularity, its limitation to one nation, is both the generating force for a vision of ethical and religious pluralism and a limitation.

Judaism and the Other Within

An instinctive appreciation for diversity and pluralism can also be seen at the epistemological level of the tradition. Diversity, contradiction and pluralism are part of the halakha's self-conscious understanding of its own processes. Adam Seligman has challenged us to consider whether revealed religious traditions have the capacity to develop an epistemology of inclusiveness based on skepticism toward its truth-claims while still maintaining a belief in revealed truth.[23] The intellectual pluralism of Talmudic thought is well known, including its affirmation of multiple, contradictory opinions about the law, as each the

---

22. Blidstein, p. 22.
23. Seligman, Adam B. 2004. *Modest Claims: Dialogues and Essays on Tolerance and Tradition.* Notre Dame: University of Notre Dame Press.

"words of God," as each having intrinsic value.[24] The halakhic tradition asserts that all opinions proffered in legitimate pursuit of the divine law bear an aspect of truth. Dissents must be recorded, in one view, because a later court may rehabilitate the rejected opinion as the law.[25] There is a clear demand then to concede the partial legitimacy of an opponent's viewpoint despite the tension this engenders. The halakhic decisor must bear not only the partial truth of his opponent but the possibility that his own view is in error.

What is the concept of truth at work here and how can the tension engendered by multiple, conflicting opinions about the law, each endowed with an aspect of truth, be endured? Some reasons given by the tradition parallel the liberal tolerator's emphasis on a free market of ideas. Diverse opinions illuminate the search for truth, sharpening debate, and clarifying the correct opinion. But others are rooted in skepticism about the possibility of human certitude, stemming either from the nature of the revelation itself or from the limits of human reason. The Talmud, in one passage, describes the revelation as itself a series of decisional options, providing an equal basis for prohibiting or permitting conduct.[26] Thus, multiplicity and contrast are features of the divine revelation itself. In this view, the essential characteristics of a legal matter are best grasped by simultaneously contemplating its negation. The mystical view of revelation as a fragmented process also emphasizes that each individual opinion reflects a partial understanding of the divine truth.

The rationalist model is no less skeptical of human certitude, but it tends to ascribe controversy and pluralism, not to inherent features of revelation, but to the extremely limited scope of revealed law, breaks in the historic chain of transmission of revelation, and individual differences in intellectual prowess and temperament. Because human reasoning is fallible, error is inevitable. But error is accounted for by the halakhic system itself, which demands not fidelity to abstract truth, but fidelity to the process of halakhic reasoning and to the halakha's own internal procedures for resolving disputes.

---

24. For a fuller discussion of this feature of Jewish thought, see Stone, Suzanne Last. 1993. In Pursuit of the Counter-Text: The Turn to the Jewish Legal Model in Contemporary American Legal Theory. *Harvard Law Review* 106:813–894.

25. Mishnah Eduyot 1:5.

26. Palestinian Talmud, Sanhedrin 4:2.

The intellectual tolerance that Judaism manifests is the exclusive province of the normative rabbinic class, however, and extends only to other recognized members of this class. Moreover, such intellectual tolerance is limited to the realm of ideas and opinions; it does not extend to action or legal practice. Behavioral pluralism, in theory, is a sin, the disregard of a binding norm or, in the absence of a binding norm, the sad consequence of the failure to reach consensus through rational discourse—the goal of the halakhic community. The author of the Sepher Ha-Hinnuch, for example, writes that an erroneous binding norm is preferable to behavioral pluralism. Given the potential for fragmentation of the law, sectarian division, legal anarchism, and the loss of the unifying force of the law in the life of the community, "it would be better to suffer an error by the rabbis than for everyone to do as he sees fit."[27] Thus, epistemological skepticism is accompanied by an equally deep appreciation for order and authority. The tension between skepticism and order is a constant feature of Jewish legal thought, reflected even in its literary output, with its cyclical production of codes of law that canonize rules and commentaries that increase the potential for pluralism and dissent.

Thus, behavioral pluralism, individual deviations from established halakhic norms, has no independent value. This raises a profound question with respect to the Jewish community's ability to bear heresy and sin. The halakha, in theory, requires harsh treatment of heretics, apostates and rebellious sinners who show, through their actions, that they reject the authority of the law. Public rejection of the authority of the law not only threatens order but is viewed as a betrayal of the community because the community itself is constituted and defined by obedience to the law.

Heretics, apostates, and rebellious sinners occupy an intermediate category between Jew and non-Jew in a sense. They are on the boundaries of the community. They are no longer "fellows" to whom mutual social obligations are owed, and they no longer enjoy rights of association with covenantal members. Social contact with them is forbidden, they are neither mourned nor eulogized, and intermarriage with them is forbidden. Maimonides writes that they are "removed from the category of Israel" in that they are not entitled to any form

---

27. Sepher Ha-Hinnuch, Commandment 408.

of social solidarity.[28] Yet, they remain Jews for purposes of incurring an obligation to God to observe the law. The status of covenantal fellow turns on conduct, and not ascription, a concept that plays a critical role in defining who is included in Jewish society, one that has assumed critical significance in modern conditions of Jewish social fragmentation.

Given the traditional definition of Jewish society as excluding deviants (including public desecrators of the Sabbath), the question arises whether secular Jews are, from the rabbinic perspective, within Jewish society. This question arose immediately on the heels of the Jewish Enlightenment, well before the creation of the state, when nontraditional denominations and secularist movements began to proliferate. As expulsion or banning was not an option, several traditional communities, instead, self-separated themselves from general Jewish society and formed segregated communities of the faithful.[29] The early settlement community in Israel raised the question in its most acute form but also spurred efforts at accommodation because the very fact of the individual's continued attachment to the idea of a Jewish nation softened the rabbinic category of rebellious sinners who reject the law.

Although one still can find contemporary rabbinic opinions holding that those who deny the divinity of Jewish law or publicly desecrate the Sabbath are no longer a part of the covenantal community,[30] most rabbinic authorities hold otherwise. These opinions reflect two different strategies of rapprochement. The first strategy is to craft conditions precedent to the invocation of the categories of rebellious sinners and apostates, so as to narrow the instances when these categories have legal effect. Rabbi Abraham Yeshayahu Karelitz, the Hazon Ish, argues broadly, for example, that the times have so changed that the traditional categories no longer even apply. Modernity is different because it is a time of God's concealment."[31] These rulings are motivated by communitar-

---

28. For a fuller discussion, see Lamm, Norman. 1992. Loving and Hating Jews as Halakhic Categories. In *Jewish Tradition and the Non-traditional Jew*, edited by J. J. Schacter. Mountvale: Jason Aronson Inc.

29. See Bleich, Judith. 1992. Rabbinic Responses to Nonobservance in the Modern Era. In *Jewish Tradition and the Non-traditional Jew*, edited by J. J. Schacter. Mountvale: Jason Aronson Inc. pp. 37–115.

30. For samples, see Lamm, p. 158 n. 22.

31. Hazon Ish 13:16, cited in Lamm, pp. 160–161.

ian concerns, and not by respect for the value of diverse forms of Jewish life or of individual choice. As such, they create a virtual fellowship, in which the primordial obligation of social solidarity exists only on one side. Still, these rulings enable continued social interaction among all Jews.

A second strategy of inclusion of apostates in Jewish society becomes possible only if attention is shifted away from the intolerable act or idea and directed, instead, toward the person. This perspectival switch is made possible by the perception that there is a good reason to excuse the person, although not the action or belief. Tolerance is advocated neither on the grounds of legitimate pluralism nor on the ground of respect for individual autonomy but, rather, on the ground that the deviant was not fully responsible for his or her actions or heretical beliefs. The individual can be tolerated because the fault for the sin lies in inferior education or upbringing, in intellectual seduction, or the like. The development of this attitude of tolerance toward persons based on a notion of excuse was extended beyond the covenantal community to justify tolerant behavior toward pagan idolaters as well.[32]

This model of tolerance builds on a constellation of concepts intrinsic to the Jewish tradition. First, it recognizes that a multiplicity of forces and social frameworks shape the self. Tolerance of persons responds to the actual, socially situated self, and not the liberal ideal, freely choosing self—that is, to the model of the self contemplated by the Jewish religious tradition itself. Second, the appeal to "bear" the sinner can be placed then within the Jewish tradition's overall approach to the ideas of repentance, mercy and *imitatio dei*. As God bears sinners, restrains his anger and is patient, in order to maintain his relationship with Israel, so humans must emulate the divine virtues, exercise restraint and patience, and preserve the sinner's relationship with the community, in the hope of eventual return and reconciliation. Bearing the sinner is not a legal duty; it is, like forgiveness and divine mercy, an act of loving-kindness outside the sphere of justice. Third, when extended toward deviant Jews, such toleration is not only motivated by an ethical concern for the tolerated person or by an ideal picture of the ethical qualities of the tolerator. In the context of

---

32. For a fuller discussion, see Ravitzky, Aviezer. 1997. The Question of Tolerance in the Jewish Religious Tradition. In *Hazon Nahum: Studies in Jewish Law, Thought, and History*, edited by Elman and J. S. Gurock. New York: Yeshiva University Press.

udaism, such toleration is also stimulated by social concerns—by the felt need o preserve the national historical community which overlaps with the theological community. Finally, retaining the heretic, the sinner or the sectarian within he horizon of the community leads inevitably to the pluralization of the community. Continued active engagement with those who hold different beliefs creates a more diverse society, in which pluralism is managed although not legitimated, and it prevents the ossification of the community into a homogeneous emnant of the faithful. A critical question is whether, over time, pluralism eases to be merely managed and actually breaks through the grounds of the ormative community, transforming it in slow and subtle ways. ◠

An Excursus: Selected Readings from the Qur'an on Issues Pertaining to Human Rights

Riffat Hassan

'he cardinal principle of Islam is belief in the absolute oneness of God, or *awhid*. In the opening chapter of the Qur'an, *Al-Fatiha*, God is described as Ar-Rahman" (The Most Merciful), "Ar-Rahim" (The Most Gracious) and Rabb al-'alamin" (The Lord of all the peoples and universes). As pointed out y Fathi Osman, in the Qur'an God is not related to any particular place or eople but to all creation.[1] In this context it is interesting to note that while the Iebrew Bible or the Old Testament refers to God as the God of Abraham, Isaac nd Jacob, the Qur'an does not refer to God as the God of any particular rophet. God is the one and only creator of everything that exists and from the nity of God comes the unity of creation. The Qur'an points out that God not nly creates and sustains all creatures but also gives moral guidance to human- y which has been made "in the best of moulds." (Surah 95: *At-Tin*: 4)

The Qur'an affirms that God "cares for all creatures" (Surah 2: *Al-Baqarah*: 68) and testifies that the message it contains is universal as may be seen from ie following verses:

> Hallowed is He who from on high, step by step, has bestowed upon His servant the standard by which to discern the true from the false, so that to all the world it may be a warning. (Surah 25: *Al-Furqan*: 1)[2]

> (The Qur'an) is but a reminder and a divine discourse, clear in itself and clearly showing the truth, to the end that it may warn everyone who is alive (of heart). (Surah 36: *Yasin*: 69–70)[3]

Osman, Fathi. 1999. *Concepts of the Qur'an*. Los Angeles: MVI Publication. p. 23.

Asad, Muhammad. 1980. *The Message of the Qur'an*. Gibraltar: Dar Al-Andalus.

Ibid.

> This (divine writ) behold, is no less than a reminder to all the worlds. (Surah 38: *Sad*: 87)[4]

> This (message) is no less than a reminder to all mankind—to every one of you who wills to walk a straight way. (Surah 81: *At-Takwir*: 27–28)[5]

The universal mission of the Prophet of Islam is also affirmed by the Qur'an as, for instance, in Surah 34: *Saba'*: 28, which states, "Now (as for the Muhammad,) we have not sent thee otherwise than to mankind at large, to b a herald of glad tidings and a warner."[6]

The non-exclusive spirit of Islam also comes through the oft-repeated teach ing of the Qur'an contained in verses such as the following:

> Verily, those who have attained to faith (in this divine writ), as well as those who follow the Jewish faith, and the Christians, and the Sabians—all who believe in God and the Last day and do righteous deeds—shall have their reward with their Sustainer; and no fear need they have, and neither shall they grieve. (Surah 2: *Al-Baqarah*: 62; this verse is repeated in almost identical form in Surah 5: *Al-Ma'idah*: 69)[7]

> And they claim, "None shall ever enter paradise unless he be a Jew"—or "a Christian." Such are their wishful beliefs! Say: "Produce an evidence for what you are claiming, if what you say is true!" Yea, indeed: everyone who surrenders his whole being unto God, and is a doer of good withal, shall have his reward with his Sustainer; and all such need have no fear, and neither shall they grieve. (Surah 2: *Al-Baqarah*: 111–112)[8]

> And be conscious of the Day on which you shall be brought back unto God, whereupon every human being shall be repaid in full for what he has earned, and none shall be wronged. (Surah 2: *Al-Baqarah*: 281)[9]

Since God is the universal creator who sends guidance to all humanity, Mu lims are commanded by the Qur'an to affirm the divine message given to all th previous Prophets. It is stated in Surah 40: *Ghafir*: 78, "And, indeed, (Muhammad,) We sent forth apostles before thy time; some of them We ha

---

4. *Ibid.*

5. *Ibid.*

6. *Ibid.*

7. *Ibid.*

8. *Ibid.*

9. *Ibid.*

ientioned to thee, and some of them We have not mentioned to thee."[10] While
nly 25 Prophets are mentioned in the Qur'an, the above-cited verse indicates
iat there have also been other Prophets. Indeed, Surah 16: *An-Nahl*: 84 tells
s that God "shall raise up a witness out of every community."[11]

Muslims are required to affirm the continuity of Islam with previous revela-
ons and Prophets and not to make a distinction among them, as can be seen
om the following verses:

> Say: "We believe in God, and in that which has been bestowed from on high
> upon us, and that which has been bestowed upon Abraham and Ishmael
> and Isaac and Jacob and their descendants, and that which has been vouch-
> safed to Moses and Jesus, and that which has been vouchsafed to all the
> (other) prophets by their Sustainer: we make no distinction between any of
> them. And it is unto Him that we surrender ourselves." (Surah 2: *Al-
> Baqarah*: 136)[12]

> Step by step has He bestowed upon thee from on high this divine writ, set-
> ting forth the truth which confirms whatever there remains (of earlier reve-
> lations): for it is He who has bestowed from on high the Torah and the
> Gospel aforetime as a guidance to mankind, and it is He who has bestowed
> (upon man) the standard by which to discern the true from the false. (Surah
> 3: *Al 'Imran*: 3)[13]

> Say: "We believe in God, and in that which has been bestowed from on high
> upon us, and that which has been bestowed upon Abraham and Ishmael
> and Isaac and Jacob and their descendants, and that which has been vouch-
> safed by their Sustainer unto Moses and Jesus and all the (other) prophets:
> we make no distinction between any of them. And unto Him do we surren-
> der ourselves." (Surah 3: *Al 'Imran*: 84)[14]

> Behold, We have inspired thee (O Prophet) just as We inspired Noah and all
> the Prophets after him—as We inspired Abraham, and Ishmael. And Isaac,
> and Jacob, and their descendants including Jesus and Job, and Jonah, and
> Aaron, and Solomon; and as We vouchsafed unto David a book of divine
> wisdom; and (We inspired other) apostles whom We have mentioned to thee
> ere this, as well as apostles whom We have not mentioned to thee; and as
> God spoke His Word unto Moses: (We sent all these) apostles as heralds of

---

Ibid.

. *Ibid.*

. *Ibid.*

Ibid.

Ibid.

glad tidings and as warners, so that men might have no excuse before God after (the coming of) these apostles: and God is indeed almighty, wise. (Surah 4: *An-Nisa'*: 163)[15]

In matters of faith, He has ordained for you that which He enjoined upon Noah—and into which We gave thee (O Muhammad) insight through revelation—as well as that which We had enjoined upon Abraham, and Moses, and Jesus: Steadfastly uphold the (true) faith, and do not break up your unity therein. (Surah 42: *Ash-Shura*: 13)[16]

One major reason why the Prophet Abraham is so important in the Islami tradition is that he is seen as a symbol of the unity of all believers implicit i Qur'anic teaching. Not only is he the Prophet most often mentioned in th Qur'an after Muhammad, but he is also regarded in a significant way as th first "Muslim" because he surrendered his whole self to God. The Qur'a repeatedly describes Abraham as "hanif"—the true in faith—or one who turn away from all that is not-God to submit to God's law and order. It also empha sizes the point that Abraham was "neither a Jew nor a Christian." Abraham regarded as a model monotheist whom the Qur'an refers to as "a friend of God" ("khalil Allah"):

Who can be better
In religion than one
Who submits his whole self
To God, does good,
And follows the way
Of Abraham the true in faith?
For God did take
Abraham for a friend (Surah 4: *An-Nisa'*: 125)[17]

Surah 37: *Al-Saffat*: 83 and 84 point out that Abraham approached Go with a heart and mind in total accord with the will of the creator and that Go recognized and rewarded the faith of Abraham. In his poetry, Muhamma Iqbal—modern Islam's most outstanding poet-philosopher—frequently pictur Abraham as an iconoclast who is shown breaking his father's idols. To Iqbal is necessary to negate all that is not-God (signified by the "la" in the "la ilah illa Allah": "There is no god but God" in the Islamic Shahadah or confessi

---

15. *Ibid.*

16. *Ibid.*

17. 'Ali, 'Abdullah Yusuf. 1989. *The Holy Qur'an*. Brentwood, MD: Amana Corporation.

f Faith) before God's existence can be affirmed. Iqbal's motif captures the ɔirit of the Qur'anic epithet "hanif" which refers not only only to a belief in ¹e one God but also a complete refusal to associate anything or anyone with ·od. Abraham is "hanif" precisely because he upheld the oneness and allness f God in the face of all opposition and obstacles.

According to the Qur'an, it is the spirit of Abraham which would enable ⁴uslims (and other believers in God) to become "witnesses for humankind" as ated in Surah 22: *Al-Hajj*: 78): "And strive hard in God's cause with all the ·riving that is due to Him: it is He who has elected you (to carry His message), ¹d has laid no hardship on you in (anything that pertains to) religion, (and ade you follow) the creed of your forefather Abraham. It is He who has ¹med you—in bygone times as well as in this (divine writ)—'those who have ⁱrrendered themselves to God,' so that the Apostle might bear witness to truth ·fore you, and that you might bear witness to it before all mankind."[18]

Among the rights given by God to all human beings which are strongly firmed by the Qur'an, the following may be regarded as particularly pertinent the context of ethical pluralism.

ᵢght to Life

¹e Qur'an upholds the sanctity and absolute value of human life and states in ᵢrah 6: *Al-An'am*: 151: "...do not take any human being's life—(the life) ¹ich God has declared to be sacred—otherwise than in (the pursuit of) justice: ᵢs has He enjoined upon you so that you might use your reason."[19] In Surah *Al-Ma'idah*: 32, the Qur'an points out that, in essence, the life of each indi-¹ual is comparable to that of an entire community and, therefore, should be ·ated with the utmost care:

> We ordained
> For the Children of Israel
> That if any one slew
> A person—unless it be
> For murder or for spreading
> Mischief in the land—

Asad.

Ibid.

It would be as if
He slew the whole people:
And if any one saved a life,
It would be as if he saved
The life of the whole people.[20]

Right to Respect

In Surah 17: *Al-Isra'*: 70, the Qur'an says: "Now, indeed, worthy of esteer because of all creation they alone chose to accept the 'trust' of freedom of th will" (Surah 33: *Al-Ahzab*: 72). Human beings can exercise freedom of the wi because they possess the rational faculty, which is what distinguishes them fror all other creatures (Surah 2: *Al-Baqarah*: 30–34). Though human beings ca become "the lowest of the low," the Qur'an declares that they have been mad "in the best of moulds" (Surah 95: *At-Tin*: 4–6), having the ability to think, t have knowledge of right and wrong, to do the good and to avoid the evil. Thu on account of the promise which is contained in being human, namely, th potential to be God's vicegerent on earth, the humanness of all human beings to be respected and considered an end in itself.

Right to Freedom

A large part of the Qur'an's concern is to free human beings from the chair that bind them: traditionalism, authoritarianism (religious, political, economic tribalism, racism, classism or caste system, sexism, and slavery.

The greatest guarantee of personal freedom for a Muslim lies in the Qur'an decree that no one other than God can limit human freedom (Surah 42: *As Shura*: 21) and in the statement that "Judgment (as to what is right and wh is wrong) rests with God alone." (Surah 12: *Yusuf*: 40)[21] As pointed out ł Khalid M. Ishaque, an eminent Pakistani jurist: "The Qur'an gives to respons ble dissent the status of a fundamental right. In exercise of their powers, ther fore, neither the legislature nor the executive can demand unquestioning obec ence.... The Prophet, even though he was the recipient of Divine revelation, w required to consult the Muslims in public affairs. Allah addressing the Proph

---

20. 'Ali
21. Asad

says: '...and consult with them upon the conduct of affairs. And... when thou art resolved, then put thy trust in Allah' (Surah 3: *Al-'Imran*: 159)."[22]

The Qur'anic proclamation in Surah 2: *Al-Baqarah*: 256, "There shall be no coercion in matters of faith," guarantees freedom of religion and worship.[23] This means that, according to Qur'anic teaching, non-Muslims living in Muslim territories should have the freedom to follow their own faith-traditions without fear or harassment. A number of Qur'anic passages state clearly that the responsibility of the Prophet Muhammad is to communicate the message of God and not to compel anyone to believe. For instance:

If it had been God's Plan
They would not have taken
False gods: but We
Made thee not one
To watch over their doings,
Nor art thou set
Over them to dispose
Of their affairs. (Surah 6: *Al-An'am*: 107)[24]

If it had been thy Lord's will
They would have all believed,
All who are on earth!
Will thou then compel mankind,
Against their will, to believe? (Surah 10: *Yunus*: 99)[25]

But if they turn away,
Thy duty is only to preach
The clear message. (Surah 16: *An-Nahl*: 82)[26]

If then they turn away,
We have not sent thee
As a guard over them.
Their duty is but to convey
(The Message). (Surah 42: *Ash-Shura*: 48)[27]

---

[22]. Ishaque, Khalid M. 1980. Islamic Law—Its Ideals and Principles. In *The Challenge of Islam*, edited by A. Gauher. London: The Islamic Council of Europe. p. 157.

[23]. Asad

[24]. 'Ali

[25]. *Ibid.*

[26]. *Ibid.*

[27]. *Ibid.*

The right to exercise free choice in matters of belief is unambiguously
endorsed by the Qur'an in Surah 18: *Al-Kahf*: 29, which states:

> The Truth is
> From your Lord:
>   Let him who will
> Believe, and let him
>   Who will, reject (it).[28]

The Qur'an also makes clear that God will judge human beings not on the
basis of what they profess but on the basis of their belief and righteous conduct,
as indicated by Surah 2: *Al-Baqarah*: 62 and Surah 5: *Al-Ma'idah*: 69.

The Qur'an recognizes the right to religious freedom not only in the case of
other believers in God, but also in the case of non-believers in God (if they are
not aggressing upon Muslims). For instance, Surah 6: *Al-An'am*: 108 states:

> Revile not ye
> Those whom they call upon
> Besides God, lest
> They out of spite
> Revile God
> In their ignorance.
>   Thus have We made
> Alluring to each people
> Its own doings.
> In the end will they
> Return to their Lord,
> And We shall then
> Tell them the truth
> Of all that they did.[29]

In the context of the human right to exercise religious freedom, it is important to mention that the Qur'anic dictum, "Let there be no compulsion in religion" applies not only to non-Muslims but also to Muslims. While those who
renounced Islam after professing it and then engaged in "acts of war" against
Muslims were to be treated as enemies and aggressors, the Qur'an does not pre-
scribe any punishment for non-profession or renunciation of faith. The decision
regarding a person's ultimate destiny in the hereafter rests with God.

---

28. *Ibid.*
29. *Ibid.*

The right to freedom includes the right to be free to tell the truth. The Qur'anic term for truth is "Haqq" which is also one of God's most important attributes. Standing up for the truth is a right and a responsibility which a Muslim may not disclaim even in the face of the greatest danger or difficulty (Surah 4: *An-Nisa'*: 135). While the Qur'an commands believers to testify to the truth, it also instructs society not to harm persons so testifying (Surah 2: *Al-Baqarah*: 282).[30]

The Qur'an regards diversity of peoples as well as religious and ethical perspectives as a part of God's design. In a remarkable passage in which reference is made to both the unity and diversity of humankind, the Qur'an states: "O men! Behold, We have created you all out of a male and a female, and have made you into nations and tribes, so that you might come to know one another. Verily, the noblest of you in the sight of God is the one who is most deeply conscious of Him. Behold, God is all-knowing, all-aware." (Surah 49: *Al-Hujurat*: 13)[31] From this verse it is clear that one of the basic purposes of diversity is to encourage dialogue among different peoples and also that a person's ultimate worth is determined not by what group he or she belongs to but how God-conscious he or she is.

That plurality of religions (and ethical viewpoints) is sanctioned by God is attested by the Qur'an in a number of verses. For example:

> To each is a goal
> To which God turns him;
> Then strive together (as in a race)
> Towards all that is good.
> Wheresoever ye are,
> God will bring you
> Together. For God
> Hath power over all things. (Surah 2: *Al-Baqarah*: 148)[32]

> To each among you
> Have We prescribed a Law
> And an Open Way.

---

30. Parwez, G.A. 1981. *Bunyadi Haquq-e-Insaniyat.* (Fundamental Human Rights), Tulu'-e-Islam, Lahore. pp. 34–35.

31. Asad

32. 'Ali

If God had so willed,
He would have made you
A single People, but (His
Plan is) to test you in what
He hath given you: so strive
As in a race in all virtues.
The goal of you all is to God;
It is He that will show you
The truth of the matters
In which ye dispute. (Surah 5: *Al-Ma'idah*: 51)[33]

And (know that) all mankind were once but one single community, and only later did they begin to hold divergent views. And had it not been for a decree that had already gone forth from thy Sustainer, all their differences would have been settled (from the outset). (Surah 10: *Yunus*: 19)[34]

The Qur'an advocates gracious conduct and tolerance toward persons who hold different religious and ethical views as a life-attitude. This can be seen clearly from verses such as the following:

When a (courteous) greeting
Is offered you, meet it
With greeting still more
Courteous, or (at least)
Of equal courtesy,
God takes careful account
Of all things. (Surah 5: *Al-Ma'idah*: 86)[35]

...If the enemy
Incline towards peace,
Do thou (also) incline
Towards peace, and trust
In God: for He is the One
That heareth and knoweth
(All things). (Surah 8: *Al-Anfal*: 61)[36]

If one amongst the Pagans
Ask thee for asylum,
Grant it to him,
So that he may hear the word

---

33. *Ibid.*

34. Asad

35. *Ibid.*

36. 'Ali

Of God; and then exhort him
To where he can be secure. (Surah 9: *At-Taubah*: 6)[37]

Call thou (all mankind) unto thy Sustainer's path with wisdom and goodly exhortation, and argue with them in the most kindly manner: for, behold, thy Sustainer knows best as to who strays from His path, and best knows He as to who are the right-guided. Hence, if you have to respond to an attack (in argument), respond only to the extent of the attack leveled against you; but to bear yourselves with patience is indeed far better for (you, since God is with) those who are patient in adversity. (Surah 16: *An-Nahl*: 125–126)[38]

And do not argue with the followers of earlier revelation otherwise than in a most kindly manner—unless it be such as are bent on evildoing—and say: "We believe in that which has been bestowed from on high upon us, as well as that which has been bestowed upon you: for our God and your God is one and the same, and it is unto Him that we (all) surrender ourselves." (Surah 29: *Al-'Ankubat*: 46)[39]

The ethical imperative central to Qur'anic teaching and the normative Islamic worldview is to enjoin the good—"*al-mar'uf*"—and forbid the evil—"*al-munkar*." Within the parameters of this categorical imperative, Islam is open to accepting and co-operating with any ethical perspective. As pointed out by Fathi Osman in his encyclopedic work, *The Concepts of the Qur'an*, "God is not biased with or against any race, ethnicity, or gender, so His guidance secures absolute justice."[40] ⌇

37. *Ibid.*

38. Asad

39. *Ibid.*

40. Osman, p. 667.

Islam and Human Rights

Khaleel Mohammed

The title of a recent book by Akbar Ahmed sums up the perception of most Muslims about the place of their religion in today's world: *Islam Under Siege*.[1] Although it may be alleged that the reason for this state of affairs is in reaction to the criminality of September 11, 2001, the evidence belies any such claim. Long before that unforgettable date, Edward Said chronicled the demonization of Islam in the 1997 edition of his *Covering Islam* thus:

> Malicious generalizations about Islam have become the last acceptable form of denigration of foreign culture in the West; what is said about the Muslim mind, or character, or religion, or culture as a whole cannot now be said in mainstream discussion about Africans, Jews, other Orientals, or Asians.[2]

Even if one can argue that the actions of authorities in Islamic and Muslim countries do little to contradict such vilification, how can one deny that like vilification ought also be directed against those who have abused the rights of Muslims the world over, not only on an individual level, but also against entire states? In the current post-honor world (a term coined by Akbar Ahmed to describe the chaotic state of affairs that has developed after September 11),[3] the human rights of Muslims everywhere seem to have disappeared. Afghanistan and Iraq have been invaded with horrible loss of life and property. And as if the Abu Ghraib scandal and other human rights violations committed by the United States Armed Forces in those occupied countries have not shocked the world enough, right here in the most fortified citadel of democracy, the Patriot

---

. Ahmed, Akbar. 2003. *Islam Under Siege*. Cambridge: Polity Press.

. Said, Edward. 1997. *Covering Islam*. New York: Vintage Books. pp. xi-xii.

. Ahmed, pp. 14, 56–57.

Act has legitimized the incarceration and deportation of thousands of Muslims, often in a manner totally at odds with due legal process.[4]

These circumstances are what make this essay on Islam and Human Rights a difficult undertaking for me, an academic and an observant Muslim who does not wish to let faith bias impinge on his academic integrity. Even as I seek to correct the draft of my essay, I am confronted with the daily news reports. And while the Nuremberg trials punished those who authorized torture, and while Saddam Hussein will be prosecuted for the horrible torture he inflicted on his own people, lawyers in the United States were attempting to make the President immune from any such charges. Under the telling caption "Lawyers sought to exempt Bush from torture law," an article in *The San Diego Tribune* details how administration lawyers in a 56-page March 2003 memorandum concluded that President Bush was bound by neither an international treaty prohibiting torture nor a federal anti-torture law because he has the authority as commander-in-chief to approve any technique needed to ensure the nation's security. Military personnel could also be immune from prohibitions against torture for a variety of reasons.[5]

Do I therefore expect anything positive that I have to say about Islam to be heeded in a country that has one of its top generals say that my god is inferior to the Judeo-Christian god of Western civilization?[6] How dare I turn a deaf ear to the cries of so many of my coreligionists whose religion is accused of fomenting terror, jihad and just about every problem that challenges human coexistence.

---

4. Books by, or in consultation with, top officials of the US Administration are best sellers in this genre. See for example: (1) Clarke, Richard. 2004. *Against All Enemies: Inside America's War on Terror*. New York: Free Press. (2) Clancy, Tom, with Anthony Zinni et al. 2004. *Battle Ready*. New York: G.P. Putnam's Sons. (3) Susskind, Ron. 2004. *The Price of Loyalty: George W. Bush, The White House and the Education of Paul O'Neill*. New York: Simon and Schuster. (4) Wilson, Joseph. 2004. *The Politics of Truth: Inside the Lies That Led to War and Betrayed My Wife's CIA Identity, a Diplomat's Memoir*. New York: Carroll and Graf Publishers. (5) Woodward, Bob. 2004. *Plan of Attack*. New York: Simon and Schuster.

5. 2004. Lawyers Sought to Exempt Bush from Torture Law. *San Diego Union Tribune*. June 8. p. A2.

6. 2003. General Casts War in Religious Terms. *Los Angeles Times*. October 16.

Yet, write this essay I must. For both academic pursuit and love for my religion compel me to examine the topic of human rights within Islam. Indeed, if most of the world was guilty of human rights abuses against Muslims that still would not excuse me refusing to examine my scripture and tradition for Islam's view on human rights. Researching the issue is, in fact, a duty since, despite the charges against Islam, as well as the violations by Muslim leaders against Muslims and non-Muslims, every believing Muslim nonetheless declares her religion to be the very bastion of human rights! In the following I will attempt to explain this seemingly dichotomous situation.

The Qur'an and Human Rights

Islam's main document is the Qur'an, accepted in the same singular form by all of Islam's various sects. The Qur'an according to Muslim belief is the word of God dictated to Muhammad in Arabic, and committed to memory and later writing, and divinely protected from corruption.[7] Many Westerners, without knowledge of Arabic, have attempted to read translations of the document, and have come away absolutely befuddled. The reason is simple: although now in book form, the Qur'an is not a "scripture" in the sense that one uses that term in reference to the Tanakh or Christian Testament. In fact, the very word "Qur'an," which comes from the word meaning "to recite," indicates why it is different from the books of the other Abrahamic religions.[8] One may read a single chapter of the Tanakh or Christian Testament and get a well-formed idea on a particular subject. In the case of the Qur'an, and the way its verses are arranged, however, one cannot usually read a single chapter to see Islam's view on a particular subject; one has to extrapolate Qur'anic views by what is known as "al-Qira'at al Mawdu'iyyah"—a thematic reading, as advocated by many scholars, most notable among them, the late Muhammad al-Ghazali.[9]

. Von Denffer, Ahmad. 2000. *Ulum al Qur'an: An Introduction to the Sciences of the Qur'an.* Leicestershire: The Islamic Foundation. p. 21.

. Von Denffer, p. 17. See also Sells, Michael. 2002. *Approaching the Qur'an: The Early Revelations.* Ashland, Oregon: White Cloud Press. p. 5.

. Al-Ghazzali, Muhammad. 1997. *A Thematic Commentary on the Qur'an.* Tr. Ashur A. Shamis. Herndon, VA: International Institute of Islamic Thought. p. 10.

The Qur'an, in such a reading, tells us that God created humankind for a single purpose: to worship (Q51:56). This worship, however, is to be understood not only as ritual forms of obeisance and adoration, but also in the way that humans relate to each other, fostering harmony and mutualism. There is no such thing as one right reified religion, to be understood in a triumphalist manner. This is best evidenced by the fact that one of the most powerful verses of the Qur'an is where piety is defined in words that constitute a repudiation of later Muslim constructs:

> Righteousness is not that you turn your faces toward East or West; but righteousness rather is to believe in God and the Last Day and the Angels and the Book and the Messengers; to spend of your substance out of love for Him, for your kin, for orphans and for the needy, for the wayfarer, for those who ask, and for the ransom of slaves; to be steadfast in prayer and practice regular charity; to fulfill the contracts which you have made; and to be firm and patient in suffering and adversity and throughout all periods of panic. Such are the people of truth, those who are God-conscious. (Q2:177)

This is supported by another verse that states:

> Those who believe, and the Jews and the Christians and the Sabians who believe in God and the Last Day and work righteousness, shall have their reward with their Lord; on them shall be no fear nor shall they grieve. (Q2:62)

The Qur'an adumbrates a recurrent theme: God does not love tyranny. The example most often used to graphically underline this message is that of Pharaoh and the Israelites. Pharaoh was the ultimate oppressor, and the Qur'an frequently repeats the narrative of how God rescued the children of Israel from his yoke, and restored to them their human existence.

The Qur'anic understanding of tyranny is not restricted to the physical enslavement of some by others. When a community or nation tries to impose its perceived values upon others, even though such imposition may done in the guise of bringing human rights, it is nonetheless, tyranny. Modern-day examples are the forced "globalization" and "democracy" that have brought more bloodshed and war than any respect for those upon whom such concepts are imposed. For the average Muslim, the picture that springs to mind is the resistance of many Afghanis and Arabs to the imposition of American values on their respective cultures. In the name of freedom and democracy, the American invaded both Afghanistan and Iraq. In the case of Iraq, the result was that a few months after an undemocratic occupation (not sanctioned by the United Nations), the very populace that the U.S. purportedly sought to rescue from Saddam Hussein's tyranny have seen the now-notorious photos from the Abu Ghraib prison, wherein Americans with their alleged higher standards have raped and tortured Iraqis. And many Iraqis have risen up in revolt against their so-called liberators, seeing them now as dictators and tyrants.

From an Islamic perspective, the issue here is not if the American values are superior to Iraqi standards; the issue is the unmitigated shamelessness and cruelty that were utilized to subjugate the Iraqi people. The Qur'an relates the story of a servant of God, Dhul Qarnayn, who came upon a people whom God had chosen not to protect from the sun; the context seems to imply that they were naked: "He came to the place of the rising of the sun, and he found that it shone upon a people from whom we had not provided a cover against it...." (Q18:90) He simply left them as they were, and proceeded to another place where, at the request of the inhabitants, he built them a wall to protect them against their enemies (Q18:94–98). In both cases, Dhul Qarnayn proceeded on his journey—not seeking to subjugate the people to his will, nor impose upon them sartorial values he thought normative. Among the lessons that can be extrapolated from the narrative is that such imposition would have been a violation of their human rights.

These verses seem to clash with those of Solomon's ultimatum to the Queen of Sheba that she and her people enter into the worship of the one God or else face the might of his armed forces (Q27:37). The Qur'anic answer to this is rather simple: for each community there are certain rules and regulations: "For each (community) of you, we have decreed a law and a method" (Q5:48).

Another issue of rights in which the Qur'an instructs is the area of spousal relations. Following the same reasoning that the Mishnah (Tractate Sanhedrin 4:5)[10] outlines for the reason why humankind is descended from a common ancestor, the Qur'an proclaims:

> O humankind! Be conscientious toward your Lord who created you from one being, and from that being, created its mate, and from them both, created many men and women.... And among His signs is that He has created from you wives from yourselves, that you may find completeness and

---

10. *Mishnah: A New Translation.* 1988. Tr. Jacob Neusner. New Haven and New York: Yale University Press. p. 591.

repose in them, and he has created love and mercy between you. Truly in his, there is a sign for those who think (Q4:1; 30:21).

This is further underlined by the verse that tells husbands, "You are as a clothing for them (wives), and they as clothing for you" (Q2:187). The Qur'an points out that it is improper to refrain from granting the other party full rights, explaining its position as "a divorce is only permissible twice; after that the parties should either hold together on equitable terms or separate with kindness" (Q2:229). It goes further:

> When you divorce women, and they fulfill the terms of their 'iddat, either take them back on equitable terms or set them free on equitable terms; but do not take them back to injure them or to take undue advantage; if anyone does that, he wrongs himself (Q2:231).

The foregoing illustrations are simply edicts from within the Qur'an, but contrary to the maximalism imputed to this document by some Muslims, Islam's holy book does not view itself as the sole repository of the sources of law and guidance. It sees other holy books as being such sources, as evidenced, for example, by the following: "We have revealed the Torah: in it there is guidance and light" (Q5:44); "It is He who has sent down the Book to you (Muhammad), with truth, confirming what came before it. He sent down the Torah and the Gospel" (Q3:3). The Qur'an goes further, even insisting that the Jews and Christians are lost unless they adhere to their scriptures: "O People of the Book! You have nothing to stand upon until you observe the Torah and the Gospel" (Q5:68). A perfect example of this Qur'anic respect for the law of another religion is illustrated in the verse that many Muslims quoted for the media in order to distance themselves from the criminality of September 11 2001:

> We ordained for the children of Israel that if anyone slew a person, unless such slaying is for homicide or spreading mischief in the land, it would be as if he slew the entire humankind, and if anyone saved a life, it would be as if he had saved the life of the entire humankind (Q5:33).

In the above verse, the Qur'an is referring to the Mishnaic tractate Sanhedrin and not the laws of the written Torah.[11] (That the Qur'an should grant this edict of the Mishnah the status of divine revelation is rather significant; a discussion on this topic, however, is beyond the scope of this essay.) This law from

---

11. *Ibid.*

a previously revealed religion has become part of the Islamic weltanschauung. Indeed the Qur'anic focus on the law of Judaism is so pronounced that the jurists adduced a source of Islamic law that they deemed as "shari'at man qablanaa"—the law of those before us. Indeed no book on classical Islamic legal theory (usul al-fiqh) is complete without a discussion of this topic.[12] As such, when the early jurists were faced with a matter that the Qur'an did not explain, they examined several solutions, one of them being Hebrew Law.

This respect for human life, and its Mishnaic antecedent, is stressed elsewhere in the Qur'an and seems particularly noteworthy as it strikes directly at the concept of suicide bombings, for which the Qur'an provides no allowance. This is perhaps the grossest violation of human rights, which is why God deems it as if the murderer has killed all of humankind. To those who say that the bombers act out of desperation, because they had no other recourse, the Qur'an states:

> When the angels come to take in death those who have wronged themselves, they ask, "what plight were you in?" They respond, "We were oppressed in the land." The (angels) will reply, "Was not God's earth spacious enough for you to move yourselves away (from evil)?" Such men will find their abode in hell. What a horrible end! (Q4:97).

A further source of human rights in Islam is in the values perceived by the community as good and normative, a sort of *ius gentium*. The Qur'an states: 'You are the best of peoples evolved for humankind, exhorting to that which is known (al ma'ruf), and forbidding that which is evil" (Q3:110). In this verse, the mar'uf (that which is known) is not by the medium of divine revelation, but rather by the collective perception of that which is correct, as if there is some natural law that is in place, hence my reference to *ius gentium*. This is also known in Islam as "al-'urf" or "al-'adah"—often translated as custom—and forms the foundation for the Islamic law maxim "al-'adah muhakkamah"— custom has legal authority.[13] It means therefore that human rights, or the interpretation of what might be deemed as human rights, might not rest solely on scriptural edicts, but on the perception of the people. Medieval Muslim thinkers addressed this issue in the problematic: Did humans, before divine revelation,

2. Ibn Quddama, Muwaffaq. 1983. *Ibn Quddama wa atharuhu al Usuliyya*. Ed. Abd al-Aziz al-Sa'id. Riyadh: Muhammad b. Sa'ud University. p. 160.

3. Al-Borno, Muhammad Siddiqui bin Ahmad. 1990. Al-Wajiz fi I dah Qawa'id al Fiqh al-Kulliyah. Riyadh: Maktabat al-Ma'arif. p. 213.

know what was good from what was bad? The conclusion was that they did, even though some parties in the debate felt that there was no reward or punishment allotted before revelation.

Any discussion of human rights in Islam would be incomplete without touching on Jihad, a concept much misunderstood by Muslim and non-Muslim alike. The Qur'an never advocates the all-out fighting against any community except in defense of human rights. Here are the verses of the Qur'an:

> To those against whom war is made, permission is given (to fight) because they are wronged and verily God is Most Powerful for their aid. (They are) those who have been expelled from their homes in violation of their rights, (for no cause) except that they say, "Our Lord is God." Did God not check one people by means of another, there would surely have been pulled down monasteries, churches, synagogues and mosques in which the name of God is commemorated in abundant measure. God will certainly aid those who aid His (cause); verily God is full of strength, exalted in might (Q22:39–40).

The Qur'an does go further, exhorting to an all-out war, with no quarter given to subdue the enemy when he is intent on the destruction not only of the Muslim community, but of humanity in general—even if that enemy is Muslim:

> If two parties among the believers fall into quarrel, make peace between them; but if one of them transgresses beyond bounds against the other, then all of you fight against the transgressor until it complies with the commands of God; but if it complies, then make peace between them in justice and be fair. God loves those who are fair and just (Q49:9).

In Chapter 9, the most explicit of all the chapters regarding conflict, the Qur'an orders Muslims to observe, even with polytheists in an all-out war, the agreements that they have made (Q9:4). Q2:177, cited earlier, equates the observance of such contracts as a form of piety. The adherence to contractual obligations and the recognition of rights, even when the enemy is bent on destroying Muslims, is based on a psychological truism. War is for the most part evil, and so the Qur'an exhorts, 'Good and evil are not equal. Repay with that which is better. Then the one with whom there existed enmity against you will become as your staunchest protector' (Q41:61).

Promoting global interaction, the Qur'an addresses humankind in words that echo the Hebrew Bible that Muhammad says he came to vouchsafe:

> O Humankind! We created you from a single (pair) of a male and a female, and made you into many nations and tribes so that you might know each

other. Truly the most honored of you in the sight of God is the one who is the most righteous. And God has full knowledge and is well acquainted (with all things) (Q49:13).

The Qur'an thus goes perhaps further than any Abrahamic scripture in recognizing pluralism (at least within the concept of monotheism). "There is no compulsion in religion," declares Q2:256, and then Q2:62 declares that heaven is open to the Jews, Christians, Sabeans, and all monotheists. Yet, the idea of pluralism, while preached, is not practiced, and the discrimination against minority religions in Islamic countries is well known.

Perhaps the greatest problem in this realm is that most of the authoritative Islamic discourse on law takes its starting point from medieval constructs, formed not from the Qur'an only, but from the extrapolations of men who certainly were servants of their time. The reality is that the concept of human rights as understood today could not have been dealt with in detail in any medieval document, of any of the world's civilizations or cultures. The contemporary understanding of human rights thus requires the use of modern thought, and the application of philosophical and exegetical constructs that are still not within the vision of traditional authorities on Islamic law. Yet, it is the case that those who seek to introduce change are ostracized, jailed and in severe cases, even killed—the prime example being Mahmud Taha, the Sudani thinker who was hanged for his views on reform.

Indeed, despite possessing a repository of values that affirm human rights, Islam, as interpreted by those in many positions of authority in nominally Islam states, is often seen as inimicable to human rights. Though this is primarily a *political* and not a *religious* problem, the problems arising from this perceived conflict are not going to disappear, and the Muslims must heed the words of the Qur'an wherein it declares, "God does not change the condition of a people unless they themselves change it" (Q13:11). Is there any prognosis for an attempt, or are there even the outlines of a way to change the system? Theories for change abound. Fazlur Rahman's concept of the "double movement theory" presents a viable solution (we must understand the text in terms of what it meant in its temporal setting, and extrapolate a philosophy that is applicable to the modern world).[14] Mohammad Arkoun's view that as we get more knowl-

---

4. Rahman, Fazlur. 1982. *Islam and Modernity: Transformation of an Intellectual Tradition.* Chicago: University of Chicago Press. p. 5.

edgeable, we must read scripture differently is unassailable in its simple logic,[15] echoing another of Fazlur Rahman's views: Humankind has reached maturity, and must now use its analysis of monotheist ethics, *mutatis mutandis*, to keep abreast with change. Abdullahi an-Na'im's[16] and Khalid Abou al-Fadl's[17] outlines for new approaches to understanding Islam are even more developed and extremely cogent. But the problem is that Fazlur Rahman, Mohammad Arkoun, Abdullahi an-Na'im, and Khalid Abou al-Fadl and similar thinkers are savants not recognized by those who hold authority for the vast masses of Muslims. Moreover, whenever the authorities in the Muslim world have assumed that the impact of any of these thinkers could be effective, they have reacted harshly and decisively.

As already noted, Mahmud Taha, teacher of Abdullahi an-Na'im, was hanged by the Sudanese government in Khartoum on charges that, if they did not clearly so state, implied that he was a heretic. And Khalid Abou al-Fadl's book wherein he criticized some of the traditional responsa rulings was banned.[18] And the Egyptian sociologist and reformer Sa'd al-Din Ibrahim was jailed in Cairo when he raised certain questions. He only enjoys freedom now because of the pressure brought to bear by the United States on the government of Egypt.

While there is the general usage of the concepts that may suggest reform and adaptability in the Muslim world, the fact is that any notion of change is stymied by neorevivalism and neo-fundamentalism, to use two of Fazlur Rahman's terms.[19] Change and adaptability are seen as heretical ideas that beckon to Westernism and secularism, making light of the permanency of God's final, immutable book.

15. Arkoun, Mohammed. 1994. *Rethinking Islam*. Tr. Robert Lee. Boulder, San Francisco, Oxford: Westview Press. pp. 35–40.

16. an-Na'im, Abdullahi Ahmed. 1990. *Toward an Islamic Reformation*. Syracuse: Syracuse University Press.

17. Abou el-Fadl, Khalid. 2003. *Speaking in God's Name*. Oxford: One World Publications.

18. Abou el-Fadl, Khalid. 1997. *The Authoritative and Authoritarian in Islamic Discourses: A Case Study*. Austin, TX: Dar al-Taiba.

19. Rahman, p. 136.

The politicization of interpretation is further exemplified by the gender issue in the world of Islamic study. It is for example significant that all of the names provided above for reform ideas are those of males—and they have been rejected by the androcentric authority figures of contemporary Islam. This only makes it clearer that the perspicacious views of female scholars such as Azizah al-Hibri, Riffat Hassan, Asma Barlas, Amina Wadud, Fatima Mernissi, etc., will face an almost impossible uphill battle for recognition. And so the process of inexorable ossification continues, while Muslim apologists and triumphalists rant about the Qur'an's peerless contribution to human rights.

For all of the foregoing pessimism, it must not be assumed that Muslim organizations do not recognize the need for reform. The International Institute for Islamic Thought (IIIT), with offices in several countries, is a think tank that seeks to bring about much-needed reform. Only in the West can they operate with full freedom, and it is not just a coincidence that some of the most dynamic thinkers of Islam now reside in Western countries.

To be sure, a new perspective on human rights in Islam will most likely come from Muslim scholars in the Western world. And, despite the general rejection of women activists and scholars within the Muslim world, the thrust of their scholarship is so compelling that, though it seems an uphill struggle, their voices will be in the not-so-distant future heard and heeded. Azizah al-Hibri is regularly consulted by Muslim organizations in the Middle East, and her advice has been offered without her compromising any of her feminist values. Professor Asma Barlas is a participant in Islamic conferences in the Arab world and not just in the West. Will these women be icebreakers for other reformers? Only time will tell.

Conclusion

At the beginning of this paper, Edward Said's observations were cited, and they are now more cogent than ever before. In North America and Europe, until the invasion of Iraq, the early polemical approach to Islam almost became tempered by a more academic outlook. In the months leading up to the invasion, however, the newspaper reports about weapons of mass destruction and the concomitant demonization of the perceived enemy's religion have resulted in a giant step back for the approaches to Islam. The recent publication in France of Jacques Ellul's virulent anti-Islamic tract, *Islam et judeo-christianisme*, with a preface by the renowned political philosopher Alain Besançon, is a particularly egregious case in point.[20] There are several books now on the market that show that Islam is opposed to Western civilization, and that in fact there is no room for harmony between Islam and the West, or that Islam is truly a blot on human civilization.[21] The only interaction can be in fact, a clash of civilizations, to use Samuel Huntington's term.[22]

The underlying message seems to be that, for all the scholarly jargon coined in research, there is still a demarcation between a civilized, righteous, intelligent and peaceful "us"—the West, with its proclaimed secular-cum-professed-Judeo-Christian values—against a barbaric, evil, unintelligent, terrorist "them"—the Muslims and their Islam. This sentiment is so deeply ingrained that, even in light of the human rights abuses that have surfaced in the Abu Ghraib scandal, even in light of the recent revelations about the error of declaring war in Iraq, U.S. Defense Secretary Donald Rumsfeld could still, on June 5, 2004, declare, "we have to find ways to persuade young Muslims that the way of the future is through education and opportunity, not through suicide and terrorism."[23] (Nowhere in his statements on his visit to Asia did he seem to reflect on the reason why so many Muslims, if they did not previously, are now beginning to harbor a grudge against the United States and its allies.)

At the root of this problem too is another misconception: that Islam is essentially non-Western, opposed to the West, and has a distinct culture. This misconception has become so widespread that it is regarded almost as a truism

---

20. Jacques Ellul, *Islam et judeo-christianisme*, Paris, Presses Universitaires de France, 2004.

21. Examples are: (1) Benjamin, Daniel, and Steven Simon. 2002. *The Age of Sacred Terror*. New York: Random House. (2) Katz, Rita. 2003. *Terrorist Hunter*. New York: HarperCollins Publishers. (3) Gold, Dore. 2003. *Hatred's Kingdom*. Washington: Regnery Publishing. (4) Gabriel, Mark. 2002. *Islam and Terrorism*. Lake Mary, Fl: Charisma Publications. (6) Gabriel, Mark 2003. *The Unfinished Battle: Islam and the Jews*. Lake Mary, FL: Charisma Publications. (7) Lindsey, Hal. 2002. *The Everlasting Hatred: The Roots of Jihad*. Murrieta, CA: Oracle House Publishing. (8) Fallaci, Oriana. 2002. *The Rage and the Pride*. New York: Rizzoli Printing. (9) Spencer, Robert. 2002. *Islam Unveiled*. San Francisco: Encounter Books. (10) Timmerman, Kenneth. 2003. *Preachers of Hate*. New York: Crown Forum.

22. Huntington, Samuel P. 1996. *The Clash of Civilizations and the Remaking of World Order*. New York: Simon and Schuster.

23. 2004. *San Diego Union Tribune*. Citing AP report, June 6, p. A16.

stemming from what Edward Said has rightfully termed "an imaginative geography."[24] For if we are referring to geographical birthplace, Judaism, Christianity and Islam all spring from the same general area. In the contemporary world, there are Muslims in every part of the globe, having cultural values that differ markedly from their co-religionists elsewhere. I, for example, coming from Guyana, South America, do not consider myself any less Muslim than my co-religionist from Saudi Arabia; yet, our cultural mores set us worlds apart. As Asma Barlas has pointed out, counter-posing Islam and the West is problematic since one is a religion and the other is a space. To represent religious and cultural diversity in terms of opposition already presumes irreducible differences, making all talk of synthesis and reconciliation moot.[25]

The result of globalization has moreover meant the imposition of European and American, i.e., "Western," values on the whole world. This has led in turn to the creation of the so-called evil axis, consisting primarily of Muslim countries wherein supposedly lies all that must be eradicated, through the process of the imposition of democracy, and this must be achieved by all means possible.

In some areas of political conflict that have a majority Muslim population, or are entirely Muslim, it is often difficult to ascertain if social conflict is caused by political and economic factors, or by religion. Secular governments in Egypt, Tunisia, Turkey and Syria have often been extremely harsh on mainstream Islamic organizations or parties that offer an alternative vision of society or are critical of government policies.[26] In fact, given that the U.S. declared war on terrorism, many countries find that it is now worthwhile to declare they are waging a battle against Islamic terrorists in order to get American aid. In April 2004, after a two-year investigation, Macedonian police spokesperson Mirjana Kontesta admitted that her country's law enforcement personnel had murdered seven innocent Pakistanis simply to impress the United States that Macedonia

---

24. Said, Edward. 1978. *Orientalism*. New York: Vintage Books. pp. 55–56.

25. Barlas, Asma. "Reviving Islamic Universalism: East/s, West/s and Coexistence." Conference on Contemporary Islamic Studies, Alexandria. Egypt. Oct 4–5, 2000 (available online at www.ithaca.edu/faculty/abarlas/papers/barlas_20031004.pdf).

26. Esposito, John. 2002. *What Everyone Needs to Know About Islam*. Oxford: Oxford University Press. p. 72.

was an ally in the war against terrorism.[27] In these cases the so-called irreconcilable conflict between the "West" and "Islam" (in quotation marks for both are fictions, created for ideological use and consumption) has in fact been internalized within the societies themselves and turned to manipulative weapons in the hands of the powers that be.

Last, in the wake of September 11, Muslims have experienced harsh attacks on both their person and their belief system. Without any knowledge of Islam, there are many "experts" who now shamelessly militate against an entire religion and its people. It is accepted as normal to produce films demonizing an entire civilization; it is normal to categorize an entire people as terrorists, as abusers of human rights. It has become acceptable to have Western media speak ill of Islam and the Muslim; but if the Muslim countries speak ill of the United States and other Western countries, they are considered to be fomenting hate and terror. In the face of what is often an unreined demonization of Islam, it is difficult to have its values understood and appreciated by a public that relies on the television and popular media for its information.

This essay has attempted no apologetic for the magnificence of Islam and its regard for human rights; it has presented neither a para-history of a glorious past nor a history of how, under the golden age of Islam, those within the Islamic state lived in wonderful harmony. That, for me, would have been unthinkable, a travesty against the honesty that is enjoined upon me by my God. For as a Muslim, although I see within the Qur'an a wonderful foundation for human rights, I hold that "Islam"—the community of Muslims—has in adopting a pan-Arab, male-centered authority system, failed to put into practice that which it professes. And while my culture and family values have always trained me not to wash dirty linen in public, the God of Islam commands me thus: "O you who believe! Be witnesses for God, upholders of Justice, even if it be against yourselves, or your parents and kin" (Q4:135). For any of my family or coreligionists then to expect me to disobey this imperative would have been to violate my human rights. ∽

---

27. 2004. Macedonia Says Police Faked Attack. *Washington Post*. April 30.

The Sources of Human Rights Ideas: A Christian Perspective[1]

Max L. Stackhouse

More than a quarter century ago, I was invited by my church to participate in ecumenical discussions and to serve as a visiting lecturer in the theological academies of sister churches in the German Democratic Republic and in South India. I became fascinated with the way in which different ideational and social traditions treated human rights, including the interpretations of the United Nations Declaration of 1947 and its subsequent "Covenants." Resistance to "Western" definitions of human rights was intense in the Marxist parties of Eastern Europe and, it turned out, in both the leadership of the Congress Party under Indira Gandhi in India, when she declared her "Emergency" in 1976, and the then-emerging Hindu Nationalist parties that have now issued in the current Hindu nationalist government. On the basis of these extended exposures to non-Western interpretations of human rights at that time, I engaged in a comparative study of the roots and conceptual framework that made modern human rights discourse possible.[2] The invitation to contribute to this forum is a welcome opportunity to rethink the issues in view of new conditions.

The new conditions are probably obvious to all. Beyond the judgment against the inhumane barbarism of Nazism, which triggered the United Nations

---

[1]. An earlier version of portions of this paper was first delivered at a conference on Religion, Tolerance, and Human Rights, held at Hebrew College and Andover Newton Theological School (Newton, MA) in October 2002, also sponsored by the Pew Charitable Trusts, and is forthcoming in the 2004 *Journal of Human Rights* 3.

[2]. Although deeply engaged in the movement for civil rights in the 1960s, as led by Martin Luther King, Jr., my experiences in India and the old East Germany in the 1970s forced the question to the level of human rights. The results of my explorations led to Stackhouse, Max L. 1981. Some Intellectual and Social Roots of Modern Human Rights Ideas. *Journal for Scientific Study of Religion* 20 (4):301–309, then to Stackhouse, Max L. 1984. *Creeds, Society, and Human Rights*. Grand Rapids: Wm. Eerdmans Publishers, and several related subsequent efforts.

Declaration, the great struggles facing issues of human rights and pluralism of the last third of the previous century had to do with racial justice, the rising parallel movements of equal rights for women, and the worldwide movements for de-colonialization. All these took place in the context of a life-and-death confrontation of the "free world" with "world communism" and the development of the idea of the "third world." The question was whether human rights were in any sense universal, especially in view of the fact of pluralism. It is not, of course, the case that the world became pluralistic all of a sudden—it had been so for as long as we have recorded history; but the direct awareness of cultures, traditions, customs, moralities, social orders and religions, brought to us by modern communication, transportation, urbanization and immigration, made the pluralistic world more present to us.

In some ways the consensus has grown that human rights are universal, at least with regard to the issues of race and sex.[3] Racism and sexism are widely condemned although they have not been abolished, and a number of regions are experiencing new diversities that evoke new forms of ethnic consciousness and conflict. Still, the suspicion remains that human rights in other areas of civil and political rights are an invention of the bourgeois West, in spite of the fact that the Soviet world has collapsed, and with it the chief advocates of this view. In some ways, their place as been taken by the rise of Islamist militancy, and with it a theocratic rather than a humanistic hope for a revolutionary change that will overthrow the influence of the world's largest religion and of the remaining superpower. This has happened in the context of massive globalization in technology, science, democratic ideals, the increased power and range of professionalism, ecological consciousness, media influence and economic interaction, all of which also bring a fresh encounter of the world religions.[4]

---

3. The problems remain in the old East Germany, and hostility to "guest workers" remains intense among the youth. And, in regard to India, the ENI (Ecumenical News Information, week of Sept 16, 2002) reported that Dalits in India rejoiced when a UN Committee had just voted to classify "casteism" as "racism." In this, caste has been recognized as evil cross-culturally, but it has not been overcome. If anything, certain current movements under the flag of "Hindutva," a virulent form of Hindu Nationalism, seem to be reinforcing caste consciousness and attempting to re-establish traditional roles for women.

4. These are the leading themes of a four-volume project, 2000, 2001, 2002, and forthcoming, *God and Globalization*. Harrisburg, PA: Trinity Press International, now underway at the Center for Theological Inquiry, Princeton.

To be sure, many people think about globalization only in economic terms. But this narrow understanding of our present situation, as if the economic challenges were not themselves largely a function of educational, technological, legal, communication, and, indeed, moral and spiritual developments, blinds us to one of the most difficult problems of universalistic principles in the face of pluralism, the conflict of values, of definitions held by the world religions of what is human and what is right. On the whole, globalization is the forming of a new and wider human interdependence, extremely complex and highly variegated, that nevertheless raises the prospect of a new world civilization, and the now unavoidable encounter of the world's cultures and societies, and the religious values on which they are based, requires us to think again about universalistic ethical principles, and whether they are possible and real, what difference they make and whether they inhibit or enhance the prospects of a genuine and principled pluralism. After all, to speak of "human" rights is to speak categorically, irrespective of social and cultural differences.

On this point, those who defend human rights as global principles have reason to be cautiously optimistic. We can be optimistic, for the wider vision of human rights ideas has, at the least, become a part of the *ius gentium*, the operating consensus as to what constitutes proper behavior by states and other formal institutions, and what counts as compelling moral argument in contemporary international discourse. Although it seemed in the middle years of the twentieth century that a neo-pagan nationalism and a militant anti-liberalism of socialist secularism, both backed by radically historicist philosophies that denied any "essentialist" normative order, could not be contained by theological, ethical or social wisdom and would bring only Holocausts, Gulags and violence to the future, it was to often-obscured Judeo-Christian ethical principles, frequently in their religiously neutered Enlightenment formulations, that the nations have increasingly adopted.[5]

---

[5] A fascinating recent account is Glendon, Mary Ann. 2001. *The World Made New: Eleanor Roosevelt and the Universal Declaration of Human Rights*. New York: Random House. Glendon mentions the religious influences on the development of human rights at several points, with special reference to the contributions of the Lebanese Protestant Charles Malik and the French Catholic Jacques Maritain. Further, Lauren, Paul Gordon. 1998. *The Evolution of Human Rights*. Philadelphia: University of Pennsylvania Press, offers a broader treatment of influences from other world religions. These studies contribute to a growing correction of an anti-religious bias in parts of the human rights community, deriving from the anti-Catholic enlightenment tradition rooted in the French Revolution (see note 19, below) even if we must recognize that several wings of the Christian traditions were complicit in the Holocaust.

The background story of how this definition of human rights came to enter the official, cross-cultural, international definition of standards, however, is only now being told. In fresh research, the British scholar-pastor, Canon John Nurser, has documented in extended detail the ways in which, from 1939 until 1947, leading Ecumenical Protestant figures not only worked with key figures in developing the Bretton Woods agreements, anticipating a post-war need for economic stability and development, but also formed the Commission for a Just and Durable Peace, the Churches' Commission on International Affairs and later the Joint Committee on Religious Liberty, all under the auspices of the Federal Council of Churches, with close connections to the emerging World Council of Churches and the International Missionary Conference. These organizations, notably led by Lutheran O. Frederick Nolde, Congregationalist Richard Fagley, Baptist M. Searle Bates, and Presbyterian John A. Mackay, among others, were dedicated to shaping what they then called a "new world order" that would honor human rights. They worked closely with Jacob Blaustein and Joseph Proskauer of the American Jewish Committee and with twelve bishops of the Roman Catholic Church to encourage the formation of the drafting committees of the U.N. Charter Committee and the committee that composed the Universal Declaration on Human Rights and deeply shaped their results. Further, they worked through their church and synagogue contacts at the local level to build the popular support for what they were doing. In fact, the more of this history that is dug out, the clearer it becomes that they supplied much of the intellectual and ethical substance that formed these so-called secular documents.[6] Such data is of particular importance, for it helps correct the secularists' slanderous treatment of religion as the cause of human rights violations.

The results of such efforts are what, at least, the leaders from most of the world's great cultures have now endorsed, and what oppressed peoples appeal to for justice, functionally recognizing principles of universal justice in the

---

6. The 'Ecumenical Movement' Churches, 'Global Order', and Human Rights: 1938–48. Forthcoming. *William and Mary Law Review.* Cf., Hill, Mark, ed. 2002. *Religious Liberty and Human Rights.* Cardiff: University of Wales Press, although some of these essays are less directly relevant to this topic.

legacy of these particular traditions.[7] Moreover, there are, at present, more people living under democratically ordered constitutions that seek to protect human rights, there is a broader public constituency interested in defending them than at any point in human history and there is little evidence of their fading from normative use soon.[8] Indeed, even those who violate human rights or plead special conditions, temporary delays or hermeneutical differences regarding the relative weight of some as compared to others, seldom deny their validity as ideals or goals.

Yet if these facts give us reason to be optimistic, it must be a cautious optimism, not only because the rights of so many people continue to be savagely violated in so many places, and the exigencies of earlier battles against domination by colonialized peoples and now against threats of terrorism in many countries seem to justify the use of means that threaten the rights of groups and persons in ways that are more than "collateral damage." For those who seek to defend civil rights and liberties and see them as a way to love their neighbors near and far, the potential erosion of the legal protections of civil rights and liberties is a matter of immediate and pressing practical concern. This is so because such erosion denies that there are inalienable human rights that stand beyond and above civil rights, which are granted by a state and thus can be withdrawn by civil authority. It makes human rights a function of state policy not a matter of universal principle.

---

[7]. Küng, Hans. 1993. Parliament of World Religions' Global Ethic. *National Catholic Reporter*, Sept. 24. pp. 11 f. See also his 1991 *Global Responsibility: In Search of a New World Ethic*. New York: Crossroad, and 1997 *A Global Ethic for Global Politics and Economics*. New York: Oxford. These are deeply related to his earlier works, one with Küng, Hans, Josef van Ess, et al. 1986. *Christianity and the World Religions: Paths to Dialogue with Islam, Hinduism, and Buddhism*. New York: Doubleday; and Küng, Hans, and Julia Ching. 1989. *Christianity and Chinese Religions*. New York: Doubleday. Similarly, the Millennium World Peace Summit of Religious and Spiritual Leaders, meeting in Moscow in November 2001, declared, "Believers have a right to make their lives conform with their beliefs. But no one has a right to use their beliefs to take the lives or violate the rights of others. No religion allows for that." [peacesummit@ruder finn.com]

[8]. See, e.g., Witte, John Jr. 2001. A Dickensian Era of Religious Rights: An Update on Religious Human Rights in Global Perspective. *William and Mary Law Review* 42 (3):707–770; and Witte, John Jr. 1999. *God's Joust, God's Justice: The Revelations of Legal History*. *Princeton Seminary Bulletin* 20 (3):295–313, which have informed views contained in this presentation at several points.

This points to a deeper threat, for it takes human rights outside the realm of universal, meta-legal norms that cannot be repealed by political authority, no matter how powerful. It is a refusal to see human rights as the same as the prohibition against murder. The world, after all, has known that murder is wrong for many centuries, and every people have laws against it. People know that murders occur, with very few "justifiable homicides." But they also know that the empirical fact that things happen does not negate the normative principles by which we judge them. Today, the threat to human rights is deeper than their sometimes violation; it is a profound intellectual and spiritual problem, for many today doubt that we can have or defend any trans-empirical principles to judge empirical life. Moreover, human rights ideas were formulated historically by those branches of the biblically based traditions, especially Jewish and Christian, that were willing to recognize, learn from and selectively embrace philosophical and legal insights from other cultures if they saw them also living under universal principles of right and wrong that they did not construct and could not de-construct.[9]

Certainly we cannot say that all of Judaism or of Christianity has supported human rights; it has been key minority traditions that have argued their case over long periods of time and become more widely accepted. Nor can we say that even these traditions have been faithful to the implications of their own heritage at all times, and the horror stories of our pasts also have to be told to mitigate any temptation to triumphalism. Still, intellectual honesty demands recognition of the fact that what passes as "secular," "Western" principles of basic human rights developed nowhere else than out of key strands of the bib

---

9. Most Christians hold that this adoption or "baptism" of non-biblical ideas that are compatible with the universalist moral and spiritual insights of the Gospel is quite possible, and sometimes able to refine what the tradition held reflexively, as anticipated in earlier portions of the Bible itself, especially in the Wisdom literature. It was extended in the traditions that developed after the fuller formation of Judaism and Christianity in the selective embrace of Greek philosophy, Roman Law, and, later, certain insights from other cultures. It is being further extended today as people from many cultures bring other philosophical, moral, social and religious insights with them into contemporary theological and ethical understanding. The famous passages in the book of Acts speak of all having "the law written on their hearts," and where all those gathered from many regions understand the preaching "each in his own language" is being re-enacted.

lically rooted religions.[10] And while many scholars and leaders from other traditions have endorsed them, and found resources in their own traditions that point to quite similar principles, today these views are under suspicion both by some Asian leaders who appeal to "Asian values" and by some communitarian and postmodern philosophers in the West who have challenged the very idea of human rights. The deepest threat comes from those intellectual leaders who have adopted anti-universalist, anti-principal perspectives.

Those who doubt the validity of human rights do so on the ground that there neither is nor can be a universalistic moral theology, master narrative or *jus naturale* to support the idea.[11] That, of course, is a universalistic claim in itself, one that ironically presses toward a universal moral relativism. Thus, they see "the West's" pressure to affirm human rights as rooted in a positive *jus civile* of a particular civilization or (in some versions) in the philosophical or religious "values" of distinct traditions or historical periods of thought, and doubt that either human-wide "first principles" or universalistic ends can be found if one turns to particular traditions, especially in the face of religious variety and cultural multiplicity. The fact of the diversity of religions and cultures is taken as an argument for a relativism in normative morality. Thus, human rights are seen as a matter of socio-historical context. While some lament that more universal principles cannot be found, many celebrate the fact, making diversity,

---

10. In this regard, the great Jewish jurist of the late nineteenth century, Georg Jellinek, was surely correct in his *Die Erklärung der Menschen- und Bürgerrechte: Ein Beitrag zur modernen Verfassungsgeschichte* (1895, Leipzig) that the roots of modern views of human rights are utterly dependent on Jewish roots and Christian developments.

11. The idea of "natural law" and its relationship to theology has been debated for centuries and is subject to many interpretations, complicated by scientific views of the "laws of nature" that have no ethical content. I intend the use most common in jurisprudence, an appeal to universal principles of justice discernable by reason, a usage that leaves open the question of whether or not they, and the capacity to discern them, are given by God. Traditions of natural law that have given rise to concepts of human rights, however, are essentially theological in nature, as we see in Roman Catholic and Calvinist thought. See the cluster of books that came out to celebrate the 50th anniversary of the United Nations Declaration of Human Rights, e.g., Tierney, Brian. 1997. *The Idea of Natural Rights*. Atlanta: Scholars Press; Haas, Guenther. 1997. *The Concept of Equity in Calvin's Ethic*. Waterloo: Wilfred Laurier University Press; Haakonssen, Knud. 1996. *Natural Law and Moral Philosophy*. Melbourne: Cambridge University Press of Australia; and the conversations of these traditions, Cromartie, Michael, ed. 1997. *A Preserving Grace: Protestants, Catholics, and Natural Law*. Grand Rapids: Wm. B. Eerdmans Publishers.

multi-culturalism, and religious distinctions themselves universally positive moral values, although on their own grounds it is difficult to see how they could defend the view, except as a cultural preference. In this situation, to insist that all people be judged according to principles of human rights is seen as an act of cultural imperialism.[12] In addition, some argue that such "values" are altogether too individualistic, and that since abstract individuals do not exist, only concrete persons-in-relationship do, we need an ethic based essentially in the particularities of specific community-embedded practices and duties.[13]

Politically, such arguments can be seen to feed the interests of those states that are the least democratic and the most likely to violate the rights of their own citizens, as recognized by the inter-faith Project on Religion and Human Rights. Nearly a decade ago they recognized that:

> To date, governmental claims that culture justifies deviating from human rights standards have been made exclusively by states that have demonstrably bad human rights records. State invocations of "culture" and "cultural relativism" seem to be little more than cynical pretexts for rationalizing human rights abuses that particular states would in any case commit. (Some) ... emulate China in appealing to ... national sovereignty....

---

12. Some of these objections to human rights are catalogued and critiqued in Henkin, Louis, Vigen Guroian, John Langan S.J., et al. 1998. Religion and Human Rights: A Discussion. *Journal of Religious Ethics* 26 (2):229–271. I attempted to address some of the key objections in my response, The Intellectual Crisis of a Good Idea, *Ibid.*, as well as in Stackhouse, Max L., and S Healey. 1996. Religion and Human Rights: A Theological Apologetic. In *Religious Human Rights in Global Perspective*, edited by J. Witte and J. v. d. Vyver. The Hague: Martinus Nijhof Publishers, 485–516; and, Stackhouse, Max L. 1999. Human Rights and Public Theology: The Basic Validation of Human Rights. In *Religion and Human Rights: Competing Claims?*, edited by C. Gustafson and P. Juviler. New York: M.E. Sharp., pp. 12–30.

13. This view is argued by Alasdair MacIntyre, who after years advocating Hegel, Marx and Nietzsche, in his 1981 *After Virtue*, Notre Dame, IN: University of Notre Dame Press, attacks both Protestantism and the Enlightenment, especially Kant, which he says generated the Modernit that led to the terrors of the twentieth century (ignoring the fact that the statism of imperial Germany, which Hegel approved, the socialism of Marx and the nihilism of Nietzsche all sought to dismantle the Christian and Enlightenment defenses of human rights against these forces of terror). Other noted critics of the rights traditions are Michael Sandel (vs John Rawls), Selya ben Habib (vs Jürgen Habermas) and Stanley Hauerwas (vs Reinhold Niebuhr). Certain parallel discussions appear in Asian philosophy; see, e.g., de Bary, William T., and Tu Wei Ming, eds. 1998 *Confucianism and Human Rights*. New York: Columbia University Press, and in perspective from other parts of the world. See Gustafson and Juviler, *op. cit.*

(Others) ... such as Saudi Arabia,... maintain that they are following Islamic human rights norms, while failing to adhere to the norms that they officially deem Islamic....[14]

Yet these critics have one valid point that fuels their argument. They are partially correct insofar as they know that abstract principles and abstracted autonomous conceptions of human nature do not and cannot supply a full ethic for humanity or provide the general theory to guide a just and peaceful civil society in a global era. They also know that particular kinds of ethical obligations, rooted in specific traditions of duty, are authentic aspects of morality and identity and that the most significant of these are rooted in commitments that have become joined to religious loyalties, and that something precious would be lost or betrayed if these were denied.

But these critics are only partly correct. They are also partly wrong when they view the matter as a situation where we must turn *either* to first principles of an abstract universalistic kind *or* to concrete networks of culturally, historically and biographically gained commitments, loyalties and expectations that shape our senses of responsibility, especially if that is how they view the highest level of religious or theological truth. In fact, most ethical issues, including those of human rights, require a synthetic judgment, one in which we must join normative first principles to the concrete matrices of experience by which we know events and read the existing ethos of our lives—that concrete network of events, traditions, relationships, commitments and specific blends of connectedness and alienation that shapes the "values" of daily experience and our senses of obligation. The classic traditions of case-study, codified in the "responsa" literature and in classic casuistry as well as the modern strictures of court procedure, exemplify this joining: they require both a finding of law, which involves the critical reflection on juristic first principles behind the law, *and* a finding of fact," which requires reliance on the experience-gained wisdom, often having to argue before a jury of peers. Moreover, they require an anticipatory assessment of the various consequences of various courses of action implied by a judgment about the interaction of principle and fact.

---

14. Kelsay, John, and Sumner B. Twiss. 1994. *Human Rights and Religion.* New York: Human Rights Watch/The Project on Religion and Human Rights, p. 38.

Indeed, it is theologically paradigmatic that following the accounts of the Decalogue in both Exodus and Deuteronomy—surely prime example of universalistic abstract principles—the next several chapters are repositories of the casuistic results of the blending of the implications of those principles with the situations that people experienced concretely in their ethos. That joining rendered judgments that are held to contribute to the well-being of the common life and to the development of a morally righteous people. Similarly, much in the prophetic tradition makes the case against the infidelities of the people and/or the people in power by identifying the enduring principles in the covenants of old, the experience of social history in the present, and the prospects for a bleak, or a redeemed, future according to human deserts and divine mercy. And, for Christians specifically, to deny that any absolute universal can be connected to the realities of concrete historical experience in ways that lead to a redeemed future is in fact a denial of the deepest insight of our faith: that Christ was both fully God and fully human, and that his life fulfilled the commands of God, was concretely lived in the midst of a specific ethos and nevertheless pointed to an ultimate future that we could not otherwise obtain.

This should be our first lesson in understanding the bases of human rights. They foster specific kinds of pluralism first of all because theologically based moral judgments are, in principle, demanding of a universalistic reference point but are simultaneously pluralistic in their internal structure. They demand critical reflection on the first principles of right and wrong, plus both the repeated analysis of the actual events and experiences of life as they occur in particular contexts, and a vision of the ultimate future—one that anticipates a more final assessment of what is right, judges what is wrong and affirms what is already good as we live toward the future.[15] The philosophies and politics of "either/or" are inevitably lopsided.

The first implications of this brief excursus about "abstractions" for our question are these: do not trust theologians, philosophers or social critics who repudiate first principles or advocate positions or policies that encourage humanity to ignore them in favor of a view that accents only the concreteness

---

15. This "ethical trinity" of moral judgment is one of the basic themes of my teaching and writing and is most recently presented in the "General Introduction" to *God and Globalization*, *op. c*

of historical experience. Similarly, do not trust those philosophers or religious leaders who do not take into account the complex matrices of experience that people have in the concrete contexts of life. Moreover, we should place both under scrutiny on the question of whether their proposals regarding the prospects for the ultimate future are a horizon in which we shall be able to discern an assessment of our proximate synthetic judgments.

Not only do I want to argue that the affirmation of such "universal absolutes" as those stated in the Ten Commandments—and less perfectly embodied in human rights provisions of our historic constitutions and such documents as the United Nations Declaration—are compatible with, and in fact seen most profoundly by, certain strands of the deeper theological heritage, I want to claim that without the impetus of theological insight, human rights concepts would not have come to their current widespread recognition, and that they are likely to fade over time if they are not anchored in a universal, context-transcending metaphysical reality.

In another way, too, I want to suggest that there is another way in which "abstraction" is required by the best of Christian and ethical views. At the practical level, persons are sometimes abstracted from their concrete historical situations and need the protection of abstract laws and rules and procedures of enforcement that say: "This person may already be alienated from his or her context of ordinary moral relationships, but the dismantling of this person's integrity must not proceed beyond specifiable limits, it is 'indivisible.' Thou shalt not torture, abuse, violate, exploit or wantonly execute even the most miserable and guilty specimen of a human being!" We can see this in one way when we are dealing with someone accused of a crime, imprisoned, subjected to slavery or forced labor, victimized by rape or torture, forced to submit to arranged marriages or liaisons, or denied the ability to participate by voice or vote in familial, political or economic institutions that decide their fate. In these imposed situations, persons are functionally alone, abstracted, as they face a dominating power they cannot control and to which they do not give honest assent. Without knowing what the race, gender, nationality, cultural background, social location, political preferences, character or network of friends of a person are, we must say, abstractly, "some things ought never to be done to them"; and if persons, to live and sustain some shred of dignity in the midst of some one or other of such situations need help, "some things ought to be done for them," as Michael Perry has put it.[16] This implies that other people and institutions must limit their powers with regard to persons, and not define the whole of the meaning of a person by the communities, traditions and habits in which they are embedded. This means also that, in some ways, a profound individualism—in the sense of the moral inviolability of each person, in contrast to only communitarian regard—is required.

At other points, people abstract themselves from the matrices of life in which they dwell ordinarily, when they choose to leave home, get married (especially if the partner is one of whom the parents do not approve for reasons, say, of ethnicity or religion), seek access to a profession other than that of the "station in life" into which they were born, decide to have or not to have a child by the use of pregnancy technology and, most critical for our discussions, decide whether to follow the faith in which they were born and raised with dedication and devotion or turn to another by overt rejection or positive conversion—that is, by joining the inchoate company of atheists or agnostics or joining another community of faith. Here, in quite a different way than in some humanly imposed violation of personhood, one stands as an individual before the deepest levels of his or her own soul and before God or the emptiness of nothingness. People may be informed by other's advice, arguments or threats, and a person's community of origin may have rules and regulations about such things, but in the final analysis the individual person stands sociologically quite alone in such moments. All the current debates about "proselytism" and hence of the freedom of religion at the personal level are at stake here.[17] Moreover, this fact of personal freedom implies the necessity of the right of people of like "chosen" faith to associate and form "voluntary associations" on religious grounds and to engage in free speech

---

16. I draw from Michael Perry's masterful treatment of the ethical implications of policies and judgments based on human rights and their religious foundations, summarized as "Some things ought not to be done to anyone, and some things should be done for everyone" (which implies "anyone"), in Perry, Michael. 1999. *Religion and Human Rights: Four Inquiries*. New York: Oxford University Press. See also the forum on this work, 1999–2000. *Journal of Law and Religion* (1):1–120.

17. John Witte, Jr. and R. C. Martin, eds., have collected a remarkable series of essays on this issue from Jewish, Christian and Islamic perspectives: 1999. *Sharing the Book: Religious Perspectives on the Rights and Wrongs of Proselytism*. Maryknoll: Orbis Books.

and press to seek to persuade others to join their faith.[18] In these two areas of life, when people are under coercion that alienates them from their communities of life, or when they choose to leave their community of origin to join an association of conscientious, committed orientation, they must have the right to do so. These two areas illustrate a certain "soul sovereignty" with regard to individual human rights that, if denied, leads to the dehumanization of humanity. From a normative Christian point of view, not always recognized by all in the tradition, each person must be free from the miseries of oppression and the threat of arbitrary destruction, and must have, at least, the basic rights to form families, to find a calling and to convert to a world-view or religion that is in accord with a personal understanding of the "best light." Christians hold that these matters ought not to be matters of coercion, and that the use of it in these areas to force or restrict a person's decisions in these areas issues in a lie in the soul and the corruption of society. In this regard, a second level of pluralism is fundamentally affirmed and advocated by this tradition.

Christians and many Jews hold this view because we believe that each person is made in the "image of God." That is, we have some residual capacity to reason, to will and to love that is given to us as an endowment that we did not achieve by our own efforts. And whereas every one of these areas of human life is at least imperfect, often distorted by sin, obscured by false desires or corrupted by exterior influences in sinful circumstances, the dignity conferred on us by the gift of the "imago" demands both a personal regard for each person and a constant drive to form and sustain those socio-political arrangements that protect the relative capacities to reason, to choose, to love that are given with this gift. Moreover, Christians hold that each person is called into particular networks of relationships in which he or she may exercise these capacities and order these networks with justice, as God guides us to be just and loving agents

---

18. I leave aside, for the moment, the question of whether humans ever make an unaided decision on these points, for whether one advocates "predestination," "prevenient grace" or "free will" the social implications are comparable. A useful collection of essays showing these public consequences and implications for the present can be found in White, R. C., and A. G. Zimmerman, eds. 1989. *An Unsettled Arena: Religion and the Bill of Rights*. Grand Rapids: Wm. B. Eerdmans. I think the evidence is convincing that the entire First Amendment to the United States Constitution, and not only the so-called establishment and free exercise clauses, derive from this theological view of human rights with these implications.

in the world. We believe that in Christ, we learn how God wants us to re-order the institutions of the common life—sacramentally, or as others say, covenantally—that are necessary to preserve humanity, and how to make them and ourselves more nearly approximate to the redemptive purposes God has for the world. Those Christians who know the history of the development of the social and ethical implications of their faith believe that the historical and normative defense of human rights derives from precisely these roots and that this particular tradition has, in principle, in spite of many betrayals of it by Christians, disclosed to humanity something universally valid with regard to human nature and the necessities of just social existence.[19]

Still a third implication of this tradition for pluralism and human rights is signaled by the direct mention of the term "church." The formation of the Christian church, anticipated in certain sociological ways, of course, in the older traditions of the synagogues and, to a degree, in the ancient Mediterranean mystery cults, was a decisive influence in the formation of pluralistic democracy and in the generation of civil society with legal protection of the rights of free association.[20] I shall not speak extensively about these matters here, except to state that I think that one of the greatest revolutions in the his-

---

19. The anti-church policies of the French Revolution with its "Declaration of the Rights of Man," asserted on anti-theological, positive law grounds, in contrast to some dominant theocratic views of Christianity of the time, prompted the established churches in Europe to resist human rights arguments for several centuries, with disastrous results. But the longer and deeper legacy of the tradition has re-asserted itself, as mentioned above. However, the major Christian traditions have recovered and recast the legacy of their deeper insights in a series of teachings and authoritative statements: Abbot, Walter, and Joseph Gallagher. 1965. *Dignitatis Humanae. Vatican Declaration on Human Freedom*; see also Weigel, George, and Robert Royal. 1991. *A Century of Catholic Social Thought*. Washington: Ethics and Public Policy Center; Hollenbach, David. 1991. *Claims in Conflict: Retrieving and Renewing the Catholic Human Rights Tradition*. New York: Paulist Press; World Council of Churches. 1976. *Human Rights and Christian Responsibility*. Geneva: World Council of Churches; Miller, Allen O., ed. 1977. *A Christian Declaration of Human Rights: Theological Studies of the World Alliance of Reformed Churches*. Grand Rapids: Wm. B. Eerdmans.; Lutheran World Federation. 1978. *Theological Studies of Human Rights*. Minneapolis: Fortress.

20. Note 1, *supra*; also, e.g., Piety, Polity, and Policy. 1987. In *Religious Beliefs, Human Rights, and the Moral Foundations of Western Democracy*, edited by C. Esbeck. Columbia: University of Missouri Press, pp. 13–26; and Christianity, Civil Society, and the State: A Christian Perspective. 2002. In *Civil Society and Government*, edited by N. Rosenblum and R. Post. Princeton: Princeton University Press, pp. 255–265.

tory of humanity was the formation of institutions differentiated both from familial, tribal and ethnic identity on one hand and from political authority (as under the Caesars, Kaisers, and Czars of history), as happened in early Christianity by slowly making the claim stick that the church was the Body of Christ with an inviolable, divine sovereignty of its own. This was gradually made more actual by those now obscure, ancient struggles between Pope and Emperor, Bishop and King, and Preacher and Prince, and again, more fully, in the modern Protestant, especially Puritan and Pietist, demanding of the right to form congregations outside of state authorization, and in the struggles for tolerance. These developments have generated a social fabric where multiple independent institutions can flourish.[21] This has not only generated a diversified society in which colleges and universities, multiple political parties, a variety of economic corporations and a mass of self-governing charitable and advocacy groups flourish, it has established the legitimacy of their claims to rights as associations with their own purposes. Indeed, it has made those parts of the world where these influences are most pronounced the safest havens for non-established and non-majoritarian religions, including non-Christian ones, to enjoy. The empirical consequence is that the Christian faith and its concrete social embodiment, for all the ambiguities, foibles and outright betrayals of Christianity's own best principles (this faith did not abolish original sin, after all), has opened the door to the development of dynamic pluralistic democratic polities that both are protected *by* human rights ideals and laws and provide the organizational infrastructure for the protection *of* human rights both of persons and of groups.

Two related problems in this area face us as we face a global future. One is the basic question as to whether we can form a global civil society that does not have a theologically based moral architecture at its core. Historically, no society has ever existed without a religion at its center, and no complex civilization capable of including many peoples and sub-cultures within it has endured without a profound and subtle religiously oriented philosophy or theology at its core. Yet some civilizations have seemed to have been repeatedly renewed by the development of doctrines and innovative social institutions based in their

---

. For primary documents see Woodhouse, A.S.P. 1938. *Puritanism and Liberty*. London: J. M. Dent. Cf. also Walzer, Michael. 1968. *The Revolution of the Saints*. New York: Athenium; and Bellah, Robert, et al. 1995. *Christianity and Civil Society: Boston Theological Institute*, edited by R. L. Peterson. Maryknoll: Orbis Books.

deepest heritage while others seem incapable of perpetual self-reformation. The present worldwide rhetoric and legal agenda of human rights, with its several "generations" of rights, is, I believe, most deeply grounded in a highly refined critical appropriation of the biblical traditions; but many of the current activists on behalf of human rights have little place for religion or theology in their conception of what they advocate. Can it endure without attention to its roots and ultimate legitimations? Doubtful!

However, if human rights are universal in principle and the biblical, theological and social legacies here identified provide a strong, possibly the only, grounds for recognizing and enacting them in the midst of a highly ambiguous social history, as I have suggested, we still have to ask what this means for those religions, philosophies and cultures not shaped by this legacy. I am personally convinced of the fact that the theological motifs here discussed are, in this area of thought and action, scripted into the deepest levels of the human soul, even if they are overlaid by obscuring other doctrines, dogmas, practices and habitual ways of thinking in many of the traditions of the world's religions, including some branches of Judaism and Christianity. Thus our task is to identify where, in the depths of all these traditions, that residual capacity to recognize and further refine the truth and justice of human rights insights lies, for this is necessary in order to overcome what, otherwise, is likely to be a "clash of civilizations." And if, God willing, we are able to survive such a clash, should it come, it is these that could, more than any other option known to me, at least provide a model for a just reconstruction of a global civil society. ∼

Human Rights and Religious Values

John Clayton

The discourse of rights is peculiarly modern and uniquely Western in origin. Talk of rights can be linked historically to the decline of the feudal order, the emergence of national states and market economies, and to the invention of the autonomous individual in the European imagination at the origins of modernity.[1] The ancient Greeks had no language for the "rights" of individuals, much less a language for "human rights" extending beyond the privileges of citizenship in the *polis*. Formative or classical Hindu, Buddhist, Jewish, Christian and Islamic sources refer more typically to religious duties than to human rights. Just such traditional duties are still liable sometimes to be cited to justify blatant violations of what in the Universal Declaration of Human Rights are heralded as inalienable.

Given this record, traditional religious communities would seem to be infertile ground in which to try to cultivate an ethos of universal human rights. In recent years, however, a number of writers in religious ethics have attempted to show, not only that traditional religious values are compatible with a strong commitment to human rights, but that the world's religious communities themselves possess resources for human flourishing which either anticipate or correct modern understandings of human rights and responsibilities.[2] For a student of religion and modernity, this phenomenon is noteworthy for at least two reasons.

---

1. For a partial history of a crucial period in the development of the language of rights, see Monahan, Arthur P. 1994. *From Personal Duties towards Personal Rights: Late Medieval and Early Modern Political Thought, 1300–1600*. Montreal: McGill-Queens University Press.

2. Rosenbaum, Alan S., ed. 1980. *The Philosophy of Human Rights: International Perspectives*. Westport: Greenwood Publishing; Swidler, Arlene, ed. 1982. *Human Rights in Religious Traditions*. New York: Pilgrim Press; Swidler, Leonard Swidler, ed. 1986. *Religious Liberty and Human Rights in Nations and in Religions*. Philadelphia: Ecumenical Press; Rouner, Leroy S., ed. 1988. *Human*

On the one hand, the very fact that those who contribute to the debate about human rights and religious values can look for *and find* positive "human rights" embedded in the traditional moral discourses of diverse religions rooted deep in a premodern past that would have lacked the linguistic and conceptual apparatus even to speak of "human rights" itself shows that the reception of traditional religious values in the present has not been left untouched by the spirit of modernity. Although those writing on virtually all religious traditions have had to work hard to accommodate the modern language of rights within traditional moral discourse, only those writing on Chinese cultural and religious traditions seem to encounter insurmountable difficulty in finding a footing for human rights within traditional texts. On the other hand, the fact that these same scholars have typically also insisted that the major religious traditions offer resources to correct some of the perceived deficiencies of modern "rights" discourse in the public domain shows that this process of reinterpretation is not mere acquiescence in the spirit of the times.

Something hermeneutically more complex than that is going on in the revision of traditional religious values to accommodate the modern discourse of human rights. The act of drawing on the resources of the past in order to come to terms with the issues of the present is the means whereby the spirit of every time creates itself anew. Suspicion of the moral discourse of modernity, with its pretensions to "neutrality" and "universality," does not in itself betray a reactionary countermodernism, as champions of what is now commonly called the "Enlightenment project" may openly fear;[3] nor does suspicion about the discourse of "human rights" automatically excuse governments from acting responsibly under the instruments of international law, as the complacent or the unscrupulous may secretly hope.

Rights and the World's Religions. Notre Dame: University of Notre Dame Press; AnNa'im, Abdullahi, ed. 1992. *Human Rights in Cross-Cultural Perspective*. Philadelphia: University of Pennsylvania Press; and AnNa'im, Abdullahi, et al., eds. 1995. *Human Rights and Religious Values: An Uneasy Relationship?* Amsterdam: Rodopi, in which appeared my Religions and Rights: Local Values and Universal Declarations, from which the present essay has been adapted.

3. For one account of that project and its unintended ironies, see my Inaugural Lecture as Professor of Religious Studies at the University of Lancaster: Clayton, John. 1992. *Thomas Jefferson and the Study of Religion*. Lancaster, England.

Such persons can certainly take no comfort from the scholars who contributed to the volumes under review here. For they all aim to make more effective the practical implementation of the legal instruments of human rights.[4] Even when the language of rights is not fully embraced, as for example in several contributions relating to East Asia, a strong emphasis is still placed on the universal import of respectfulness toward others or compassion for human well-being.[5] However much they may differ on matters of strategy, their common aim appears to be to push beyond modernity and its ironies in order to achieve an enhanced vision of common life on a shared and fragile planet. In pursuing that goal, many discover elements in the religions surveyed that would contribute to enrichment of life in a global context, while allowing that no one religion has all the answers or lives up to its own professed ideals.[6]

To judge from the vast volume of literature on human rights to have appeared in recent years,[7] the subject has never been more topical. Nor does one have to reflect long on the current geopolitical situation to see why this might be the case. Yet only a handful of the thousands of publications to have appeared in the past few years consider the positive role religions might play in defining, undergirding and implementing human rights.

The assumption is widespread that religious convictions are more often a factor in the infringement than a force in the implementation of human rights or that religious communities are only interested in protecting the rights of religious communities.[8] It is easy enough to think of instances when religious

---

4. This aim is never far from sight, but it is made explicit in the "Workshop Statement" agreed at Amsterdam in 1993 and published as *Human Rights and Religious Anthropologies in Human Rights and Religious Values*, pp. 26–79.

5. See, e.g., Unno, Taitetsu, *Personal Rights and Contemporary Buddhism*, and de Bary, W. Theodore, *Neo-Confucianism and Human Rights in Human Rights and the World's Religions*, pp. 129–147, 183–198.

6. See, for instance, the carefully balanced account of Buddhist limitations and contributions to the contemporary debate about human rights in Thurman, Robert A. F., Social and Cultural Rights in Buddhism. In *Human Rights and the World's Religions*, pp. 148–163.

7. To give some impression of the vast volume of work in the area, one electronic database I consulted held 51,100 records of books on human rights published over a two-year period [OCLC FirstSearch WorldCat; the search was limited only to books published in 1991–92].

8. A topic addressed by the contributors to *Religious Liberty and Human Rights*.

authority has been invoked in order to justify the violation of human rights, not least the rights of women.[9] It is also easy to think of further instances when religious rivalries have exacerbated conflicts that may have other, more specifically economic or social origins, even if one lacks the confidence clearly to distinguish cause and effect in conflicts as tangled as, say, the protracted struggle in the north of Ireland or in the Balkan states.

Even so, many scholars who have looked sympathetically at the evidence have come to the view that most religious communities not only have an interest in the quality of human life on this earth, but may also have resources to enhance life beyond the minimalist expectations of some advocates of human rights. When measured against the image of the good life projected in the authoritative texts of many religious traditions, more than one contributor has remarked, the narrowly secular discourse of rights looks comparatively thin.[10]

Why have those allegedly richer resources not been taken more seriously by advocates of human rights? One main reason why the positive role religions can play in defining and enforcing human rights has tended to be ignored in international discussions on human rights must surely be sought in the popular presumption that the "public" discourse of rights is *universal* in scope and ideologically neutral in respect to underlying principles. The "private" discourses of religious communities are perceived in contrast as parochial or *local* in scope and as being grounded in context-specific commitments. Moreover, there is such diversity of opinion within the religious communities themselves about the interpretation of their own moral codes that it is difficult to know what would count as, say, the Jewish approach to "human rights."[11] Whether viewed from the out-

---

9. See Cook, Rebecca J., ed. 1994. *Human Rights of Women: National and International Perspectives*. Philadelphia: University of Pennsylvania Press.

10. See Vroom, Hendrik. Religious Ways of Life and Human Rights, pp. 24–42, and de Silva, Padmasiri. Human Rights in Buddhist Perspective, pp. 133–143, in *Human Rights and Religious Values*. See also Thurman, Robert A. F., *loc. cit.*, and Ames, Robert T. Rites as Rights: The Confucian Alternative. In *Human Rights and the World's Religions*, pp. 199–216, esp. 213.

11. A point perceptively made by Abraham Kaplan: Human Relations and Human Rights in Judaism. In *The Philosophy of Human Rights*, pp. 54–85; though Michael Fishbane speaks confidently of "the Jewish position" in his contribution to *Human Rights and the World's Religions* on The Image of the Human and the Rights of the Individual in Jewish Tradition, pp. 17–32. For a wide-ranging bibliographical survey, see Breslauer, S. Daniel. 1977. *Judaism and Human Rights in Contemporary Thought*. Westport: Greenwood Publishing.

side or the inside, so to say, the moral discourses of the disparate religious communities carry conviction for some people at some time and in some place, but they cannot be expected to carry conviction for all people at all times or in all places. They are at best expressive of the tradition-constituted values of a limited community of interest and thereby fail to achieve the generality of the moral discourse required for the recognition and implementation of human rights.

This is a commonsense view and it is not without justification. For human rights—entitlements all persons are supposed to possess simply by virtue of being persons—would seem by definition to be rights whose authority cannot be contingent upon limiting circumstances, historical or cultural. Human rights are presumed to trump any place-specific privileges to which persons may be entitled by virtue of their membership in a group or a society.[12]

The diverse moral discourses of religious groups more typically spell out duties which are specific to the members of their own communities and which often could not even in principle be reasonably extended as requirements for persons beyond their borders. And legitimation of group-specific duties derives ultimately from some authority that is accepted as authority by that group alone. Such discourses can be said to express group-specific norms, but not universal maxims, whether in a Kantian or some other sense.

Any talk of "human rights" and religious values must, therefore, deal with the dilemma of universal and local in at least these two interrelated aspects: first, how group-specific duties relate to human rights and, second, how human rights are legitimated. In regard to legitimation, the issue is whether human rights claims must always be backed by reasons that can be reasons for everyone, or if they might also be backed by reasons that are accepted as such only by participants in some localized community of interest.

This dilemma faces anyone engaged in a discussion of human rights, but it is made more acute by the extravagant claims religious groups often make for their moral code and its unique authority. Of course, every group's religious code is in a *weak* sense unique, in that it is the code of that group and not of another. But some religious groups claim for themselves uniqueness in a *strong* sense: namely, their code exclusively provides a reliable guide to the good life in virtue of its

---

12. See Dworkin, Ronald. 1977. *Taking Rights Seriously*. London.

authority as revealed law. Its code is claimed to have universal validity, even if its authority is not acknowledged beyond the membership of the community. When a religious group claims universal validity for its own code, its authority is in practice still restricted to the group that acknowledges its laws as binding. However sweeping the claim on the code's behalf, its authority remains localized to the group for whom it is acknowledged as revealed law. For such religious groups, therefore, the tension persists between the universal entitlement to human rights and more localized group-defined duties and liberties.

What sorts of strategy might be adopted by religious communities to deal with that tension? Variations on at least five distinct but often overlapping strategies have found advocates among those writing in the volumes under examination here.

1. Some hold that the concept of "human rights" is a kind of shared universal, arrived at by different cultural routes but expressing nonetheless a kind of *consensus gentium*. In terms of this strategy, the main contribution of religious communities to human rights has typically less to do with setting standards than with providing motives for adopting and implementing independently established standards[13] or reasons for ecumenical cooperation.[14]

Various moves are possible, but this strategy might take the form of proposing a reading of traditional texts to show that they somehow anticipate the concept of human rights, or that they are at least compatible with what is now understood by that concept. One could search the base texts or ritual practices of some religious tradition, for instance, selecting those passages or practices that seem to commend behavior or attitudes similar to those engendered by the modern discourse of human rights.[15] When dissonance is registered, harmony is

---

13. See Fortman, Bas de Gaay. Human Rights, Entitlements Systems and the Problem of Cultural Recaptivity. In *Human Rights and Religious Values*, pp. 62–77.

14. Although this topic crops up in other volumes (not least in *Human Rights and Religious Values*) the ecumenical dimension is thematized systematically in all the contributions to *Human Rights in Religious Traditions*.

15. Compare, for instance, the contributions by Polish, Daniel F. Judaism and Human Rights; and Hassan, Riffat. On Human Rights and the Qur'an Perspective. In *Human Rights in Religious Traditions*, pp. 40–66. See also Keddie, N.R. The Rights of Women in Contemporary Islam. In *Human Rights and the World's Religions*, pp. 76–93.

restored if possible by reinterpreting the traditional text or practice. But in cases of irreconcilable conflict between traditional moral codes of some religion and modern norms of human rights, this strategy suggests that old, established custom should be restyled to accommodate modern sensibilities.[16]

2. Whereas advocates of the first strategy allow "universal" reasons to trump "local" ones, those of the second reverse the direction, insisting that group-specific reasons be given priority over general ones. Both the concept and practice of human rights are measured by criteria that have been established by some authoritative religious standard.[17] What are allowed as rights and what count as their grounds are derived from resources uniquely available to some religious tradition, not from some "universal" or "independent" concept of rights.

This kind of strategy leads necessarily to considerable variety in practice. One community might want to ground human rights in the sovereignty of God,[18] whereas another might do so in a "transanthropocentric" sense of the sacredness of life.[19] Both of them might with equal vigor oppose the anthro-

---

16. As in, e.g., AnNa'im, Abdullahi. 1990. *Toward an Islamic Reformation: Civil Liberties, Human Rights and International Law.* Syracuse: Syracuse University Press; and his more recent essay Toward an Islamic Hermeneutics for Human Rights. In *Human Rights and Religious Values*, pp. 229–242.

17. Contrast the firmly traditional stance adopted in the Universal Islamic Declaration of Human Rights (1401 AH/CE 1981) or in Sultananhussein Tabandeh's 1970 Muslim Commentary on the Universal Declaration of Human Rights. London; with AnNa'im, Abdullahi's radically reformist "anthropological approach" in which shari'a is seen as more nearly human than divine. Regarding the complexity of the debate within Islam about human rights, see Dwyer, Kevin. 1991. *Arab Voices: The Human Rights Debate in the Middle East.* London: University of California Press; and Mayer, Ann Elizabeth. 1991. *Islam and Human Rights: Tradition and Politics.* London: Westview Press; as well as her contribution to *Human Rights and the World's Religions* on The Dilemmas of Islamic Identity, pp. 94–110.

18. See Aad van Egmond's uncompromising essay on Calvinist Thought and Human Rights in *Human Rights and Religious Values*, pp. 192–202, as well as the Universal Islamic Declaration of Human Rights and the philosophically more sophisticated contribution to the 2001 *The Philosophy of Human Rights: Readings in Context*, edited by P. Hayden. New York: Paragon House, by Seyyed Hossein Nasr, The Concept and Reality of Freedom in Islam and Islamic Civilization, pp. 95–101. Stanley S. Harakas grounds the duty within Eastern Orthodoxy to protect the rights of others in the duty to imitate in our social action God's graceful compassion toward humankind. Harakas, Stanley S. Human Rights: An Eastern Orthodox Perspective. In *Human Rights in Religious Traditions*, pp. 13–24.

19. See Abe, Masao. The Buddhist View of Human Rights. In *Human Rights and Religious Values*, pp. 144–153.

pocentrism of the ancient dictum (attributed to Protagoras) that "man is the measure of all things." But the one would do so in the name of a *theo*centrism, and the other in the name of a *zoe*centrism. Just such differences inform not just the foundations of rights, but their edifice as well. Two such communities might still be able to cooperate on many human rights issues, but their cooperation would remain limited and strategic and would have no basis in an agreement about the nature or the grounds of such rights.[20]

3. Advocates of a third strategy promise a way between the first two by insisting that the underlying principles of human rights are universal, while allowing that the language of rights varies according to local preference.[21] In line with the first strategy, religions are viewed as providing motives to implement the relevant international legal instruments; in line with the second, however, there is a recognition that particular rights might be given different priorities according to the demands of local circumstance. The main difficulty facing this strategy arises whenever an attempt is made to explicate the common principles that are supposed to underlie the variety of moral discourses that function in different religious and cultural contexts. It then becomes evident that different kinds of construction are supported by different sorts of foundation.

4. Whereas the third strategy assumed common underlying principles for diversely formed human rights, a fourth uncovers differently laid foundations to support a limited set of core rights that transcend their local provenance and achieve universal consensus.[22] These core rights, however few in number, are often treated as self-evident and generally as "nonnegotiable."

---

20. This is the pragmatic line recommended, for instance, by Schwöbel, Christoph. 1990. Particularity, Universality, and the Religions. In *Christian Uniqueness Reconsidered*, edited by G. D'Costa Maryknoll: Orbis Books, pp. 30–46, esp. pp. 42–45.

21. This strategy dominates Bas de Gaay Fortman's approach in Human Rights, Entitlement System and the Problem of Cultural Receptivity, in *Human Rights and Religious Values*.

22. See de Silva, Padmasiri. Human Rights in Buddhist Perspective. In *Human Rights and Religious Values*, pp. 133–143. Peter K. Y. Woo tries to show how the Chinese can from their own rich, if sometimes locally despised, philosophical tradition provide rational foundations for a respect for universal human rights, despite the fact that Chinese has no character for the person. See A Metaphysical Approach to Human Rights from a Chinese Point of View in *The Philosophy of Human Rights*, pp. 114–124. See again the two contributions on Confucian traditions in *Human Rights and the World's Religions*, pp. 167–216.

The problem confronting this fourth option, however, is similar to that which faced the third. When people attempt to agree to a list of core rights, it becomes all too clear that consensus is less universal than might be thought. Can one identify a single "core right" that would win universal support? If a person were to name, for example, the prohibition against killing one's mother as an example of a universal moral value, then we could imagine a second calling attention to some society in which it is a duty to ease the way of one's elderly parents into the next world when they are no longer capable of looking after themselves in this one.[23]

Different foundations of human rights support different kinds of value structures. Even a right, such as the right to life, that may be reasonably expected to appear on virtually everyone's list of "core rights" will not be understood by everyone to have precisely the same entailments. There is no consensus about when "the right to life" actually begins (at conception or at birth or at some moment in between?), nor about its proper bearers (individuals only or also groups?), nor about the circumstances, if any, in which it may be justifiably infringed (combatants in battle?) or lawfully forfeited (capital punishment?) or even perhaps voluntarily relinquished (euthanasia?). And a Buddhist or a Hindu would want to insist that the right to life extends beyond the limits of the species-specific discourse of narrowly human rights.

5. Difficulty in identifying a common "core" would seem to require at least a modification in strategy. Perhaps one should draw back slightly and see if, even in the absence of consensus, there might still remain some degree of overlap between major traditions as to what would count as "core rights."

Such rights might be said to overlap in either of two ways. On the one hand, there is the tighter, Rawls-like overlap expected by those who insist there must be some point, however fine, at which agreement is achieved in order for a right to qualify as a core right. On the other hand, there is the looser kind of overlap sufficient for those who, possibly in a more Wittgensteinian mood, are content

---

23. See the discussion of this point by Johannes S. Reinders in Human Rights from the Perspective of a Narrow Conception of Religious Morality, in *Human Rights and Religious Values*, pp. 19–20. Cf. Green, R. M. 1988. *Religion and Moral Reason*. Oxford: Oxford University Press, p. 9f, and Reinders' Ethical Universalism and Human Rights, in Musschenga A., ed. 1992. *Morality, Worldview and Law*. Assen/Maastricht: VanGorcum and Co., pp. 868–869.

to find a relatively coherent pattern of the kinds of rights that appear on different lists of core rights, even if no one right appears on every list or has the same sense when it does appear on different lists. This latter sense of overlapping softens the claim that particular rights are universal and creates more room for maneuver when approaching the dilemma of universal rights and local values.

That dilemma, in the form stated above, presumed that secular rights discourses were in some strong sense universal and neutral and that the competing moral discourses of determinate religions are local and partisan, being confined to the communities of interest that embrace them. Yet the secular discourse of "rights" (including that of human rights) is itself a construction of a specific historical and cultural circumstance,[24] as is the concept of the autonomous self as rightsbearer.[25] And the idea of "rights" encoded in such discourse is also tied to the place in which it is formed or gains endorsement. *Human rights are historical constructions, not natural kinds.*

For instance, John Locke, a major contributor to the modern formation of rights discourse, could by subverting the idea of rights defend in his *Second Treatise of Government* the institution of slavery, according to which persons "are by right of nature subjected to the absolute dominion and arbitrary power of their master."[26] A later upholder of the Lockean tradition of human rights may have been more ambivalent in his attitude toward the institution of slavery, but Thomas Jefferson cannot have had foremost in mind his own slaves

---

24. In his brief essay on A Catholic View of Human Rights: A Thomistic Reflection, in *The Philosophy of Human Rights*, pp. 87–93, R. J. Henle is right to say that the idea of a "right" is a construction, even if he stands on shakier ground when he goes on to claim that the language of rights is itself grounded in a more fundamental objective *justum*, which is not itself also a social construction.

25. The notion of the sovereign self as rightsbearer has to be seen in terms of the modern "turn to subjectivity," which from a variety of motives and to disparate ends has become a major concern in recent philosophical literature within both Anglo-American "analytic" or postanalytic philosophy and so-called "Continental" philosophy. Where one chooses to enter that discussion is largely a matter of preference, but a good place to begin for the historical background is Taylor, Charles. 1989. *Sources of the Self: The Making of the Modern Identity*. Cambridge: Harvard University Press.

26. Locke, John. 1952. *The Second Treatise of Government*. New York: Macmillan Publishing. VII, p. 85.

when he extolled in one of the most eloquent documents of his age the "unalienable" rights of life, liberty and the pursuit of happiness.[27]

Surely none could claim that Locke's or Jefferson's understanding of rights was "universal," whether in the sense of being an equal entitlement to everyone or in the sense of gaining general endorsement by everyone. Nor could one reasonably think that its underpinning was ideologically neutral. Human slavery may not yet be entirely eradicated, but it no longer has morally earnest defenders. What has changed since John Locke's or Thomas Jefferson's time to make slavery indefensible, however, is not just that a further item or two has been added to the shortlist of so-called core rights. What has occurred, more crucially, is a transformation of what is meant by a "right" and what it is to be a "rightsbearer."

Every understanding of "rights" is bound to a time and place. This holds for our own notion of human rights as much as it does for that of Locke or Jefferson. Over time, the concept of rights may develop or be stretched or be altered to fit some new circumstance or it may be finally abandoned as outmoded. But it does not stay fixed in stone. The discourse of human rights is itself temporal and not "eternal," local and not "universal." And this applies to the Universal Declaration of Human Rights, no less than it does to the American Declaration of Independence or the French Déclaration des droits de l'homme et du citoyen, the datedness of which may be more readily evident.

The 1948 Universal Declaration was a historic document. It is rightly regarded as a key moment in shaping the postwar world. In the meantime, however, it has become also a historical document. It can now be seen to mirror the concerns of that time and to embody its asymmetry of political power. The understanding of what count as "human rights" presumed by it has now been altered and stretched and developed by ensuing Charters, Conventions, Decla-

---

7. Jefferson's public remarks on slavery were so ambivalent that his authority was later invoked by both sides in the abolition debate in America in the decades leading up to the War between the States. See Borstin, Daniel J. 1981. *The Lost World of Thomas Jefferson*. Chicago: University of Chicago Press; and Miller, John C. 1991. *The Wolf by the Ears: Thomas Jefferson and Slavery*. Charlottesville: University of Virginia Press.

rations and Protocols.[28] The discourse of rights has continued by this means to construct itself anew. And rival conceptions of human rights compete for wider endorsement within an increasingly global "culture of rights."[29]

This feature of the modern discourse of rights ironically brings it nearer to the competing moral discourses of the determinate religious communities which, according to the Enlightenment self-image, the tradition-neutral language of rights was itself supposed to supersede. The dilemma of universal and local seems, therefore, to end in a proliferation of localized norms, vying with one another in the world's marketplace, with at best a hope of being judged to be "generalizable."[30]

Any challenge to the universality of human rights norms raises the specter of relativism. During the 1993 World Conference on Human Rights held in Vienna, the U.S. Secretary of State warned against allowing cultural relativism to become the last refuge of repression.[31] But some delegates listening to Warren Christopher on that occasion may have harbored their own worry that such insistence on universality could easily become the last refuge of imperialism. Many thoughtful people from mainly Asia and Africa, including no doubt most of those who attended the conference in Vienna, could find just cause to complain that the West in general or the United States in particular uses its preferred priorities in "human rights" as a means of imposing its own political ideology and economic policy on the rest of the world. It would be misguided to hear their complaint as no more than a defense, opportunistic or otherwise, of some variety of "relativism."

---

28. See the Council of Europe Directorate of Human Rights 1992 compilation of basic texts concerning *Human Rights in International Law*. Strasbourg: Council of Europe Publishing; Brownlie, Ian, ed. 1992. *Basic Documents on Human Rights*. Oxford: Oxford University Press; and Bilder, Richard B. 1992. Overview of International Human Rights Law. In *Guide to International Human Rights Practice*, edited by H. Hannum. Philadelphia: University of Pennsylvania Press.

29. Lacey, Michael J., and Knud Haakonssen, eds. 1992. *A Culture of Rights: The Bill of Rights in Philosophy, Politics, and Law, 1791–1991*. Cambridge: Cambridge University Press.

30. See Chattopadhyaya, D.P. Human Rights, Justice, and Social Context, in *The Philosophy of Human Rights*, pp. 169–193, esp. pp. 191f. Of the books surveyed here, the contributions to *Human Rights and the World's Religions* seem most acutely aware of these difficulties.

31. U.S. Stresses a Rights Code. 1993. *The International Herald Tribune*, 15 June, p. 2, cols. 1–3.

In any case, resorting to relativism is ultimately self-defeating. It fails to provide adequate reasons for adopting some position and it fails to provide a convincing account of how claims (epistemic or moral) can be contested across cultural boundaries. The case against relativism, and the course of the debate about rationality generally, is too familiar to require being rehearsed here.[32] That debate, moreover, has grown stale by virtue of having been conducted too much at the level of high theory and too little at the level of the practical operations of reason in different contexts. The tension in human rights discussions between universal declarations and local values, by contrast, exhibits practical reason at work where it really counts.

More significant than the perceived threat of "relativism" in matters moral is the simple fact that the discourse of rights has become in modern times, and preeminently since World War II, the recognized global currency in which to negotiate our different views about what weighting attaches to competing entitlements due to persons. In this fact, rather than in some defense of relativism, is to be found the key to undo the deadlock between local and universal in regard to religious traditions and human rights.

This is not to say that there is a consensus about the rights we have or the values which underpin them. Nor is it to ignore the fact that the spread of the language of rights from West to East and from North to South was both enabled and tainted by colonialism, whether political or economic or cultural.[33] The discourse of rights has nonetheless established itself as the language in which competing values are publicly justified and, in the face of opposition, publicly contested. Protagonists on both sides of the abortion debate, for example, will claim to be champions of "human rights" and will define their posi-

---

2. To cite some of the most obvious collections: Wilson, Bryan R., ed. 1970. *Rationality*. Oxford: Blackwell Publishers; Hollis, Martin, and Steven Lukes, eds. 1982. *Rationality and Relativism*. Oxford: MIT Press; Meiland, Jack W., and Michael Krausz, eds. 1982. *Relativism: Cognitive and Moral*. Notre Dame: University of Notre Dame Press; Krausz, Michael, ed. 1989. *Relativism: Interpretation and Confrontation*. Notre Dame: University of Notre Dame Press.

3. This theme does not come to the fore as much as one might have expected in the volumes considered here, though at least one contribution per volume can be counted on to raise the issue of imperialism/colonialism. In *Human Rights and the World's Religions*, for instance, there are two: John B. Carman, Duties and Rights in Hindu Society, pp. 113–128, and Anne Elizabeth Mayer, The Dilemmas of Islamic Identity, pp. 94–110.

tion in terms of competing rights, typically summed up as "the right to life" and "women's rights." Their dispute in effect has to do with which kind of right has the greater claim to priority.

"Human rights" has been able to become a universal discourse in large measure because of its elasticity. The concept of rights has been expanded and stretched to encompass aspects of human life that were once beyond its limits. In addition to an individual's civil and political rights that constitute its traditional center, the concept of "human rights" has been extended to cover not only economic, social, cultural and other group rights, but also environmental rights and the rights of "future generations."[34]

For philosophers, this makes up an untidy series of disparate goods. For jurists, the list presents difficulties of a different kind, since such diverse rights cannot all be honored at one time in equal measure. Above all, it poses for everyone a problem of priorities. The 1981 "African Charter," for instance, places the collective rights of peoples alongside the personal rights of individuals without indicating how the two kinds of rights relate to one another or how their competing entitlements are to be reconciled when they come into conflict. Which human rights, and in what circumstances, are to be allowed to trump other human rights?

In response to that question, it is not helpful to insist, as Western public officials are sometimes inclined to do, that the priorities fit for one's own local constituency have inherently universal validity. No one who has regularly read reports of Amnesty International could deny that the most appalling violations of human rights regularly occur in every part of the world—violations that are beyond all reasonable defense, no matter which set of norms and priorities are adopted in respect to human rights. But there are also genuine disputes among peoples about the proper order of priorities among human rights in differing circumstances. During the "Cold War," it was sometimes observed (a little simplistically, but not without justification) that in the West or the "First World," civil and political rights were given highest priority; in the Communist East or

---

34. See Gort, Jerald D. The Christian Ecumenical Reception of Human Rights, in *Human Rights and Religious Values*, pp. 203–228.

"Second World," economic and social-welfare rights were ranked first; and in the South or "Third World," group rights or development rights tended to take precedence over individual rights or social rights.[35] Our world no longer looks just like that, but the point remains that differing local circumstances can influence the hierarchy of human rights.

For this reason, it is more helpful to treat such disputes over priorities as differences within the discourse of rights, than to regard them as conflicts between those who are committed to human rights and those who are not. It is more helpful not least because the language of rights itself provides a public medium within which disparate communities of interest, religious and secular alike, can test the soundness of the other's position and have their own position contested in return. For instance, if one wished to argue for the priority of personal rights over, say, development rights, then one might try to show that the curtailment of individuals' civil and political rights impedes economic development and that the developing countries that have the best record in protecting civil rights show also the highest rates of economic development, and so forth.[36] Or if one wished to argue for the priority of group rights over individual rights, then one might try to show that in, say, pluralistic societies the protection of the rights of minority groups is the best way to protect individuals' rights against majoritarian tyranny.[37]

Such moves do not occur in some neutral space. Nor are they generated by value-free reasoning. There is no place that is not some place in particular, and there are no reasons that are not reasons for someone. Such moves cannot be expected to lead to global consensus on prioritization in the hierarchy of rights. But they remain strategies that can be pursued within the public discourse of rights. The price of gaining access to that language is *not* agreement to set aside all attachments and commitments in order to achieve universality and neutral-

---

35. Vincent, John. 1992. Modernity and Universal Human Rights. In *Global Politics: Globalization and the Nation-State*, edited by A.G. McGrew. Cambridge: Blackwell Publishers, pp. 280–286.

36. Cf. Dasgupta, Partha. 1995. *An Inquiry into Well-Being and Destitution*. Oxford: Oxford University Press.

37. Cf. Kymlicka, Will. 1995. *Multicultural Citizenship*. Oxford: Oxford University Press.

ity. The price of entering into that realm of discourse is no more than a willing-
ness to be a reasonable partisan.

*Testing and being contested by this means, the discourse of rights constructs
itself anew and the hierarchy of rights is subjected to public scrutiny. By this
means, basic human rights are more likely to be implemented than if one insists
on prior consensus about the hierarchy of specific rights.* ∿

Interreligious Center on Public Life

Mission Statement

Religion has played a significant role in the evolution of American culture and society. It is therefore fitting and timely that the diverse faith communities whose ideas have so enriched this land establish an Interreligious Center on Public Life. The Center will serve both as a forum for the dissemination of religious principles and perspectives as these relate to the great issues of the day, domestically and internationally, and as a vehicle for research and dialogue among the faiths.

The enormous technological and scientific advances of our age, ranging from cloning to the new frontiers of the information explosion, require a concurrent exploration and articulation of spiritual and ethical insights that can be applied to these momentous accomplishments and those that will follow in the years ahead. The Center sees as its mandate the pursuit of these goals along with addressing perennial dilemmas of church–state relations.

Through its deliberations, colloquia and workshops, along with its engagement with secular thinkers and policy makers, the Center hopes to convey the values drawn from a wide range of religious beliefs to those entrusted with the resolution of the broad gamut of public policy concerns. In so doing, the Center dedicates its efforts to the enrichment of civic life and discourse and the betterment of the human condition. ∼

International Summer School on Religion & Public Life

Mission Statement

Executive Summary

The International Summer School on Religion and Public Life (ISSRPL) is an annual international, interreligious summer school of approximately two weeks that meets in a different country every year. It provides a framework where students, civic leaders and prominent academics from different countries can explore the issues of religion and the public sphere with an aim to develop new strategies of tolerance and pluralism while maintaining a commitment to tradition and religious identity. The program is centered around three academic courses together with the processes of group building and the construction of working relationships across religious and ethnic identities. The didactic goals of the school are thus not solely cognitive but social as well.

The ISSRPL is a unique initiative. It combines a global perspective on religious thought with social scientific research on tolerance, civil society and a pluralistic approach to pedagogic practice. Its goal is to transform both the theoretical models and concrete practices through which religious orientations and secular models of politics and society engage one another. Its guiding principle is that in order to build relations of tolerance and understanding between groups and to shape a civil society, the perceived barrier between secular, modern and more traditional religious values must be broken down. Rather, political orientations and social practices must be developed that will draw on both religious traditions and the insights of secular modernity in new and creative ways.

Narrative—International Summer School on Religion and Public Life

In the modern world most ideas of tolerance and pluralism rest on liberal and secular ideas of self and society. These ideas can be briefly summarized as follows: a) the establishment of a secular public sphere, b) the privatization of religion, c) a politics of rights rather than a politics of the good, d) a secular idea of the individual as a self-regulating moral agent. In most of the world, however, these ideas simply do not hold. In most parts of the world the public sphere is not secularized, religion remains a public and not a private matter, politics are articulated along visions of a truth community and the self is seen as constituted by collective definitions and desiderata rather than by purely individual pursuits and interests. This is true not only in Southeast Asia and the Indian subcontinent, but also in the Balkans, the Middle East, Ireland, North Africa, Turkey and even in parts of that most secular of enclaves, Western Europe. In Lodi, in North Italy in October 2000, for example, local Catholic inhabitants poured pig urine on a site that was to be consecrated for the building of a Mosque. Religious identities continue to matter.

Given the continued, if not renewed, salience of religious identities worldwide, as well as their potential to form a focus of conflict and to provide a dangerous legitimation for existing conflicts (in the Israeli/Palestinian case, for example), it is crucial to take religion seriously. This means seeing the potential of religion to provide resources for tolerance and mutual acceptance and not solely for conflict and oppression. The ISSRPL is devoted to furthering these goals within an educational milieu. It will provide the educational context for the intensive training of students in those areas where religious thought and secular Enlightenment concepts of self and society overlap as well as where they conflict. Training will include not solely the cognitive or intellectual component of text study, but also an experiential or social component—creating relationships and building group interactions predicated on the dual sources of religious and more secular civil society traditions. In so doing it will "model" the broader social goals of the project and develop allegiances and networks of individual committed to the enterprise.

Locale

The goal of ISSRPL is to meet each year in a different country. In line with it commitment to substantive dialogue across traditions and a mutual engagement of different perspectives, the changing physical location is of paramount importance given the educational strategy and philosophical purpose of ISSRPL. Meetings will be held in the Balkans, the Middle East, Europe and elsewhere.

The ISSRPL mission is to educate a new cadre of religious and civic leaders who, while maintaining their religious identities and affiliations, will provide much-needed leadership in bridging the worlds of religious and secular communities. Along these lines we have selected as locales for the Summer School those countries where religious and secular worlds, commitments and desiderata, are often in conflict, or alternatively, where different religious civilizations face one another across a divide of hatred and intolerance and violence. In some cases, the reasoning behind the site selection needs no explanation. The war against Bosnia of 1992–1995 was one in which the religious sentiments and commitments of Catholic, Serbian Orthodox and Muslim populations played a significicant role.

As we prepare the coming ISSRPL formats the populations of Israel and the Palestinian Authority remain in a state just short of all-out war as the generations-old conflict around the Jewish presence in Palestine continues. While rooted in conflicting national claims, no one can question the increasing radicalization of the conflict along religious lines, as religiously articulated Muslim and Jewish identities play an increasingly greater role on both sides in defining the nature of the conflict and in positing often irreconcilable goals. Here too the ISSRPL works with religiously committed yet political democratic and pluralistic groups of both Jews and Muslims, working together in educational initiatives toward the time when joint work of construction will be possible.

The 2003 Summer School was held in Bosnia i Herzegovina and in Croatia. It was dedicated to the role of religion in the 1992–1995 wars. The 2004 Summer School will also be held in Bosnia, dedicated to Muslims in Europe. In 2005 the Summer School will meet in Jerusalem, around the theme of religion in the Israeli-Palestinian conflict.

Participants

The participants, faculty and students are international. Students in the first summer school were community activists and religious educators committed to the goals and agenda of the summer school. To these were added graduate students or their equivalents from the countries of Western and Eastern Europe, the Balkans, the Middle East, India, and North and South America.

Faculty is drawn from the leading scholars in the fields of law, social science, religious studies, philosophy and public policy from different countries. The language of the summer school is English.

Criteria for participation include the following: a) knowledge of English, b) assessment that students can participate productively in the school, c) interest in the two loci of religious and civil society traditions, d) expectations that students will apply what they learned in their ongoing career and life work. Assessments are based on written essays supplemented where possible with interviews.

Format

In the first year of operation the summer school had 22 students, 11 teachers and 4 administrative staff members.

The school was held over a two-and-a-half-week period (17 days). There were 10 working days, bracketed by weekends at either end and one weekend in the middle. The weekends were used for more unstructured interaction, the meeting of religious obligations for those so obliged, relaxation and local touring.

Students take three courses. Each course meets for two academic hours a day. Last year, the courses were as follows:

Course 1: Religion and Civil Society dealt with the overarching theoretical issues of religion and civil society. It brought together different sources, traditions and intellectual perspectives to explore areas of overlap, conflict and potential dialogue between religious traditions and more secular, modern worldviews.

Course 2: Religion, Pluralism and Democracy in Southeast Europe was devoted to religion, pluralism, democracy, tensions and conflicts in Southeast Europe. This course was taught by experts in Southeastern European issues.

Course 3: Religion and Public Life presented an arena in which to explore different ways of bringing the theoretical issues discussed in the other courses into practical application. The different faculty of this course reflected on their own professional experience and presented models by which the insights of the Summer School could be realized in different institutional spheres.

This year the second course will be structured around the theme of Islam in Europe.

Needless to say the structure of the courses is not set in stone and will change from year to year as we learn from our experience (of faculty, students and the dynamics of short but intensive group meetings). The principle of having one course devoted to local issues is, however, an essential component of the program.

Students are expected to do the bulk of the reading before the start of the summer school. Reading material is made available to students both in hard copy and via the internet. During the course of the summer school, teachers assign no more than 20 pages a day of reading per course.

Each work day consists of approximately 6 hours of school and 2 hours of reading. The program is intensive and demands a high degree of commitment from both faculty and students.

Outcomes

Four major outcomes of the summer school are envisioned:

1. Transformation of awareness and perception of the participants. While not attenuating in any way their commitment to their own religious traditions, the school hopes to open the participants to other religious traditions and view them not solely as a threat.

2. Enhance understanding of what has generally been viewed as a tension between modern secular and more traditional understandings of self and society.

3. Build in the participants an understanding of this tension as a "creative" one, rather than an unbridgeable obstacle to understanding. Hence, too, to inculcate in the participants an understanding that to shape a truly civil society, devoted to tolerance and the plurality of the human experience, we need to draw on religious traditions as well as modern secular thought and practice.

4. Finally, recruit the participants into an ongoing effort and dialogue around these themes that will build on the experience of the summer school to establish ongoing relationships, networks of interaction and contact during the year around the continued sharing of material and publications, as well as social and political experience.

The following have provided financial support for the organization and implementation of the ISSRPL:

- Energoinvest (Sarajevo, Bosnia);

- City of Sarajevo (Sarajevo, Bosnia);

- Interreligious Center on Public Life (Boston, USA);

- International Forum Bosnia (Sarajevo, Bosnia);

- Canton Sarajevo, Ministry of Culture and Sport (Sarajevo, Bosnia);

- Ministry of Science and Technology of the Government of the Republic of Croatia (Zagreb, Croatia);

- University of Verona (Verona, Italy);

- Council of Ministers of Bosnia and Herzegovina (Sarajevo, Bosnia).

⁓

BED AND BREAKFAST
IN CALIFORNIA

"Picturesque lodgings are visible in all 403 entries in this enlarged guide. . . . Strong provides helpful tips, traveler's checklist, bed & breakfast association names, and an index."
  —*Books of the Southwest*

"Offers some excellent choices."
  —*Los Angeles Times*

"The book lists a wide variety of accommodations . . . a welcome addition to an inn-goer's library."
  —*Yellow Brick Road*

"The first comprehensive guide to such inns in the state."
  —*Times-Press Recorder*, San Luis Obispo, California

"Much advice is added by this veteran B&B hostess."
  —*Family Travel Times*

BED AND BREAKFAST
IN CALIFORNIA

Fifth Edition

by
Kathy Strong

A Voyager Book

Old Saybrook, Connecticut

Illustrations in this book have been reproduced from establishments' brochures or literature, with the permission of the establishment. Special credit and thanks are given to the following individuals, agencies, or inns: The Gosby House, Carol Simmons Ragle; The Ryan House, Helen Kendall; River Rock Inn, Carol Mathis; White Sulphur Springs Ranch, Janet Gogue; Golden Ore House, Dan Schilling; Petersen Village Inn, Richard Yaco; Eastlake Inn, Ed Alejandre; Bluebelle House, Ann Serra; Heritage Park B&B, Tillie Morse/Sun Graphics; La Mer, Sara Fine; Donnymac Inn, Joe Romano; Ten Inverness Way, Jacquetta Nisbet; The Cobblestone Inn, Nancy Taylor; The Darling House, Daniel R. Dicicco; Camellia Inn, Sonoma County Atlas of 1877; Hope-Merrill & Hope-Bosworth Houses, Steve Doty; Beazley House, Mandy Fisher; The Plough & the Stars Country Inn, Patricia Bason; Philo Pottery Inn, Brian McFann; The Grey Whale Inn, Bob Avery; Big River Lodge, Larry Eifert; Joshua Grindle Inn, Dick Smith; Elk Cove Inn, Judith Brown; Old Thyme Inn; The Victorian on Lytton, Susan Elwart-Hall; Simpson House Inn, Elissa Peters; Christmas House Bed & Breakfast Inn, Bill Baldwin; B. G. Ranch and Inn, Marsha Mello; Chalet de France, Lili Vieyra; Raford House, Robert Matson; Heritage Inn, The Publicity Mill; Little Inn on the Bay, Bob Bates; Old Town Bed & Breakfast Inn; The Gingerbread Mansion; Howard Creek Ranch; Mendocino Hotel & Garden Cottages; Whitegate Inn; Harbor House; North Coast Country Inn; Abrams House Inn; Ye Olde Shelford House; The Haydon House; Calderwood; Scarlett's Country Inn; Wine Way Inn; Erika's Hillside; Villa St. Helena; The Wine Country Inn; Magliulo's; Victorian Garden Inn; Arbor Guest House; Napa Inn; The Old World Inn; The Feather Bed; Annie Horan's Bed & Breakfast; Lincoln House Bed & Breakfast; The American River Inn; The Driver Mansion Inn; Court Street Inn; The Robin's Nest—A Country Inn; Holly Tree Inn; Marsh Cottage, Wendy Schwartz; Art Center Bed & Breakfast; The Mansion Hotel; Marina Inn; Petit Auberge; Gramma's Inn; Garratt Mansion; The Pillar Point Inn; Centrella Hotel; The House of Seven Gables Inn; Old Monterey Inn; The J. Patrick House; The Village Inn; Snow Goose Bed & Breakfast Inn; The Glenborough Inn; Avalon House; An Elegant Victorian Mansion, Arlee Marshal; Bayview Hotel Bed & Breakfast Inn; Gatehouse Inn; Green Gables Inn; Country Rose Inn; The Babbling Brook Inn; Pleasure Point Inn; Karen's Bed & Breakfast Yosemite Inn; The Gables Bed & Breakfast; The Hidden Oak Inn; Zaballa House, Corky Wahl; The Goose & Turrets B&B, Alex Koronatov; The Chateau Tivoli; The White Swan Inn; Casa del Mar; Rancho San Gregorio; Chaney House; Lulu Belle's; Inn on Summer Hill, Janice Blair; Channel Road Inn; Blue Lantern Inn; Red Castle Inn, D. R. Graffis; The Inn on Mt. Ada; Strawberry Creek Inn; Pelican Cove Inn; Britt House.

Cover photo: Sean Kernan & Cover design: Barbara Marks

Library of Congress Cataloging-in-Publication Data

Strong, Kathy, 1950-
    Bed and breakfast in California / by Kathy Strong. — 5th ed.
        p. cm.
    "A Voyager book."
    Includes index.
    ISBN 0-87106-189-9
        1. Bed and breakfast accommodations—California—Guide-books. 2. California
—Description and travel—1981- —Guide-books.
I. Title
TX907.3.C2S77 1992
647.94794'03—dc20   91-32677
                                                                                CIP

Manufactured in the United States of America
Fifth Edition/Second Printing

*With special appreciation to the innkeepers
for their assistance and good wishes;
may your winter Mondays all be "full."*

CONTENTS

INTRODUCTION

This fifth edition of *Bed & Breakfast in California* is a must for any avid b&b traveler or for those who are considering sampling this exciting and personal way of touring the state. This thoroughly updated edition includes new information on inns listed previously plus entries on more than thirty new establishments—more than four hundred in all! You will also find many new, attractive illustrations to help you choose your perfect bed & breakfast. The new b&b listings include many interesting and historical landmark structures, gracious mansion estates, new oceanside luxury inns, mountain retreats surrounded by fir and cedar trees, "theme" b&bs with guest rooms from Hollywood's glamorous 1920s, a cottage nestled in the heart of the city, and Gold Country farmhouses that are surrounded by gold-mine remainders, to name just a few!

Bed & Breakfast in California invites you to venture out of your predictable and perhaps dull traveling routine and discover this gracious world of individuality, comfort, and warmth where you can indulge your dreams of opulence for a day or step back in history to relive days gone by. Sounds like a large promise? You'll find it isn't once you've ventured into the "unknown," for the underlying message in *Bed & Breakfast in California*, whether you're discovering a gold-rush hotel, a picturesque Victorian house, or a glass-enclosed suite overhanging the Pacific, is the certainty of a highly personalized and comfortable stay. After all, in this rapid-paced, computerized life nearly everyone is searching for a world that moves more slowly and relates more personally.

Bed & Breakfast in California encourages you to experience these overnight adventures, as varied and vast as the California scenery. If you've already sampled bed & breakfast travel here, you're undoubtedly yearning for more, for it's an exciting discovery that gives a whole new dimension to touring the "sunshine" state. Although bed & breakfast is hardly new (it was born and is practiced widely in Europe, is synonymous with New England America, and is more than twenty years old in California), it is still gaining momentum and high popularity in the West. And, as always, California has its own unique qualities to lend and blend with the old, established traditions known to bed & breakfast travel. That's where *Bed & Breakfast in California* shines as the adventure it truly is.

If bed & breakfast travel is such a glorious and fulfilling experience, then why, you may ask, is it currently enjoyed by only a small (be it rapidly growing) portion of the traveling community? One

Introduction

explanation is that the majority of bed & breakfast establishments in the state are still in their infancy, having mushroomed about countryside and cityside in the last decade faster than almost anyone can recall. The second reason is ironic yet true. Bed & breakfast travel is so varied in California that many travelers are timid about pioneering into this unknown territory, which seemingly lacks uniformity in any respect. If you are one of these reluctant but curious pioneers, *Bed & Breakfast in California* will help you to become a courageous explorer discovering those special places in and about California's alluring valleys, peaks, deserts, and coastlines, reserving confidently and arriving enthusiastic about the very differences you are about to find. The following pages will guide the most cautions of you through the sometimes confusing and overwhelming aspects of what to expect, what to ask, and what to watch for, culminating with a detailed *Bed & Breakfast in California* "Traveler's Checklist" for especially easy reference.

The "Bed & Breakfast Directory" herein contains more than four hundred California b&b establishments and is the largest, most up-to-date directory available. A simple key with each b&b listing offers basic information about that particular establishment to help you narrow your search in any specific geographic area. But *Bed & Breakfast in California* highly recommends that you personally contact each establishment you are considering and request a brochure and/or additional information. It is the aim of *Bed & Breakfast in California* to present you with the most complete guide to b&b travel rather than to be selective for you. A routine b&b to one may be a fantasy come true to another! The descriptions of the bed & breakfasts in this book are as accurate as possible. Sometimes, however, situations and/or owners change, and if you should find any accommodation not measuring up to your expectations, the author would very much appreciate your letting her know. Most bed & breakfast travelers find, however, that once they know what to expect, disappointments are rare.

So, venture out into one of California's few remaining frontiers. The experiences you will have are sure to add spice and spirit to your travel and, above all, restore your belief that personal comforts, individuality, and hospitality are still part of California living.

PART ONE

EXPLORING CALIFORNIA
BED & BREAKFASTS

THE VARIETY OF CALIFORNIA'S
BED & BREAKFAST ESTABLISHMENTS

Drawing from Europe's popular and quaint *pension*, enterprising and always-innovative Californians have produced a bounty of that intimate and hospitable form of lodging in almost every imaginable size, style of architecture and furnishings, and location. In other words, you name it, and California bed & breakfast has it (or will very soon!). To give you an idea of the creative bed & breakfasts awaiting you, let's explore a sampling.

Size and Type

The size of bed & breakfast establishments ranges from the large inn, with as many as fifty rooms, to the small private home, with one or two rooms. Some of the inns contain amenities associated with hotels, and, indeed, some were at one time traditional hotels or boardinghouses. Within these you may find restaurants, pools, spas, large lounges, and other hotel-type offerings. Smaller homes make up the majority of bed & breakfast establishments in the state and were, for the most part, single-family homes originally. Each inn is operated primarily as a bed & breakfast business with more businesslike hours, staffing, policies, and routine in general than is usually found in a private-home situation.

A cottage or guest house may be found in conjunction with an inn or may be an overnight rental all by itself in back of a private home. This separate dwelling inherently provides more privacy, often is more family-oriented, and sometimes offers cooking facilities.

Although local zoning regulations that discourage bed & breakfast use in residential areas are on the rise, private homes offering from one to four bed & breakfast accommodations still exist in large numbers around the state. A few private homes with guest rooms are listed in the directory in this book, primarily those that remain independent from referral agencies. But the bulk of home listings can be found by contacting one of the several agencies also listed in this book that specialize in finding you bed & breakfast accommodations in private homes for either a membership or placement fee or at no cost to you at all.

California's Bed & Breakfasts

Architecture and Period

The California concept of the b&b ranges architecturally from an 1888 Eastlake Victorian mansion to a 1920s Italian stone villa with Gothic arches to a real working lighthouse to a new Cape Cod or Mediterranean structure overlooking the Pacific. In other words, you'll find a bed & breakfast representative of almost every type of California's architecture whether it be turn-of-the-century, Gothic, Tudor, early frontier, contemporary, or brand-new built to "look" old. You'll also discover bed & breakfasts with unusual historic uses, such as a former fishery, a 1920s yacht club, a hospital, a tree house nestled in the woods, and a former bordello.

Furnishings and Accessories

Just as the architecture of California bed & breakfasts varies, the furnishings within also provide variety and, sometimes, surprises. Many b&b travelers assume bed & breakfast is equivalent to "antique." True, many of the bed & breakfasts concentrate on re-creating the past in California, often consistent with the establishment's turn-of-the-century or late-1800s vintage. But some bed & breakfast owners choose an eclectic decorating style, often blending harmoniously the old and new to create a very individual feel. Some establishments feature guest rooms that not only carry out different themes but offer quite different decors. One Gold County inn accomplishes this by offering some rooms in antiques, some with very contemporary furnishings, and others that are just "unique," with hanging beds that swing you to sleep. Representing a handful of totally contemporary establishments is one exceptional Victorian b&b in San Francisco whose surprisingly contemporary interior could be in an issue of *Architectural Digest*—an exciting contrast to say the least!

Family heirlooms, pottery or paintings, and the innkeeper's hobbies, such as a rare doll collection, add a personal touch to many establishments. Though the decor is endlessly varied, you'll find a common element in all the bed & breakfasts statewide: a desire to provide a hospitable and comfortable environment, whether it be accomplished with fresh flowers, candy, a decanter of wine or sherry, fresh fruit, bright and cheerful wall coverings, or soft and inviting colors and patterns.

Bed & Breakfast Settings

The "country inn" is synonymous with the bed & breakfast concept, but many of California's b&bs have sprung up in the city and downtown areas. These "urban inns" are a mixture of hotels and former factories turned bed & breakfast, large homes or mansions, row houses, and even private homes and cottages offering a room or two. *Convenience* is the key word in this urban setting for the tourist and the businessperson alike. Fine restaurants, civic centers, shopping, and cultural events are often just a walk away. Many of the city establishments that were once hotels also offer a wider range of services such as telephones, television, and business-meeting facilities.

Nestled among lilacs and ancient oaks, perched atop a mountain with patchwork fields stretched out for miles, or ensconced in a peaceful suburban neighborhood, the bed & breakfast in the country offers diverse, and often rural, settings. Many western ranches in the state have adopted bed & breakfast traits while also offering the ranch-style amenities of animals, casual dress, and hearty meals. California's rapidly growing wine industry goes hand in hand with its expanding b&b business, as shown not only in the number of bed & breakfasts surrounding wineries, but also by the many b&bs on the vineyard grounds. What could be more unique to California bed & breakfast travel than the opportunity to sleep and breakfast among verdant vines and oak barrels, sampling the latest harvest in your room before retiring?

Residential-area b&bs range from tree-lined Victorian neighborhoods to a California 1950s tract to a custom wood-and-glass structure reaching out to the Pacific Ocean. You'll find large mansions and estates and modest private homes located in all sorts of residential areas, some more rural than others, but all with something special to offer.

FINDING THE RIGHT
BED & BREAKFAST

Scouting the Whereabouts of Bed & Breakfasts

The directory in this book is the most complete guide currently available to bed & breakfast establishments in California. Of course, new b&bs are opening constantly as this idea gains greater and greater popularity from seashore to desert, from mountains to cities. For that reason, if you care to stay completely abreast of new finds, you'll want to keep a watchful eye on other sources as well.

Travel Publications

To the delight of bed & breakfast travelers, travel articles in newspapers and magazines are focusing more and more on bed & breakfast developments these days. Many new establishments gain their audience this way, so openings are often announced in travel editors' columns or the "Letters to the Travel Editor" section on Sunday. Keep an eye on Jerry Hulse's *Los Angeles Times* travel section each Sunday. Both Mr. Hulse's column and letters section are, more often than not, sprinkled with the latest in b&b openings and reader reviews.

Tourist Bureaus

If you're traveling to a specific area and want an update on possible new bed & breakfasts, a call, letter, or visit to the local chamber of commerce or tourist center is usually a good start. These offices keep up with new businesses in general, especially those that cater to the tourist. Often they will distribute a brochure, if available, on the inn.

A knowledgeable travel agent will scout out a b&b at a client's request or maybe even make a suggestion of one for a special trip. Although many travel agents are not deterred by the fact that not every California b&b currently gives a commission for the booking, some may be influenced by this fact. If your trip is being planned by a travel agent, you may want to do the suggesting. You will find, however, that many of the larger b&bs will offer travel-agent commissions.

Referrals and Associations

Following the directory in this book is a listing of referral agencies based in California and primarily involved in b&b accommodations within the state. These referral agencies work in a variety of ways: Some choose to charge the inn or home owner for each room they book; others require a membership fee, usually annual, which gives the member a descriptive listing of their offerings from which to choose; and still others sell the listings only, and you handle the booking arrangements. Some of these referral agencies deal with selected inns only, but a majority offer listings in private homes. Indeed, more home b&bs choose this alternative rather than soliciting guests on their own. The private homes listed in this directory are those that do not rely solely on a referral agency for their trade.

The bed & breakfast associations also listed following the directory in this book are organizations formed by the innkeepers within that region. The associations have many and varied functions, such as forming standard guidelines for membership inns, advertising jointly, and offering referrals, but all of the groups mentioned in this guide publish or give out the names of their association members. Most of these associations will send you a brochure or pamphlet with the names and descriptions of their member inns and require only that you first send a self-addressed stamped envelope. Several of the associations now offer toll-free numbers for a quick referral.

Of course, let's not overlook the very valuable "personal referral" when searching for new b&bs. Bed & breakfasts survive mainly on word of mouth, and a new establishment's opening spreads among innkeepers and avid b&b-goers like fresh butter on a steaming hot croissant. So when staying at a bed & breakfast, talk to your fellow guests and pump your innkeeper for new information. It's by far the most delightful way to enlarge your Directory.

If becoming a bed & breakfast sleuth is not your cup of tea, then the solution to keeping current is simple—just watch your bookstore carefully for the next updated edition of *Bed & Breakfast in California*! Even you super-sleuths may find a few more.

What You Should Ask About a Bed & Breakfast

What could be less personal than dialing some anonymous person 2,000 miles away on an even more anonymous "800" number and reserving a room in a chain motel by answering a quick, memo-rized list of questions? We have all performed this rather mindless act (perhaps hundreds of times), and it is simple to guess we are apt to receive the same impersonal greeting upon our arrival. We know what the room will look like except for the rather unexciting sur-prise of what the color scheme will be this time. If guessing the color of the bedspread and drapes is the most intrigue you derive from travel, then you're in for *thrills* traveling b&b style in California! Right from the moment you place your first call or receive a handwritten response to your inquiry, you'll discover researching b&bs is not only easy to do, but fun at the same time—as long as you know what sorts of things to ask. For, before travel-ing to California bed & breakfasts, you get to ask the questions and mold your stay into the adventure and experience for which you've been longing.

Description of the B&B

By studying the directory in this book, you may have a good idea which establishments in any given area you would like to know more about. If time allows, you may want to write a note briefly stating your specific questions; or if you are in a hurry, you will want to call the establishment directly and speak with the innkeeper or clerk. You will notice that some b&bs now offer fac-simile (fax) machines for quick responses. In either case, you will most likely be delighted with the very personal and warm response you receive. A common trait among innkeepers is their basic fondness for people, and this results in a gracious and helpful attitude. They are eager to answer your smallest question. If you telephone your innkeeper at a busy moment (the phone always rings when he or she is just about to serve ten guests with perfect three-minute eggs), ask him or her to call you back. Generally, the busiest times are during breakfast and early evening, but since some innkeepers close at midday to take care of cleaning, shop-ping, washing, and the like, it is difficult to guess the best time to call—just keep trying.

Whether writing or phoning, be sure to request a brochure, rate card, postcard, or whatever descriptive pieces are available. A brochure is the b&b's best tool for informing you and saving both of you time. One of the most common questions an innkeeper hears is "Can you tell me about your inn?" Because the very nature of a bed & breakfast is its uniqueness and individuality throughout, from its handsewn quilts to its stuffed teddy bear collection, the question can be overwhelming. In comes the brochure, the most convenient and descriptive way of telling you about all the little extras, as well as the cost, rules, and policies.

Accommodations

Although the trend in California b&bs is oversized beds (king or queen) due to guests' demands in the last few years, you may want to double-check just in case a larger bed is important to you or if you prefer twin beds. Some inns have compromised by putting a larger bed and twin in the same room, which also satisfies requests for three to a room. But this situation is not common, and roll-aways are not always available, so be sure to check. Some inns will offer a special rate for three traveling together in exchange for allowing three to a room, especially during nonpeak times. No matter what the size, comfort is usually a foremost consideration, and the beds are often outfitted with delicate sheets and plump comforters for an unforgettable night's rest.

Shared Baths: Those about to venture into b&b travel for the first time are usually the most hesitant about the next topic: the "shared bath." It actually prevents some from experiencing many places they would have otherwise cherished. The majority of California b&bs in this directory offer all private baths, but shared-bath situations do exist. "Shared bath" is not as easily defined as "private bath" because there are several degrees of "sharing" to be found. For instance, many shared-bath accommodations have within the guest room itself a "vanity area," generally consisting of a sink, mirror, plug-in, and appropriate towels and soap. Vanity areas cut down considerably on the use of the baths by allowing you to complete the more time-consuming tasks of makeup application, shaving, toothbrushing, hairstyling, and so on in your own room. If sharing the bath worries you, be sure to ask about the ratio of rooms to a bath. Often it is as low as two rooms to one bath or perhaps four rooms to a bath, but even the latter is rarely a problem. Remember, too, that bed & breakfast travelers are, for the most part, a very considerate lot who know to leave the bath promptly and as neat as when they entered. If you're still skittish, most establishments do offer some private, if not all private, bath accommodations. But if you do insist on a private bath, be sure to peek at the shared baths before you leave. You may be pleasantly surprised to find them more elegant and spacious or decorated more authentically in claw-foot tubs, pedestal sinks, and pull-chain toilets. A few California inns offer twin claw-foots for bathing side by side!

Handicapped: Many cities and counties in California have adopted strict building and operating requirements for the handicapped guest at bed & breakfast inns, but the rules are far from uniform and rarely apply to private residences. If climbing stairs is the main concern, be sure to specify downstairs accommodations if available. The inn's ability to accommodate a wheelchair guest is noted in the "key" information. Because this relates to wheelchair-equipped units primarily, please check with the individual inn for possible accommodations "with assistance."

Rules and Policies

You'll discover many similarities in the rules and general policies of bed & breakfast establishments throughout the state. But you're also sure to find some exceptions and "bending of the rules." Bed & breakfasts can do that since they're dealing on such a personal level. The more professional the establishment, however, the more rigid it will tend to be regarding key policies, especially those regarding smoking and pets, which affect other guests.

Children: A recent amendment to the federal Civil Rights Act prohibits bed & breakfast and other lodging establishments from discriminating against children. For this reason there is no reference in this book to each b&b's policy regarding children. It is important to note, however, that many California b&bs are not equipped to handle small children easily, and a great many establishments cannot accommodate more than two people in a room. Guests traveling with children should therefore check carefully with the b&b regarding specific arrangements. Of course, you will discover many fine inns within this book that are perfect for family travel and offer many wonderful adventures for children, such as sleeping lofts, playrooms, nature trails, and backyard play areas.

Smoking: Smoking is a controversial subject everywhere these days. Most of the b&bs in this directory do not allow smoking inside the establishment; several others permit smoking in specific rooms only. This policy should be spelled out in the establishment's literature, but if not, be sure to ask. If you are a smoker, please abide by the rules of the house to avoid embarrassment to yourself and your obliging innkeeper. Try to keep in mind that a no-smoking policy is often due to a variety of factors that include the protection and longevity of delicate fabrics and expensive antiques as well as the proximity of areas and the general risks involved.

Pets: There are few exceptions to the "no pets" rule at bed & breakfasts in California. If you plan to travel with a pet, be sure to ask in advance. Unless otherwise stated in the descriptive material on each listing, pets are not allowed.

Days and Hours of Operation, Minimum Stays

Some bed & breakfasts operate nearly as motels/hotels: open seven days a week, management on duty twenty-four hours, and so forth, but this is far from the norm. Indeed, some are open only when business is there, some on weekends only, and some only during certain seasons. Therefore it is important to determine if a particular establishment is open for business when you care to visit, as well as if a minimum stay is required. It is not unusual for a b&b to require a minimum stay of two nights during peak times: weekends, holidays, and special local events. Also, it is critical to indicate your approximate time of arrival so that proper arrangements are made for your check-in, especially if you are arriving later or earlier than the establishment's normal check-in timetable.

Rates

If you're traveling bed & breakfast style in California on the premise that you'll save a lot of money—sorry! You'll discover that California inns are actually very similar in cost to the nicer motels in the same area, but don't overlook all the extras you receive traveling b&b style. You probably will decide it is a bargain of sorts. Also, the rates in private homes are generally lower than those in the local motels, so genuine bargains do exist.

Some bed & breakfasts charge a flat fee per room, while others will give a separate rate for single occupancy, this averaging about $5.00 less than the double fee. Since commercial business is not the mainstay of most bed & breakfast establishments, many do not offer commercial rates. If you are traveling on business, do make the request. More and more establishments are beginning to realize the value of the business patron and are offering a special rate, especially in urban areas and on weekdays.

It is not unusual for a bed & breakfast to offer special room rates at different times of the year: lower midweek rates, winter or off-season reductions, weekly discounts, or holiday increases. Often this information is not stated on the rate card, so be sure to inquire.

The tax imposed on lodging in California is referred to as "bed tax," and this tax amount varies from area to area, ranging anywhere from 6 percent to 11 percent of the room rate, with the average being around 8 percent. Rates quoted for bed & breakfast accommodations are "without tax," so be sure to ask for the total amount when making advance payment for your lodging.

Deposits: In order to secure a reservation, many establishments require that the first night's stay be paid in advance; others require that the entire stay be paid before arrival. When credit cards are accepted, the credit card number can usually be taken for confirmation. It is important to ask what form of payment is acceptable at your bed & breakfast because many establishments deal only in cash and checks.

Cancellations: Because a majority of bed & breakfasts in California operate on a relatively small scale in comparison to hotels and motels, they must also impose much stricter cancellation policies. Most b&bs offer a total refund if a cancellation is made within a certain amount of time prior to your stay, ranging from forty-eight hours to seven days. The cancellation policy should be stated clearly in the establishment's literature; if it isn't, be sure to ask. If circumstances require that you cancel your reservation at the last minute, do notify your b&b immediately. If the room remains vacant, you may be charged, although most innkeepers will be lenient for extenuating circumstances or may move your stay to another agreed date. A handful of b&bs will charge you a cancellation fee for time and trouble regardless of when the cancellation was made.

Other Considerations

Breakfast: Breakfast is of course a common element in all the b&bs around, but it can take many delicious forms. Some establishments serve an "extended continental breakfast," consisting of juice, fruit, coffee or tea, and baked goods, but the trend is certainly toward a full, often gourmet, cuisine. A "full" breakfast might add eggs, pancakes, waffles, or crepes to the above; a simpler continental fare might delete the fresh fruit. Guests may delight to such breakfast delicacies as stuffed French toast, lemon-shirred eggs, apple–ricotta-cheese pancakes, or fried apples.

If *where* breakfast is served is important to you, be sure to ask. Many establishments with a dining room serve all guests there during a certain period of time, such as from 8:00 to 10:00 A.M. Some offer both the dining room (or parlor) and patio, as well as in-room service, while others offer only the latter. Some b&bs literally offer "breakfast in bed," but most in-room breakfasts are served on a table provided in the room at a specific time. Breakfast in your room can be fun, but many avid b&b travelers delight in the communal dining situation, which allows for interesting exchanges with fellow guests and innkeepers.

Refreshments: Although it's not a requirement for being defined as a bed & breakfast, many b&bs in California offer refreshments apart from breakfast; and they have found many ways of accomplishing this pleasant repast. You'll discover anything from wine and hors d'oeuvres in the evening to an in-room basket of goodies to cookies and tea at midday. Many b&bs now offer late evening desserts in addition to evening or afternoon light snacks.

Televisions, Telephones, and Transportation: Contrary to common belief, some California b&bs do have television in the rooms. In fact, many of the newer inns have provided televisions and VCRs in each guest room. When available, televisions are usually cleverly concealed in an armoire. Some inns offer televisions in a lounge area.

Telephones are found more commonly in the Inn/Hotel situation and also are becoming more frequent in smaller b&bs. Indeed, many of the new establishments in this directory offer in-room phones or jacks.

Since most b&bs are small operations, pickup service is often not available, but some do offer transportation from airports, train depots, or bus stations with prior notice. Those that do not are usually happy to assist in arranging alternative ways of getting you there via bus or taxi. Parking availability at your b&b is an important question, especially at those in San Francisco or other larger city areas where there may be an additional charge for parking.

Special Arrangements

Bed & breakfasts, with all their inherent charm, are catching on as attractive places to hold small functions such as weddings, receptions, business retreats, and reunions. Some establishments do not encourage group functions, while others are eager to arrange and assist in the various details.

Because California b&bs provide ideal settings for special times such as birthdays, honeymoons, and anniversaries, many establishments offer champagne or some other very special provision, often on a complimentary basis, with prior notice. If you are staying on such an occasion, be sure to mention it when making your reservation.

Gift certificates are becoming a very popular offering of California b&bs. There are some very attractive certificates available, and you may decide it's a perfect gift idea for a relative, friend, or work associate.

RESERVE, PACK, AND ARRIVE
WITH CONFIDENCE—THEN ENJOY

Reserving, Confirming, and Arriving

When traveling bed & breakfast style in California, a reservation is almost a must in that some establishments operate only on advance reservations, but all prefer and recommend that method. Don't allow this fact to dissuade you from a spur-of-the-moment trip, because cancellations do occur, and b&bs need a high occupancy rate to survive. Do make it a habit to reserve as early as possible to avoid disappointment, however, since it is not unusual for a b&b to be booked several weeks (even months) ahead, especially on weekends. Not only are you apt to obtain a reservation early, but you will also have a better pick of the guest accommodations: that cozy fireplace room or the bed that "the general" slept in.

The Reservation and Deposit

You may reserve your room by phone or mail, but in either case, be specific. Less confusion is apt to arise if you choose to phone, which allows for clear, immediate deposit instructions from your b&b, back-up room selections, and a quick acknowledgment of a vacancy. Once an accommodation is decided upon, the next step is the deposit that will secure your reservation. Many establishments, especially those that do not accept credit cards, require either the first night's tariff or the amount for the entire stay in advance. On the average this amount is due within five to seven days from the date the reservation is made. If you forget, you may discover your room has been given away. On your deposit check be sure to indicate the dates of your stay as a cross-check and an easy reference. If your b&b accepts credit cards, usually VISA or MasterCard, then often the number and date of expiration will hold your reservation. If you need to cancel and do not notify your innkeeper, do not be surprised to find the amount on your next charge-account statement. In defense of bed & breakfasts, every room is crucial to financial prosperity when working on such a small scale, and b&bs are one of the few lodging establishments that will loyally hold that room for you no matter what unless they hear otherwise.

Confirmation and Arrival

Upon receiving your check or after noting your charge number, the b&b should send you a confirmation note, usually handwritten,

14

along with a brochure if you do not already have one. Included somewhere should be the "rules of the house," and you should read these carefully, especially points regarding their cancellation policy, smoking, and check-in times.

When you reserve your room, make it clear what time you plan to arrive. Bed & breakfasts often close as early as 8:00 P.M. and may also close around midday. Late arrivals can usually be handled efficiently with advance warning; early arrivals may at least be able to leave luggage and freshen up with prior arrangements.

Another item to keep in mind when placing your reservation is advance tour or dinner arrangements that your b&b host might be happy to handle for you. If there is a special event or very popular dining spot in town, ask if the b&b would handle reservations for you ahead of time.

Emergency Provisions

As pleasant as bed & breakfast travel is in California, problems and emergencies can arise. To avoid a panic situation, be sure to acquaint yourself with emergency provisions upon checking in: Is there a resident manager? Where can he or she be found after closing time? Is an emergency phone available and where? If no resident manager is on the premises, how can the owners be reached? Are phone numbers posted? Ask whom you should see if you lose your key in the night or the toilet backs up or your next-door guests decide to have an all-night party. The chances are good that you will have a marvelous, romantic stay without a hint of a problem, but it is good to be prepared.

A common problem centers on the security of the b&b, which often involves locking doors up tight at a certain time of the night. If you find yourself arriving late without notifying the bed & breakfast, then look for a late box with a key or a number to call or just knock loudly! Of course, you should always call when possible if you're arriving later than the indicated office hours. If you're a guest already and you lose your key, the same applies. As a note, keys are handled quite differently at various establishments. Some issue you a key to your room and the front door, others just to the front door if your guest room has an inside latch. Still others deal with no keys at all. I know of a few inns with a curfew, but luckily those are a rarity—staying at "grandmother's" can be taken to extremes.

Checking Out

Most bed & breakfast check-outs, like motels and hotels, are at noon or 11:00 A.M. If you haven't paid in full, do so and also remember to return the keys. Always bid farewell personally and sign the guest book if you like. It's great fun to read the guest book, too. Should you tip? Some b&bs ask that you do not tip, but others leave that up to the guest; it is rarely expected. Do what pleases you, but add a name if the tip is for a specific person (otherwise the house-keeper may assume it is just for her or him). Some b&b travelers prefer more creative tipping such as a bottle of wine or a bouquet of flowers for the host. As a bed & breakfast owner, my favorite gratuity was always a heartfelt note of thanks with a promise to return.

Packing for Your Stay at a Bed & Breakfast

Just two words of advice here: Pack lightly! A recent California University survey on state bed & breakfasts reveals the average stay to be two nights, so most likely you won't pack for a week unless you're in transit. In that case, prepare ahead with a small suitcase for your b&b stop and leave the rest in the car. It is not at all unusual to discover your beautiful, antique-filled room is missing a closet, and in its place are a few ornate brass hooks or perhaps a tiny turn-of-the-century armoire. Of course, some b&bs have lovely, large closets, but you might want to check if you're traveling with an entire wardrobe.

Once you've determined how much to tote, you'll need to give thought to what to bring along. When you're sharing the bath, a robe of some sort is a necessity. Some gracious inns do supply a robe if you forget yours, but you wouldn't want to depend on that. A small cosmetic or toiletry bag for sundry items will also make your "trip down the hall" much more efficient and comfortable. Although most guest rooms will have a mirror, and indeed many are equipped with full vanity/sink areas, it is wise to carry a traveling standup mirror. Then, if the bath is occupied or you are nervous about taking a few extra minutes on your coiffure, you can proceed in the privacy of your room.

Many of the b&b inns and inn/hotels in California are, if not historic, definitely older—circa 1900. The turn-of-the-century renovated structures provide a unique and elegant stay, but they do not always provide impressive heating, air conditioning, plumbing, and electrical situations. This is not to say you will be uncomfortable; most likely you won't even notice. But if you chill or overheat easily, then pack a sweater or a few lighter pieces of clothing. Also, the use of higher voltage electrical appliances, such as your hair dryer, can be affected. If not using your blower would be a disaster, then you had better ask ahead.

If you plan to travel with a supply of cold drinks or refreshments and your accommodations do not include a refrigerator, then ask about using the establishment's own refrigerator. Some places will offer happily, while others prefer not to extend this service due to several factors. Motels and hotels have trained the California traveler into the "ice-machine habit," but not one such machine exists in the state's b&b offerings. A few of the larger inn/hotels may have an ice dispenser, but your "ice machine" will most likely be a carton of cubes brought out graciously by the innkeeper at your request.

Enjoying Your Stay to the Fullest

The grand, spiraling staircase may conjure up childhood fantasies of sliding down its smooth walnut banister, and the painted, carved carousel horse in the parlor has your mind wandering to playful, simpler times. Yet a California bed & breakfast can do more than bring nostalgic thoughts to mind, especially if you prepare to enjoy all it has to offer.

Enjoying a bed & breakfast can be an end in itself, but often you'll want to explore its setting as well. As your own "personal tourist bureau," the b&b is ideally suited to recommend and even chart out a day's or week's activities. Many establishments are equipped with area brochures, maps, and, most important, are managed by an innkeeper or a host with very knowledgeable ideas of what's worthwhile.

The Breakfast

The breakfast is a most enjoyable other half of the b&b; and it's great fun to discover the unique ways different establishments accomplish this meal. As discussed earlier, locales and types of breakfasts can vary from in-bed trays to formal dining rooms, from juice and croissants to homemade country feasts. To make the most of your breakfast, check your options and try several if you're staying longer than a day. Be sure to mention any special dietary requirement upon arrival. The personal touch at a b&b mirrors the desire to please whenever possible. Don't be surprised to find a copy of the morning paper alongside your coffee cup.

Refreshments and Other Offerings

Picture yourself arriving at your bed & breakfast destination exhausted from a long drive; the next thing you know, a chilled glass of wine or a hot cup of tea is there to soothe your traveler's woes. Or perhaps you are escorted to your room to freshen up and presented with a basketed "care package" of fresh fruit or cookies. Or you go downstairs in the late afternoon to gather with fellow guests for champagne, hors d'oeuvres, and warm conversation. Many establishments now offer late-night snacks or after-dinner desserts. In any circumstance, the refreshment offering practiced by most California b&bs is a most enjoyable and refreshing gesture.

Breakfast is not necessarily the only meal offered at California bed & breakfasts. With advance notice many establishments will pack a homemade picnic lunch for your day's outing or will prepare a special gourmet dinner. Of course, many of the larger inn/hotels have their own adjoining restaurants that are open to guests and the public on a regular basis.

The Extras

The extra services you'll find at California b&bs are almost too numerous to mention, as you are sure to notice when reading the descriptions in this edition. In terms of recreation and relaxation, you'll find bicycles for exploring (both on a complimentary basis and rentals), spas, saunas, hot tubs, and pools—all a part of the California scene. Turn-of-the-century gazebos, lawn croquet, ponds, creeks, and flower-filled gardens abound in both country and urban settings. Some newly opened inns offer such extras as dance lessons, bay cruises, touring in vintage autos, massages, private beaches and coves, and fishing or whale-watching expeditions.

Within your bed & breakfast you'll almost always find some sort of sitting room, parlor, or library with comfy nooks, lots of reading material, and, at times, a television, radio, or player piano. These relaxation spots often feature a fireplace to sip by or challenging games for one or more.

The newest diversions at California's b&bs involve "theme" weekends. Guests may participate in a weekend-long mystery murder and rendezvous for clues at midnight at the gazebo, enjoy a real Western barbecue and shoot-out in Gold Country, or enjoy an inn's box seats at Dodger Stadium a short stroll away.

Guest-Room Frills

Within the privacy of your room, you may discover a decanter of sherry, fruit, or candies to fill your cravings. Many b&b accommodations include refrigerators, wet bars, and even whole kitchens for you to stock with your favorites. With an emphasis on comfort, it is not unusual to find yourself relaxing in beds adorned with plush comforters, down pillows, and fancy sheets. Ask for extra blankets or pillows if you like. If you enjoy reading in bed, then ask for a reading light; ask for an alarm clock for a special wake-up time. If your room has a fireplace, check to be sure it's working, and find out how to use it. Some establishments prefer to start your fire for you or may have simple instructions available. You may return from the evening out to discover that a sweet elf has lovingly turned down your bed and left an elfin treat of candies or sherry, freshened your towels, and maybe even shined your shoes!

The Bed & Breakfast in California
Traveler's Checklist

1. Choosing your bed & breakfast
- ☐ Request a brochure, rate card
- ☐ Check policies regarding smoking, credit cards, cancellations
- ☐ Minimum-stay requirement
- ☐ Days and hours of operation, arrival time

2. Reserving with confidence
- ☐ Total deposit required? When?
- ☐ Form of payment accepted
- ☐ Confirmation received
- ☐ Late or early arrival
- ☐ Advance tour or dinner reservations
- ☐ Parking
- ☐ How to get there
- ☐ Public transportation, pickup service

3. Packing for your stay
- ☐ Robe
- ☐ Tote
- ☐ Electrical appliances

4. Checking in and out
- ☐ Breakfast options
- ☐ Emergency provisions
- ☐ Office hours
- ☐ Keys
- ☐ Guest book

5. Enjoying your stay
- ☐ Personal tourist information
- ☐ Refreshment time
- ☐ Picnics, lunches, dinners
- ☐ Bicycles
- ☐ Spas, saunas, pools, hot tubs
- ☐ Patios, gardens, gazebos
- ☐ Parlor/library: books, games, fireplaces, pianos
- ☐ Shared bath: bubble bath, robes, cleaning supplies
- ☐ Room comforts: reading lights, alarm clocks, extra pillows/
  blankets, refreshments, fireplace use
- ☐ Telephone
- ☐ Television

PART TWO

BED & BREAKFAST IN CALIFORNIA DIRECTORY

HOW TO USE THE DIRECTORY

Geographic Areas: All the b&b establishments listed in the Directory have been categorized geographically into one of the following six areas, each displayed with a map highlighting pertinent communities and described in a brief list of things to do and see:

- **Northern California:** Northernmost California, primarily the north coast and redwood country
- **California Wine Country:** Napa and Sonoma counties
- **California Gold Country:** Sacramento and adjoining Gold Country including Tahoe and the Sierra Foothills
- **San Francisco Bay Area:** The City and surrounding Bay communities
- **Central California:** Santa Cruz–Monterey Bay south through San Luis Obispo County and the San Joaquin and Owens valleys
- **Southern California:** Santa Barbara County south through San Diego

Individual Listings: Each bed & breakfast listing in the directory is followed by basic information about that particular b&b.

Reading the key:

1. *Inn*—Operates primarily as a bed & breakfast inn
2. *Inn/Hotel*—Is an inn as well as a hotel, usually offering other services such as an adjoining restaurant
3. *Cottage*—Usually a small cottage in back of a home or an inn
4. *Home*—A private home renting from one to four rooms (most bed & breakfast homes can be found by checking with the referral agencies at the end of this directory)

Number of Guest Rooms: This is the total number of units available and many include cottages as well as suites.
Rates: Rates have been categorized in the following fashion based upon double occupancy, on-season rates before tax:
1. Inexpensive: up to $60
2. Moderate: $61–$110
3. Superior: $111–$160
4. Deluxe: $161 and up
Smoking:
1. OK—Permitted in general
2. Limited—Permitted in certain rooms only

3. No—Not allowed inside the establishment (most establishments have provisions for *outside* smoking)

Children: (See information on page 10.)

Credit Cards: When credit cards are accepted, the most common cards are MasterCard and VISA. Check with the establishment if traveling with any other charge card.

Pets: This item is *not* listed, because almost all b&bs within this guidebook do not allow pets. If pets are allowed, an indication of this may be listed in the description.

Handicapped Access: This refers primarily to wheelchair access. Check with the establishment for possible access "with assistance."

NORTHERN CALIFORNIA

Rugged coastlines, isolated stretches, "Cape Cod" villages, steep mountains, giant redwoods, old lumber and fishing towns, and farmland are the essence of California's scenic northern section. The inland areas here, housing towns such as Boonville and Garberville, are marked by warmer, drier weather, orchards, and the mighty redwood forests. The Skunk Train, which departs near coastal Fort Bragg, travels the redwood area as a popular tourist attraction. The nineteenth-century coastal towns of Mendocino and Little River offer dramatic cliffs with ocean-view bluffs, meadows, rocky beaches, and architecture reminiscent of a New England fishing village. Colorful gardens, artists' galleries and craft shops, water recreation, and bountiful driftwood collections are all a part of northern California, a year-round travel destination.

Fensalden

33810 Navarro Ride Road, P.O. Box 99, Albion, CA 95410
Phone: (707) 937–4042
Key: Inn; 8 units; Moderate–Superior; No smoking; Credit cards; No handicapped access

Built originally in the 1860s as a stagecoach stop and tavern and later used as a farmhouse until its recent renovation to a b&b, this inn is situated on twenty acres of meadowland sweeping downward. The inn's name translates appropriately to "land of the mist and sea." The interiors of the b&b are a pleasant melding of antique and traditional decor punctuated with fine art. Special touches in the guest rooms, all with private baths, include handmade pottery sinks, cozy down-filled quilts, and impressive ocean and countryside views. Home-baked breads and muffins, fruit, freshly squeezed juice, and coffee or tea are served in the "Tavern Room" or in the parlor. Complimentary wine and hors d'oeuvres are served at sunset in this tranquil and inspiring spot.

The Plough and the Stars Country Inn, Arcata

The Plough and the Stars Country Inn

1800 Twenty-seventh Street, Arcata, CA 95521
Phone: (707) 822–8236
Key: Inn; 5 units; Moderate–Superior; Credit cards; Handicapped access, 1 unit, Limited smoking

This mid-1800s farmhouse was once the center of a 140-acre ranch and housed a local entrepreneur's family of fourteen children. The lovingly restored country inn sits on two acres filled with lawns and herb and flower gardens and is bordered on three sides by a working bulb farm abloom with lilies and daffodils. The two upstairs guest rooms share a bath and an upstairs sitting room with views of the southern pasture. Three guest rooms downstairs offer full baths with showers and range in style from a summer sleeping porch to an elegant Victorian-designed room with a cozy woodstove. A full breakfast is served family style in the country kitchen. Three common rooms filled with books, games, antiques, and country touches such as teddy bears and locally made baskets are for lounging and socializing. Guests enjoy the inn's croquet lawn and a relaxing hot tub.

Anderson Creek Inn

12050 Anderson Valley Way, P.O. Box 217, Boonville, CA 95415
Phone: (707) 895–3091
Key: Home; 4 units; Moderate–Superior; Limited smoking; Credit cards; No handicapped access

This sprawling house on sixteen acres of land with two streams is nestled deep within Anderson Valley and is surrounded by mountains and nature. Each spacious guest room at this ranch b&b has its own serene view and unique antique decor with both shared- and private-bath accommodations available. Guests here enjoy a game room with pool table, an indoor spa, and a 20-by-40-foot in-ground pool surrounded by a large deck; bicycles are available. The full breakfast is served on the patio, in the dining room, or in the privacy of the guest room. Free shuttle service is provided to and from the nearby airport.

Toll House Inn

15301 Highway 253, P.O. Box 268, Boonville, CA 95415
Phone: (707) 895–3630; **Fax:** (707) 895–3632
Key: Inn; 5 units; Superior–Deluxe; No smoking; Credit cards; Handicapped access, 1 unit

This private and secluded resort sits on 360 scenic acres—perfect for walking, jogging, and bird-watching. Guests may choose from five accommodations, all with private baths and sitting areas. Two guest rooms boast cozy fireplaces. Guests may soak in the open-air hot tub or relax on one of many decks. The stay at Toll House includes a full country breakfast; the inn now has a bar and restaurant open to the public.

Timberhill Ranch

35755 Hauser Bridge Road, Cazadero, CA 95421
Phone: (707) 847–3258; **Fax:** (707) 847–3342
Key: Inn/Cottages; 10 units; Deluxe; Limited smoking; Credit cards; Handicapped access, 1 unit

This small country resort surrounded by 6,000 acres of state parkland offers ten private cedar cottages for two and includes a gourmet breakfast and dinner; lunch is available for purchase. The cottages, with redwood decks, sit on former Kashia Pomo Indian ground, now home to horses and llamas, a pond with wild ducks, and spring wildflowers. Each carefully appointed cottage boasts a romantic wood-burning fireplace, handmade quilt, and tiled bath. Special amenities include a 40-foot pool, a Jacuzzi with views of the hills, and world-class tennis courts. Trays of homemade breads, fruit, juice, and beverages are served in each cottage in the morning, a lunch may be enjoyed poolside, on one of the main decks, in the lodge dining room, or elsewhere by picnic basket. The intimate main lodge is the locale of the fireside dinner, which features six courses with a generous choice of entrees and homemade desserts. Each cottage boasts its own fully stocked refrigerator, and beverages are offered by the pool and at the tennis courts throughout the day.

Elk Cove Inn

6300 S. Highway One, P.O. Box 367, Elk, CA 95432
Phone: (707) 877–3321
Key: Inn/Guesthouses; 7 units; Moderate–Superior; No smoking; No credit cards; Handicapped access, 3 units

Elk Cove Inn, Elk

This early 1800s Victorian house with four cabins offers three guest rooms on the second story. These rooms all have dormer windows with window seats and private baths; rooms share a common area upstairs with a deck overlooking the ocean. The cabins boast queen-size beds, bay windows with window seats, and private baths; two cabins have cozy fireplaces. A full breakfast featuring German and French specialties is served in the oceanview dining room each morning. Guests enjoy a secluded beach, numerous scenic trails, a living room with fireplace, and a wine cellar with select local wines available for purchase.

Green Dolphin Inn

6145 S. Highway One, P.O. Box 132, Elk, CA 95432
Phone: (707) 877–3342
Key: Inn/Guesthouse; 3 units; Moderate–Superior; No smoking; No credit cards; No handicapped access

This small inn, commanding spectacular views of the ocean and boulders off the coast, offers one room in the main house and guest accommodations on both floors of an adjacent carriage house. All accommodations boast private baths and country-antique furnishings. The house provides a common area and a full library with massive fireplace. The complete breakfast, served with sea views in the upstairs dining room, is delightfully different each day. Guests also enjoy a hot tub.

Elk

Griffin House at Greenwood Cove

5910 S. Highway One, P.O. Box 172, Elk, CA 95432
Phone: (707) 877–3422
Key: Inn/Cottages; 7 units; Moderate–Deluxe; No smoking; Credit cards; No handicapped access

This turn-of-the-century inn offers private, cozy cottages with views of the ocean and cove. The individual cottages offer a step into the past. Some units feature sitting rooms or decks overlooking the ocean. Breakfast is always unique and features such specialties as apple-stuffed pears with maple-syrup-cream sauce. For special occasions guests may receive a surprise candlelit champagne breakfast! A social hour is held in the main house each evening and features beverages and regional specialty hors d'oeuvres.

Harbor House, Elk

Harbor House

5600 S. Highway One, P.O. Box 369, Elk, CA 95432
Phone: (707) 877–3203
Key: Inn/Cottages; 10 units; Superior–Deluxe; Limited smoking; No credit cards; No handicapped access

This entirely redwood-constructed main building of the 1916 inn sits on a bluff overlooking a once-busy lumber port. The tranquil setting offers accommodations in the redwood structure as well as in adjacent cottages. All guest quarters host private baths and either fireplaces or Franklin stoves and have private-beach rights. Guests at the small inn are served both breakfast and dinner in the ocean-view dining room as a part of the overnight stay, making the b&b a moderate splurge.

The Carter House & Hotel

1033 Third Street, Eureka, CA 95501
Phone: (707) 445-1390
Key: Inn; 7 units; Moderate–Deluxe; No smoking; Credit cards; Handicapped access, 1 unit

This b&b calls itself "a modern tribute to the splendor of Victorian architecture." The three-story new structure, built from 1884 house plans, is just that. Victorian furnishings, marble and hardwood floors, oriental carpets, and fresh flowers decorate throughout, and the third-floor b&b room offers views of Old Town and the marina. A full gourmet breakfast is included in the stay as well as evening wine and hors d'oeuvres and after-dinner cookies and cordials. The main floor of the building houses an art gallery. The Carter Hotel sits across from the inn and offers guest rooms and suites; breakfast is also included in the stay. The exceptional hotel restaurant has been featured in several national magazines praising the cuisine.

Chalet de France

1406 "C" Street, Eureka, CA 95501
Phone: (707) 444-3144/442-5594
Key: Home; 2 units; Deluxe; No smoking; Credit cards; No handicapped access

Perched atop a 3,000-foot mountain, this chalet commands unparalleled panoramic views of the Pacific Ocean and is an hour's

Chalet de France, Eureka

drive through forest from Eureka. The remote setting, surrounded by a thousand miles of ranch and timberland, brings a touch of "Switzerland," complete with its yodeling mountaineer host and Belgian hostess who specializes in French cuisine, to its chalet architecture befitting a Swiss-Tyrolean chalet. The interior of the chalet boasts rich woods, tole-painted detailings, and intricate carvings. One suite offers a queen-size French rococo brass bed and the other, an antique iron double bed. The walls are filled with original artwork and etchings, and antique firearms, cut crystal, and china decorate throughout. The full breakfasts include eight different main courses featuring such delights as eggs Benedict and omelettes à la Provence along with champagne, fresh fruit, juice, and freshly baked muffins and breads. The morning meal is served either in the dining room or on the south deck, with 30-mile views. For an additional charge guests may enjoy the "gourmet experience," which includes French gourmet meals and escorted drives around the ranchlands in the inn's antique 1928 automobiles. The b&b accepts advance reservations only.

An Elegant Victorian Mansion

1406 "C" Street, Eureka, CA 95501
Phone: (707) 444–3144/442–5594
Key: Inn; 4 units; Moderate; No smoking; Credit cards; No handicapped access

    This Queen Anne–influenced Eastlake Victorian mansion is on the National Register of Historic Places and is well noted for its turn-of-the-century opulence and ornate architecture. Built in 1988, the carefully preserved and restored 4,000-square-foot home now offers four unique guest rooms to b&b travelers. Inside, the inn boasts wallpaper from Bradbury and Bradbury, wool carpets, the mansion's original wood trim, gas, and electric lighting fixtures, custom-made Lincripta and Anaglypta wall and ceiling coverings, and a mixture of 1890s antiques and reproduction pieces. A tuxedoed butler and hosts in period attire greet guests and serve afternoon wine and cheese with crackers or summertime ice-cream sodas. The full-morning fare includes freshly squeezed juice, fruit, cereals, baked fruit in sauce, home-baked breads, rolls, and croissants, and a special entree such as eggs Benedict or quiche. Late-evening gourmet desserts are also offered. Guests enjoy the inn's parlors, library, and sitting room along with its

An Elegant Victorian Mansion, Eureka

veranda, croquet field, bicycles, and fleet of antique touring cars available for guided tours of historic Eureka. Swedish massages and Finnish saunas are also available in the hospitable inn.

Heuer's Victorian Inn

1302 "E" Street, Eureka, CA 95501
Phone: (707) 442–7334
Key: Inn; 3 units; Moderate; No smoking; Credit cards; No handicapped access

This Victorian inn, built in 1894, was completely restored in 1980. The Rose Room offers a private bath, while the Blue and Gold rooms share a bath. The continental breakfast is served in the kitchen. Guests may enjoy all areas on the first two floors of the house as their own.

House of Francis

1006 Second Street, Eureka, CA 95501
Phone: (707) 443–3632
Key: Home; 3 units; Inexpensive; Limited smoking; No credit cards; No handicapped access

Built in the late 1800s and moved to its site two blocks from the Carson Mansion several years ago, the b&b is near the shops of Old Town. This home can accommodate up to six adults and one child in its comfortable suites, which consist of a living room, bedroom, and bath. The stay includes a full breakfast of two kinds of fruit and a choice of whole-wheat waffles, blueberry muffins, fruit muffins, French toast, French pancakes or popovers, and a soufflé omelette. Guests enjoy wonderful in-town views of the bay and marina.

Iris Inn Bed & Breakfast

1134 "H" Street, Eureka, CA 95501
Phone: (707) 445–0307
Key: Inn; 4 units; Inexpensive–Moderate; Limited smoking; Credit cards; No handicapped access

A few blocks from Old Town is this elegantly restored Queen Anne–Victorian b&b built for Humboldt's first county clerk. Guests may relax on the large Colonial Revival porch or in the sunny yard with flowering fruit trees. Inside, guests enjoy the pleasant blending of contemporary art and Victorian antiques throughout, a music room used as an art gallery, and a library and parlor, both with fireplaces. The restored home also boasts a profusion of stained-glass windows and an elegant dining room. The four guest rooms include one accommodation with private bath and boast expertly arranged flowers. The full gourmet breakfast with main courses such as crepes, soufflés, quiche or omelettes, berries and cream, juice, and baked pastries is served in the dining room with fine china, crystal, and silver or in the privacy of the guest room. An elegant afternoon tea and evening nightcap of cordials and hand-dipped chocolate truffles is presented in the parlor. Extras at Iris include the afternoon newspaper and bed turndown service; picnic baskets are available. The inn loves children and accepts collect calls.

Old Town Bed & Breakfast Inn

1521 Third Street, Eureka, CA 95501
Phone: (707) 445–3951
Key: Inn; 7 units; Moderate; No smoking; Credit cards; No handicapped access

Built in 1871, this inn was the original home of the Carson family and is the last remaining structure of the Bay Mill. The Greek Revival Victorian was moved to its present location near the Carson Mansion in 1915. The restored inn, recently upgraded throughout, offers seven guest rooms with private and shared baths; Sumner's Room boasts an antique brass double bed and private bath. The inn's decor combines period pieces with homey touches, and every bed has its own teddy bear. The antique claw-foot tubs

Old Town Bed & Breakfast Inn, Eureka

are outfitted with bubble bath and "rubber duckies." The inn serves a country gourmet breakfast, with such specialties as Timber Beast Breakfast Pie and Eggs Derelict, served family style around the antique oak table. Guests relax in the Raspberry Parlor by the fireplace for beverages and cheese each evening and enjoy a new deck with hot tub.

The Ferndale Inn

619 Main Street, Ferndale, CA 95536
Phone: (707) 786–4307
Key: Inn/Cottage; 5 units; Moderate–Superior; No smoking; Credit cards; No handicapped access

Built in 1859 as the third house in Ferndale, the structure was nicknamed the "Carpenter Gothic" because of its unique style. The Victorian grounds include a one-hundred-year-old spreading chestnut tree; a large, colorful flower garden; and a redwood deck overlooking Francis Creek. Accommodations at the inn feature a suite with queen bed, carved oak headboard, sundeck, and full bath, as well as both shared- and private-bath guest rooms. The inn also offers a private honeymoon cottage. Guests may relax in the parlor with nineteenth-century antiques or in the music room with varied antique instruments. The dining room, in turn-of-the-century decor, is the site for breakfast, which features freshly squeezed orange juice, homemade oatmeal blueberry-banana pancakes, fresh muffins, and the inn's own blend of coffee. Tea and brownies are served each afternoon at the inn, and bedstand treats include hand-dipped truffles.

The Gingerbread Mansion, Ferndale

The Gingerbread Mansion

400 Berding Street, Ferndale, CA 95536
Phone: (707) 786–4000
Key: Inn; 9 units; Moderate–Deluxe; No smoking; Credit cards; No handicapped access

This storybook Queen Anne–Eastlake-style Victorian mansion with turrets, gables, and "gingerbread" galore is surrounded by colorful English gardens. Guests enjoy the turn-of-the-century elegance of four parlors with two fireplaces and nine large and romantic guest rooms, all with private baths. Four feature claw-foot tubs in the room.

Both the Gingerbread Suite and the Fountain Suite offer two tubs for "his and her" bubble baths! Before-breakfast trays of coffee and tea may be taken in the room. A generous continental breakfast is served in the formal dining room overlooking the garden. Guests at this inn are pampered with afternoon tea and cakes, bicycles for exploring, chocolates, bathrobes and bubble bath, and even boots and umbrellas when it rains! The Gingerbread Mansion is a member of Special Places, as well as the Great Inns of America, Unique Northwest Country Inns, and the Country Inn and Backroads Association.

The Shaw House Inn

703 Main Street, P.O. Box 1125, Ferndale, CA 95536
Phone: (707) 786–9958
Key: Inn; 6 units; Moderate–Superior; No smoking; Credit cards; No handicapped access

This gabled, Gothic-style house was built by the town's founder in 1854. The exterior is enhanced by two old-fashioned porches, bays, and numerous balconies. Rooms inside are decorated in wall coverings, antiques, art, and memorabilia. The Honeymoon Room offers an unusual canopied ceiling plus a private bath with claw-foot tub and shower. Tea is served by the fire in the library, and breakfast is enjoyed in the formal dining room of the house. Shaw House is listed on the National Register of Historic Places.

Avalon House

561 Stewart Street, Fort Bragg, CA 95437
Phone: (707) 964–5555
Key: Inn; 6 units; Moderate–Superior; Smoking OK (rooms only); Credit cards; No handicapped access

This 1905 Craftsman house, situated in a quiet residential neighborhood, is just three blocks form the ocean and two blocks from the popular Skunk Train attraction. The carefully restored home, while maintaining its antique character, has been equipped with modern luxuries and conveniences, such as soundproofed walls, ade-

Avalon House, Fort Bragg

quate bedside lighting, comfortable seating, and modern bathroom fixtures. The six unique guest accommodations are furnished in an attractive mix of antique and willow furnishings and boast some fireplaces, canopy beds, ocean-view decks, and stained-glass windows; the Yellow Room has an in-room whirlpool bath. Bathrooms, all private, host extra-thick towels and sparkling tile walls, and several contain whirlpool tubs, dressing tables, and stained-glass windows. A large breakfast is served in the living room and adjoining parlor; the morning fare may include such delicacies as sour cream pancakes along with sausage, fruit, and home-baked muffins or perhaps hominy grits with eggs, ham, fried apples, and biscuits. The inn's spacious living room is furnished with antiques, lots of paintings, and a cozy wood-burning fireplace.

Cleone Lodge

24600 N. Highway One, Fort Bragg, CA 95437
Phone: (707) 964–2788
Key: Inn/Cottage; 11 units; Moderate; Smoking OK; Credit cards; No handicapped access

Located in a rustic lumbering area, this ranch-style country inn is situated on five and one-half wooded acres conducive to strolling and relaxation. Lodge guest rooms, with private baths, have cabin-like interiors; some offer fireplaces, kitchens, sitting areas, television, antiques, and decks. A separate country cottage and beach house are also available. This lodge "becomes" a b&b establishment with an optional plan of services that can include, along with the continental breakfast, a hot tub and beverage and snack service.

Country Inn

632 N. Main Street, Fort Bragg, CA 95437
Phone: (707) 964–3737
Key: Inn; 8 units; Moderate–Superior; No smoking; Credit cards; Handicapped access, 1 unit

The early 1890s-built home, within walking distance to town and the Skunk Train, has been beautifully renovated. All guest rooms boast king- or queen-size brass or iron beds, private baths (one with an antique claw-foot tub), wallpapers, and colorful touches. Two guest rooms have cozy fireplaces. The redwood sun deck and skylighted sitting room with potbelly stove and art pieces are there for the guests' relaxation. A glass of complimentary wine is served each evening, and morning brings home-baked fruit and nut breads, Don's Prize Muffins, cheese, and fresh fruit. The inn offers a special train package, including two nights' stay, dinners, and Skunk Train tickets.

Glass Beach Bed & Breakfast Inn

726 N. Main Street, Fort Bragg, CA 95437
Phone: (707) 964–6774
Key: Inn; 9 units; Inexpensive–Moderate; Smoking OK; Credit cards; Handicapped access, 1 unit

This renovated 1920s home offers uniquely decorated guest accommodations both upstairs and down. Rooms range from an Asian-wicker motif to a Victorian attic room; all have private baths with shower/tub combinations. The sitting room with reading material and games is the locale of evening wine and snacks, as well as the generous breakfast, which also may be taken to the room. Guests enjoy a private hot tub.

The Grey Whale Inn, Fort Bragg

The Grey Whale Inn

615 N. Main Street, Fort Bragg, CA 95437
Phone: (707) 964–0640 / (800) 382–7244
Key: Inn; 14 units; Moderate–Superior; No smoking; Credit cards;
Handicapped access, 1 unit

Built in 1915 in the classic style of old-growth redwood, this
stately, historic building served as the Redwood Coast Hospital
until 1971 but leaves no hint of its former identity. The carefully
renovated inn boasts beveled glass and interesting local art throughout. The spacious and airy guest rooms offer views of the town and
hills or the ocean, as well as private baths and telephones; a favorite
is the Fireside Rendezvous Room. A new honeymoon suite boasts a
special whirlpool tub. Guests gather in the ground-floor conference
room, in the television/VCR room, and in the lounge with fireplace.
The delightful breakfast buffet includes juices, seasonal fruit, homemade coffee cakes, cereal, and a special entree that may range from
egg-and-sausage casserole to bacon-and-egg breakfast pie. The inn is
close to the ocean and the Skunk Train.

Noyo River Lodge

500 Casa del Noyo Drive, Fort Bragg, CA 95437
Phone: (707) 964–8045; (800) 628–1126
Key: Inn/Cottage; 13 units; Moderate–Superior; Limited smoking;
Credit cards; Handicapped access, 1 unit

Fort Bragg

This inn was originally built in 1868 as a residence and reveals the fine woodwork and craftsmanship of the period throughout. Situated on two and one-half acres of cypress trees and flower gardens, the b&b overlooks the Noyo River and village. Guest accommodations include spacious, carpeted guest rooms with antique private baths, antique furnishings, and views (two guest rooms have fireplaces), and an attached cabin with a king-size bed, skylights, and fireplace. Suites at the inn feature such amenities as gas fireplaces, over-sized tubs, queen beds, decks, and step-down sitting areas with ocean views. The continental breakfast is served in the main lodge building, which has fireplaces in its lounge and restaurant.

Pudding Creek Inn

700 N. Main Street, Fort Bragg, CA 95437
Phone: (707) 964–9529
Key: Inn; 10 units; Inexpensive–Moderate; No smoking; Credit cards; No handicapped access

Two 1884 Victorian homes connected by an enclosed garden court make up this b&b built by a Russian Count with an infamous past. Each guest room is uniquely decorated in a country-style motif; all offer private baths, some with original turn-of-the-century fixtures, and two feature working fireplaces. Guests enjoy a full buffet breakfast in the breakfast rooms, furnished with individual tables and displays of the inn's original cast-iron stove, antique utensils, and old-fashioned water pump. A small country store with gifts and antiques is located in one of the houses. The inn is an easy walk from beaches, the train ride, shopping, restaurants, and historical sites.

Green Apple Inn

520 Bohemian Highway, Freestone, CA 95472
Phone: (707) 874–2526
Key: Inn; 4 units; Moderate; No smoking; Credit cards; No handicapped access

This New England–style farmhouse built in 1862 is located on five acres in a designated historic district. The inn is furnished with some family pieces from the 1700s, and the cheery rooms, which boast private baths, look out on the countryside. Guests enjoy a parlor with fireplace and a full breakfast. Recreation is all close by, with many fine restaurants, family wineries, biking, horseback riding, and canoeing available in this spot near the Russian River and the Pacific Ocean.

North Coast Country Inn, Gualala

North Coast Country Inn

34591 S. Highway One, Gualala, CA 95445
Phone: (707) 884–4537
Key: Inn/Cottage; 4 units; Superior; No smoking; Credit cards; No handicapped access

Overlooking the Pacific Ocean is this cluster of restored redwood buildings with rugged shake roofs nestled into a redwood and pine forest. The hillside property that houses the b&b was once part of a coastal sheep ranch; below the buildings is a colorful country garden with lawn, brick pathways, and fruit trees. Guest accommodations range from a private guest house with deck, fireplace, skylights, and a four-poster bed to rooms with such details as French doors, fireplaces, beam ceilings, French and European antiques, and ocean-view decks. All accommodations boast private baths and kitchens. Guests at the inn enjoy breakfast served on individual trays in the room; the full fare consists of a hot entree, fresh fruit, and freshly baked muffins, cinnamon rolls, or croissants. A freshly brewed pot of coffee is also included in the morning meal, but all guest rooms are stocked with a coffeepot, coffee, and juice. A favorite spot at the inn is the upper garden at the top of the hill, surrounded by towering pines and offering ocean vistas.

The Old Milano Hotel

38300 Highway One, Gualala, CA 95445
Phone: (707) 884–3256
Key: Inn/Cottage; 9 units; Moderate–Superior; No smoking; Credit cards; Handicapped access, 1 unit

This hotel, which began as a 1905 rest stop and pub alongside the railroad, has been refurbished throughout. Accommodations include six guest rooms and two baths upstairs with ocean or garden views; a suite with a hand-painted canopy bed; and a vine-covered cottage with bath, sitting area, and potbelly stove. The inn's most unusual accommodation is the Caboose, with deck, refrigerator, potbelly stove, and sitting area. Guests enjoy the hotel's gardens and hot tub, perched above a cove. The complimentary continental breakfast consists of home-baked breads, a fresh fruit dish, and locally roasted coffee. The inn's chef offers gourmet dinners Wednesday through Sunday.

St. Orres

P.O. Box 523, Gualala, CA 95445
Phone: (707) 884–3303/884–3335
Key: Inn/Cottages; 19 units; Inexpensive–Deluxe; Smoking OK; Credit cards; Handicapped access, 11 units

Inspired by Russian architecture and constructed of one-hundred-year-old timbers, the inn with restaurant is a unique b&b offering. Accommodations include eight rooms in the inn, each with double bed and handmade quilt and some with stained-glass windows and balconies, as well as a cabin and ten cottages. One cottage has a full kitchen; the others offer a wet bar, refrigerator, and coffeepot. The seven creek-side cottages enjoy use of the exclusive creek-side spa area with hot tub, sauna, and sundeck. A full breakfast is included in the stay, and dinner is available in the restaurant.

Whale Watch

35100 Highway One, Gualala, CA 95445
Phone: (707) 884–3667; Fax: (707) 884–4815
Key: Inn; 18 units; Superior–Deluxe; No smoking; Credit cards; Handicapped access, 2 units

Located on two cliff-side acres overlooking Anchor Bay with breathtaking views of the Mendocino coastline is this contemporary inn with beach access. Five buildings compose the inn and offer eighteen unique guest accommodations that feature such varied amenities as fireplaces, skylights, queen-size beds, down comforters, whirlpool tubs, two-story units, fully equipped kitchens, sitting areas, private decks, and private baths. Guests enjoy a large lounge with ocean views and a generous breakfast served in the room; wine is available. The bountiful breakfast fare might include frittatas, blintzes, quiche, or Belgian waffles.

The Estate

13555 Highway 116, Guerneville, CA 95446
Phone: (707) 869–9093
Key: Inn; 10 units; Moderate–Deluxe; No smoking; Credit cards; Handicapped access, 1 unit

The three-story, Mission Revival country home, a Sonoma County Historical Landmark, sits on six acres with redwood groves, gardens, and apple orchards; the grounds feature a large, terraced heated pool and spa. The 1922-built stucco structure with tile roof offers ten guest rooms with private baths, antique decor, and queen beds. Special touches include freshly cut flowers, imported soaps and toiletries, down pillows and comforters, remote color television, telephones, and evening turn-down service with chocolates. Common rooms at the inn include a solarium with bay-window views, a Great Room, a Breakfast Room, and a large, formal dining room with French doors opening onto the pool and gardens. The lower level of the inn contains a sitting room and library with balcony and covered porch. The full breakfast of juice, French-roast coffee, and specialties such as sausages and apple-stuffed French toast with local apple syrup is served in the solarium, breakfast or main dining rooms, or by the pool. Dinners and wine are available certain nights.

Ridenhour Ranch House Inn

12850 River Road, Guerneville, CA 95446
Phone: (707) 887–1033
Key: Inn; 8 units; Moderate–Superior; No smoking; Credit cards; Handicapped access, 1 unit

This eleven-room country house built at the turn of the century is within walking distance of the Korbel Winery's champagne cellars. The carefully restored inn offers guest rooms decorated individually in country English and American antiques with quilts, flowers, plants, and decanters of wine. Guests may stroll under the redwoods, soak in the hot tub, or relax in front of the comfortable living room's fireplace. The country kitchen, formal dining room, or garden terrace provides the setting for the full, creative breakfast by the owner/chef; breakfast features homemade marmalade and eggs gathered by the guests. Five-course gourmet dinners are available at an additional cost.

Santa Nella House

12130 Highway 116, Guerneville, CA 95446
Phone: (707) 869–9488
Key: Home; 4 units; Moderate; Limited smoking; Credit cards; No handicapped access

Formerly the winemaster's residence of the circa-1880 Santa Nella Winery, this b&b offers guests overnight lodging along with a full champagne breakfast. The house sits among the redwoods with the Korbel vineyard in view and Pocket Creek passing through the frontage. The guest rooms boast Victorian decor, private baths, and plush red carpeting; two rooms have fireplaces. Guests may relax in the parlor with its wood-burning fireplace, sun on the large wrap-around veranda, and enjoy the hot tub under the redwoods.

Murphy's Jenner by the Sea

10400 Coast Highway One, P.O. Box 69, Jenner, CA 95450
Phone: (707) 865–2377
Key: Inn/Cottage; 11 units; Moderate–Deluxe; No smoking; Credit cards; No handicapped access

   This inn, offering a variety of guest rooms, suites, cottages, and vacation homes, is surrounded by 15 miles of sandy beaches and acres of state parkland. Situated at the meeting point of the Russian River and the Pacific, the b&b complex offers hiking, fishing, whale watching, and canoeing. Guest accommodations have antique and wicker decor, plants, and private baths, and many boast handmade quilts, private entrances, view decks, and wood-stoves; suites include living rooms, kitchens, and bedrooms. The stay at Jenner by the Sea includes a generous continental breakfast served in the parlor, breakfast room, or piano room. A restaurant on the premises serves continental cuisine, featuring local sea-foods and wines.

Glendeven

8221 N. Highway One, Little River, CA 95456
Phone: (707) 937–0083
Key: Inn; 11 units; Moderate–Superior; No smoking; Credit cards; No handicapped access

   This small inn within an 1867-built, Maine-style farmhouse overlooks meadows and the bay. Guest accommodations are located in the main farmhouse and also in the barn house, which hosts suites with private baths. Half the rooms have fireplaces, and two accommodations share baths. Guest rooms are decorated with antiques and contemporary artwork. A brick terrace, gardens, and sitting room provide relaxation. The spacious sitting area with fireplace and baby grand piano is the locale of the morning breakfast unless in-room service is requested. Guests enjoy the inn's own art gallery featuring contemporary art and crafts.

Little River

Heritage House

5200 Highway One, Little River, CA 95456
Phone: (707) 937–5885
Key: Inn/Cottages; 70 units; Superior–Deluxe; Smoking OK; No credit cards; Handicapped access, 10 units

This country inn expands on the b&b concept by serving a full breakfast and a six-course dinner along with the overnight stay. The Maine-style complex perched on the dramatic coastline consists of an 1877 farmhouse (now office), with dining room, kitchen, and a handful of guest rooms, and sixty-seven guest cottages that blend in with the landscape. Accommodations are furnished with local historical pieces, and all quarters enjoy beautiful views and peaceful surroundings.

The Victorian Farmhouse

7001 N. Highway One, P.O. Box 357, Little River, CA 95456
Phone: (707) 937–0697
Key: Inn; 10 units; Moderate; No smoking; Credit cards; No handicapped access

An apple orchard, flower gardens, School House Creek, and nearby Buckhorn Cove offer relaxation and recreation to this 1877 farmhouse's guests. Guest rooms all have king- or queen-size beds covered with quilts from the innkeeper's collection, private baths, and period antiques; six rooms boast a fireplace. Some rooms offer ocean vistas or views of forest redwoods and ferns. Breakfast is brought to the room each morning, and for evening enjoyment sherry is placed in the parlor, which has a bay window and fireplace.

McCloud Guest House

606 W. Colombero Drive, P.O. Box 1510, McCloud, CA 96057
Phone: (916) 964–3160
Key: Inn; 5 units; Moderate; Limited smoking; Credit cards; No handicapped access

Giant oaks, pines, and lawns surround this 1907 country inn and restaurant on the lower slopes of Mount Shasta. The entire guest house has been restored to its turn-of-the-century elegance with wallpapers, original chandeliers, claw-foot tubs, and pedestal sinks. Upstairs, the five spacious guest rooms are furnished with antiques, reproductions of brass and white-iron queen-size beds, and original beveled mirrors. Each accommodation boasts its own bath and a sitting area, which opens to the guest parlor with fireplace and antique pool table. The continental breakfast of assorted fruit, pastries, juice, and coffee or tea is served in the upstairs parlor; sherry may be sipped in the parlor each evening. Four mountain bikes are available for afternoon rides; the inn is only 6 miles from Mt. Shasta Ski Park and near several golf courses and trout-fishing spots. The first floor of the guest house is a well-known dinner house open to the public on weekends in the winter and six days a week the remainder of the year; reservations are suggested.

Agate Cove Inn, Mendocino

Agate Cove Inn

11201 Lansing Street, P.O. Box 1150, Mendocino, CA 95460
Phone: (707) 937–0551
Key: Inn/Cottages; 10 units; Moderate–Superior; No smoking; Credit cards; No handicapped access

When guests check into this tiny "village" of Cape Cod–style cottages surrounding an 1860s-built farmhouse, they receive a complimentary decanter of sherry from the innkeeper to enjoy on their own cottage deck. The main house, built by the first brewer of Mendocino Beer in the country, is the innkeeper's residence as well as the locale of the sumptuous full country breakfast, prepared before guests on the antique wood-burning stove. Guests enjoy this repast while viewing the splendor of the crashing waves below. Each individual cottage, painted an ocean blue with white trim, features quaint wall coverings above the wainscoting, a four-poster bed, cozy fireplace, color television, and private bath (some with double tubs or double showers). Fresh flowers and ocean views past red passion vines and marigolds make these cottages extra special. Guests enjoy a common room decorated with antiques and a colorful garden.

B. G. Ranch and Inn, Mendocino

B. G. Ranch and Inn

9601 Highway One, Mendocino, CA 95460
Phone: (707) 937–5322
Key: Inn, 4 units; Moderate; No smoking; No credit cards; No handicapped access

This coastal ranch house, built in the late 1800s, is surrounded by fourteen acres of redwood forest, gardens, and meadows and overlooks the inn's own stream-fed pond and wildlife-filled woods. The upstairs of the house consists of two bedrooms for guests that share a bath and offer such detailing as the original polished redwood floors, picture-window views, and skylights. The two downstairs guest rooms also share one bath. The hearty continental breakfast of juice, homemade muffins, and more is served in the large country kitchen with views of the pond. Guests at the ranch may watch deer from the living room with its cozy fireplace or take a leisurely walk to the ocean.

Big River Lodge, Mendocino

Big River Lodge—The Stanford Inn by the Sea

P.O. Box 487, Mendocino, CA 95460
Phone: (707) 937–5615; **Fax:** (707) 937–0305
Key: Inn; 23 units; Superior–Deluxe; Limited smoking; Credit cards; Handicapped access, 11 units

This lodge on a hillside overlooking the town and the ocean is surrounded by forests and meadows. The spacious guest rooms, uniquely decorated in country antiques, flowers, and art, feature color television, private entrances and baths, and wood-burning fireplaces or stoves. The morning breakfast includes special Irish coffee cakes, yogurt, cereal, juices, fruit, and champagne. A carafe of wine awaits guests in each room. The inn is proud of its flower and vegetable gardens, and guests enjoy the friendly llamas that graze nearby, as well as a swimming pool, Jacuzzi, and sauna. Plans are underway to add additional suites at the lodge.

Brewery Gulch Inn

9350 Coast Highway One, Mendocino, CA 95460
Phone: (707) 937–4752
Key: Inn; 5 units; Moderate–Superior; No smoking; Credit cards; No handicapped access

This 1860s-built white farmhouse on two flower- and tree-filled acres is serenely bordered by pastures, forests, and the rugged coast of the Pacific Ocean. Paths wander through the flower gardens on the old farm, which was once a dairy as well as a beer-brewing operation. The quiet interiors of the inn are filled with Victorian decor; all five guest rooms offer a country warmth with queen-size beds, homemade quilts, and down pillows. Two rooms boast fireplaces, and all the guest accommodations grant peaceful views, some of which include the ocean. A full country breakfast of such delicacies as Spanish eggs and fried apples or cheese blintzes with ham and blueberries is served at the guest's convenience either in the common room or in the garden.

The Headlands Inn

Howard and Albion streets, P.O. Box 132, Mendocino, CA 95460
Phone: (707) 937–4431
Key: Inn/Cottage; 5 units; Moderate–Superior; No smoking; Credit cards; Handicapped access, 1 unit

This inn, overlooking an English-style garden, with its spectacular white-water ocean views, was originally built in 1868 as the town's barbershop and then moved and expanded in later years. Restoration has preserved its charm and added present-day comforts. The five guest accommodations each feature a queen- or king-size bed, village or ocean views, private bath, and wood-burning fireplace (one unit offers an old-fashioned parlor stove on a raised hearth).

The Headlands Inn, Mendocino

Guests may relax in two parlors. The full breakfast consists of fresh fruit, two home-baked breads or muffins, a hot entree, and beverage and is served in the room on a tray along with the morning *San Francisco Chronicle*.

Joshua Grindle Inn

44800 Little Lake, P.O. Box 647, Mendocino, CA 95460
Phone: (707) 937–4143
Key: Inn/Cottage; 10 units; Moderate–Superior; No smoking; Credit cards; No handicapped access

This 1879 home, within walking distance of shops and the beach, is on two acres and offers views of the village, bay, and ocean. Guest rooms, each with private bath, are light and airy and are decorated in a New England–country motif with selected antiques. In addition to the inn's accommodations, two guest rooms are located in a cottage and three are in a water-tower building. Many rooms boast ocean views, and some have a fireplace. Breakfast is served each morning at the pine harvest table in the dining room; the full fare might include quiche, scones, and frittatas, along with cereal and fresh fruit.

MacCallum House

45020 Albion Street, P.O. Box 206, Mendocino, CA 95460
Phone: (707) 937–0289
Key: Inn/Cottages; 21 units; Inexpensive–Deluxe; Smoking OK;
Credit cards; No handicapped access

The large house with gardens was built in 1882. The inn now
offers guest accommodations, in the main house and in several
buildings on the grounds, as well as a restaurant and bar. Fireplaces,
original Tiffany lamps, Persian rugs, period photos, and antiques create a nostalgic feeling in all the cheerful guest rooms. Separate
accommodations are found in the converted carriage house, water
tower with split-level lodging, child's playhouse nestled in a bed of
geraniums, and barn; many feature Franklin stoves. A continental
breakfast is included in the stay except during winter months when
offered on weekends and holidays only.

Mendocino Hotel & Garden Cottages, Mendocino

Mendocino Hotel & Garden Cottages

45080 Main Street, P.O. Box 587, Mendocino, CA 95460
Phone: (707) 937–0511; **Fax:** (707) 937–0513
Key: Inn/Hotel/Cottages; 51 units; Inexpensive–Deluxe; Limited
smoking; Credit cards; Handicapped access, 1 unit

The historic hotel, established in 1878, offers elegantly restored
lodging, a restaurant, and a lounge overlooking Mendocino Bay. Four
cottages have been added in the English garden overlooking the
Pacific Ocean. The guest rooms are furnished in Victorian decor
with four-poster and brass beds, armoires, and assorted antiques;

many rooms boast a balcony, fireplace, or marble bath. Extras at the inn include telephones, televisions, and turn-down service each night. Breakfast, lunch, and dinner are served daily in the hotel's intimate dining rooms."

Mendocino Village Inn

44860 Main Street, P.O. Box 626, Mendocino, CA 95460
Phone: (707) 937–0246
Key: Inn; 12 units; Inexpensive–Superior; Limited smoking; Credit cards; No handicapped access

Originally built as a doctor's residence in 1882, the home belonged to three more doctors and their families and thus received the appropriate nickname of "the house of doctors." The interiors of the inn are a pleasant blend of Victorian and country decor with contemporary art throughout. The twelve guest accommodations are located upstairs, downstairs, and in the attic. The two attic rooms share a bath on the second floor; all remaining rooms have private baths. Many guest rooms grant ocean views, and some offer fireplaces. The full gourmet breakfast varies each day with specialties such as herbed cheesecake or blue cornmeal pancakes. The inn hosts an evening wine hour.

1021 Main Street Guest House

P.O. Box 803, Mendocino, CA 95460
Phone: (707) 937–5150
Key: Inn/Cottages; 3 units; Superior; Limited smoking; No credit cards; No handicapped access

Built by shipwrights around 1861, this farmhouse with barn and outbuildings overlooking Jackson State Forest, Big River Beach, Mendocino Bay, and the Pacific affords spectacular views in all directions. The inn offers two private cottages: one a garden cottage and the other with panoramic views of the ocean. Cottages contain refrigerators and iron fireplaces. The one suite within the inn is self-contained with an outside entrance and boasts panoramic views of the ocean and a fireplace. All units have queen-size beds and luxurious private baths. A homemade continental breakfast is included in the stay.

Mendocino

Sea Gull Inn

P.O. Box 317, Mendocino, CA 95460
Phone: (707) 937–5204
Key: Inn; 9 units; Inexpensive–Moderate; Limited smoking; No credit cards; Handicapped access, 1 unit

This one-hundred-year-old residence, within walking distance of town, became an inn in the 1960s. A garden lush in fuschias and boasting a century-old rosemary bush surrounds the quaint inn, which offers nine guest accommodations. The neat guest rooms offer private baths and views of the headland and ocean. A generous continental breakfast is included in the stay.

Sea Rock

11101 N. Lansing, P.O. Box 286, Mendocino, CA 95460
Phone: (707) 937–5517
Key: Inn/Cottages; 16 units; Moderate–Superior; Smoking OK; Credit cards; No handicapped access

Originally a trailer court, this b&b on a 70-foot cliff with spectacular white-water views now offers individual cabins set amidst a cypress grove. Along with views of the Mendocino headlands, the blue-gray cabins with white trim offer private flower gardens, fireplaces, color cable television, and brewed in-room coffee. Some have antiques and kitchens. The buffet breakfast is served downstairs in the office; guests may enjoy their meal in the room or outside. Guests enjoy a lawn area and a private beach and cove, where they may wade through tidal pools, collect shells, or fish for abalone.

Whitegate Inn

---

499 Howard Street, P.O. Box 150, Mendocino, CA 95460
Phone: (707) 937–4892
Key: Inn; 5 units; Moderate–Superior; No smoking; No credit cards; No handicapped access

Whitegate Inn, Mendocino

The 1880 home, overlooking the town park, has been refurbished and is decorated totally in antiques. The guest rooms all feature their own sitting areas, and all have private baths and fireplaces. A full breakfast greets guests in the dining room each morning; a parlor decanter of wine is shared in the early evening. The inn recently turned a former guest room into a double parlor/dining room; guests also enjoy a deck and gazebo. The inn is available for small weddings.

Highland Dell Inn

21050 River Boulevard, P.O. Box 370, Monte Rio, CA 95462-0370
Phone: (707) 865–1759 / (800) 767–1759
Key: Inn; 11 units; Moderate–Deluxe; Limited smoking; Credit cards; No handicapped access

This 1906-built original hotel also hosted the big bands of the 1940s; today it is a quiet bed & breakfast inn on the south side of the Russian River, surrounded by tall redwoods. The Germanic-style inn boasts a lobby with soaring ceiling, a grand staircase, stained-glass windows, and a large lobby fireplace. The decor features many of the heirloom furnishings collected by previous owners, including an impressive collection of local historic photos.

Monte Rio

Each of the inn's accommodations, offering both private and shared baths, is uniquely decorated; the third-floor Bohemian Suite features a king-size brass bed, an over-sized sunken tub, two antique wood-burning stoves, and its own sitting and dressing areas. The living room with comfortable seating is the locale of the buffet breakfast that always includes a hot offering along with fruits, juices, and baked goods. Guests may also relax in the sun room with its view of the river; out of doors, guests enjoy the inn's swimming pool among the redwoods. The inn is available for small conferences and retreats; four-course dinners are offered biweekly. Pets are welcome with a security deposit.

The House of a Thousand Flowers

P.O. Box 369, Monte Rio, CA 95462
Phone: (707) 632–5571
Key: Home; 2 units; Moderate; No smoking; Credit cards; No handicapped access

The 1967 house on a bluff overlooks the Russian River and is surrounded by flowering trees and gardens and sunny decks. The comfortably furnished guest rooms each have a private entrance and impressive forest and valley views. Guests enjoy a warm spa on the outside, enclosed deck, plus a large living room, with fireplace and concert grand piano, stocked with books and music. Coffee is served in-room each morning, and a full breakfast of omelettes, bread, and fruit is offered in the dining room. A library-music room and greenhouse–sitting room have been added. Collie dog, Annie, is on hand to greet guests.

Philo Pottery Inn

8550 Highway 128, P.O. Box 166, Philo, CA 95466
Phone: (707) 895–3069
Key: Inn/Cottage; 5 units; Moderate; No smoking; Credit cards; No handicapped access

This historic house, constructed entirely of redwood in 1888, was once a stagecoach stop on the way to the north coast. The guest rooms and cottage are furnished with antiques, and the beds are cov-

Philo Pottery Inn, Philo

ered with patchwork quilts and cozy down comforters. Guests enjoy the inn's living room with woodstove and library. A full breakfast is served in the dining room each morning and features seasonal fresh fruit or hot fruit compote, cream cheese-stuffed French toast, sausages, homemade baked goods, and juices. Tea and homemade cookies are offered in the evening; a complimentary bottle of wine is also included in the stay. From the willow furniture on the front porch, guests may relax and enjoy the English garden.

The Faulkner House

1029 Jefferson Street, Red Bluff, CA 96080
Phone: (916) 529–0520
Key: Inn; 4 units; Inexpensive–Moderate; No smoking; Credit cards; No handicapped access

This beautiful Queen Anne–Victorian home on a vintage tree-lined street still retains its original molding, leaded-glass windows, and outside porches. Guests are invited to enjoy the parlor, the living room, and the dining room, all tastefully decorated in antiques. The guest rooms also are furnished in period pieces and feature old-fashioned high ceilings. The Arbor Room boasts a European-carved bedroom set and private bath; the Wicker Room is sunny and light; the Tower Room is cozy; and the Rose Room features a brocade fainting couch. The three accommodations share a bath. Evening refreshments are served to guests; the full morning meal is offered from 8:00 to 9:00 A.M. in the dining room.

Palisades Paradise

1200 Palisades Avenue, Redding, CA 96003
Phone: (916) 223–5305
Key: Home; 2 units; Inexpensive; No smoking; Credit cards; No handicapped access

Just 30 feet from the banks of the Sacramento River in a quiet residential area is this contemporary home b&b with 60-foot patio, redwood deck with spa overlooking the city and river, and well-groomed lawns. The two guest accommodations, professionally decorated with traditional furnishings, share one bath. The spacious Sunset Suite offers a sitting area and sliding glass doors to the back lawn and deck. Drinks and snacks are offered upon arrival, and breakfast is served in the dining area. The morning meal varies, but an extended continental fare is served weekdays, and a full breakfast is offered each weekend. This b&b is a perfect retreat for outdoor enthusiasts: guests may choose to sit by a fire in the living room or relax on the old-fashioned porch swing under the oak tree.

Scotia Inn

P.O. Box 248, Scotia, CA 95565
Phone: (707) 764–5683
Key: Inn; 11 units; Inexpensive–Superior; Limited smoking; Credit cards; No handicapped access

Surrounded by forested hills and nestled along the Eel River, this historic inn has been in operation since 1888. Beautifully renovated in 1985, the b&b boasts a polished redwood lobby with comfortable seating and eleven guest rooms, each with private bath. The spacious guest accommodations include king- and queen-size beds, antiques, European silk wall coverings, and original claw-foot tubs. The Bridal Suite features an adjoining Jacuzzi room. The homemade continental breakfast is served in the lobby from 7:30 to 10:00 A.M., and complete dining, cocktail, and banquet facilities are available.

The Lost Whale Inn

3452 Patrick's Point Drive, Trinidad, CA 95570
Phone: (707) 677–3425
Key: Inn; 6 units; Moderate–Superior; No smoking; Credit cards; No handicapped access

This Cape Cod–style inn with wood-planked floors and country decor was built in 1989 as a b&b inn. The Lost Whale boasts spectacular ocean views along with a private beach and 2 miles of private cove. The inn caters to families and offers lots of child-related recreation such as spacious grounds with playhouse, playground, and berries ripe for picking. The inn also provides a Great Room filled with books, puzzles, and games, as well as sleeping lofts perfect for children in two of the suites. Guests may choose from four unique suites with private baths and ocean views and two guest rooms with shared baths. Stays include a hearty country breakfast of casseroles and quiches, home-baked muffins, fresh fruit, and locally smoked salmon. Afternoon tea with wine, beverages, and snacks is also served. Guests enjoy an ocean-view hot tub, a wooded-trail stroll to the inn's private cove filled with tide pools and sea lions, and bicycling over coastal roads on the inn's bikes.

Oak Knoll Bed & Breakfast

858 Sanel Drive, P.O. Box 412, Ukiah, CA 95482
Phone: (707) 468–5646
Key: Home; 2 units; Moderate; No smoking; No credit cards; No handicapped access

This contemporary redwood-and-glass home sits on a knoll studded with oak trees and enjoys views of the hills, valley, and vineyards on all sides. A 3,000-square-foot deck with tables and chairs is the site of the morning meal. Both guest accommodations feature a queen-size bed and fresh flowers and share a bath and adjacent sitting room with games and color television. The house is decorated in wall coverings, chandeliers, and oriental rugs; guests may enjoy fireside relaxation, or the living room, with its piano. Breakfast, served on fine china, includes fruit, juice, homemade breads, and pastries; eggs and bacon are available. Wine and cheese are offered in the evening.

Sanford House

306 South Pine Street, Ukiah, CA 95482
Phone: (707) 462–1653
Key: Inn; 5 units; Moderate; No smoking; No credit cards; No handicapped access

In the heart of the Mendocino wine country is this 1904-built Queen Anne–Victorian home that was the residence of Senator John Sanford and his family until 1944. A rare bird's-eye-maple fireplace warms the antique-filled parlor of the inn. Also, the library is a popular gathering spot with its cozy window seat. The five individually decorated guest rooms, all named after presidents who served between 1904 and 1928, are located upstairs and feature quaint wallpaper prints, fresh flowers, antique decor, and private baths. A chilled bottle of local wine is served to guests upon arrival. The complimentary full breakfast is served either in the dining room on fine china and crystal or in the privacy of your room; the fare includes fresh seasonal fruit, homemade breads and muffins, and an egg dish. Guests are encouraged to relax on the large porch furnished with nostalgic wicker furniture.

Vichy Springs Resort & Inn

2605 Vichy Springs Road, Ukiah, CA 95482
Phone: (707) 462–9515
Key: Inn/Cottages; 14 units; Moderate–Superior; No smoking; Credit cards; Handicapped access, 1 unit

A former playground for the rich and famous, this 1890s-built spa resort offers historical charm with updated conveniences. Guests may stay in one of the resort's two original cottages built in 1854, with kitchens and private porches, or in the completely renovated inn offering a dozen guest rooms with hardwood floors and Waverly floral prints, as well as private baths and phones. The stay includes an extended continental breakfast, use of the mineral baths and mineral swimming pool, and enjoyment of the 700-acre grounds for hiking, picnicking, mountain biking, and nature explorations. The resort's famous grotto, offering sparkling "champagne" baths from effervescent, 90-degree mineral waters, is its special attraction. Massages are available at an additional cost.

Bowen's Pelican Lodge & Inn

38921 N. Highway One, P.O. Box 35, Westport, CA 95488
Phone: (707) 964-5588
Key: Inn/Cottage; 7 units; Inexpensive–Superior; Smoking OK; Credit cards; No handicapped access

Formerly the Cobweb Palace Inn, the lodge and inn now has new owners. This western Victorian inn, reminiscent of the 1890s, also has an old-time dining room for full-course dinners at an additional charge and a full bar, which has recently been remodeled. Guest rooms are located in the inn and in the house and offer views of the sea and mountains in this remote setting; some have balconies. A separate Honeymoon Cabin hosts a queen-size bed and a charming loft. The continental breakfast included in the stay consists of fresh fruit, homemade muffins, preserves, and juice. The inn is located just 200 yards from the ocean.

Howard Creek Ranch

40501 N. Highway One, P.O. Box 121, Westport, CA 95488
Phone: (707) 964-6725
Key: Inn/Cottages; 7 units; Inexpensive–Moderate; No smoking; Credit cards; No handicapped access

Rolling mountains, wide sandy beaches, and tranquility surround this ranch, which was first settled in 1867. The farmhouse and cottages, built in 1871, sit on twenty acres of land, encompassing beach, mountain, creek, pond, lawn, and flower-garden settings. A small herd of deer, a porcupine, foxes, raccoons, and an occasional elk or bobcat frequent the property, which also hosts horses for feeding and petting; a naturalist offers tours of the grounds. The inn's antique-furnished guest rooms and cottages are scented with home-

Howard Creek Ranch, Westport

made potpourri and offer views of the surrounding scenery. Suites
and cabins have microwave ovens and refrigerators; most have private baths. Guests enjoy late-afternoon refreshments, including herb
teas from the garden; a hearty ranch breakfast is served in the dining
room. This unique "health spa" has a hot tub, sauna, and pool set in
the mountainside; massages are available by advance reservation.

The Doll House Bed & Breakfast

118 School Street, Willits, CA 95490
Phone: (707) 459–4055
Key: Inn; 3 units; Moderate; Limited smoking; No credit cards;
Handicapped access, 1 unit

This restored Queen Anne cottage is just one block from Main
Street and within walking distance of shops and the Skunk Train
Depot. The gingerbread-laden house, surrounded by colorful flowering shrubs and gardens, offers guest rooms with cheery wall coverings and handmade quilts. The downstairs room features a private
bath, and the two upstairs bedrooms, oversized, offer quaint dormer
windows. Guests enjoy a dining room with nearby antique piano, a
living room with bay window and period furniture, and the Doll
Room, filled with more than 500 dolls that overflow into other
rooms of the house. The full, country-style breakfast served on fine

china includes such down-home specialties as fresh orange juice, bacon and sausage, scrambled ranch eggs, bran muffins, homemade jam, and coffee or tea; early-morning beverage and newspaper are delivered to each guest room.

CALIFORNIA WINE COUNTRY

Endless fields of grapes that stretch out to picturesque mountain slopes, historic town squares, country roads dotted with quiet communities, natural hot springs, and renowned wineries all define the Wine Country of the Napa and Sonoma valleys and the Russian River. Add the popular sport of ballooning to vineyard vistas, ideal picnic scenery, lakes, and spas, and this area becomes a natural haven for travelers. This by far is the most popular region for bed & breakfasts, and it is no wonder, what with the perfect settings that abound: ranches, wineries, and quiet Victorian towns. The history of the area is apparent in the town of Sonoma, with its plaza and Mission, and in Yountville's unusual shopping complex reminiscent of its winery origins, vintage 1870. Calistoga still offers mud baths, mineral-spring spas, and the nearby Old Faithful Geyser with its regular eruptions. Country serenity, wine picnicking, and gracious bed & breakfast stops throughout— Wine Country is a relaxing and most pleasurable vacation spot.

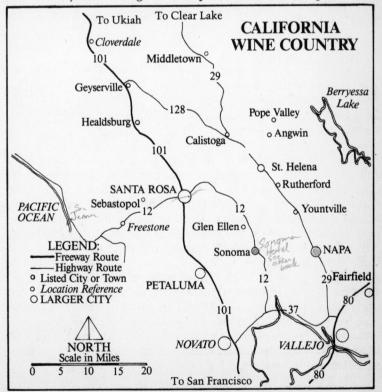

Forest Manor

415 Cold Springs Road, Angwin, CA 94508
Phone: (707) 965–3538; **Fax:** (707) 965–3516
Key: Inn; 3 units; Moderate–Deluxe; No smoking; Credit cards; No handicapped access

This majestic English Tudor estate on twenty secluded acres is nestled among the hillside forests and vineyards above St. Helena. The manor features massive hand-carved beams, fireplaces, a 53-foot-long pool with Jacuzzi, and spacious suites with private baths, decks, refrigerators, and coffeemakers. One suite offers a private Jacuzzi, fireplace, and king-size bed. The generous continental breakfast may be served in the dining room, on the tree-shaded deck, or in the room. Guests enjoy walking trails and nearby tennis.

Brannan Cottage Inn

109 Wapoo Avenue, Calistoga, CA 94515
Phone: (707) 942–4200
Key: Inn; 6 units; Moderate–Superior; No smoking; Credit cards; Handicapped access, 1 unit

This 1860 Greek Revival inn with graceful arches, gingerbread, and original palm tree is the last remaining Sam Brannan–built cottage at his Calistoga Hot Springs Resort and is listed on the National Register of Historic Places. The carefully restored structure is decorated in Victorian country style with light-oak floors, pine furnishings, and white wicker. The six guest rooms and suites boast the original hand-done flower stenciling as well as private baths and entrances, queen-size beds, down comforters, ceiling fans, and central air conditioning. The elegant parlor is furnished in rose and gray with a grapevine stencil border, etched oval window, cozy fireplace, and sherry and port. Afternoon tea is served fireside in cool weather. The full breakfast is served in the enclosed courtyard under the lemon trees on sunny mornings. The tranquil cottage inn is surrounded by lawns and gardens and is within walking distance of Calistoga's hot springs, restaurants, and shops.

Foothill House

3037 Foothill Boulevard, Calistoga, CA 94515
Phone: (707) 942–6933
Key: Inn/Cottage; 3 units; Moderate–Deluxe; No smoking; Credit cards; No handicapped access

Nestled among the western foothills north of Calistoga is this turn-of-the-century farmhouse surrounded by trees and wildlife. Each room is individually decorated with country antiques, a handmade quilt, and a four-poster bed. The two guest rooms offer queen-size beds, private baths and entrances, refrigerators, and fireplaces or stoves as well as air conditioning. The Evergreen Suite cottage boasts a king-size bed, a two-person Jacuzzi, and an oversized shower, as well as a private garden with waterfall and sun deck. An ample continental breakfast is served in the room, on the sun porch, or on the terrace, and guests may partake of wine and cheese each evening.

Larkmead Country Inn

1103 Larkmead Lane, Calistoga, CA 94515
Phone: (707) 942–5360/(415) 254–0304
Key: Inn; 4 units; Moderate; Smoking OK; No credit cards; No handicapped access

This California Victorian was built as a home for one of the first wine-producing families of Napa Valley. The inn is situated on a quiet country road and is surrounded by vineyards and trees. The guest rooms are tastefully furnished with antiques, Persian carpets, and old paintings and are centrally air-conditioned. All guest rooms have private baths. Breakfast, served in the dining room or on the porches, consists of fresh fruit, brioche, and French rolls.

Meadowlark Country House & Inn

601 Petrified Forest Road, Calistoga, CA 94515
Phone: (707) 942–5651
Key: Inn; 4 units; Moderate–Superior; No smoking; Credit Cards; No handicapped access

Calistoga

Twenty acres of woods, creeks, and mountains surround this country house. Guests of the inn enjoy pastures of Arabian horses, pastoral trails, and a large swimming pool, as well as a spacious and comfortable living room with French windows and a relaxing veranda. The two-story farmhouse, built in 1886, has been completely renovated and is decorated tastefully with country prints and a pleasing combination of English country pine antiques and early American furnishings. The four guest rooms of the home offer private baths, nostalgic-print comforters, and antique touches. The inn serves a generous country breakfast of eggs, breads, fresh fruit, and juice each morning; the refrigerator is stocked with refreshments for guests' use.

Mount View Hotel

1457 Lincoln Avenue, Calistoga, CA 94515
Phone: (707) 942–6877; **Fax:** (707) 942–6904
Key: Inn/Hotel; 34 units; Moderate–Superior; Smoking OK; Credit cards; No handicapped access

This 1917 hotel has been restored in the Art Deco style and is on the National Register of Historic Places. Much of its furniture, lighting, and bath fixtures is original. The Mount View has Fender's, a full-service lounge with entertainment nightly and Sunday-afternoon jazz. The dining room serves Napa Valley cuisine at breakfast, lunch, Sunday brunch, and dinner. A full breakfast is included in the stay and served in the main dining room. All rooms offer private baths, and guests enjoy nightly turn-down service, a heated pool, and a Jacuzzi.

The Pink Mansion

1415 Foothill Boulevard, Calistoga, CA 94515
Phone: (707) 942–0558
Key: Inn; 5 units; Moderate–Superior; Limited smoking; Credit cards; Handicapped access, 1 unit

This meticulously restored 1875 Victorian home, painted a pale pink, belonged to the innkeeper's aunt for many years. Her many and varied collections are reflected tastefully throughout the house; collections of angels, cherubs, and Victorian and Oriental treasures adorn many of the rooms. The inn offers five uniquely decorated guest rooms, each with a private bath, queen-size bed, central heating and air conditioning, and valley or forest views. The corner Angel Room features many pieces of the angel collection, a turn-of-the-century brass bed, an airy bathroom with claw-foot tub, and a window seat with views of Mt. St. Helena and the Palisades. Guests at the inn enjoy the use of the spacious Victorian parlor, a drawing room, dining room, and breakfast area. The stay at Pink Mansion includes a gourmet breakfast and afternoon wine tasting by the indoor heated pool.

Scarlett's Country Inn, Calistoga

Scarlett's Country Inn

3918 Silverado Trail, Calistoga, CA 94515
Phone: (707) 942–6669
Key: Inn/Cottage; 3 units; Moderate–Superior; Smoking OK; No credit cards; No handicapped access

This cottage b&b is separate from the main two-story farmhouse, and it is located in a quiet canyon off the road. A suite with private bath has a queen-size, wood-carved bed, French country antiques, and claw-foot tub. Two other suites overlooking the vineyards also are available and also boast queen-size beds; the larger suite has a fireplace. Guests enjoy a pool and a homemade continental breakfast served under the apple trees by the pool or in the suite. This hospitable b&b welcomes families.

Trailside Inn

4201 Silverado Trail, Calistoga, CA 94515
Phone: (707) 942–4106
Key: Inn; 3 units; Moderate; Smoking OK; Credit cards; No handi-
capped access

This inn has three suites for guests; one attached to the one-
story, 1930s farmhouse, the other two within the fifty-year-old barn.
Two guest rooms feature an antique, brass double bed in the bedroom, and one suite hosts a queen-size bed; a living room with twin
daybeds; and a private entrance, bath, and porch with views of the
vineyards. The complete kitchens in each are stocked with homemade fruit bread, orange juice, butter, eggs, fruit, wine, mineral
water, tea, and coffee for both breakfast and refreshment time. Each
unit will accommodate up to four people; there is no charge for children under twelve.

Wine Way Inn, Calistoga

Wine Way Inn

1019 Foothill Boulevard, Highway 29, Calistoga, CA 94515
Phone: (707) 942–0680
Key: Inn/Cottage; 6 units; Moderate–Superior; No smoking; Credit
cards; No handicapped access

The inn, built in 1915 as a family home, is located within walking distance of shops yet offers deck views of the mountains and forests of the area. Guest rooms, all with central air conditioning and private baths, have recently been redecorated with antiques; three guest rooms offer queen-size beds. A separate cottage offers a private bath and spectacular views. The patio or dining room is the site of morning breakfast. A full breakfast featuring such specialties as huevos rancheros and/or crepes is served in the dining room, on the patio, or in the intimate gazebo. A delightful arbor has recently been added.

Zinfandel House

1253 Summit Drive, Calistoga, CA 94515
Phone: (707) 942-0733
Key: Home; 3 units; Moderate; No smoking; No credit cards; No handicapped access

This home is situated on a wooded hillside overlooking vineyards and the mountains across the valley. The three guest rooms boast private baths, down pillows and comforters, and handmade quilts. During warm weather breakfast is served on the deck, with majestic views, and in the solarium during the winter. Wine is offered in the late afternoon.

Abrams House Inn

314 North Main Street, Cloverdale, CA 95425
Phone: (707) 894-2412
Key: Inn; 4 units; Moderate; No smoking; Credit cards; No handicapped access

Originally built by the Abrams family in the 1870s, this Victorian inn also includes a circa-1860s brick building on the premises that may have been the town's first jail. The restored home sits amid lawns; flower, herb, and vegetable gardens; and mature trees that include a one-hundred-year-old olive. Each of the four guest rooms is uniquely decorated with antiques and small-print wallpapers; the Private Suite features a king-size four-poster bed, private bath, and private porch. The other guest rooms share

Abrams House Inn, Cloverdale

two baths but have in-room sinks. Guests may enjoy the inn's upstairs parlor with books and games, as well as a more formal downstairs sitting room and parlor with an original oak-mantled fireplace. The antique-furnished dining room is the locale of the full breakfast meal, which consists of fresh fruit, freshly squeezed juice, a main entree, and homemade breads. Extras at the inn include complimentary cookies and refreshments served upon arrival and use of the inn's bicycles.

Ye Olde Shelford House

29955 River Road, Cloverdale, CA 95425
Phone: (707) 894–5956
Key: Inn; 6 units; Moderate; No smoking; Credit cards; Handicapped access, 1 unit

Bordering on acres of vineyards is this late-1800s home near the Russian River. The completely restored interiors of this intimate b&b feature antiques, cozy window seats, quaint wall coverings (on the ceilings, too), and several relaxing niches including an outside wraparound porch, a game room, a parlor, an upstairs sitting room, a swimming pool, and a hot tub. Those wanting more activity may borrow the inn's "bicycle built for two." The guest rooms offer homemade quilts, antiques, and fresh flowers and plants; four guest

Ye Olde Shelford House, Cloverdale

rooms have private baths. A full homemade breakfast is included in the stay. Guests may help themselves to refreshments and old-fashioned oatmeal cookies from the kitchen. Reservations are advised for the inn's popular "Surrey & Sip" horse-drawn surrey rides as well as antique car tours to the wineries. Picnic lunches are available at an additional cost.

Campbell Ranch Inn

1475 Canyon Road, Geyserville, CA 95441
Phone: (707) 857–3476
Key: Inn/Cottage; 5 units; Moderate–Superior; No smoking; Credit cards; No handicapped access

This hilltop contemporary home looks out onto vineyards and the ranch's own colorful flower gardens. This 35-acre "miniresort" treats guests to tennis, swimming, hiking, Ping-Pong, a hot tub, and bikes, as well as a living-room fireplace. The spacious rooms feature king-size beds, balconies, fresh flowers, fruit, and private baths. The inn's separate cottage features a wood-burning stove. Besides the full gourmet breakfast, fresh pie and coffee are offered before bedtime, and unlimited iced tea and lemonade are served poolside.

The Hope-Bosworth House

21238 Geyserville Avenue, P.O. Box 42, Geyserville, CA 95441
Phone: (707) 857–3356
Key: Inn; 5 units; Moderate; No smoking; Credit cards; No handi-
capped access

This 1904 Victorian home was earlier called the "Palms"
because of the many palm trees once lining the street. All the guest
rooms are decorated in wallpapers, antique light fixtures, and period
antiques. A formal dining room is the site of the morning full country breakfast featuring the innkeeper's prize-winning coffee cake.
Beer and wine are sold at the inn. Guests at the inn enjoy a colorful,
fragrant Victorian garden and use of the swimming pool.

The Hope-Merrill House

21253 Geyserville Avenue, P.O. Box 42, Geyserville, CA 95441
Phone: (707) 857–3356
Key: Inn; 7 units; Moderate–Superior; No smoking; Credit cards;
Handicapped access, 1 unit

The 1885 home was restored completely and carefully in 1980
with authentic wall coverings and woodwork and the original

Lincrusta-Walton wainscoting. Guests may relax with a glass of wine on the wraparound porch or in the parlor. A country breakfast featuring homemade breads, fresh fruit, and eggs is served in the dining room. Dinners are available upon prearrangement (when the entire inn is booked by a group). Individually decorated guest rooms at the inn feature such varied touches as a fireplace, bay-window views, unusual antiques, Bradbury wallpapers, and antique bath fixtures in the all-private baths, which include two whirlpool tubs. The inn offers a unique wine tour called Stage-a-Picnic that visits three wineries via a one-hundred-year-old stage drawn by two Belgian horses and also includes a gourmet picnic. Guests enjoy a garden swimming pool and a gazebo in the vineyards.

Isis Oasis

20889 Geyserville Avenue, Geyserville, CA 95441
Phone: (707) 857–3524
Key: Inn/Cottage; 19 units; Inexpensive–Moderate; Smoking OK; Credit cards; Handicapped access, 1 unit

This 10-acre lodge and cultural center includes a honeymoon cottage with a private hot tub and fireplace, a two-story water tower with a guest room, and a farmhouse that accommodates a dozen guests. The grounds of the informal retreat also host three "yurts" (Mongolian tent structures) and one wine-barrel room. Guests of Isis enjoy a heated pool, a sauna, and a small zoo with some new additions. Breakfast is offered each morning in the dining pavilion.

Beltane Ranch

11775 Sonoma Highway, P.O. Box 395, Glen Ellen, CA 95442
Phone: (707) 996–6501
Key: Inn; 4 units; Moderate; No smoking; No credit cards; No handicapped access

This 1892 house is situated on mountain-slope property with sweeping views of the Sonoma Valley vineyards. The active ranch raises grapes, and its comfortable guest accommodations all boast private baths and entrances. One guest room features a fireplace, and two suites offer separate sitting rooms and the ability to accommodate three guests. A generous breakfast, along with views, is served on the porch on warmer days. Guests enjoy a tennis court.

Glenelly Inn

5131 Warm Springs Road, Glen Ellen, CA 95442
Phone: (707) 996–6720
Key: Inn; 8 units; Moderate–Superior; No smoking; Credit cards; No handicapped access

This b&b was built in 1916 as an inn and was a popular summer retreat for city dwellers in the 1920s. The inn, restored carefully to its original glory, offers to guests once again its long verandas with wicker furniture, an acre of shady lawn, and Common Room with cobblestone fireplace and French leaded-glass windows. The eight individually decorated guest rooms all boast private baths and entrances as well as iron, brass, or four-poster beds (except one trundle unit), some Laura Ashley linens, and pleasantly coordinated prints. The Grand Cru room features a unique queen-size, pewter-and-brass bed; two rooms feature fireplaces. Each afternoon guests may sample local wine and cheeses, and the full breakfast is offered each morning on the veranda under a large oak tree or, on chilly days, by fireside in the Common Room.

Belle de Jour Inn

16276 Healdsburg Avenue, Healdsburg, CA 95448
Phone: (707) 433–7892; **Fax:** (707) 431–7412
Key: Cottages; 4 units; Moderate–Deluxe; No smoking; Credit cards; No handicapped access

This garden b&b offers fresh white cottages nestled in six private acres with panoramic views of the countryside. The guest rooms, decorated in antiques, are situated in separate cottages and offer private baths and queen- or king-size beds. Special details in some of the accommodations include woodstoves, a fireplace, oversized showers, and three whirlpool tubs for two. A sumptuous breakfast is included in the stay; picnic baskets are available on arrangement, as is winery touring via a 1923 Star vintage car.

Calderwood, Healdsburg

Calderwood

25 West Grant Street, Healdsburg, CA 95448
Phone: (707) 431–1110
Key: Inn; 6 units; Moderate–Superior; No smoking; Credit cards; No handicapped access

This finely restored Victorian is nestled among spruce, cedar, and redwood trees. The inn has a turn-of-the-century-feeling; it is decorated throughout with fine English and American antiques and boasts fully restored interiors. A full breakfast is served each morning and features fruit, freshly baked breads, egg dishes, and meat. Guests may also snack on afternoon tea and refreshments such as sandwiches and scones; coffee is served on the porch. Calderwood is available for group rentals at group rates.

Camellia Inn, Healdsburg

Camellia Inn

211 North Street, Healdsburg, CA 95448
Phone: (707) 433–8182
Key: Inn; 9 units; Moderate–Superior; No smoking; Credit cards;
Handicapped access, 1 unit

Built in 1869, this Italianate–Victorian townhouse is just two
blocks from the town plaza. The guest rooms are decorated in
antiques, inlaid hardwood floors, chandeliers, and oriental rugs;
six rooms feature private entrances and baths, and two rooms
boast whirlpool tubs for two and gas fireplaces. Guests are encouraged to enjoy the villa-styled swimming pool and the double parlors with twin marble fireplaces and ceiling medallions. The
breakfast of fresh fruit, eggs, nut breads, and juice is served in the
dining room.

Grape Leaf Inn

539 Johnson Street, Healdsburg, CA 95448
Phone: (707) 433–8140
Key: Inn; 7 units; Moderate–Superior; No smoking; Credit cards; No
handicapped access

This 1902 Queen Anne–Victorian home has been completely restored and offers seven guest accommodations, all with private baths, skylight roofs, and antiques. Four of the guest rooms and suites feature tiled whirlpool tubs. Guests read, play games, or just relax in a parlor with antiques and a living room/dining room with fireplace and comfortable seating. A full breakfast featuring egg dishes and home-baked breads is served in the dining room. Wine and cheeses are offered in the evening.

The Haydon House, Healdsburg

The Haydon House

321 Haydon Street, Healdsburg, CA 95448
Phone: (707) 433–5228
Key: Inn/Cottage; 8 units; Moderate–Superior; No smoking; Credit cards; No handicapped access

A short walk from the Russian River and downtown shops takes you to this lovely Queen Anne–Victorian home in a quiet residential area. The one-time convent has been meticulously restored to its 1912 vintage and dons such period detailing as picture moldings, chair rails and baseboards, stenciling, and wallpapering. The light and airy rooms are furnished in antiques, handmade rugs, lace curtains, and pastels. The cheerful guest rooms feature a favorite of honeymooners, the Attic Suite with skylights, and all are individually decorated in French and American antiques, dhurrie rugs, Laura Ashley prints, and custom-made down comforters. Claw-foot tubs grace several of the rooms. A bountiful breakfast featuring frittatas is offered in the large dining room each morning. Two accommodations are located in a separate Victorian-style cottage that boasts pine floors, double whirlpool tubs with skylights, and romantic laces.

Healdsburg Inn on the Plaza

116 Matheson Street, P.O. Box 1196, Healdsburg, CA 95448
Phone: (707) 433–6991
Key: Inn; 9 units; Moderate–Superior; No smoking; Credit cards; Handicapped access, 1 unit

This renovated 1900-built Wells Fargo building hosts quaint shops and a guest lobby below and attractive b&b guest rooms above. Rooms at the inn feature huge skylights, bay windows, pressed-wood paneling, and Victorian and Eastlake decor. Three guest rooms boast fireplaces, and all accommodations have private baths. The gingerbread-adorned brick building looks over the historic plaza and offers an all-weather solarium and roof garden for socializing. A full breakfast with home-baked breads and a hot entree is served in the solarium. Wine and popcorn are offered in the evening.

Madrona Manor

1001 Westside Road, P.O. Box 818, Healdsburg, CA 95448
Phone: (707) 433–4231/433–4433/(800) 258–4003; **Fax:** (707) 433–0703
Key: Inn/Hotel; 21 units; Moderate–Deluxe; Limited smoking; Credit cards; Handicapped access, 1 unit

This lavish 1881 Victorian mansion is surrounded by eight acres of wooded and landscaped grounds. Today, the ornate hotel and gourmet restaurant offer guest rooms and suites decorated in antiques, Persian carpets, and hand-carved rosewood. All rooms boast air conditioning and private baths, and all but three guest rooms have fireplaces. The acclaimed restaurant at the mansion has an extensive wine list and serves dinners nightly as well as Sunday brunch. A full breakfast is included in the stay.

The Raford House, Healdsburg

The Raford House

10630 Wohler Road, Healdsburg, CA 95448
Phone: (707) 887–9573
Key: Inn; 7 units; Moderate–Superior; No smoking; Credit cards; No handicapped access

This 1880s home, formerly the Wohler Ranch, is a beautifully restored Victorian farmhouse with thirteen rooms and six baths surrounded by vineyards. The seven guest rooms are decorated in period pieces; two have working fireplaces, and most offer private baths. A large front porch overlooks the vineyards and orchards as well as the inn's rose bushes, which number more than one hundred. A light breakfast of rolls, breads, fruit, and juice is served in the formal dining room.

Big Canyon Inn

11750 Big Canyon Road, Middletown, CA 95461
(P.O. Box 1311, Lower Lake, CA 95457)
Phone: (707) 928–5631
Key: Inn; 2 units; Inexpensive; No smoking; No credit cards; No handicapped access

Middletown

This secluded mountain home on twelve acres of pines and oaks is surrounded by recreational opportunities ranging from wildflower viewing in spring to wine tasting to boating on nearby Clear Lake. Guests are accommodated in a suite with private porch, entrance, and bath as well as kitchenette, air conditioning, and cozy woodstove. Accommodations also boast a nice front porch view overlooking the valley. A continental breakfast of pastry and fruit is served each morning. As a special service, private pilots flying into local Hoberg Airport and staying at the inn will be picked up by the hosts.

Arbor Guest House, Napa

Arbor Guest House

1436 G Street, Napa, CA 94559
Phone: (707) 252–8144
Key: Inn; 5 units; Moderate–Superior; No smoking; Credit cards; Handicapped access, 1 unit

Trumpet vines and hanging fuchsia cover the arbor that connects this award-winning Victorian home and carriage house. A garden motif is featured inside the inn with wall coverings, period antiques, and etched glass. Guest rooms in the main house and in the carriage house are beautifully appointed with antiques, private baths, and queen-size beds. Rose's Bower features a romantic fireplace faced by rose-patterned French chairs; another accommodation boasts a whirlpool tub for two and a fireplace. Guests are served a generous breakfast of fresh fruits, quiche, or an egg dish, and baked goods in the room, in the dining room, or on one of the inn's three patios surrounded by fruit and cedar trees.

Beazley House, Napa

Beazley House

1910 First Street, Napa, CA 94559
Phone: (707) 257–1649
Key: Inn/Cottage; 10 units; Moderate–Deluxe; No smoking; Credit cards; Handicapped access, 1 unit

   This mansion with converted carriage house sits on one-half acre of landscaped grounds. Its turn-of-the-century character is expressed throughout in stained glass, inlaid floors, and antique-furnished rooms. Some guest rooms feature fireplaces, and the carriage-house accommodations have private spas and baths. All guest rooms have private baths. The spacious living room is equipped with a tea cart full of beverages. A full breakfast is served in the dining room each morning.

Coombs Residence Inn on the Park

720 Seminary Street, Napa, CA 94559
Phone: (707) 257–0789
Key: Inn; 4 units; Moderate–Superior; No smoking; Credit cards; No handicapped access

This gracious 1852 Victorian home faces the park and is framed by trees, year-round blooms, and lawn. Guests enjoy a swimming pool, Jacuzzi, and bicycles for riding around the park. The inn has been completely restored and furnished with American and European antiques. All guest rooms except one share baths and offer down quilts and pillows, featherbeds, lace sheets, and terry robes. The full breakfast of juice, fruits, and such specialties as quiche, Belgian waffles, or blueberry pancakes is served in the living room on the poolside deck; the morning fare is presented on fine china with silver and linens. Sherry and port are available in a formal parlor complete with fireplace and stereo. Guests may help themselves to sodas in the kitchen any time at this hospitable b&b.

Country Garden Inn

1815 Silverado Trail, Napa, CA 94558
Phone: (707) 255–1197; Fax: (707) 255–3112
Key: Inn/Cottage; 10 units; Superior–Deluxe; No smoking; Credit cards; Handicapped access, 2 units

This nineteenth-century coach house on the Silverado Trail is a true English-style country inn on one and one-half acres of mature woodland and riverside property with rose gardens, fountains, lawns, and abundant with maple trees. The b&b is furnished throughout in English pine antiques and family heirlooms; the romantic oak-beamed public rooms boast pastel colors, a carved fruitwood fireplace, and French doors that open onto a deck and terrace overlooking the river. The spacious and elegant guest rooms feature private baths (two with Jacuzzis), air conditioning, oversized beds, and color-coordinated linens; three rooms boast private river-view decks. A separate cottage with wood-burning fireplace and private Jacuzzi is available. The recently completed Rose House offers three new guest rooms, all with fireplaces, Jacuzzis, and river- or rose garden-view decks. The Morning Room is the site of a full champagne breakfast that includes a fruit buffet, homemade scones and coffee cake, and a hot entree such as eggs Benedict. Guests at this hospitable inn also are treated to in-room wine, afternoon tea, late-evening desserts, and a happy hour before dinner with hors d'oeuvres. A fleet of Silver Shadow Rolls Royces is available for winery touring.

The Goodman House

1225 Division Street, Napa, CA 94558
Phone: (707) 257–1166
Key: Inn; 4 units; Moderate–Superior; No smoking; Credit cards; No handicapped access

This late-1870s house combines both old and new to create a comfortable b&b. The spacious guest rooms boast private baths, and two have fireplaces; one offers a two-person whirlpool tub. The dining room is the site of the full breakfast, while the upstairs kitchen is available to guests for a cup of coffee and literature to peruse for sight-seeing ideas. The Red Room offers relaxation with a grand piano and fireplace. Guests enjoy wine each evening.

La Belle Epoque

1386 Calistoga Avenue, Napa, CA 94558
Phone: (707) 257–2161
Key: Inn; 6 units; Moderate–Superior; No smoking; Credit cards; No handicapped access

This Queen Anne–Victorian home boasts impressive stained-glass windows and has been refurbished throughout with tasteful antiques, oriental rugs, and fine linens. The b&b offers six guest rooms, all with private baths, and offers a selection of queen-size, double, or king-size beds. Guests at the inn are invited to taste premium vintage wines in the wine cellar and are served a generous full breakfast in the sunny garden room or in the formal dining room.

La Residence Country Inn

4066 St. Helena Highway, Napa, CA 94558
Phone: (707) 253–0337
Key: Inn; 20 units; Moderate–Deluxe; No smoking; Credit cards; Handicapped access, 4 units

This 1870 Gothic Revival home called the Mansion and a French country barn called the Cabernet Hall offer guest rooms and suites with private baths, fireplaces, and French and English pine and American oak antiques. Modern amenities include central air conditioning, a heated swimming pool, and a spa. Guests at La Residence enjoy evening wine and a full breakfast served by the innkeepers.

Napa Inn, Napa

Napa Inn

1137 Warren Street, Napa, CA 94559
Phone: (707) 257–1444
Key: Inn; 5 units; Moderate–Superior; No smoking; Credit cards; No handicapped access

This turn-of-the-century home is in a tree-lined residential section of town yet convenient to the local winery, shopping, ballooning activities, and the Wine Train, a three-hour excursion on a restored antique train going from Napa to St. Helena and back again. The spacious rooms offer queen-size beds, private baths, and sitting areas; two accommodations are suites. Guests enjoy the inn's living room furnished with antiques, as well as the inn's outstanding collection of antique memorabilia, ranging from phonographs and clocks to hand-painted china. A full breakfast is served in the antique-furnished dining room each morning.

The Old World Inn, Napa

The Old World Inn

1301 Jefferson Street, Napa, CA 94559
Phone: (707) 257–0112
Key: Inn; 8 units; Moderate–Superior; No smoking; Credit cards; No handicapped access

This 1906 home with shady porches and beveled glass contains interior decor inspired by Swedish artist Carl Larrson. A fireside parlor has bright Scandinavian colors and offers soft classical music. The guest rooms, in French blues, pinks, peaches, and greens, feature Victorian and antique furniture, private baths with mostly claw-foot tubs, some canopy beds, and skylights; one guest room offers a private Jacuzzi. Special amenities for all guests include evening wine in the room, and international cheeses and a selection of homemade goodies before retiring. The generous breakfast is served in the Morning Room with old-fashioned hospitality; afternoon tea is poured.

Sybron House

7400 St. Helena Highway, Napa, CA 94558
Phone: (707) 944–2785
Key: Inn; 3 units; Superior; No smoking; Credit cards; No handicapped access

Napa

This new Victorian–style home, built in 1978, is situated on a hill with panoramic views of Napa Valley. Guests may enjoy the whole house, including the wet bar stocked with wine, cheese, crackers, coffee, tea, and hot chocolate. The continental breakfast features croissants and nut breads as well as juice and fresh fruit. A tennis court and spa are also available to guests at the inn.

Tall Timbers Chalets

1012 Darms Lane, Napa, CA 94558
Phone: (707) 252–7810
Key: Cottages; 8 units; Moderate; No smoking; Credit cards; No handicapped access

This country retreat on two wooded acres is composed of eight separate cottages, all individually decorated and recently refurbished in a rustic motif with original oil paintings. Each features a living room with sofa bed, bedroom with queen-size bed, bathroom, breakfast nook, television, and air conditioning and heating. Refrigerators in the cabins are stocked with champagne, breakfast muffins, and yogurt.

Rancho Caymus Inn

1140 Rutherford Road, P.O. Box 78, Rutherford, CA 94573
Phone: (707) 963–1777
Key: Inn/Hotel; 26 units; Superior–Deluxe; Smoking OK; Credit cards; Handicapped access, 2 units

This unique early California–style inn with red-tile roof encircles a small, quiet central garden. The twenty-six guest rooms contain two levels featuring sitting rooms with polished oak floors, wool rugs, comfortable seating, and (in some of the first-floor rooms) hand-sculpted adobe fireplaces. Guests step up to the bedroom with black-walnut queen-size beds, other handworked furnishings, and French doors that open onto a private garden patio or balcony. All rooms feature hand-hewn beams, eighty-year-old handmade doors, air conditioning, color television, telephones, refrigerators, wet bars, and luxurious bathrooms with stoneware basins and hardwood countertops. Four Getaway master suites offer full kitchens, stained-glass windows, and Jacuzzi tubs. The Caymus Kitchen restaurant, open for breakfast and lunch, serves a "Hacienda" continental breakfast in the room or in the award-winning garden.

Ambrose Bierce House

1515 Main Street, St. Helena, CA 94574
Phone: (707) 963-3003
Key: Inn; 2 units; Moderate–Deluxe; No smoking; Credit cards; No handicapped access

Vines climb lazily on the 1872-built house that was once the residence of poet, essayist, and witty author Ambrose Bierce. In a residential area with well-tended gardens and lawn, this small b&b inn offers guests a spacious sitting room and bedroom suites named after late-1800s Napa Valley personalities. Each history-filled guest room contains antiques, a queen-size brass bed, Laura Ashley wallpaper, and an armoire. The private bathrooms are Victorian with claw-foot tubs and brass fittings. A formal, two-course breakfast greets guests in the morning; complimentary sherry is offered in the evening.

Bartels Ranch & Country Inn

1200 Conn Valley Road, St. Helena, CA 94574
Phone: (707) 963-4001 / (800) 932-4002; **Fax:** (707) 963-5100
Key: Inn; 3 units; Superior–Deluxe; Limited smoking; Credit cards; Handicapped access, 2 units

This intimate country inn is set within a 100-acre valley with vineyard views. The ranch, surrounded by hills, pines, and oaks, offers three guest rooms, all with private baths, and entrances. Terry robes, picnic baskets, and blankets are provided. Guest accommodations are decorated with antiques, wicker, and contemporary prints. The new Heart of the Valley Suite features a sunken, heart-shaped Jacuzzi tub for two, a separate shower and sauna, a stone fireplace, a private redwood deck with vineyard views, silver service, a refrigerator, a stereo, a satellite television, and a VCR. Guests enjoy a library, sundeck lounging, a barbecue grill, a guest refrigerator, and a recreation room with fireplace, billiards, television, and Ping-Pong. They may also sip champagne under the stars by the swimming pool at this romantic retreat. A continental breakfast and evening wine, fruit, and cheese are included in the stay; after-dinner popcorn is also offered. Ten-speed bicycles are available, and the hospitable innkeepers are happy to prepare personalized itineraries for their guests.

Chestleson House

1417 Kearney Street, St. Helena, CA 94574
Phone: (707) 963–2238
Key: Inn; 3 units; Moderate–Superior; No smoking; No credit cards; No handicapped access

This early 1900s Victorian home offers a big front porch with mountain views in a quiet residential neighborhood. Guest rooms boast private baths and are furnished with antiques and are decorated in pastel colors; a downstairs room features a separate entrance. The cozy living room offers a fireplace, and each evening complimentary beverages with pâtés or cheeses are served. A gourmet breakfast is served at 9:00 A.M.; both breakfast and refreshments are offered on the large veranda, weather permitting.

The Cinnamon Bear

1407 Kearney Street, St. Helena, CA 94574
Phone: (707) 963–4653
Key: Inn; 4 units; Moderate–Superior; No smoking; Credit cards; No handicapped access

This charming 1904 house sits in a quiet residential neighborhood. The homey atmosphere is created by comfortable antiques and, yes, lots of bears, mainly of the stuffed variety. All guest rooms have a bath of their own, and guests enjoy a large parlor and dining room. The Relatives suite on the main floor offers two rooms, a queen-size bed, a large claw-foot tub, and lots of privacy. Complimentary wine and hors d'oeuvres are served in the early evening; the full homemade breakfast varies each morning.

Creekside Inn

945 Main Street, St. Helena, CA 94574
Phone: (707) 963-7244
Key: Inn; 3 units; Moderate; No smoking; Credit cards; No handicapped access

The pleasant murmurs of White Sulphur Creek and ancient oaks give a country setting to this inn located in the heart of the town. The individually decorated guest rooms feature an antique oak poster bed and white iron beds, all with a French country feel; all beds are queen-size. Guests are served a full breakfast each morning in the sun room or creekside on the patio. Innkeepers will cater a candlelight dinner in the dining room upon arrangement.

Deer Run

3995 Spring Mountain Road, St. Helena, CA 94574
Phone: (707) 963-3794
Key: Home/Cottage; 3 units; Moderate; No smoking; No credit cards; No handicapped access

This small b&b offers a secluded mountain retreat overlooking the valley vineyards. Both of the home guest accommodations have a private bath; one features a fireplace. A carriage-house accommodation is available featuring a private entrance and bath; breakfast is served in the cottage. The extended continental breakfast is served each morning offering fresh fruit, juice, bran or blueberry muffins, cereals, and fruit breads.

St. Helena

Elsie's Conn Valley Inn

726 Rossi Road, St. Helena, CA 94574
Phone: (707) 963–4614
Key: Home; 3 units; Moderate; No smoking; Credit cards; No handicapped access

Four miles outside of town is this country retreat with lawns and gardens as well as views of the vineyards and rolling hills. The home b&b with stone pillars in front offers three comfortable bedrooms to guests, each with a garden view and one with a private bath. Upon arrival guests are given a basket of fruit, cheeses, and crackers to accompany a bottle of Napa Valley wine. The full breakfast offering, served inside or on the patio, comprises homemade breads and pastries, an egg dish, fruits, juices, and beverages. Guests at Elsie's may relax by the fire, watch television in the guests' own family room, or stroll along country roads to nearby Lake Hennessey.

Erika's Hillside, St. Helena

Erika's Hillside

285 Fawn Park Road, St. Helena, CA 94574
Phone: (707) 963–2887
Key: Inn; 3 units; Moderate–Deluxe; No smoking; No credit cards; No handicapped access

This Swiss chalet inn on three acres of beautifully landscaped grounds enjoys views of the vineyards and wineries. The spacious guest accommodations include rooms and a suite, all with private entrances and views of the valley. The continental breakfast served on the patio or deck or in the garden room, features German specialties. Guests are welcomed with refreshments.

Harvest Inn

One Main Street, St. Helena, CA 94574
Phone: (707) 963–9463; **Fax:** (707) 963–4402
Key: Inn/Hotel; 54 units; Moderate–Deluxe; Smoking OK; Credit cards; No handicapped access

This large Tudor–style inn was built in 1978 on the grounds of a 21-acre working vineyard. Besides enjoying the grounds, guests may swim in the pool during the summer and relax in the spa year-round. All guest rooms have king- or queen-size beds, color television, telephone, and antique decor; and most also have fireplaces, wet bars, and refrigerators. A continental breakfast of pastry and rolls, fresh fruit, and juices is served. The hotel has been featured in *Smithsonian* magazine.

Hotel St. Helena

1309 Main Street, St. Helena, CA 94574
Phone: (707) 963–4388; **Fax:** (707) 963–5402
Key: Inn/Hotel; 18 units; Moderate–Deluxe; No smoking; Credit cards; No handicapped access

The 1881 hotel on the town's Main Street has been completely renovated and carefully restored. Today, the hotel offers guest rooms upstairs decorated in antiques, authentic wallpapers, quilted spreads, armoires, and carpeting. A suite with sitting room can accommodate four people. The downstairs is devoted to shops and a comfortable sitting area where the morning breakfast buffet is served. A wine bar is available in the lobby.

The Ink House

1575 St. Helena Highway, St. Helena, CA 94574
Phone: (707) 963–3890
Key: Inn; 4 units; Superior; No smoking; No credit cards; No handi-
capped access

The historic 1884 home is Italianate Victorian and boasts 12- and
11-foot-high ceilings. The guest rooms, with private bath, have
handmade quilts, lace curtains, queen-size beds, and antiques.
Guests may enjoy two parlors, one featuring a restored 1870 pump
organ, as well as an upstairs observatory granting 360-degree views.
A continental breakfast of juice and home-baked nut breads is
served buffet-style in the dining room.

Judy's Bed & Breakfast

2036 Madrona Avenue, St. Helena, CA 94574
Phone: (707) 963–3081
Key: Home; 1 unit; Moderate; No smoking; Credit cards (American
Express only); No handicapped access

Vineyards surround this ranch–style b&b on three sides. The one
suite consists of a bedroom, sitting room, and private bath and
entrance. The quarters are decorated in antiques with a queen-size
brass bed, air conditioning, wood-burning stove, and color television. Freshly baked goodies are served in the room or by the pool,
which is available to guests. The suite is supplied with beverages,
cheese, fruit, and candies.

Judy's Ranch House

701 Rossi Road, St. Helena, CA 94574
Phone: (707) 963–3081
Key: Home; 2 units; Moderate; No smoking; Credit cards (American
Express only); No handicapped access

This spacious ranch–style b&b boasts a unique open-air courtyard in the center of the house, a large living room with fireplace, and magnificent views of the valley countryside. Guests may either sip assorted beverages and enjoy cheese, crackers, and fruit on the front porch overlooking the oaks and creek or unwind in the Jacuzzi spa with pasture views. Each of the guest accommodations, furnished in a combination of contemporary and antique decor, offers an oversized bed, ceiling fan, private bath, and hillside views. A complimentary continental breakfast of orange juice, fresh fruit, pastries, and coffee or tea is served in the sunny country kitchen.

Milat Vineyard

1091 St. Helena Highway So., St. Helena, CA 94574
Phone: (707) 963-2612
Key: Guest house; 2 units; Moderate; No smoking; No credit cards; Handicapped access, 1 unit

Surrounded by the family-operated vineyard, this guest cottage boasts both privacy and spectacular views. Guests enjoy a continental breakfast each morning served in the guest house or on the private patio. Guests enjoy wine tasting at the family winery.

Oliver House

2970 Silverado Trail, St. Helena, CA 94574
Phone: (707) 963-4089
Key: Inn; 4 units; Moderate–Deluxe; No smoking; Credit cards; No handicapped access

This Bavarian–style farmhouse b&b sits in the foothills overlooking vineyards. Each room is decorated in antiques, and three accommodations boast French doors leading to balcony views of the countryside. An old-fashioned parlor adjoins the guest rooms and offers relaxation in front of the fireplace. The generous continental breakfast featuring berries or fruit fresh from the garden is served in the country kitchen or on the balcony. The inn is within easy walking distance of eight wineries.

Prager Winery B&B

1281 Lewelling Lane, St. Helena, CA 94574
Phone: (707) 963–3720
Key: Home/Cottage; 2 units; Superior; Smoking OK; No credit cards; Handicapped access, 1 unit

This home b&b with separate guest accommodation is located right on the winery premises. The Winery Suite is situated above the barrel-aging cellar and offers a private entrance, bath, bedroom, living room, and a veranda with views of the vineyard and mountains. The Vineyard Suite, attached to the house, offers a private entrance and bath as well as a comfortable living room with piano. The home-baked breakfast is served in the suite, and guests enjoy a personal tour of the winery.

Spanish Villa

474 Glass Mountain Road, St. Helena, CA 94574
Phone: (707) 963–7483
Key: Inn; 3 units; Moderate–Superior; No smoking; No credit cards; No handicapped access

The two-story Spanish–style villa is surrounded by country roads and woods. Its Mediterranean design features an enclosed patio and a spacious sitting room with arched windows. The guest rooms all have king-size beds, private baths, and handmade glass replicas of famous Tiffany lamps. An extended continental breakfast is included in the stay at this tranquil retreat.

Villa St. Helena

2727 Sulphur Springs Avenue, St. Helena, CA 94574
Phone: (707) 963–2514
Key: Inn; 3 units; Superior–Deluxe; Limited smoking; Credit cards; No handicapped access

Villa St. Helena, St. Helena

This 12,000-square-foot, three-level brick mansion on a secluded wooded hillside offers panoramic views of Napa Valley and twenty acres filled with walking trails and a courtyard. The former (1940s and 1950s) celebrity hideaway gives its b&b guests a luxurious retreat. The beamed-ceilinged living room and its massive stone fireplace was featured in television's "Falcon Crest" filming. A generous, homemade continental breakfast is served in a solarium. The three guest rooms, with private baths and private entrance verandas, have a country elegance accomplished by the use of antiques and muted, earth-tone color schemes. Some of the rooms feature fireplaces. Guests also are treated to the inn's private-label wine. The inn claims to be one of two homes in California designed by renowned architect Robert M. Carrere.

The White Ranch

707 White Lane, St. Helena, CA 94574
Phone: (707) 963–4635
Key: Home; 1 unit; Moderate; No smoking; No credit cards; No handicapped access

This farmhouse, built in 1865, offers sherry on the front porch and a picnic table for lunch or supper. The guest suite, decorated in antiques, has a bedroom, dressing room, and private bath. Guests may enjoy the fireplace in the parlor. The morning continental breakfast consists of juice, homemade breads and jams, and espresso coffee.

St. Helena

Wine Country Cottage

P.O. Box 295, St. Helena, CA 94574
Phone: (707) 963–4633
Key: Home/Cottage; 2 units; Moderate; Limited smoking; No credit cards; No handicapped access

This charming cottage and Victorian house nestled among the elms and pines provides guests with privacy and quiet. The cottage contains a bedroom/living room, complete kitchen, bath, and patio. Guests also enjoy an accommodation in the turn-of-the-century house located on four and one-half acres. The light and airy room is decorated with Laura Ashley prints and has a private bath. Guests choose between a complimentary continental breakfast, in bed or on the patio, or a champagne feast for an additional charge. Innkeepers will also arrange for mud baths or massages, hot-air ballooning, and dinner.

The Wine Country Inn, St. Helena

The Wine Country Inn

1152 Lodi Lane, St. Helena, CA 94574
Phone: (707) 963–7077
Key: Inn/Hotel; 25 units; Moderate–Deluxe; Smoking OK; Credit cards; Handicapped access, 4 units

The small country hotel is located off a busy highway in a peaceful setting. Most of the guest accommodations boast rural views, and some have patios, balconies, or fireplaces usable fall through spring. All rooms have private bath and telephone and are decorated uniquely in country antiques and fresh colors. A buffet-style continental breakfast is served each morning. A beautiful pool and spa have been added for guests' enjoyment.

The Gables Bed & Breakfast Inn, Santa Rosa

The Gables Bed & Breakfast Inn

4257 Petaluma Hill Road, Santa Rosa, CA 95404
Phone: (707) 585–7777
Key: Inn/Cottage; 6 units; Moderate–Deluxe; No smoking; Credit cards; No handicapped access

Fifteen gables crown the unusual keyhole-shaped windows of this High Victorian Gothic Revival inn nestled on three and one-half acres of former dairy pasture land. The elegant 1877-built home with 12-foot-high ceilings, Italian marble fireplaces, and a mahogany spiral staircase offers guests accommodations with comfortable antique furnishings, brass beds, and private baths. The William and Mary's Cottage, next to Taylor Creek, which traverses the grounds, is a private country retreat with woodstove, kitchenette, and sleeping loft. Breakfast at The Gables is a three-course country feast served in the spacious dining room with a warm sunny-rose and light-green decor; the meal begins with freshly squeezed juices and a fresh-fruit dish, such as baked apple crisp. Entrees might include such specialties as custardy French Toast Souffl_ with Grand Marnier Sauce or Zucchini and Three-Cheese Frittata, all served with just-baked pastries, muffins, and breads. Home-baked cookies and tea are offered each afternoon. Guests at the inn enjoy a formal sitting room as well as a deck with views stretching across the Sonoma Valley.

Gee-Gee's B&B

7810 Sonoma Highway, Santa Rosa, CA 95405
Phone: (707) 833–6667
Key: Home/Cottage; 4 units; Moderate; No smoking; Credit cards; No handicapped access

This converted farmhouse and cottage situated on a full acre offers guests a swimming pool, decks, and a sitting room with television and fireplace. Two of the guest accommodations are located in the main house and share one bath, and the other two are housed in the separate cottage. One guest room offers its own sitting area with television. A tasty, full breakfast is served on the deck overlooking orchards, vineyards, and mountains. Bicycles are complimentary.

Hilltop House B&B

9550 St. Helena Road, St. Rosa, CA 95404
Phone: (707) 944–0880
Key: Home; 3 units; Moderate–Deluxe; No smoking; Credit cards; Handicapped access, 1 unit

This contemporary ranch house is located on top of a high ridge overlooking the historic Mayacama Mountains on 135 acres of unspoiled wilderness. The home offers panoramic views of the peaceful surroundings and spectacular sunrises and sunsets from its large deck outside the guest rooms. The entire house is decorated with beautiful antiques. Guests enjoy a spacious common room with stereo, television, woodstove, guest refrigerator, and library. Guests enjoy the Sunrise Suite with private deck, sky-lights, queen-size bed, and private bath. Included in the stay at Hilltop House is a generous continental breakfast served on the outside deck or in the dining room, afternoon refreshments, evening sherry, wine at check-in, and use of a hot tub under the stars. Guests also enjoy numerous hiking trails, picnic areas, and occasional guest-involved mystery plays put on by the entertainer/innkeeper.

Melitta Station Inn

5850 Melita Road, Santa Rosa, CA 95409
Phone: (707) 538–7712
Key: Inn; 6 units; Moderate; No smoking; Credit cards; No handi-capped access

In the late 1880s the railroad station was a stagecoach stop, then went on to be a freight station, general store, boardinghouse, and antique shop. Carefully converted to a b&b inn and home, the inte-riors reflect a country feel with antiques and hand stencilings. The comfortably furnished guest rooms have private or shared baths. A sitting room features a wood-burning stove and French-door views of the countryside. The full breakfast including homemade scones, muffins, and fruit is served on the deck. Guests enjoy the inn's beautiful setting, which is surrounded by parks offering hiking and other forms of recreation.

Pygmalion House

331 Orange Street, Santa Rosa, CA 95401
Phone: (707) 526–3407
Key: Inn; 5 units; Inexpensive–Moderate; No smoking; Credit cards; No handicapped access

This historic Victorian home with 12-foot-high ceilings is near downtown Santa Rosa. The five guest rooms all have private baths with old-fashioned claw-foot tubs or showers and an eclectic country decor. Guests enjoy a parlor with fireplace and television and evening sparkling apple cider, tea or coffee, cheese, and nuts. The full breakfast served in the country kitchen includes such delicacies as cereals, muffins, croissants, ham, egg dishes, and the inn's own blend of brewed decaffeinated coffee.

Vintners Inn

4350 Barnes Road, Santa Rosa, CA 95401
Phone: (707) 575–7350; (800) 421–2584; **Fax:** (707) 575–1426
Key: Inn/Hotel; 44 units; Moderate–Deluxe; Limited smoking; Credit cards; Handicapped access, 3 units

A small French "village," with a central plaza and fountain surrounded by four separate stucco and red-tile-roof buildings with arched windows, has been created in the middle of a working vineyard as a unique b&b offering. The hotel offers forty-four individually decorated, spacious guest rooms furnished in a country French motif with antique pine furniture; some have wood-burning fireplaces, custom-made pine beds, beamed ceilings, color television, telephones, private baths, and balcony or patio views of the plaza or vineyards. A common building contains a library and breakfast area, where the morning fare of Belgian waffles, cereals, croissants, nut breads, and juices is served. The inn can accommodate executive conferences, with separate conference and dining rooms also available. Guests enjoy a large sun deck with spa, as well as the John Ash & Co. restaurant, specializing in Sonoma regional cuisine.

Chalet Bed & Breakfast

18935 Fifth Street West, Sonoma, CA 95476
Phone: (707) 996–0190/938–3129
Key: Inn/Cottage; 7 units; Moderate–Superior; No smoking; Credit cards; No handicapped access

This farmhouse with three cottages is situated on three acres where fruit, nuts, and eggs are produced, just 3/4 mile from the town of Sonoma. In the main house, two upstairs rooms share a sitting room and bath, as do the two downstairs rooms. The private cottages offer baths and wood-burning stoves; two feature lofts. An expanded continental breakfast of juice, fruit, granolas, pastries, and cereals is included in the stay, as is use of the hot tub. Guests may stroll around the property of the farm, alive with ducks, geese, and chickens.

The Hidden Oak, Sonoma

The Hidden Oak

214 E. Napa Street, Sonoma, CA 95476
Phone: (707) 996-9863
Key: Inn; 3 units; Moderate–Superior; No smoking; Credit cards (American Express only); No handicapped access

Situated just a block and one-half from Sonoma's historic Plaza is this 1913-built California Craftsman bungalow. Totally redecorated in 1988, the brown-shingled structure was originally used as a refectory. The three spacious and airy guest rooms feature private baths and queen-size beds. Room decor is a blend of wicker and antiques with floral prints and fluffy comforters. Guests enjoy the parlor with early-morning newspaper and coffee, as well as fireside reading in the library. A full breakfast, served in the dining room, consists of fresh fruit and juice, pastries, and an egg dish with breakfast meat. Afternoon refreshments are also offered. Guests may use the inn's bicycles for touring nearby wineries.

Magliulo's, Sonoma

Magliulo's

691 Broadway, Sonoma, CA 95476
Phone: (707) 996–1031
Key: Inn; 5 units; Moderate; No smoking; Credit cards; Handicapped access, 1 unit

This late-1800s Victorian residence with restaurant of the same name next door is within walking distance of Sonoma Plaza and boasts beautifully landscaped yards. The guest rooms at the inn, in shades of rose, offer fresh flowers, fine antiques, quilts, ceiling fans, iron and brass beds, and both private and shared baths. Guests enjoy an outdoor cabana and a cozy parlor with glowing fireplace. Drinks and hors d'oeuvres are available from the restaurant upon request. A generous continental breakfast is served in the inn's own dining room each morning.

Sonoma Hotel

110 West Spain Street, Sonoma, CA 95476
Phone: (707) 996–2996
Key: Inn/Hotel; 17 units; Moderate; Smoking OK; Credit cards; No handicapped access

The exact age of the old hotel is unknown, but records show it to be at least of 1870s vintage. The hotel has been completely restored; the guest accommodations have been furnished with authentic items from the days of the Barbary Coast and the Gay Nineties. Interesting antiques include a bedroom suite owned by General Vallejo's sister and the original chandeliers. A restaurant addition to the establishment offers dinners and brunches, with menus changing biweekly; the restaurant is closed on Wednesdays.

Thistle Dew Inn

171 West Spain Street, Sonoma, CA 95476
Phone: (707) 938-2909
Key: Inn; 6 units; Moderate; No smoking; Credit cards; Handicapped access, 2 units

The inn is located in a quiet residential neighborhood just three doors off the main plaza. It consists of two one-story Victorian houses surrounded by lawns and gardens and decorated in collector's pieces of Mission style. The guest rooms, all with private bath, have washstands, ceiling fans, and air conditioning. A full breakfast is served in the dining room, and appetizers and beverages are offered on the deck each evening, weather permitting. Bicycles and picnic baskets are available for guests' use; a relaxing heated spa is nestled between the two buildings.

Trojan Horse Inn

19455 Sonoma Highway, Sonoma, CA 95476
Phone: (707) 996-2430
Key: Inn; 6 units; Moderate–Superior; No smoking; Credit cards; Handicapped access, 1 unit

This 1887 Victorian, farm-style home sits on the banks of Sonoma Creek. The inn, painted three shades of blue, has been completely renovated. Outside features include two levels of well-kept gardens and patios, beautiful old trees, and a spa. The inn is furnished in English and French antiques, and guest rooms offer queen-size beds, plush linens and bedspreads, ceiling fans, air conditioning, and private baths; one guest room offers a fireplace, and another boasts a whirlpool tub for two. A full breakfast with home-baked goodies and a hot dish is served graciously in the dining room each morning; wine and hors d'oeuvres are offered in the early evening.

Victorian Garden Inn, Sonoma

Victorian Garden Inn

316 E. Napa Street, Sonoma, CA 95476
Phone: (707) 996–5339
Key: Inn; 4 units; Moderate–Superior; Limited smoking; Credit cards; No handicapped access

This 1880s farmhouse with water tower features a secluded acre with meandering walks through creekside Victorian gardens. Guest rooms are individually furnished in antiques with quaint wall coverings, and all but one have private baths. One guest accommodation has a fireplace, private entrance, and claw-foot tub. A generous California breakfast may be enjoyed in the dining room or carried on a wicker tray to the room. During the day guests may swim in the garden-set pool, walk to shops, or relax on the creek-side patio. The inn is one and one-half blocks from local wineries.

Bordeaux House

P.O. Box 3274, Yountville, CA 94599
Phone: (707) 944–2855
Key: Inn; 6 units; Moderate–Superior; Smoking OK; Credit cards; No handicapped access

The formal red-brick structure situated among lush gardens and large pines is secluded from the main highway yet convenient to the famous wineries in the area. The spacious rooms in hues of camel and wine reds are air-conditioned and also boast fireplaces, private baths, and patios for the evening glass of wine. A continental breakfast is served each morning.

Burgundy House

P.O. Box 3156, Yountville, CA 94599
Phone: (707) 944–0889
Key: Inn; 5 units; Superior; No smoking; Credit cards; No handicapped access

This country French stone structure was built in the early 1870s of local fieldstone and river rock. Starting out as a brandy distillery, the structure went on to house a winery, a hotel, and an antiques warehouse until its present function as a fine bed & breakfast inn. Antique country furnishings accent the unique 22-inch-thick walls and hand-hewn beams of the inn. The five guest rooms all offer private baths, quilted bedspreads, fresh flowers, and a decanter of wine. The inn serves a full breakfast in the "distillery," or guests may dine in the intimate garden surrounded by hedges, roses, and trees.

Magnolia Hotel

6529 Yount Street, P.O. Drawer M, Yountville, CA 94599
Phone: (707) 944–2056
Key: Inn/Hotel/Cottage; 12 units; Moderate–Deluxe; No smoking; No credit cards; Handicapped access, 2 units

This 1873 hotel features a large swimming pool and Jacuzzi spa on the grounds. The guest rooms, all with private bath, are furnished in antiques. Some rooms boast balconies, fireplaces, patios, extra-high ceilings, or bay windows; accommodations are available in the main hotel or in the garden court. A carriage-house suite is a favorite of guests. A full breakfast is served promptly at 9:00 A.M. each morning; a crystal decanter of port wine is available in each guest room.

Napa Valley Railway Inn

6503 Washington Street, P.O. Box 2568, Yountville, CA 94599
Phone: (707) 944–2000
Key: Inn; 9 units; Moderate–Superior; Smoking OK; Credit cards;
Handicapped access, 1 unit

Nine brightly painted, turn-of-the-century railroad cars from several different railway lines sit alongside the original Napa Valley Railroad tracks and have been renovated to form this unique inn. The three cabooses and six railcars overlooking vineyards offer nine guest-room suites, all with private baths, queen-size beds, and sitting rooms with velvet love seats. Many rooms feature skylights and bay windows. This cozy bed and "hospitality" inn offers in-room coffee and tea at all times. Breakfast may be enjoyed at one of several restaurants in the adjacent vintage 1870 complex of shops but is not included in the stay.

Oleander House

7433 St. Helena Highway, P.O. Box 2937, Yountville, CA 94599
Phone: (707) 944–8315
Key: Inn; 4 units; Superior; No smoking; Credit cards; No handicapped access

This spacious, two-story home located at the entrance to Napa Valley offers four guest rooms. Each accommodation features high ceilings, queen-size brass beds, antiques, private bath, balcony, and fireplace; all guest rooms are uniquely decorated with Laura Ashley wallpapers and prints. Guests enjoy an ample breakfast served around the large table in the dining room.

The Webber Place

6610 Webber, P.O. Box 2873, Yountville, CA 94599
Phone: (707) 944–8384
Key: Inn; 4 units; Moderate; No smoking; Credit cards; No handicapped access

This converted farmhouse, within walking distance of town shops, features guest rooms furnished in antiques, two with in-room claw-foot tubs. The Veranda Suite has a private, latticed veranda and unusual woodwork. In keeping with farmhouse living, a full country breakfast is served each morning featuring freshly baked biscuits and home-baked dishes. Wine is served in the afternoon.

CALIFORNIA GOLD COUNTRY

Communities born of the gold-rush days, old mines, vineyards, rolling hills with oaks, lakes, museums, the Sierras' grandeur, unlimited recreation, and the cornucopian fields of the great Central Valley make up this region's diverse character. The traveler may still pan gold here or tour the state's preserved gold-rush town, Columbia, or a thriving historic town, such as Sutter Creek, Amador City, Jackson, or Nevada City—all steeped in the history of the "golden days." Nestled high in the Sierra Nevada are the communities of Tahoe City, Kings Beach, and Olympic Valley, which, still rich in history, are better known for their nearby casinos, skiing, and lake sports and beaches. The state's capital, Sacramento, offers history in the making as well as its Old Town to explore. History, the lure of gold-rush days, recreation, and scenic paradise— Gold Country's generous offerings are waiting.

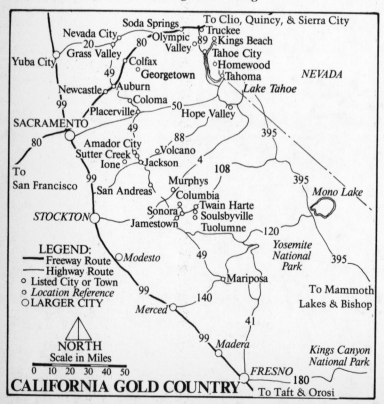

The Mine House Inn

P.O. Box 245, Amador City, CA 95601
Phone: (209) 267–5900
Key: Inn; 8 units; Inexpensive–Moderate; Smoking OK; No credit cards; No handicapped access

This most unusual hostelry is the one-hundred-year-old former Keystone Consolidated Mining Office Building, and each guest room is named after its original use: the Mill Grinding Room with the original shaft supporters, the Vault Room with the original bullion safe, and so on; all rooms boast private baths. Guests enjoy a swimming pool, a sitting room, and an art gallery/gift shop. A complete continental breakfast consisting of orange juice, breakfast rolls, and coffee, tea, or hot chocolate is served to each guest in the morning. The inn is well equipped for families.

Lincoln House Bed & Breakfast, Auburn
(See listing next page)

Lincoln House Bed & Breakfast

191 Lincoln Way, Auburn, CA 95603
Phone: (916) 885–8880
Key: Home; 3 units; Moderate; No smoking; Credit cards; No handi-capped access

Guests enter this storybook–style, 1933-built home by crossing a footbridge over koi-filled fish ponds. Terraces are surrounded by lush lawns, and a garden-lined swimming pool grants views of the Sierras and the American River canyon. The interior of the house is filled with soft pastel colors, family antiques, and selected 1930s and 1940s pieces. The three guest rooms, each with a private bath, are decorated in antiques, soft colors, and cozy quilts. Guests enjoy complimentary beverages each afternoon in the fireside sitting room and a homemade breakfast in the dining room with majestic views. The morning meal features such delectables as French toast, waffles, and homemade muffins.

Power's Mansion Inn, Auburn

Power's Mansion Inn

164 Cleveland Avenue, Auburn, CA 95603
Phone: (916) 885–1166
Key: Inn; 13 units; Moderate–Deluxe; Limited smoking; Credit cards; No handicapped access

This century-old Victorian mansion was built from a gold fortune and has been fully restored to its past elegance. The thirteen authentically decorated guest rooms at the inn boast private baths with brass and porcelain fixtures, air conditioning, big brass beds covered in satin comforters, windows trimmed in lace, and antique furniture. A full gourmet breakfast prepared by the innkeeper is served each morning. Gold-panning tours and special events are offered at this Victorian retreat.

Victorian Hill House

195 Park Street, P.O. Box 9097, Auburn, CA 95604
Phone: (916) 885–5879; **Fax:** same as phone
Key: Inn; 4 units; Moderate; No smoking; Credit cards; Handicapped access, 2 units

This 115-year-old home nestled amid oaks, pines, and flower gardens overlooks the historic gold-rush town. The hilltop Victorian has been completely renovated and offers four guest rooms. Rooms are individually decorated and feature double or queen-size beds, central heating and air conditioning, full or half baths, and a charming, nostalgic decor. Guests may relax in the gazebo hot tub, swim in the pool, or enjoy the comfortable library. The inn serves a full country breakfast on fine china; the meal includes an egg casserole or omelettes with bacon, sausage, or ham, as well as seasonal specialties. Breakfast may be enjoyed in the formal dining room, in the room, or in the serene garden; afternoon beverages are also provided. The inn is available for weddings and meetings in fair weather.

White Sulphur Springs Ranch

P.O. Box 136, Clio, CA 96106
Phone: (916) 836–2387
Key: Inn/Cottage; 8 units; Moderate–Superior; No smoking; Credit cards; No handicapped access

First established as a stagecoach stop in 1852 and later as a family-run ranch and hotel, the b&b is open to guests once again after the complete restoration of the house and its furnishings. The ranch, on

White Sulphur Springs Ranch, Clio

forty acres of hillside timber, is surrounded by the old ranch buildings, such as a blacksmith shop, and has a warm sulphur-spring-fed, olympic-size pool. The interior of the home contains many of the original 1800s furnishings; the parlor features a pump organ and a piano that came around Cape Horn. The guest rooms are uniquely decorated in a variety of antiques and turn-of-the-century wall coverings and grant views of the Mohawk Valley. Accommodations include the Dairy House, an original building that now offers a quaint cottage with bedroom, bath, living room, and dining area, and the new Hen House cottage with two bedrooms and a complete kitchen. The homemade full breakfast and early morning coffee are offered to guests in the parlor. The Attic Museum is now open at the inn featuring family heirlooms and ranch antiques.

The Coloma Country Inn

345 High Street, P.O. Box 502, Coloma, CA 95613
Phone: (916) 622–6919
Key: Inn; 5 units; Moderate; No smoking; No credit cards; No handicapped access

Surrounded on all sides by history is this quiet house built in the 1850s. Sutter's Mill and pioneer churches sit alongside the inn, and many attractions, including the Marshall Gold Discovery Park and white-water rafting, are within walking distance of the gold-rush home. The inn has been carefully renovated, and the eleven rooms, including five guest rooms, are decorated in a pleasing combination of American antiques, primitives, quilts, and stenciling. The home-made breakfast, which includes muffins, fruit with whipped cream, fruit juice, and coffee, is served in the room or in the formal dining room. The inn offers special champagne–hot-air-ballooning tours over the American River valley; gourmet picnics and wine-tasting tours may also be arranged with advance notice.

Vineyard House

P.O. Box 176, Coloma, CA 95613
Phone: (916) 622–2217
Key: Inn/Hotel; 7 units; Moderate; Smoking OK; Credit cards; No handicapped access

A famous vintner of the period built this four-story, 11,000-square-foot house in 1878. It consists of a ballroom, four dining rooms, a front parlor, old wine cellar, and jail cell (the latter two now form a saloon with entertainment). Guest rooms are upstairs, share a modern bath at the end of the hall, and are furnished in period pieces. Hotel guests are served a continental breakfast of juice, coffee, muffins, and breads and may also enjoy dinners in the public dining room. A guest lounge and gift shop are located on the premises. The inn now offers banquet and wedding facilities.

City Hotel

P.O. Box 1870, Columbia, CA 95310
Phone: (209) 532–1479
Key: Inn/Hotel; 9 units; Moderate; Limited smoking; Credit cards; No handicapped access

A part of the Columbia Historic State Park, a historic 1800s town, this hotel is a combined living museum, training center for hotel management, restaurant, and b&b establishment. Each luxuriously appointed guest room, with balcony or sitting area, has a private half bath and authentic antiques. Overnight lodging includes a continental breakfast each morning. Other meals are available in the restaurant; check for hours of operation when visiting in non-summer months.

Fallon Hotel

P.O. Box 1870, Columbia, CA 95310
Phone: (209) 532–1470
Key: Inn/Hotel; 14 units; Inexpensive–Moderate; Limited smoking; Credit cards; Handicapped access, 1 unit

The state of California finished restoration of the 1857-built Fallon Hotel in the historic park of Columbia in 1986. The lodging establishment with brick facade and wooden balcony is a "living museum," boasting many of its original furnishings and other antiques as well as authentic wallpaper reproductions that return it to its Victorian grandeur. Most of the guest rooms offer half baths and share showers, and accommodations range from the intimate hall rooms to the elaborate Balcony Suite. Five rooms open onto the balcony for a bird's-eye view of the charming town. The complimentary continental breakfast includes fresh breads, sweet rolls, juices, and coffee or tea and is served to guests only in the parlor on the first floor. The hotel participates in a number of special events year-round and offers special lodging, dinner, and theater packages. The Fallon is partially staffed by hospitality-management students from Columbia College.

The American River Inn

Main at Orleans Street, P.O. Box 43, Georgetown, CA 95634
Phone: (916) 333–4499; **Fax:** (916) 333–9253
Key: Inn; 25 units; Moderate; Smoking OK; Credit cards; Handicapped access, 3 units

This totally restored 1853 miners' boardinghouse and 1907 Queen Anne home is a former stagecoach stop nestled in the Sierra

The American River Inn, Georgetown

Nevada foothills. It offers guests strolls through Victorian gardens, a dove aviary, and a unique antique shop. Guests enjoy local wines in the parlor each evening and may relax in a refreshing mountain-stream pool or the Jacuzzi. Bicycles are provided, as are picnic lunches on prior arrangement. Guests may stay in the Woodside Mine structure with one- and two-bedroom suites or in the turn-of-the-century house. (The five-bedroom house may be rented as a whole for groups.) The guest rooms at the inn feature turn-of-the-century decor and private as well as shared bath accommodations. A full breakfast is served in the dining room or on the patio. Games in the garden include croquet, badminton, Ping-Pong, and horseshoes; the inn is only ten minutes from white-water rafting, which the inn will arrange.

Annie Horan's Bed & Breakfast

415 W. Main Street, Grass Valley, CA 95945
Phone: (916) 272–2418
Key: Inn; 4 units; Moderate; No smoking; Credit cards; No handicapped access

In terms of unique design and workmanship, this 1974 residence remains virtually unchanged since its early days. The interior of the inn, just a stroll away from Main Street shops, is decorated in antiques representing the gold-rush era. The four guest rooms, all with private baths, are individually decorated, and the old parlor of

Annie Horan's Bed & Breakfast, Grass Valley

the house is now a guest room with pretty Queen Anne furnishings. The dining room, with its original architecture, and a spacious deck are breakfast locales. The full breakfast includes homemade granola, muffins, bread, an egg dish, fruit, juice, and coffee or tea.

Golden Ore House Bed & Breakfast

448 South Auburn Street, Grass Valley, CA 95945
Phone: (916) 272–6872
Key: Inn; 7 units; Moderate; No smoking; Credit cards; Handicapped access, 1 unit

This turn-of-the-century home with lots of charm is a short walk from the scenic Empire Mine State Park. The lovingly restored home is filled with fine antiques and abundant natural woodwork. It has two living rooms with fireplaces and an extra kitchen for guests, as well as a large second-story deck for lounging. The seven antique-

Golden Ore House Bed & Breakfast, Grass Valley

decorated guest rooms include unusual attic rooms with skylights. A delicious, full breakfast, served in the dining room between 8:00 A.M. and 10:00 A.M., may include fruit, juice, muffins, eggs, waffles, and blintzes.

Murphy's Inn

318 Neal Street, Grass Valley, CA 95945
Phone: (916) 273–6873
Key: Inn; 8 units; Moderate–Superior; No smoking; Credit cards; Handicapped access, 1 unit

Originally the 1866 inn was the personal estate of a gold baron. Today the well-maintained Victorian sits within walking distance of town shops and restaurants. Guests may relax on the spacious veranda graced with ivy baskets, take a dip in the swimming spa, or enjoy a cozy fire in one of the sitting rooms. Guest rooms have private baths, and all are furnished in period pieces, lace curtains, antique brass beds, and floral wall coverings. The inn's three suites and one of the guest rooms boast cozy fireplaces. A full breakfast awaits guests in the breakfast room or is presented in the room.

Swan-Levine House

328 South Church Street, Grass Valley, CA 95945
Phone: (916) 272–1873
Key: Inn; 4 units; Inexpensive–Moderate; No smoking; Credit cards;
No handicapped access

The Victorian mansion, built before 1880, has been restored by the artist/owners. The main house features upstairs guest rooms, including one suite with private bath and parlor, others with oak bedsteads and wicker, and even a small room with bunk beds for children. The carriage house has been renovated and is used as a printmaking studio. Reservations are required. Guests enjoy an outdoor pool surrounded by redwood decks and a tree-shaded yard at this family-oriented inn.

Rockwood Lodge

5295 West Lake Boulevard, P.O. Box 226, Homewood, CA 95718
Phone: (916) 525–5273; **Fax:** (916) 525–5949
Key: Inn; 4 units; Moderate–Superior; No smoking; No credit cards;
No handicapped access

Hand-hewn beams, restored golden-pine paneling, and local rock exteriors are featured in this former "summer home" built in the 1930s. Located among tall pines near the west shore of Lake Tahoe, the b&b offers rooms decorated in a pleasing mixture of European and American antiques and Laura Ashley fabrics. Guest rooms feature large feather beds, down comforters, pillows, and sitting areas. Two of the guest accommodations share a large bath with a 7-foot Roman tub; pedestal sinks grace each room. The other rooms boast private, tiled baths. The full breakfast, featuring juice, muffins, croissants, and special entrees such as Dutch Baby or fruit crepes, is served in the dining room or on the terrace in the summer. Wine and cider are enjoyed by the cozy stone fireplace in the living room, as are late-night port and sherry. Guests also enjoy a large stone patio with outside fireplace in front of the inn.

Sorensen's Resort

Highway 88, Hope Valley, CA 96120
Phone: (916) 694–2203 / (800) 423–9949; **Fax:** (916) 694–2204
Key: Inn/Cottages; 23 units; Inexpensive–Deluxe; No smoking;
Credit cards; No handicapped access

This 165-acre resort in the High Sierra meadowland was home-steaded by Danish sheepherders in 1876. The guest cabins are nestled in a grove of aspens, and each cabin is uniquely appointed with such details as freestanding, wood-burning stoves, cathedral ceilings, lofts, and kitchenettes. Three units at the resort offer a complimentary breakfast; in the remaining twenty rooms, the continental breakfast, ordered from a reasonably priced menu, is an additional charge, but this bed & "hospitality" establishment provides a complimentary glass of wine as well as coffee, tea, or hot cocoa throughout the day. Unlimited recreation at the resort includes volleyball, horseshoes, barbecues, two on-site creeks, and river rafting as well as trail-walking tours that include meals, lodging, and tour guides. The resort also offers cross-country skiing with its own trails, rentals, and lessons.

The Heirloom

214 Shakeley Lane, P.O. Box 322, Ione, CA 95640
Phone: (209) 274–4468
Key: Inn; 6 units; Inexpensive–Moderate; No smoking; No credit cards; Handicapped access, 2 units

The home of one of the earliest settlers in the Ione Valley, this Greek Revival structure is situated on nearly two acres of secluded grounds. The private grounds, full of ancient trees, shrubs, and gardens, provide lawns for croquet, a gazebo, and hammocks, as well as umbrella tables and swings. Guests may relax in the living room of the house with its fireplace and 10-foot-high ceilings and in the dining room with a crystal chandelier and fireplace. The rooms are all furnished with family heirlooms and antiques; several guest rooms boast balconies or fireplaces. Afternoon refreshments are served, and a full breakfast is served in bed, on the balcony, in the garden, or in the dining room.

Ann Marie's Country Inn

410 Stasal Street, Jackson, CA 95642
Phone: (209) 223-1452
Key: Inn/Cottage; 5 units; Moderate; Limited smoking; Credit cards;
No handicapped access

This authentic country Victorian with bay windows was constructed in 1892 during the gold-mining days. The guest rooms are full of quality antiques and are decorated with wallpaper prints and old lace and linens. Two of the accommodations have brass beds; a separate cottage is a romantic retreat with queen-size brass bed, potbelly stove, and bath. Guests enjoy a parlor with games, a Victorian-style wood-burning stove, and music, as well as complimentary beverages. A full "harvest" breakfast of perhaps eggs Benedict, omelettes, or quiche with fried potatoes and fresh fruit is served at 9:00 A.M. each morning. Baby-sitting is available at this inn, which welcomes children.

Broadway Hotel

225 Broadway, Jackson, CA 95642
Phone: (209) 223-3503
Key: Inn/Hotel; 13 units; Inexpensive–Moderate; Smoking OK;
Credit cards; No handicapped access

From the gold-rush days through 1942, the hotel served as a haven for miners. Today, the b&b inn captures days gone by with its restored guest rooms, all with private bath, air conditioning, and bright, airy colors. The two-bedroom suite at this reasonable hotel is especially suited for families. Guests enjoy the hotel's garden, gazebo, and covered Jacuzzi. Breakfasts of prize-winning nut breads and a fresh-fruit bowl greet guests.

Court Street Inn

215 Court Street, Jackson, CA 95642
Phone: (209) 223-0416
Key: Inn/Cottage; 7 units; Moderate–Superior; No smoking; Credit cards; Handicapped access, 1 unit

Court Street Inn, Jackson

This fully restored 1870 Mother Lode home with cottage is listed on the National Register of Historic Places. Fine antiques, lace curtains, fluffy down comforters, and abundant fresh flowers are some of the special touches here. Guest accommodations in the house include three rooms downstairs with private baths and two rooms upstairs which share a bath and a half bath. One guest room boasts an oak fireplace. The Indian House cottage, originally built as a museum to house Native American artifacts, offers two bedrooms and a spacious living room. The inn offers complimentary hors d'oeuvres in the evening. The generous morning fare, which is served in the dining room, usually consists of fresh fruit, the inn's own version of Orange Julius, potatoes, meat, and a special entree, such as seafood in a pastry ring or eggs Benedict.

The Gate House Inn

1330 Jackson Gate Road, Jackson, CA 95642
Phone: (209) 223–3500
Key: Inn/Cottage; 5 units; Moderate–Superior; No smoking; Credit cards; No handicapped access

The Victorian inn and separate summerhouse are a step into the past created with lots of early American pine and oak furnishings with a few French accent pieces. Guest rooms in the house all have private baths and brass or early American queen-size beds. The summerhouse's two-room suite offers a wood-burning stove and a bath with claw-foot tub and pull-chain toilet. Guests are invited to relax on the porches and in the picnic area and to enjoy the swimming pool. A full breakfast in the formal dining room is served on English country china.

The Wedgewood Inn, Jackson

The Wedgewood Inn

11941 Narcissus Road, Jackson, CA 95642
Phone: (209) 296–4300
Key: Inn/Cottage; 6 units; Moderate; No smoking; Credit cards; No handicapped access

This turn-of-the-century–designed inn was built in 1987 as a b&b and is situated on five private acres dotted with pines and oaks. The main "Victorian" house with colorful flower boxes boasts a wraparound porch with a swing and a balcony off the two upstairs guest rooms. Inside the nostalgic house, which is furnished with European and American antiques, including stained-glass and Victorian lace lamps, guests also enjoy a sitting parlor with grand piano and cozy wood-burning stove; the dining room has an interesting tapestry collection. Guest rooms in the house all have private baths (many with antique claw-foot tubs) and are decorated individually with fine antiques; three guest rooms boast wood-burning stoves. The Carriage House Suite, the largest accommodation at the inn, is decorated in a country theme, hosting four generations of family heirlooms; it has a carved queen-size bed as well as a white wrought-iron day bed. Coffee is available for early risers, and a full gourmet breakfast is graciously served on fine bone china in the formal dining room. Upon arrival guests are served a cheese-and-beverage snack.

Windrose Inn

1407 Jackson Gate Road, Jackson, CA 95642
Phone: (209) 223–3650
Key: Inn/Cottage; 8 units; Moderate–Superior; No smoking; Credit cards; No handicapped access

A footbridge over a babbling creek leads to this Victorian farmhouse with wraparound porch. Sitting adjacent to the historic Kennedy Gold Mine, the grounds of the restored country home also hold a hand-dug Chinese well that served the mine, as well as hundreds of daffodils and irises, wild roses, fruit trees, a fish pond, and an arbor. The interior of the inn boasts all the original floors and moldings; the parlor offers a 1903 wood-burning stove with nickel plating. The spacious guest accommodations, all with private bath, are located in the main house as well as in a newer structure and in a rustic, ivy-covered cottage. Guests will find such amenities as bedroom/bathroom fireplaces, step-down Jacuzzi or claw-foot tubs, and unique contemporary or period decor. The generous country breakfast may be served in some of the rooms, in the glass solarium, or on the side patio and gazebo when weather permits. Guests feast on fresh fruit, egg dishes or a main entree such as double French toast layered with marmalade or a Dutch Baby apple pancake, juice, breads and muffins, and a special sausage or bacon from a local meat market. Beverages and hors d'oeuvres are served each evening. Windrose Inn is a leisurely stroll away from fine restaurants; guests enjoy picnics and croquet on the inn's grounds.

Jamestown Hotel

P.O. Box 539, Jamestown, CA 95327
Phone: (209) 984–3902
Key: Inn/Hotel; 8 units; Inexpensive–Moderate; Smoking OK; Credit cards; No handicapped access

This historic hotel with adjoining restaurant and saloon offers rooms and suites that have been restored to reflect the gold-rush period and the early days of the Sierra Railroad. All accommodations have private Victorian baths and antiques, and some have separate sitting rooms. Guests are invited to relax or sunbathe on the outdoor deck. A continental breakfast is served each morning.

Royal Hotel

18239 Main Street, P.O. Box 219, Jamestown, CA 95327
Phone: (209) 984–5271
Key: Inn/Hotel/Cottage; 19 units; Inexpensive–Moderate; Smoking OK; Credit cards; Handicapped access, 1 unit

This hotel in historic Jamestown was built in 1922. The gold-mining town has been the locale of many movies and television series. Victorian–style guest rooms are in the main building, and a honeymoon cottage is in the rear. Guests are encouraged to use the patio, gas barbecues, gazebo, and old-fashioned balconies. A continental breakfast is served on weekends only. The inn is located one block from a historic state park with steam-powered trains.

Dick and Shirl's

4870 Triangle Road, Mariposa, CA 95338
Phone: (209) 966–2514
Key: Home/Cottage; 2 units; Inexpensive; Smoking OK; Credit cards; No handicapped access

This b&b home/guest house offers a quiet country setting surrounded by pines for travelers on their way to Yosemite National

Park. The main-house accommodation with private bath also includes a full breakfast each morning served in the dining room or on the patio. The cottage accommodation features a private entrance, a bedroom with a queen-size bed, and a bathroom. Guests breakfast in the main house.

Granny's Garden

7333 Highway 49 North, Mariposa, CA 95338
Phone: (209) 377–8342
Key: Home; 2 units; Moderate; Limited smoking; Credit cards; No handicapped access

This small Victorian farmhouse near Yosemite National Park boasts a large garden area with fresh produce and more than one hundred rose bushes. The 1896 inn is decorated in comfortable antiques. Both guest rooms offer a private bath. A generous morning meal is served on the sun porch or in the dining room. A cellar porch with 7-foot skylights is decorated with kitchen and mining utensils. This cheerful and home air-conditioned inn is open May through October but closed in the winter due to lack of central heating. Guests enjoy an outdoor spa.

Meadow Creek Ranch

2669 Triangle Road, Mariposa, CA 95338
Phone: (209) 966–3843
Key: Inn; 4 units; Moderate; No smoking; Credit cards; No handicapped access

This original 1858 overnight stagecoach stop is on eight acres of land and contains the main two-story ranch house and a country cottage. Innkeepers greet guests with refreshments and encourage them to take a relaxing stroll around the grounds, which feature an old waterwheel. The four comfortable guest rooms have European and country antiques, original art, and lots of plants. The Country Cottage room offers a private bath with two-person, claw-foot tub, gas fireplace, and queen-size canopy bed. The full breakfast is served family style in the dining room or on the patio.

Mariposa

The Pelennor

3871 Highway 49 South, Mariposa, CA 95338
Phone: (209) 966–2832
Key: Home; 4 units; Inexpensive; No smoking; No credit cards; No handicapped access

This hospitable b&b with a Scottish theme offers a two-story b&b building with two baths and a common room as well as two rooms in the innkeeper's adjoining home. The 15-acre country setting offers serenity and pretty gardens. The decor is basic but features some tartan touches; the innkeepers will play a few tunes on the bagpipes upon request. A full breakfast with an egg dish, a meat, muffins, croissants, homemade breads, juice, cereal, and fruits will satisfy any appetite. Guests enjoy the home's lap pool and spa.

Dunbar House

271 Jones Street, P.O. Box 1375, Murphys, CA 95247
Phone: (209) 728–2897
Key: Inn; 4 units; Moderate; No smoking; Credit cards; No handicapped access

This restored 1880 Italianate-style home was Calaveras County's first b&b and offers a homey atmosphere. All guest rooms at the inn have private baths, wood-burning stoves, and small refrigerators. Rooms also feature down comforters, air conditioning, family antiques, and light, cheery wall coverings; rooms are also supplied with a small bottle of wine. Guests enjoy summertime lemonade in the parlor, stocked with games and books, and a full breakfast served fireside in the dining room, on the porch, or in the garden.

Flume's End Bed & Breakfast Inn

317 South Pine Street, Nevada City, CA 95959
Phone: (916) 265–9665
Key: Inn; 4 units; Superior; No smoking; Credit cards; No handicapped access

The historic flume beside this 1863-built Victorian inn brought Sierra mountain waters of good fortune rushing to gold miners in the 1800s. Flume's End rests on a picturesque hillside, sloping down to the natural waterfalls of a 3-mile-long winding creek. The restored home offers four comfortable accommodations, including a honeymoon suite with Jacuzzi tub and the Garden and Creekside rooms, which share a large deck over a waterfall and a secluded sitting room with television, wet bar, and refrigerator. Guests relax in the inn's large common rooms with piano and fireplaces. Stays at the inn include a generous buffet breakfast and early-morning coffee or tea.

Grandmere's Inn

449 Broad Street, Nevada City, CA 95959
Phone: (916) 265–4660
Key: Inn; 7 units; Moderate–Superior; No smoking; Credit cards; No handicapped access

This three-story Colonial Revival home with a two-story carriage house is listed in the National Register of Historic Places as the Sargent House. The 7,300-square-foot home is surrounded by rolling lawns and Victorian gardens that present an ideal area for weddings and parties, for which a commercial kitchen and staff are available. The elegant guest rooms at the inn feature private baths and queen-size beds, and three have double sofa/sleepers as well. The inn is furnished in a country French motif with lots of antique pine, baskets, and American art. Guests enjoy a living room and dining room, where the full breakfast is served at 9:00 A.M.

Piety Hill Inn

523 Sacramento Street, Nevada City, CA 95959
Phone: (916) 265–2245
Key: Inn/Cottages; 7 units; Moderate; No smoking; Credit cards; Handicapped access, 1 unit

Nevada City

Originally built as an autocourt in the 1930s, this renovated enclave of guest cottages sits in a quiet residential neighborhood. The individual cottages surround a tree-shaded garden and lawn and are decorated, in an eclectic blend of the antique and the contemporary, with brass beds, hand stenciling, antique quilts, original art, and homey touches. Cottages also possess modern touches such as private baths, king-size beds, cable television, and refrigerators. The full breakfast is brought to the cottage and consists of a basket of pastries, fruit, juice, and hot beverages. A gazebo-crowned hot tub is nestled under a towering cedar at the edge of the garden.

Red Castle Inn, Nevada City

Red Castle Inn

109 Prospect Street, Nevada City, CA 95959
Phone: (916) 265–5135
Key: Inn; 7 units; Moderate–Superior; No smoking; Credit cards; No handicapped access

Atop a hill overlooking picturesque Nevada City sits this four-story Gothic Revival structure resembling a castle. The impressive, 1859-built brick mansion is a well-photographed historical landmark and has been an inn since 1963. It offers lush, terraced gardens, verandas, and interiors filled with period antiques. The uniquely furnished guest rooms offer some historical treasures, fresh flowers, private baths, and sweets. The entire top floor of the inn comprises the Garret Suite, featuring two guest rooms that share a sitting room and bath; the suite is ideal for families or two couples. The bountiful breakfast, featuring a dish from the gold-rush days, an egg specialty, meat, fruit, and juice is served from 8:00 to 10:00 A.M. in the elegant parlor; afternoon Victorian refreshments of sweets and beverages are also served in the parlor, with its 1880s pump organ. After breakfast on Saturday mornings, the inn offers an optional horse-and-buggy tour of the historic district.

National Hotel

211 Broad Street, Nevada City, CA 95959
Phone: (916) 265–4551
Key: Inn/Hotel; 42 units; Inexpensive–Moderate; Limited smoking; Credit cards; Handicapped access, 9 units

Claiming to be the "oldest continuously operating hotel west of the Rocky Mountains," this registered historical landmark offers both hospitality and old-fashioned comfort. The hotel, with its distinctive cupola, boasts a swimming pool filled with mountain water and a lobby with a square grand piano that journeyed around Cape Horn. Most guest rooms and suites have a private bath (twelve rooms share baths) and are decorated in antiques from the gold-rush days that include some canopy beds. The hotel has a complete Victorian restaurant and bar with banquet, reception, and meeting facilities available; during summer, lunch and dinner are served on the two-story veranda. Complimentary coffee only is offered each morning at this bed and "hospitality" inn.

The Chichester House

800 Spring Street, Placerville, CA 95667
Phone: (916) 626–1882
Key: Inn; 3 units; Moderate; No smoking; Credit cards; No handicapped access

A gold mine is hidden under the dining area of this lovingly restored 1892 Victorian home located on a hillside. California oaks, flower gardens, and a 60-foot tulip tree surround the inn and its carriage house. The interior of the home features antique furnishings and a storybook doll collection, and the library and parlor offer fireplaces and cozy reading nooks. The guest rooms are furnished in period pieces, and each has its own half bath. A full gourmet breakfast awaits guests each morning and features goodies such as eggs Benedict, German apple pancakes, crepes, and quiche.

River Rock Inn, Placerville

River Rock Inn

1756 Georgetown Drive, P.O. Box 827, Placerville, CA 95667
Phone: (916) 622–7640
Key: Inn; 4 units; Moderate; No smoking; No credit cards; No handicapped access

Guests may fish or pan for gold in the front yard of this wood-and-glass inn faced with river rock. The river and trees provide the views from three of the rooms and the 140-foot deck that also offers a sun-room and hot tub. The interior of the comfortable inn is furnished in antiques and a country decor; guests enjoy the living room with television and large fireplace. Breakfast, served in the dining room by fireside in the winter and in the sun-room in summer, features eggs Benedict and apple crepes.

The Rupley House

2500 Highway 50, Placerville, CA 95667
Phone: (916) 626–0630
Key: Inn; 3 units; Moderate; No smoking; No credit cards; No handicapped access

This 1929 Pennsylvania Dutch–style farmhouse is surrounded by an acre of estate gardens and fourteen acres of pastures. The country inn offers restful gardens, gold panning, and farm animals. The accommodations include three guest rooms with queen-size beds and one with private bath and balcony. The living room reflects the innkeepers' collection of Western-movie-star collectibles and photos. The full breakfast may include such delectables as mammoth sourdough French toast with fresh fruit and home-baked muffins.

The Feather Bed

542 Jackson Street, P.O. Box 3200, Quincy, CA 95971
Phone: (916) 283–0102
Key: Inn/Cottage; 7 units; Moderate; No smoking; Credit cards; No handicapped access

Situated near downtown Quincy and surrounded by the trees and meadows of a national forest is this 1893 Queen Anne home with 1905 Greek Revival touches. The b&b with a cozy cottage honeymoon suite has a large turn-of-the-century parlor with wood columns and a formal dining room, where winter breakfast is served. The antique-filled guest rooms all have private baths with

The Feather Bed, Quincy

brass fixtures and claw-foot tubs as well as showers. The unique accommodations range from Edward's Room, with antique windows and nonfunctioning fireplace, to the corner Morning Room, with private balcony. A generous full breakfast featuring baked pears and apples and buttermilk-oatmeal, raspberry walnut pancakes is served on the flower-filled patio in the spring and summer and in the room year-round. The inn offers a cross-country skiing package as well as fishing poles, bicycles, and day packs for guests' use.

Amber House

1315 22nd Street, Sacramento, CA 95816
Phone: (916) 444–8085 / (800) 755–6526; **Fax:** (916) 447–1548
Key: Inn; 8 units; Moderate–Deluxe; No smoking; Credit cards; No handicapped access

This recently expanded inn now offers deluxe accommodations in two meticulously restored vintage structures. The inn's Poets' Refuge is a Craftsman–style home touched with period elegance, such as beveled glass, boxed-beam ceilings, a clinker-brick fireplace, and hardwood floors. Its five guest rooms feature wallpapers, antiques, stained-glass or French windows, and all have private baths, one with a skylight and large antique tub and one with a Jacuzzi tub for two. The Artists' Retreat is a fully restored 1913 home with columns and beveled and leaded glass; it offers three luxurious guest rooms with marble-tiled baths and Jacuzzi tubs for two. The Renoir Room features a sitting area and framed Renoir prints. All guest accommodations at the inn include hidden televisions and VCRs, clock radios, telephones, and central air conditioning. A full gourmet breakfast including fresh fruit, a special entree, and homemade pastries is served in the formal dining room, in the room, or on the veranda. Bikes are available; a meeting or reception facility for small groups may be reserved. The inn, located in a residential neighborhood, is just a few blocks from shops, restaurants, and the capitol.

Aunt Abigail's

2120 "G" Street, Sacramento, CA 95816
Phone: (916) 441–5007
Key: Inn; 5 units; Moderate–Superior; No smoking; Credit cards; No handicapped access

This 1912 Colonial Revival mansion in the fashionable Boulevard Park area is framed by massive cedar and elm trees and boasts a former carriage area that is now a small park. The elegant interiors offer 10-foot-high ornate ceilings, antiques, and a warm, friendly feel. All five guest rooms have private baths, and many have brass beds, antique armoires, and decorator sinks. The full breakfast, with award-winning coffee cakes and muffins, is served in the sunny dining room. Guests may relax in the spacious living room with fireplace, in the sitting room with its piano and games, or in the secluded, flower-filled garden with hot tub.

The Bear Flag Inn

2814 "I" Street, Sacramento, CA 95816
Phone: (916) 448–5417
Key: Inn; 5 units; Moderate–Superior; No smoking; Credit cards; No handicapped access

Sacramento

Just two blocks from Sutter's Fort in a downtown residential area is this meticulously restored 1910 California Craftsman home. The b&b offers five guest rooms, all with private baths, furnished in period pieces, William Morris–designed wall coverings, and queen- or twin-size brass, iron, pine, or cherrywood beds. Guests enjoy a refreshment hour each evening and books in the room as well as a comfortable living room with fireplace. A full gourmet breakfast is served in the dining room or in the garden in summer months.

The Driver Mansion Inn, Sacramento

The Driver Mansion Inn

2019 Twenty-first Street, Sacramento, CA 95818
Phone: (916) 455–5243 / (800) 456–2019; Fax: (916) 455–6102
Key: Inn; 10 units; Moderate–Deluxe; No smoking; Credit cards; No handicapped access

A high degree of care has gone into preserving this 1899 family mansion with corner tower in the heart of downtown. A sweeping staircase and stately entry lead to the parlor and dining room with leaded glass, fireplaces, and a refinished 1907 grand piano. The guest rooms, spacious and beautifully appointed in unusual walnut and mahogany pieces, original art, rare Victorian lighting, and oriental carpets, have private marble-tiled baths with Victorian fixtures. All guest rooms feature such modern touches as wall-to-wall carpeting, private phones, and central air and heat. The inn features deluxe master suites and spas and a restored carriage house boasting fireplaces and Jacuzzis. The stay includes a full breakfast and complimentary beverages. Guests enjoy the landscaped gardens with Victorian gazebo and proximity to city entertainment and the capitol.

River Rose, A Country Inn

8201 Freeport Boulevard, Sacramento, CA 95832
Phone: (916) 665–1998 / (800) 695–1998
Key: Inn; 10 units; Moderate–Deluxe; No smoking; Credit cards; Handicapped access, 1 unit

This 1989-built inn situated across the street from the Sacramento River in the quiet town of Freeport offers ten guest accommodations featuring king-size beds, Jacuzzi tubs for two, and some private balconies. The early American–style inn in Delta country serves guests a full country breakfast in the dining room or in the guest room, as well as late afternoon refreshments in the sitting room or on the veranda. If fishing is on the agenda, the inn will arrange a guided fishing expedition on the river. The River Rose is a popular spot for weddings and special events such as luncheons, dinners, Sunday buffet brunches, workshops, and baby and wedding showers. Old Sacramento and golfing are a short drive away.

The Robin's Nest—A Country Inn

247 W. St. Charles Street, P.O. Box 1408, San Andreas, CA 95249
Phone: (209) 754–1076; **Fax:** (209) 754–1076
Key: Inn; 9 units; Moderate; No smoking; Credit cards; No handicapped access

This relaxed country estate consists of an 1895 Queen Anne–Victorian home with views of the Sierra foothills and charming gardens. The spacious inn, within walking distance of shops and restaurants, features a large parlor, sitting room, dining room, and

The Robin's Nest, San Andreas

music room with antique grand piano. An extensive library is available. The guest rooms are named and decorated after turn-of-the-century modes of transportation. The Buggy Room is a gabled suite with a 17-foot-high ceiling and views of the countryside. The full breakfast includes such items as quiches, crepes, and frittatas; champagne is offered on special occasions. Iced tea and wine are served on arrival; after-dinner coffee and brandy are offered. This creative inn offers many specialty weekends, including innovative mystery weekends with guest participation and country-western weekends with shoot-outs, barbecues, and country breakfasts.

High Country Inn

Highway 49 at Bassetts Corner, HCR 2, Box 7, Sierra City, CA 96125
Phone: (916) 862–1530
Key: Inn; 4 units; Moderate; Limited smoking; Credit cards; No handicapped access

Spacious decks surround this mountain home granting spectacular views of the majestic Sierra Buttes and the aspen- and pine-filled acreage of the estate. The Yuba River is a mere 45 feet from the house; Howard Creek borders the other side of the house; and guests also enjoy the inn's private pond, stocked by the innkeepers. Guests congregate in the 30-foot-long living room with cathedral ceiling and stone fireplace and also in the library/music area with pool table. The spacious guest rooms, decorated with interesting antiques and collectibles, all boast deck views as well as both private and shared baths. The Sierra Buttes Suite offers tall windows, a private bath with antique tub and modern shower, a dressing room, fireplace, and king-size bed. A full gourmet breakfast featuring homemade muffins and breads, egg dishes, fresh fruit and juices, and breakfast meats is served on the deck in the summer, or at the dining table with fabulous morning views of the Sierra Buttes; coffee and tea carafes are delivered outside each room early in the morning. In addition to fishing, guests enjoy cross-country skiing, snowmobile riding, hiking, golfing, and biking within a few miles of the inn. The inn has been featured in *Bon Appétit* magazine.

Barretta Gardens Inn

700 So. Barretta Street, Sonora, CA 95370
Phone: (209) 532–6039
Key: Inn; 5 units; Moderate; No smoking; Credit cards; No handicapped access

This turn-of-the-century inn offers guest rooms with queen-size beds, private baths, antiques, and color schemes that complement the flowers in the gardens. Complimentary beverages are served each evening and may be enjoyed in the three guest parlors and on the sun porch or the wraparound porch. The full breakfast, served in the dining room, breakfast room, or on the front porch, consists of fresh fruit and such delicacies as French toast, quiche, or crepes. The inn is located on an acre of terraced gardens and offers beautiful views; it is within walking distance of downtown.

Gunn House

286 S. Washington Street, Sonora, CA 95370
Phone: (209) 532–3421
Key: Inn/Hotel; 25 units; Inexpensive–Moderate; Smoking OK; Credit cards; No handicapped access

Sonora

This 1850 residence was the first two-story adobe built in Sonora. The original adobe makes up the core of the restored hotel. All the guest rooms are decorated in priceless antiques but have the modern conveniences of electric heat, air conditioning, and television. Guests enjoy a pleasant patio area and a heated swimming pool. A continental breakfast is served each morning, and cocktails are available in the Josephine Room.

Lulu Belle's Bed & Breakfast, Sonora

Lulu Belle's Bed & Breakfast

85 Gold Street, Sonora, CA 95370
Phone: (209) 533–3455
Key: Inn; 5 units; Moderate; No smoking; Credit cards; Handicapped access, 1 unit

This restored Victorian home two blocks from historic downtown Sonora is surrounded by peaceful lawn and garden areas, complete with gazebo and antique carriage. The individually decorated guest rooms, all with private bath, include some four-poster beds, family antiques, and garden views. Guests may stay in the two rooms in the main house or in the converted garage annex with three additional units. A hearty breakfast is served each morning in the rustic country kitchen or in the garden; breakfast also may be served in the room upon request. Guests at Lulu Belle's are welcome to play instruments provided in the music room or to select a book from the living-room library.

The Ryan House, Sonora

The Ryan House

153 S. Shepherd Street, Sonora, CA 95370
Phone: (209) 533–3445
Key: Inn; 3 units; Moderate; No smoking; Credit cards; No handicapped access

This gold-rush home, built in the 1850s and winner of a historic-preservation award, is framed by lovely rose gardens and is within walking distance of town. Guest rooms are furnished in antiques and antique reproductions and boast a constant supply of fresh flowers from the garden; all rooms feature queen-size beds and private baths. The full breakfast, with such specialties as banana-walnut pancakes or chili egg puff along with homemade breads, is served each morning. Guests are invited to relax in front of the fire at the end of the day and enjoy afternoon refreshments.

Serenity

15305 Bear Cub Drive, Sonora, CA 95370
Phone: (209) 533-1441
Key: Inn; 4 units; Moderate; Limited smoking; Credit cards; No handicapped access

This period home nestled in the pines offers uniquely decorated rooms with many handmade items. Each room has its own bath and either a queen-size bed or twin beds. Fireside refreshments are served in the Commons or on the veranda each evening, and a hearty breakfast featuring homemade preserves is offered in the dining room. Guests are invited to enjoy the game table or library, which features mother-lode reading material.

The Foxes in Sutter Creek

77 Main Street, P.O. Box 159, Sutter Creek, CA 95685
Phone: (209) 267-5882; **Fax:** (209) 267-0712
Key: Inn; 6 units; Moderate–Superior; No smoking; Credit cards; No handicapped access

This inn was built in 1857 during the gold-rush days. Accommodations include suites that are furnished in specially selected antiques and have dining and sitting areas as well as private baths, queen-size beds, and air conditioning. The downstairs suite boasts a fireplace and large bath with crystal chandelier and claw-foot tub, as well as private entrance and porch. Three accommodations at the inn boast fireplaces. The bountiful country breakfast is served on a silver service, along with the morning newspaper, in the suite or on the tree-roofed gazebo surrounded by colorful azaleas. Guests enjoy covered parking and courtesy pickup at the airport.

The Gold Quartz Inn

15 Bryson Drive, Sutter Creek, CA 95685
Phone: (209) 267-9155; **Fax:** (209) 267-9170
Key: Inn/Hotel; 24 units; Moderate–Superior; No smoking; Credit cards; Handicapped access, 2 units

The Gold Quartz Inn, Sutter Creek

This "new" Queen Anne–Victorian-style inn is painted white with gray trim and is situated on the outskirts of town. The spacious antique-filled parlor of the inn offers a fireplace, a television (hidden in a cabinet), and games and is the site of afternoon tea. The inn's two dining rooms host the breakfast of freshly squeezed juice, muffins, and cereal for early risers as well as the full breakfast, which includes all of the above as well as two entrees, and is served from 8:30 to 10:30 A.M. Guests have use of the guest refrigerator, which is stocked with soda and juice, as well as a courtesy washer and dryer. The rooms at the inn are individually decorated and boast such special touches as antique plates on the walls, fresh flowers, hair dryers, televisions in cherrywood cabinets, telephones, and mostly king-size beds; honeymoon suites offer four-poster beds and claw-foot tubs. The inn can accommodate weddings and special events with a chef on staff, a catering department, and a banquet room.

The Hanford House

61 Hanford Street, P.O. Box 1450, Sutter Creek, CA 95685
Phone: (209) 267–0747
Key: Inn; 9 units; Inexpensive–Moderate; No smoking; Credit cards; Handicapped access, 1 unit

The inn is a newer brick structure built around a Spanish cottage and is reminiscent of a turn-of-the-century San Francisco warehouse. In the same way, the furnishings at the b&b blend both the old and new with a country feel. All the guest rooms offer private baths and ceiling fans and are bright and spacious. The suite features a fireplace. Guests relax on a large redwood deck that affords breathtaking views of the countryside. The inn serves a hearty continental breakfast. The Hanford House boasts a collection of more than 400 teddy bears.

Sutter Creek Inn

75 Main Street, P.O. Box 385, Sutter Creek, CA 95685
Phone: (209) 267–5606
Key: Inn/Cottages; 19 units; Inexpensive–Superior; Limited smoking; No credit cards; No handicapped access

The 1859-built inn, the biggest house in town, offers accommodations upstairs and in several outbuildings in the rear of the house that have been totally refurbished. The unusual colors and eclectic decorating schemes include swinging beds (which can be stabilized), fireplaces, Franklin stoves, canopies, and brightly colored wicker. Guests may relax in the living room or on outside hammocks. An imaginative country breakfast is prepared and served in the spacious old kitchen. Handwriting analysis is done upon request at this hospitable inn, as are professional massages or reflexology.

Cedar Tree Guest House

P.O. Box 7106, Tahoe City, CA 95730
Phone: (916) 583–5421
Key: Home; 3 units; Inexpensive; No smoking; No credit cards; Handicapped access, 1 unit

This contemporary wood-shingled house near the lake, a sandy beach, and pier offers three comfortable guest rooms with queen- or twin-size beds, one with private bath. Guests may relax on large decks in the front, in the hot tub on the back deck, or in the loft with television and VCR. Homemade rolls and muffins, fresh fruit, and coffee or tea are served in the dining area each morning. Bicycles and a barbecue are available at this guest house close to town. The b&b is now open year-round.

Chaney House, Tahoe City

Chaney House

4725 W. Lake Boulevard, P.O. Box 7852, Tahoe City, CA 95730
Phone: (916) 525–7333; **Fax:** (916) 525–4413
Key: Inn; 3 units; Moderate; No smoking; No credit cards; No handicapped access

This historic stone lakefront home was built in the 1920s by Italian stonemasons. The distinct European-style construction boasts 18-inch-thick stone walls throughout the house, a massive fireplace extending to the cathedral ceilings, and Gothic stone arches and walls outlining the paths around the three patios. The guest accommodations, offering private and shared baths, all have down comforters, warm wood paneling, and some family antiques. A small apartment is also available. Breakfast is served on the lake-view patio or in the formal dining room; the house specialty is Grand Marnier Oven French Toast served with homemade hot blackberry sauce and crème fraiche. Evening refreshments are offered by fireside. Guests at the Chaney House enjoy a private beach and pier and abundant recreational opportunities year-round.

The Cottage Inn

1690 W. Lake Boulevard, P.O. Box 66, Tahoe City, CA 95730
Phone: (916) 581–4073
Key: Inn/Cottages; 15 units; Moderate–Superior; No smoking; Credit cards; Handicapped access, 1 unit

Six knotty-pine-paneled cottages on two acres of pine trees provide fifteen lodging accommodations at this b&b on the west shore of Lake Tahoe. The cottages cluster around a central garden area and boast private baths, European pine furniture, Scandinavian color schemes, cozy Pendleton blankets, and adjustable heating. Guests may choose either suites with living rooms or studios or the Honeymoon room with wood-burning fireplace. The main-house sitting room with its stone fireplace and piano is for guests' enjoyment, and breakfast is offered in the house dining room or in the cottage. The generous morning fare includes juice, fruit, granola, a cooked entree, and bread or muffins. Refreshing beverages are offered at the inn, along with complimentary espresso and a "twenty-four-hour" cookie jar!

Mayfield House

236 Grove Street, P.O. Box 5999, Tahoe City, CA 95730
Phone: (916) 583–1001
Key: Inn; 5 units; Moderate; No smoking; Credit cards; Handicapped access, 1 unit

This wood-and-stone inn with pretty gardens and patios offers a living room with cozy fireplace and individually decorated guest rooms. The guest accommodations share three centrally located baths. Beds are covered with down comforters and pillows and fine linens. Breakfast, served in the room, on the patio, or in the breakfast area, includes such delectables as Finnish pancakes, Portuguese toast, apple strudel, and sweet-potato muffins. The menu changes daily, and all meals are served on fine china with fresh flowers. The b&b is one-half block from the lake and convenient to major ski resorts.

Alpenhaus Country Inn

6941 W. Lake Boulevard, P.O. Box 262, Tahoma, CA 95733
Phone: (916) 525-5266; **Fax:** (916) 525-4434
Key: Inn/Cottages; 14 units; Moderate–Superior; Limited smoking; Credit cards; No handicapped access

This completely renovated inn with a fine European-style restaurant and cozy bar boasts an Alpine decor and a swimming pool surrounded by trees and gardens. The interior of the inn features warm pine walls, Bavarian and Swiss imports, and bell-shaped lantern light fixtures. The inn offers six cottages with kitchens and fireplaces, guest rooms, and a two-bedroom suite with full kitchen. The guest rooms, all with private baths, have hand-painted pine headboards, cozy comforters, pine closets, and country wallpaper prints. Guests may enjoy a comfortable lounge with a small bar and rock fireplace. The full breakfast (not served to cottages guests) changes daily but might include omelettes, blueberry muffins, juice, and fresh fruit. The restaurant, featuring Swiss-Austrian cuisine, is open nightly in summer months and on Fridays and Saturdays in winter.

Richardson House

Spring & High streets, P.O. Box 2011, Truckee, CA 95734
Phone: (916) 587-5388
Key: Inn; 7 units; Inexpensive–Moderate; Limited smoking; Credit cards; No handicapped access

This large Victorian home built in the 1870s has been completely restored and is highlighted by a hand-carved picket fence, rich pine woodwork, and unusual leather wainscoting in the hall. Five guest rooms share a bath upstairs and are decorated in soft tones and handmade Amish quilts; two rooms downstairs share a bath and can be a family suite. The dining room is the site of the full breakfast featuring omelettes, waffles, eggs Benedict, quiche, or French toast. The parlor serves as the locale for evening wine and cheese; guests enjoy a Jacuzzi on the outside deck.

Truckee Hotel

P.O. Box 884, Truckee, CA 95734
Phone: (916) 587–4444
Key: Inn/Hotel; 37 units; Inexpensive–Moderate; No smoking; Credit cards; No handicapped access

This 1873 hotel nestled high in the Sierras is just a minute's walk from Amtrak and a few steps from the town's historic commercial center. The guest rooms, with private and shared baths, are a step into nineteenth-century California with sepia-toned portraits, oak antiques, and lace curtains. The bottom floor of the hotel features a fine restaurant and a saloon, and hotel guests receive a complimentary breakfast. Free guided tours of the hotel take place every day, and champagne is added for special occasions.

Oak Hill Ranch

18550 Connally Lane, P.O. Box 307, Tuolumne, CA 95379
Phone: (209) 928–4717
Key: Inn/Cottages; 5 units; Moderate; No smoking; No credit cards; Handicapped access, 2 units

This rural Victorian ranch house with cottage sits on fifty-six acres and looks out onto pastures, ponds, and the Sierras. The house guest rooms have been carefully restored and are authentically decorated in antiques. These accommodations feature two rooms with private baths and two with shared baths, one with a claw-foot tub. The Cow Palace cottage, also in antiques, is totally private; has a rock fireplace, two queen beds, and a furnished kitchen; and can accommodate groups up to five. A full gourmet breakfast, featuring such dishes as Normandy crepes, crustless Swiss quiche, crunchy French toast, or Eggs Fantasia, is served in the dining room; prebreakfast coffee, in the old-fashioned gazebo.

Twain Harte's Bed & Breakfast

18864 Manzanita Drive, Box 1718, Twain Harte, CA 95383
Phone: (209) 586–3311
Key: Inn; 6 units; Inexpensive–Moderate; No smoking; Credit cards;
No handicapped access

This b&b with lots of decks and walkways is situated in a
wooded setting yet is within walking distance of downtown. Each
guest room has its own decor and sink. One guest accommodation
boasts a private bath, and another offers a complete family suite
with living room and bath. Guests enjoy a cozy living room with
fireplace and antiques, a recreation room with pool table and bar,
and a breakfast room, where the country-style breakfast is served.
Excellent restaurants are within walking distance.

The Harkey House

212 "C" Street, Yuba City, CA 95991
Phone: (916) 674–1942
Key: Home; 4 units; Moderate; No smoking; No credit cards; Handi-
capped access, 1 unit

This Victorian home, built in 1874, has four guest rooms. The
Harkey Suite has a queen-size brass bed, fireplace, and balcony; the
Yellow Wicker Room features white-wicker decor, fresh flowers,
and quilts. Besides breakfasting in the sunny dining room, guests
may rent bikes for touring or enjoy the swimming pool and spa.
Harkey House guests also enjoy a basketball court, a piano, and an
art gallery.

SAN FRANCISCO BAY AREA

Synonymous with Fisherman's Wharf, cable cars, and Chinatown, the city also offers numerous cultural activities, fine restaurants, and splendid examples of Victorian architecture blended with the ultramodern edifices. The communities that surround San Francisco, all just minutes away, bring suburban and country settings. Nearby Berkeley reflects the University of California campus with small coffeehouses and boutiques, as well as stately homes. The suburban communities of Sunnyvale and Los Gatos are home to commuters, but each has retained its own identity. Just over the Golden Gate Bridge lies Sausalito with its hillside homes perched over the bay and its many tourist shops and art galleries. Over by the coast, but still within a modest drive, are communities such as Muir Beach, Tomales Bay, Olema, Point Reyes, and Inverness. They offer forests with hiking, seafood stops, beautiful beaches, and wilderness areas.

LEGEND:
— Freeway Route
— Highway Route
○ Listed City or Town
○ Location Reference
◯ LARGER CITY

NORTH
Scale in Miles
0   5   10   15   20

SAN FRANCISCO BAY AREA

Garratt Mansion

900 Union Street, Alameda, CA 94501
Phone: (510) 521–4779
Key: Inn; 6 units; Moderate–Superior; No smoking; Credit cards; No handicapped access

This Colonial Revival residence was built in 1893 for W. T. Garratt, a turn-of-the-century industrialist. The splendor of the twenty-seven-room Victorian residence has been brought to life through extensive renovation. The mansion features a sweeping carved wood staircase with orchestra balcony, lots of stained- and leaded-glass windows, and a ceiling three stories high. Nestled in a quiet residential neighborhood filled with other interesting homes, this b&b welcomes guests to its second floor common room, which is usually outfitted with plates of cookies and fresh fruit. The guest rooms, hosting both shared and private baths, have sitting areas with comfortable reading chairs; the four rooms on the third floor feel ultraprivate and have private phones. A generous continental breakfast of muffins, croissants, mini-quiches, fruit, and juices is served to guests who wish to dine in the room, and a full breakfast with varying entrees is served each morning in the dining room. The inn is able to host weddings and other functions on its main floor and regularly schedules teas and musical events.

Captain Dillingham's Inn

145 East "D" Street, Benicia, CA 94510
Phone: (707) 746–7164 / (800) 544–2278
Key: Inn; 10 units; Moderate–Superior; Limited smoking; Credit cards; Handicapped access, 2 units

This 1853-built former home of a seafaring captain is located in the town's historic waterfront district, just one-half block from the marina. The restored, yellow, Cape Cod–style home is surrounded by lush gardens and offers spacious guest rooms, including one suite. Guest accommodations all feature private baths with Jacuzzi tubs (except for the Mate's Quarters with its claw-foot tub), antique decor, and modern amenities such as television, radio, refrigerators, telephones, and air conditioning. The Captain's Quarters features a working onyx fireplace; several rooms offer garden-view decks. The abundant hot and cold buffet breakfast, served in the country dining room or on one of the outside decks, includes fresh fruits, breads, pastries, cheeses, meats, cereals, yogurts, juices, and the inn's special blend of coffee. Complimentary wine-and-cheese trays are brought to the rooms each afternoon. The inn also has three apartment suites, complete with baths, kitchens with microwaves and coffee makers, sitting rooms, and daily maid service; the complimentary breakfast may be enjoyed in the suite or at the inn, a few hundred yards away.

The Union Hotel

401 First Street, Benicia, CA 94510
Phone: (707) 746–0100; **Fax:** (707) 746–6458
Key: Inn/Hotel; 12 units; Moderate–Superior; Limited smoking; Credit cards; No handicapped access

This 1882 hotel with spectacular views of the bay has been completely restored with modern conveniences such as soundproofing, an elevator, phones, television, and private baths with Jacuzzi tubs. Each one of the guest rooms reflects a less-than-modern era ranging from late-1800s Americana through nineteenth-century Louis XVI to 1920s art deco. A restaurant on the premises specializes in California cuisine and serves the continental breakfast, which is included in the stay. The inn is located two blocks from the new marina.

Gramma's Inn

2740 Telegraph Avenue, Berkeley, CA 94705
Phone: (510) 549–2145; **Fax:** (510) 549–1085
Key: Inn; 30 units; Moderate–Deluxe; Limited smoking; Credit cards; Handicapped access, 4 units

Two side-by-side, turn-of-the-century homes with gardens, a carriage house, and garden house form this b&b not far from the University of California campus. The Queen Anne original b&b structure offers two parlors, a fireplace, ornate moldings, inlaid

Gramma's Inn, Berkeley

floors, and chintz fabrics and antiques. The adjacent Fay House has marble fireplaces, hand-painted ceilings, stained-glass windows, and oriental rugs. The unique, enlarged guest accommodations with private baths offer such amenities as antiques, fireplaces, private decks, armoires, and stained-glass windows. The breakfast of croissants, muffins, fruit platters, Gramma's granola, and juice is served in the dining room, the garden, or the greenhouse. The inn is a favorite locale for weddings and serves a gourmet Sunday brunch at a reduced rate for b&b guests.

New Davenport Bed & Breakfast

31 Davenport Avenue, Davenport, CA 95017
Phone: (408) 425–1818/426–4122
Key: Inn; 12 units; Inexpensive–Moderate; No smoking; Credit cards; Handicapped access, 4 units

Housed in one of the town's original old buildings, the inn is within walking distance of local craft studios and close to a popular whale-watch spot. The guest rooms, all with private bath, are furnished with antique iron beds, oak dressers, colorful rugs, and art and are located above the restaurant with ocean views or in an adjacent house with patio and sitting room. Champagne is offered on arrival, and the continental breakfast featuring home-baked cinnamon rolls is served in the Cash Store Restaurant next door.

Cypress Inn on Miramar Beach

407 Mirada Road, Half Moon Bay, CA 94019
Phone: (415) 726–6002 / (800) 832–3224; **Fax:** (415) 726–1138
Key: Inn; 8 units; Superior–Deluxe; No smoking; Credit cards;
Handicapped access, 1 unit

This 1989-built contemporary beach house, situated directly on
a 5-mile-long sandy beach, offers spectacular ocean views from
every guest room. The pole-structure inn is decorated with colorful folk art and boasts terra-cotta tile floors covered with Indian
rugs throughout. The eight luxurious guest accommodations feature queen-size beds with comforters, fireplaces, private baths and
decks, and shuttered windows. Guests awake to a full breakfast of
freshly squeezed orange juice, just-baked croissants, and a gourmet
entree such as Peaches and Cream French Toast, served in the
main room. A continental breakfast is available in the room.
Guests enjoy tea and hors d'oeuvres at sunset. The Cypress Inn
offers massages by its own in-house massage therapist. Within ten
minutes of the inn, guests may enjoy sailing, fishing, whale-
watching, horseback riding, biking, golfing, and wine tasting.

Old Thyme Inn

779 Main Street, Half Moon Bay, CA 94019
Phone: (415) 726–1616
Key: Inn; 7 units; Moderate–Deluxe; No smoking; Credit cards; No
handicapped access

Located in Main Street's historic district, this 1899-built b&b
is within walking distance of quaint boutiques and restaurants. In
the rear of the redwood-constructed Victorian is an herb garden
with more than fifty varieties of sweet-smelling herbs. Guests
may explore the garden, which provides garnishes and breakfast
ingredients. The many return guests to this b&b may choose from
seven individual accommodations ranging from the cozy
Chamomile Room, with antique American decor, to the plush
Thyme Room, with double-size whirlpool tub, a fireplace, and a
queen-size canopy bed. Four guest rooms feature private baths.

Old Thyme Inn, Half Moon Bay

The inn offers a suite with its own private entrance through the herb garden; the suite boasts a four-poster bed, a fireplace, a whirlpool tub for two, a television, a VCR, and a refrigerator stocked with beverages. The English-style morning fare typically includes such specialties as fresh juice, coffee, homemade scones, cold meats, and English cheeses as well as homemade French cherry flan; the menu varies each morning. Both breakfast and evening wine and sherry are served in the lounge by a cozy fire. Well-behaved pets are allowed.

San Benito House

356 Main Street, Half Moon Bay, CA 94019
Phone: (415) 726–3425
Key: Inn/Hotel; 12 units; Inexpensive–Moderate; Limited smoking; Credit cards; No handicapped access

This upstairs historic hostelry is filled with European antiques and fresh flowers from the English garden. Guest rooms bordering the garden boast more elaborate decor. The continental breakfast is served in the room or on the sunny redwood deck, which is dressed with flower boxes and a massive firepit for the evening cognac. A "nonhistoric" sauna is available as well as lunch and dinner in the hotel's Garden Deli and San Benito House Restaurant.

Half Moon Bay

Zaballa House

324 Main Street, Half Moon Bay, CA 94019
Phone: (415) 726–9123 / (800) 772–6248
Key: Inn; 9 units; Moderate–Superior; No smoking; Credit cards; No handicapped access

This historic structure at the entrance to Main Street is described as the "oldest building still standing in Half Moon Bay." Constructed by early city planner Estanislao Zaballa around 1863, the renovated bright and cheery inn now welcomes guests with period comfort. All guest accommodations are decorated individually with antiques, wall coverings, and art; many feature 10-foot-high ceilings. Comforts include over-sized comforters, fresh flowers, and fluffy towels. The private bathrooms are imaginative with some double-size whirlpool tubs or deep old-fashioned claw-foot tubs with brass fixtures. Family-style "all you can eat" breakfasts are served in the open kitchen and include juices, fruit or cereals, muffins or breads, and a hot-dish specialty, such as apple crepes. Guests may enjoy wine or sherry in the parlor each evening; the refrigerator is available for guests' use. Fine restaurants and shops are all within walking distance of the Zaballa House; flower gardens for strolling are located both next door and behind the inn. Well-behaved pets are allowed.

The Ark

180 Highland Way, P.O. Box 273, Inverness, CA 94937
Phone: (415) 663–9338
Key: Cottage; 1 unit; Superior; Smoking OK; No credit cards; Handicapped access, 1 unit

Tucked away up the ridge from Inverness is this two-room artist's retreat nestled in the forest. The spacious main room boasts a cathedral ceiling, sunny forest-view windows, a woodstove, a queen-size bed, and a sleeping loft with futon. A smaller room adorned with the artwork of past visitors offers twin beds, a tape deck and stereo, and reading material. The cottage offers both toilet and sink, but guests bathe Japanese style in a separate octagonal shower and bathhouse with big Victorian tub and skylights. The full kitchen is stocked with breakfast fixings of eggs, juice, fresh fruit, granola, pastries, scones or muffins, braided egg bread, and home-made jams. A few steps outside the cottage, an area for picnics and barbecues awaits guests.

Blackthorne Inn

266 Vallejo Avenue, P.O. Box 712, Inverness Park, CA 94937
Phone: (415) 663–8621
Key: Inn; 5 units; Moderate–Deluxe; No smoking; Credit cards; No handicapped access

The multilevel wood-and-glass inn resembles a tree house nestled in a rustic, tree-filled canyon. Guest rooms perched from top floor to bottom yield views as well as added privacy and lead to a deck offering spectacular views and a hot tub for guests' use. An A-frame living room is for guests' enjoyment, as is a 3,000-square-foot sun deck. A buffet breakfast consisting of quiche, coffee cakes, juice, and fresh fruit salad with toppings is served at 9:30 A.M.

Rosemary Cottage

75 Balboa Avenue, P.O. Box 619, Inverness, CA 94937
Phone: (415) 663–9338
Key: Cottage; 1 unit; Superior; Smoking OK; No credit cards; No handicapped access

Located on Inverness Ridge is this French country cottage with hand-crafted cabinets and tile. The b&b offers a large bedroom with queen-size bed; a main room with high ceilings, wood-burning stove, and panoramic picture-window views of the forest; additional sleeping areas; a full kitchen; and a bath with tub and shower. A full breakfast of juice, seasonal fruit, granola, fresh eggs (guests cook their own), pastries or muffins, and sometimes hot crepes is offered each morning. A large deck nestled under an old oak overlooks the herb garden at this secluded getaway near Point Reyes National Seashore and Tomales Bay.

Ten Inverness Way, Inverness

Ten Inverness Way

10 Inverness Way, P.O. Box 63, Inverness, CA 94937
Phone: (415) 669–1648
Key: Inn; 4 units; Moderate–Superior; No smoking; Credit cards; No handicapped access

This inn is designed for avid readers and hikers and is ideal for anyone who appreciates colorful gardens and seclusion near the Point Reyes National Seashore. A flagstone path leads to a wisteria-covered arbor and the sweet smells of blooms and fruit trees. The comfortable rooms of this 1904 guest house boast the original Douglas fir floor and paneling; the guest rooms have white wainscoting, sloped ceilings, and an abundance of windows. Most of the accommodations offer queen-size beds, and all rooms have private baths, handmade quilts, and, of course, flowers from the garden. Breakfast, served in the sun-room, includes specialties such as blackberry-buttermilk-buckwheat pancakes with fresh berries or French toast. Guests can also enjoy a mug of tea or other refreshments by the stone fireplace in the living room. Guests may soak in a private hot tub in the garden cottage; guests sign up for its use.

The Goose and Turrets B & B, Montara

The Goose and Turrets B&B

835 George Street, P.O. Box 937, Montara, CA 94037-0937
Phone: (415) 728–5451
Key: Inn; 5 units; Moderate; No smoking; Credit cards; No handicapped access

The inn's two mascot geese, Mrs. Goose and Mr. Turrets, float contentedly on the pond of the one-acre villa. Built circa 1908 the Italian villa-style b&b surrounded by gardens is tucked into a hillside. The five-guest-room inn offers a comfortable decor with a common lounge area outfitted with woodstove, piano, game table, and library of books for every taste. Guest rooms enjoy individual motifs; the Goose Room and the Whale Room both boast beds that once belonged to the Teddy Roosevelt family. The Hummingbird Room offers a sitting room with wood-burning stove. All rooms are furnished with a German down comforter, an English towel warmer, and bath robes. One accommodation has a private bath, and the other four share two and one-half baths. Guests enjoy a four-course breakfast in the dining room with such delicacies prepared as Dutch Baby, filled with strawberries or wild blackberries from the garden, or Southwest Corn-Pepper Pancakes garnished with salsa and sour cream. Afternoon tea is special at the inn, with varying delights such as homemade Scottish shortbread or Italian Squares topped with melted gorgonzola.

Montara B&B

1125 Tamarind Street, P.O. Box 493, Montara, CA 94037
Phone: (415) 728–3946
Key: Home; 1 unit; Moderate; No smoking; Credit cards; No handicapped access

This home b&b, nestled in a quiet coastal town just twenty-five minutes from downtown San Francisco, offers guests a myriad of surrounding activities, such as beach-going, whale-watching, horseback riding, and hiking. The redwood-and-glass contemporary home offers a sunny solarium overlooking a colorful garden, which is the locale of the full morning breakfast featuring the inn's own honey. The one guest accommodation is a suite with private bath and entrance; a redwood sunning deck; a private, connecting sitting room, where evening sherry and nuts are provided; and either a king-size bed or twin beds made from a trundle. The suite offers comfortable furnishings, television, and stereo, as well as a sitting room with fireplace and ocean view.

The Pelican Inn

Muir Beach, CA 94965
Phone: (415) 383–6000
Key: Inn; 7 units; Superior; Smoking OK; Credit cards; No handicapped access

This Tudor-style farmhouse with pub and restaurant captures the spirit of sixteenth-century England yet is just twenty minutes from San Francisco. English antiques, a hearty English breakfast, and British ales, fine ports, wine, and tea carry out the theme. Luncheon service is available Tuesday through Saturday; a Sunday buffet lunch and dinner are also available. Lodging reservations are taken from 9:30 A.M. to 4:30 P.M.

Bear Valley Bed & Breakfast

88 Bear Valley Road, P.O. Box 33, Olema, CA 94950
Phone: (415) 663–1777
Key: Home; 3 units; Moderate; No smoking; Credit cards; No handicapped access

This two-story Victorian ranch house is just ¹/₂ mile from Point Reyes National Park, which offers many recreational activities and exhibits. The 1899-built inn is surrounded by gardens and fruit trees and offers guests a relaxing parlor with oak floors, wallpaper, overstuffed seating, and a cozy woodstove. The three individually furnished guest accommodations include some family antiques and a shared bath with the ranch's original claw-foot tub. A typical breakfast here might offer quiche, juice, home-baked muffins, and coffee or tea. The inn rents mountain bikes, cameras, and binoculars to interested guests.

The Victorian on Lytton, Palo Alto

The Victorian on Lytton

555 Lytton Avenue, Palo Alto, CA 94301
Phone: (415) 322–8555; **Fax:** (415) 322–7141
Key: Inn; 10 units; Moderate–Deluxe; No smoking; Credit cards; Handicapped access, 1 unit

Palo Alto

This historic inn, built in 1895 as a private residence, also provides accommodations in an addition in the rear; the grounds are graced by a fragrant English country garden with more than 700 perennials. The ten unique guest rooms are named after Queen Victoria and her nine children and offer such "royal" touches as separate sitting parlors, private baths, canopy or four-poster queen- or king-size beds, romantic laces, down comforters, claw-foot tubs, and fine antiques. The Queen's Room features a unique step-down bathroom. A generous continental breakfast is served in the room between 7:00 and 9:00 A.M. along with the morning paper; complimentary port and sherry are served each evening. Guests may relax in the tastefully decorated parlor with classical music; coffee, tea, and biscuits are available throughout the day. The service-minded hosts at this b&b near Stanford University will often offer special courtesies when their guests need assistance.

Holly Tree Inn, Point Reyes Station

Holly Tree Inn

3 Silverhills Road, P.O. Box 642, Point Reyes Station, CA 94956
Phone: (415) 663–1554
Key: Inn/Cottage; 6 units; Moderate–Deluxe; No smoking; Credit cards; No handicapped access

This b&b inn is located on nineteen acres of land and is surrounded by fir, bay, and oak trees; fragrant gardens; lilacs in the spring; and festive holly trees just in time for Christmas. The 4,000-square-foot inn with beamed ceilings and fireplaces offers four guest rooms, a living room with fireplace and comfortable seating, and a dining room, as well as a back deck that joins a hillside draped in heather. The guest accommodations offer plush carpeting, antique furnishings, Laura Ashley prints, garden views, and private baths. The generous country breakfast of farm-fresh eggs, homemade poppy-seed bread, juice, and fruit is served by the cozy curved hearth in the dining room. Sherry is served in the afternoon. The inn also offers a cottage with privacy and views of the gardens, creek, and forest. One cottage boasts a sitting room/library, wood-burning stove, king-size bed, kitchenette (for self-serve breakfast), bath with claw-foot tub, and patio. The inn's new Sea Star Cottage is an intimate rustic house built out over the tidal waters of Tomales Bay with unobstructed views in all directions; the cottage features a 75-foot-long dock leading to the front door, a cozy living room with fireplace, a four-poster queen-size bed, a full kitchen, bath, and solarium with hot tub.

Jasmine Cottage

P.O. Box 56, Point Reyes Station, CA 94956
Phone: (415) 663–1166
Key: Cottage; 1 unit; Superior; No smoking; No credit cards; Handicapped access, 1 unit

This complete little house is surrounded by a country garden at the top of a hill north of Point Reyes Station. The cottage is a pleasant five-minute walk from town and a five-minute drive from the national seashore. The romantic hideaway is situated among aromatic blooms, a vegetable garden, an herb garden, fruit trees, and wandering chickens (which provide eggs for breakfast). The retreat offers a fully equipped kitchen, sleeping arrangements for up to four adults and a baby, a garden room with deck and library, and a woodshed well stocked for the cottage's cozy woodstove. The stay includes a full breakfast laid out in the kitchen before guests arrive. The bountiful offering consists of eggs, muffins, homemade jams, cheese, fruit, coffees, teas, and cereals. The owners also rent a cottage, Gray's Retreat, but food and linens are not provided.

Marsh Cottage, Point Reyes Station

Marsh Cottage

P.O. Box 1121, Point Reyes Station, CA 94956
Phone: (415) 669–7168
Key: Cottage; 1 unit; Moderate; No smoking; No credit cards; No handicapped access

This forty-year-old restored cottage sits amid untamed wild roses, grasses, fir trees, mint, and blackberry brambles. Jasmine entwines the front porch, and a relaxing deck overlooks marsh wetlands dotted with cattails, an old pier, the bay, and hills. An ideal retreat for bird-watchers, this b&b, with its own driveway and entrance, offers complete privacy. The one main room of the gray wooden cottage boasts a freestanding fireplace, sitting area, queen-size bed and futon, and full kitchen. The hallway leads to an adjoining shower, tub bathroom, and closet. The sunny room with white wooden walls is decorated in beige, teal, and terra-cotta shades with coordinating country print fabrics. The kitchen is stocked at all times with tea, coffee, and sherry; breakfast in the cottage consists of fresh orange juice, home-baked breads and muffins, fresh fruits, granola, a basket of fresh eggs, cheeses, and French-roast coffee. Families are welcome; a Porta-crib is available.

Thirty-Nine Cypress

P.O. Box 176, Point Reyes Station, CA 94956
Phone: (415) 663–1709
Key: Home; 3 units; Moderate; No smoking; No credit cards;
Handicapped access, 1 unit

Situated on a bluff above Tomales Bay, this home offers views of
grazing cattle and evergreen hills. Each guest room is furnished in
family antiques, oriental rugs, and original works of art. The two
upstairs guest rooms have their own baths but host unique shower
arrangements outside the rooms' sliding glass doors; the downstairs
room offers a full conventional bath. Guests are offered a glass of
wine on the patio as well as a full breakfast each morning.

East Brother Light Station

117 Park Place, Point Richmond, CA 94801
Phone: (510) 233–2385
Key: Inn; 4 units; Deluxe; No smoking; No credit cards; Handi-
capped access, 2 units

A unique b&b accommodation, this restored 1874 lighthouse station offers a total package of overnight lodging, continental breakfast, a five-course California/French dinner with wine, and boat
transportation from the yacht harbor to the island. The entire station, on the National Register of Historic Places, serves as a living
museum of American maritime history and offers many Victorian
buildings to explore.

The Pillar Point Inn

380 Capistrano Road, Princeton-by-the-Sea, CA 94018
P.O. Box 388, El Granada, CA 94018
Phone: (415) 728–7377; **Fax:** (415) 728–8345
Key: Inn; 11 units; Superior–Deluxe; No smoking; Credit cards;
Handicapped access, 1 unit

The Pillar Point Inn, Princeton-by-the-Sea

Located on the only harbor between San Francisco and Santa Cruz is this Cape Cod–style b&b that proves a haven for homesick New Englanders. The inn was built to blend with the architecture of the quaint fishing village and offers eleven luxurious guest accommodations, all with views of the harbor, Half Moon Bay, and the Pacific Ocean. Each room offers a fireplace, private bath, European-style feather mattress, and bay or window seat, as well as VCR, concealed television, radio, and refrigerator. Five of the rooms boast a private steam bath. A public dining room and living room share an open fireplace and are furnished in country pine and maple; a separate conference room accommodates up to sixteen persons. The full and varied complimentary morning fare, which is served in the dining room, includes eggs, meat, bread, and fruit dishes. Guests enjoy a harbor-view terrace as well as afternoon tea.

Alamo Square Inn

719 Scott Street, San Francisco, CA 94117
Phone: (415) 922–2055; **Fax:** (415) 931–1304
Key: Inn; 12 units; Moderate–Deluxe; No smoking; Credit cards;
Handicapped access, 1 unit

This large 1895 Queen Anne–Victorian and atrium-adjoining 1896 Tudor Revival b&b overlooks Alamo Square and the city skyline. Oak floors, a grand staircase, period decor, and Oriental accents create an elegant setting for this b&b. Guest accommodations range from intimate double rooms to deluxe suites, most with private baths. Telephones are available in all rooms, and parking is available on the premises. The garden and solarium complex also offers several common rooms with fireplaces, where guests may linger over late-afternoon wine and snacks or evening sherry. The hearty full breakfast includes home-baked breads prepared by the resident chef. Catered dinners are available on arrangement.

Albion House

135 Gough Street, San Francisco, CA 94102
Phone: (415) 621–0896
Key: Inn; 8 units; Inexpensive–Moderate; Limited smoking; Credit cards; No handicapped access

Built after the great earthquake of 1906, the inn near Symphony Hall has gone through many periods of decor. The three-story building hosts a restaurant on the bottom floor and the b&b inn on the two upper levels. Each guest room offers a combination of Victorian, Oriental, and Californian decor and features many carved wooden antiques and brass beds. Several guest rooms have private sun decks, and all have private baths. Sherry is served fireside in the spacious living room, and breakfast in the dining room includes croissants, boiled eggs, fresh fruit, and juice.

San Francisco

The Andrews Hotel

624 Post Street, San Francisco, CA 94109
Phone: (415) 563–6877 / (800) 926–3739 (CA); **Fax:** (415) 928–6919
Key: Inn/Hotel; 48 units; Moderate; Smoking OK; Credit cards; No handicapped access

This neat and cheerful b&b is simply furnished with white wrought iron beds, desks, European lace curtains, and plants. This gracious European-style hotel also offers color television, private baths, and telephones in each room. Fresh fruit, baked goods, and coffee or tea are served on each floor in the morning. The inn is within walking distance of restaurants, stores, and theaters and is two blocks from Union Square. Complimentary wine is offered in the hotel's Italian restaurant. Parking is available for an additional charge.

The Archbishops Mansion Inn

1000 Fulton Street, San Francisco, CA 94117
Phone: (415) 563–7872
Key: Inn; 15 units; Moderate–Deluxe; Limited smoking; Credit cards; No handicapped access

Built for the archbishop of San Francisco in 1904, this elegantly restored mansion with open, carved mahogany staircase, stained-glass dome, and spacious country-manor guest suites is a luxurious b&b offering. The guest rooms, all with carved queen-size beds, private baths, sitting areas, and fireplaces, are filled with oriental carpets, museum-quality French antiques, canopies, oil paintings, and period chandeliers. As a salute to the nearby opera house, each guest room is named after a nineteenth-century opera. Guests gather for wine tastings in the late afternoon, and a French picnic basket packed with gourmet croissants, jams, juice, and beverages is delivered to the room at guests' specified time each morning.

Art Center Bed & Breakfast, San Francisco

Art Center Bed & Breakfast

1902 Filbert Street, San Francisco, CA 94123
Phone: (415) 567–1526
Key: Inn; 5 units; Moderate–Superior; No smoking; Credit cards; No handicapped access

Constructed in 1857 on a fresh-water lagoon that was used as a washerwoman's cove, the French Provincial building first accommodated gold-seeking guests en route from Yerba Buena (San Francisco) to the Presidio. The Wamsley Art Center now houses art workshops and suites complete with color television, radio, full kitchen with microwave oven (one with a "coffee bar" only), and, of course, original artwork. The private accommodations off a garden and a sunny patio include two with fireplaces, and all have two entrances. Breakfast is self-serve in your own kitchen with eggs, croissants, cereals, juice, and coffee, tea, or hot chocolate provided. A coffee maker also is furnished, along with easels for the artist-guest on the deck. The inn is conveniently located in the marina area between the bay and Union Street.

San Francisco

The Bed and Breakfast Inn

4 Charlton Court, San Francisco, CA 94123
Phone: (415) 921–9784
Key: Inn; 10 units; Moderate–Deluxe; No smoking; No credit cards;
No handicapped access

This ten-room inn, located in a quiet mews near Union Street, is filled with family antiques and fresh flowers and offers garden views. Above the main house is a private suite with living room, kitchen, latticed balcony, and a spiral staircase leading to a loft bedroom. Six of the cozy guest rooms boast private baths.

Bock's Bed and Breakfast

1448 Willard Street, San Francisco, CA 94117
Phone: (415) 664–6842
Key: Home; 3 units; Inexpensive–Moderate; No smoking; No credit cards; No handicapped access

This lovely Edwardian home in a residential section of the city is two blocks from Golden Gate Park and the University of California Medical Center. Guests may choose from accommodations with private or semiprivate bath, in-room coffee and tea, television, and telephone. Guests also have access to the refrigerator; a deck is available. A continental breakfast is served in a dining room with original redwood paneling and magnificent views of the city. A two-night minimum stay is required; weekly rates are available.

Casa Arguello

225 Arguello Boulevard, San Francisco, CA 94118
Phone: (415) 752–9482
Key: Inn; 5 units; Inexpensive; No smoking; No credit cards; No handicapped access

Located in a residential area just ten minutes from the center of the city, this inn offers simple yet comfortable accommodations. A mixture of decor can be found throughout the spacious b&b, with an emphasis on the old. The complimentary breakfast is served in the dining room. The hosts at the inn are fluent in Spanish.

Casita Blanca

330 Edgehill Way, San Francisco, CA 94127
Phone: (415) 564–9339; **Fax:** (415) 566–4737
Key: Cottage; 1 unit; Moderate; No smoking; No credit cards; No handicapped access

This country-style retreat, in the middle of the city near Golden Gate Park, sits high on a hill among the trees overlooking the city and bay. The one-bedroom cottage offers twin beds, an alcove with desk, and a fireplace, as well as a separate bathroom with stall shower and a fully-equipped kitchen. A continental breakfast is provided in the kitchen, ready for guests to assemble in the morning. Guests enjoy proximity to restaurants and city attractions, as well as a peaceful, private patio adjacent to the approximately sixty-year-old white "casita."

The Chateau Tivoli, San Francisco

The Chateau Tivoli

1057 Steiner Street, San Francisco, CA 94115
Phone: (415) 776–5462; **Fax:** (415) 776–0505
Key: Inn; 7 units; Moderate–Deluxe; No smoking; Credit cards; No handicapped access

This 1892 Victorian townhouse has been completely restored to its original splendor with hardwood floors, a grand oak staircase, stately columns, and double parlors. The historic building, located in the Alamo Square Historic District of the city, stands out with its more than twenty-color paint scheme highlighted by 23-karat gold-leaf trim. The interior of the inn is abundant with impressive, original antiques, including a $10,000 French canopy bed. The five guest rooms and two suites feature such amenities as marble baths, balconies, city views, stained glass, towers and turrets; four accommodations share two baths. The Luisa Tetrazzini Suite features a canopy bed, marble bath, balcony, and private parlor with fireplace. The elegant inn offers a generous continental breakfast each morning, which includes fresh fruit salad, cereal, yogurt, juice, and croissants, served in the dining room. Complimentary beverages are available; the inn will make arrangements for champagne, desserts, or roses on request. The Chateau also provides a romantic setting for small weddings, parties, meetings, or receptions.

Edward II Inn

3155 Scott Street, San Francisco, CA 94123
Phone: (415) 922–3000 / (800) 473–2846; **Fax:** (415) 931–5784
Key: Inn/Hotel; 31 units; Moderate–Deluxe; Smoking OK; Credit cards; No handicapped access

Located in the marina district, this 1915-vintage hotel offers proximity to the shopping areas of Chestnut and Union streets. Decorated throughout in an English country mood, the inn offers accommodations from the quaint to the deluxe. Six luxurious suites in the hotel and in a nearby carriage house are offered with canopy beds, wet bars, whirlpool baths, and more; kitchens and Jacuzzis are offered in some suites. Nineteen guest rooms boast private baths. The continental breakfast, hosted in the lobby area, is served by Café Lilly, located on the premises; the café also serves light luncheon fare. Also in the lobby of the hotel is a quaint pub open to the public as well. Parking is available in the surrounding neighborhood. Deluxe "Romance Packages" are available featuring champagne breakfast in bed and more.

Dorothy Franzblau

2207 Twelfth Avenue, San Francisco, CA 94116
Phone: (415) 564–7686
Key: Home; 1 unit; Moderate; No smoking; No credit cards; No handicapped access

Situated on top of Golden Gate Heights, this home b&b offers panoramic views of the bay. The private guest room has twin beds and bath. The comfortable stay includes a large breakfast and a late-day snack. Guests enjoy ample street parking and are close to public transportation.

Inn on Castro

321 Castro Street, San Francisco, CA 94114
Phone: (415) 861–0321
Key: Inn; 5 units; Moderate–Superior; No smoking; Credit cards; Handicapped access, 1 unit

This Victorian b&b offers a surprise of contemporary furnishings splashed with bright colors, vibrant paintings, and an abundance of exotic plants and fresh flowers. Guests are served a breakfast of orange juice and fine pastries in the upstairs dining room, also decorated in a contemporary yet hospitable motif. The inn is situated on a hill with views of the city and bay.

The Inn San Francisco

943 South Van Ness Avenue, San Francisco, CA 94110
Phone: (415) 641–0188 / (800) 359–0913; **Fax:** (415) 641–1701
Key: Inn/Cottage; 22 units; Moderate–Deluxe; Limited smoking; Credit cards; No handicapped access

This twenty-seven-room 1872 Victorian mansion with guest house has been restored to its original grandeur and features cozy, spacious rooms. All guest rooms are furnished in antiques and boast fresh flowers, telephones, refrigerators, and televisions; several rooms offer private Jacuzzi tubs. Accommodations include a two-room guest house with fireplace and balconies, as well as a luxury suite with spacious parlor, kitchen, bathroom, sun deck, and private use of the garden Jacuzzi. The flower-filled garden with gazebo and hot tub, as well as the rooftop sun deck with panoramic city views, provide a pleasant retreat for guests. Each morning a deluxe continental buffet breakfast is served in the double parlors. Limited reserved parking is available.

The Inn at Union Square

440 Post Street, San Francisco, CA 94102
Phone: (415) 397–3510; **Fax:** (415) 989–0529
Key: Inn/Hotel; 30 units; Superior–Deluxe; Smoking OK; Credit cards; Handicapped access, 2 units

Each guest room has been decorated with Georgian furnishings and colorful fabrics; most have king-size beds and sitting areas. Each floor hosts its own intimate lobby with a fireplace; these relaxing areas provide the sites for the morning breakfast of juice, fresh fruit, croissants, muffins, and scones and the afternoon tea with cakes and cucumber sandwiches. Wine and hors d'oeuvres are served after tea. A sixth-floor suite has a fireplace, bar, whirlpool bath, and sauna. Other extras at the inn include terry robes in the room and the Wall Street Journal and San Francisco Chronicle outside each door in the morning.

The Mansion Hotel

2220 Sacramento Street, San Francisco, CA 94115
Phone: (415) 929–9444; **Fax:** (415) 567–9391
Key: Inn/Hotel; 29 units; Moderate–Deluxe; Smoking OK; Credit cards; No handicapped access

The Mansion Hotel recently joined with The Hermitage House, another well-known area b&b, and now offers a larger historic b&b enclave, which also includes a restaurant, a theater, and a sculpture

The Mansion Hotel, San Francisco

park. Located in a fine residential neighborhood, the inn boasts elegant period furnishings filled with tapestries, paintings, crystal chandeliers, and an array of historic memorabilia. Each guest room is uniquely furnished, some with terrace views of Golden Gate Bridge; all accommodations feature private baths, telephones, fresh flowers, candies, and piped-in classical music. Guests enjoy fine wine in the parlor, a billiard room, and a full breakfast served in the country kitchen or in bed. The Mansion's intimate Cabaret Theatre is the setting for nightly events, including "ghostly" concerts. The hotel's stained-glass dining room hosts dinner on weekends and some weekdays.

Marina Inn B&B

3110 Octavia Street, San Francisco, CA 94123
Phone: (415) 928–1000; **Fax:** (415) 928–5909
Key: Inn/Hotel; 40 units; Inexpensive–Moderate; No smoking; Credit cards; Handicapped access, 1 unit

This four-story Victorian hotel on the corner of Octavia and Lombard streets welcomes guests with its elegant marble lobby in country furnishings. The extensively renovated and redecorated inn with bay windows offers a second-floor sitting room, which is the locale of the morning continental breakfast and afternoon sherry; a microwave is provided here as well. Each of the forty

Marina Inn B & B, San Francisco

rooms boasts pastel-flowered wallpaper, forest green carpet, quilts, pine furnishings, poster beds, and a full bath with marble sink. Guest baskets, televisions, and telephones are also available in each guest room.

Millefiori Inn

444 Columbus Avenue, San Francisco, CA 94133
Phone: (415) 433–9111; **Fax:** (415) 362–6292
Key: Inn/Hotel; 14 units; Moderate; Smoking OK; Credit cards; No handicapped access

This continental-style hotel is located in the heart of North Beach. Stained-glass windows, brasswork, chandeliers, hardwood furniture, and European bath fixtures decorate throughout. Rooms have individual flower themes and boast private baths, televisions, and telephones. A patio courtyard is the setting for a continental breakfast.

Moffatt House

431 Hugo Street, San Francisco, CA 94122
Phone: (415) 661–6210
Key: Inn; 4 units; Inexpensive; Smoking OK; Credit cards; No handicapped access

The 1910 Edwardian house near Golden Gate Park and the University of California Medical Center offers a casual, friendly retreat with its light interiors and flowering plants. Guests gather in the cheery kitchen for tourist information and a self-catered, generous continental breakfast of neighborhood-produce-market fruit, juice, home-baked muffins, toast, Danish, cheeses, and boiled eggs. The four guest rooms (two may accommodate four people) share baths. Queen-size, twin, and double beds are offered, and a crib is available for a one-time, nominal charge at this reasonable b&b.

The Monte Cristo

600 Presidio Avenue, San Francisco, CA 94115
Phone: (415) 931–1875 / 626–8777
Key: Inn/Hotel; 14 units; Moderate; Smoking OK; Credit cards; No handicapped access

The 1875-vintage inn is located just two blocks from restored Victorian shops. The spacious rooms are pleasantly furnished in authentic period pieces of early American and English antiques, wallpapers, down comforters, and fragrant potpourri. A popular guest accommodation is the Oriental Room with Chinese wedding bed and sunken tub. The breakfast includes fresh juice, home-baked breads and muffins, and cereals.

Petite Auberge

863 Bush Street, San Francisco, CA 94108
Phone: (415) 928–6000; **Fax:** (415) 775–5717
Key: Inn/Hotel; 26 units; Moderate–Deluxe; Limited smoking; Credit cards; No handicapped access

Petite Auberge, San Francisco

This romantic French country inn in the heart of downtown is a finely restored mansion offering an ornate, Baroque exterior design and warm, burnished woods on the interior. An antique carousel horse and fresh flowers greet guests, and an antique-filled lounge with fireplace is a cozy retreat. The twenty-six guest rooms all feature private baths, French wallpapers, antiques, handmade pillows, and quilted bedspreads; eighteen rooms boast fireplaces. A garden-view dining area offers a generous continental fare each morning, as well as afternoon tea. Among the special services extended to the pampered guests at the b&b is expert shoe polishing by inn "elves" each night.

The Queen Anne

1590 Sutter Street, San Francisco, CA 94109
Phone: (415) 441–2828 / (800) 227–3970; **Fax:** (415) 775–5212
Key: Inn/Hotel; 49 units; Moderate–Superior; Smoking OK; Credit cards; Handicapped access, 2 units

In the heart of the Civic Center area, this nineteenth-century refurbished guest house is a classic Queen Anne example with a cascading staircase, glass skylights, and window settees. Room furnishings blend the old and new with marble sinks, brick fireplaces, and antiques. The continental breakfast, along with the morning newspaper, is served in the room; afternoon tea and sherry are offered in the parlor. Laundry and business services (such as a conference facility, fax machine, and special corporate rates) are available.

The Red Victorian

1665 Haight Street, San Francisco, CA 94117
Phone: (415) 864–1978 / 864–1906; **Fax:** (415) 863–3293
Key: Inn/Hotel; 18 units; Inexpensive–Superior; No smoking; Credit cards; No handicapped access

This small upstairs hotel is as colorful as the well-known Haight-Ashbury neighborhood in which it resides. Teddy bears, red rugs, and lace curtains grace the inn and its uniquely decorated shared- and private-bath guest accommodations. A continental breakfast of croissants, muffins, and coffee is served in the bay-windowed "peace gallery." The bed & breakfast accommodations are a part of an entire complex that includes an art gallery, a human-relationship center, and a staff-training program.

Stanyan Park Hotel

1750 Stanyan Street, San Francisco, CA 94117
Phone: (415) 751–1000; **Fax:** (415) 668–5454
Key: Inn/Hotel; 36 units; Moderate–Deluxe; Smoking OK; Credit cards; Handicapped access, 2 units

This hotel of the early 1900s has been meticulously restored to its early glory, including the reconstruction of its rare cupola and roof balustrade. The thirty-six guest rooms and suites are individually decorated in Victorian furnishings, four-poster beds, brass chandeliers, and patterned wall papers and have the modern amenities of phones, color television, and private tiled bathrooms with pedestal sinks. Many of the guest accommodations overlook Golden Gate Park, and guests may park across the street from the b&b in an attended lot. Coffee, juice, croissants, and sweet rolls are served in the hotel dining room each morning.

Union Street Inn

2229 Union Street, San Francisco, CA 94123
Phone: (415) 346-0424
Key: Inn/Cottage; 6 units; Superior–Deluxe; No smoking; Credit cards; No handicapped access

The nineteenth-century Edwardian home-turned-inn has a garden setting within the city's downtown. The European-style decor includes canopy and brass beds, armoires, and private baths. A carriage house is separated from the inn by a garden and hosts a Jacuzzi for carriage-house guests' use only. The continental breakfast is served in the parlor, the garden, or the room.

Victorian Inn on the Park

301 Lyon Street, San Francisco, CA 94117
Phone: (415) 931–1830; Fax: (415) 931–1830
Key: Inn; 12 units; Moderate–Superior; Smoking OK; Credit cards; No handicapped access

Near Golden Gate Park in an area famed for its Victorian architecture, the 1897 inn also reflects turn-of-the-century San Francisco in its furnishings. Each room offers fresh flowers, comforters, down pillows, and private bath; some guest rooms boast fireplaces. Along with fruit and home-baked croissants comes a daily newspaper in the oak-paneled dining room each morning. Phones and television are available on request; the inn is able to accommodate small meetings.

The Washington Square Inn

1660 Stockton Street, San Francisco, CA 94133
Phone: (415) 981–4220
Key: Inn/Hotel; 15 units; Moderate–Deluxe; Limited smoking;
Credit cards; No handicapped access

   The small hotel is located in the heart of the city's Italian district
on historic Washington Square. Most guest rooms, decorated individually in English and French antiques, boast private baths, and all
have telephones. A complimentary breakfast of croissants, fresh
orange juice, and coffee is served in bed or by the hearth. Guests also
enjoy afternoon tea, as well as wine and hors d'oeuvres for guests
and their visitors.

The White Swan Inn

845 Bush Street, San Francisco, CA 94108
Phone: (415) 775–1755; **Fax:** (415) 775–5717
Key: Inn/Hotel; 26 units; Superior–Deluxe; Limited smoking; Credit
cards; No handicapped access

   This totally renovated b&b is filled with English country charm
created by the use of rich, warm woods, soft wallpapers, and an
abundance of cozy fireplaces. The uniquely decorated guest rooms
and two-room suite feature fireplaces, refrigerators, private baths,
telephones, and color televisions as well as bay windows, fresh flowers and fruit, antiques, and overstuffed chairs. Guests will enjoy the
generous breakfast in the dining room or in the solarium off the
courtyard-sheltered garden. An English tea is served each afternoon
in the peaceful English garden; a fireside living room and library
offer restful retreats as well. Innkeepers at this downtown b&b pam-
per guests by making sure guests' shoes are polished, their guest-
room fire is kindled, and the morning newspaper waits outside each
door.

The Willows

710 Fourteenth Street, San Francisco, CA 94114
Phone: (415) 431–4770
Key: Inn/Hotel; 11 units; Moderate; Smoking OK; Credit cards; No handicapped access

Convenient to downtown and Union Square, the inn also provides parking for guests. Rooms are individually furnished in "gypsy willow" furniture designed for the inn, antiques, armoires (with robes), Laura Ashley prints, and private phones. The continental breakfast, served in bed or in the sitting room, arrives with a morning paper. The "Hour of Apertif" each afternoon offers cheese and chilled wine to guests. The inn gives priority reservations to guests at its small French restaurant. The Willows has a gay and lesbian clientele.

Rancho San Gregorio, San Gregorio

Rancho San Gregorio

Route 1, Box 54, 5086 San Gregorio Road, San Gregorio, CA 94074
Phone: (415) 747–0810
Key: Inn; 5 units; Moderate–Superior; No smoking; No credit cards; No handicapped access

Oaks and pine-covered hills surround this country retreat on fifteen acres of ranchland, just forty-five minutes from San Francisco. The Spanish mission-style home with arches, heavy redwood beams, terra-cotta tile floors, and cactus-planted courtyard is furnished with carved oak antiques and homey memorabilia. The guest rooms are individually decorated and named for local creeks; all rooms have access to the upper deck, which affords spectacular views of valley farmland and wooded hills. Both private and semiprivate bath accommodations are available. Guests at Rancho San Gregorio enjoy badminton, volleyball, horseshoes, and lawn croquet; the complimentary morning fare includes fresh juice and fruit, home-baked breads and muffins, and a specialty of the day, such as apple-filled crepes or Swedish egg cake with wild blackberry sauce. The inn is also available for weddings, small groups, picnics, and barbecues.

The Panama Hotel & Restaurant

4 Bayview Street, San Rafael, CA 94901
Phone: (415) 457–3993
Key: Inn/Hotel; 17 units; Inexpensive–Moderate; Smoking OK; Credit cards; No handicapped access

This urban inn is situated in the central shopping area of town. Accommodations include cozy rooms, many with balconies. Most rooms have televisions and direct-dial telephones; ten units have private baths. Seven of the guest rooms have kitchenettes, but all rooms at this b&b/restaurant have access to the kitchen. The restaurant at the inn serves lunches and dinners but is closed on Mondays. The complimentary extended continental breakfast is offered to b&b guests only each morning, either in the restaurant or on the patio.

The Madison Street Inn

1390 Madison Street, Santa Clara, CA 95050
Phone: (408) 249–5541/249–6058
Key: Inn; 5 units; Moderate; No smoking; Credit cards; No handicapped access

This restored Queen Anne home in grays and blues is situated in a quiet residential area and has a pretty yard with red-brick pool, redwood deck, and hot tub. Guests enjoy a parlor decorated in oriental rugs and comfortable antiques, and its fireplace. The five antique-filled guest rooms with high ceilings are wallpapered and have plush peach carpeting. Three of the guest rooms have private baths, and the two rooms that share a bath have sink/vanity areas; one of the rooms is a family suite with queen-size bed and sofa bed. Breakfast treats at the inn may include Belgian waffles, eggs Benedict, and fresh blueberry muffins; the repast may be enjoyed in your room, on the patio, or in the dining room. A television, VCR, and movies are available, as are bicycles. Complimentary sherry is offered at all times, and dinner is available with advance reservation. The inn offers package stays for room, dinner, and tickets to the Winchester Mystery House.

Casa Madrona Hotel & Restaurant

801 Bridgeway, Sausalito, CA 94965
Phone: (415) 332–0502 / (800) 288–0502; **Fax:** (415) 332–2537
Key: Inn/Hotel/Cottages; 32 units; Moderate–Deluxe; Smoking OK;
Credit cards; Handicapped access, 1 unit

This historic 1885 Victorian is located fifteen minutes north of San Francisco across the Golden Gate Bridge. Situated on a hillside overlooking the harbor, the hotel is within walking distance of quaint town shops. Guest accommodations, located in the main house as well as in cottages, include sixteen modern, designer-decorated rooms with views. The award-winning restaurant at the inn features American cuisine, and guests enjoy a complimentary continental breakfast. Guests may also use the private Jacuzzi.

Sausalito Hotel

16 El Portal, Sausalito, CA 94965
Phone: (415) 332–4155
Key: Inn/Hotel; 15 units; Moderate–Deluxe; Smoking OK; Credit cards; No handicapped access

Located in the downtown area, this historic hotel offers free parking to its guests. All the guest rooms are decorated in Victorian antiques, but most notable is the Marquis de Queensbury Room, which allows occupants to sleep in General Ulysses Grant's bed by fireside. A continental breakfast is included.

Casa del Mar, Stinson Beach

Casa del Mar

37 Belvedere Avenue, P.O. Box 238, Stinson Beach, CA 94970
Phone: (415) 868-2124
Key: Inn; 5 units; Moderate–Deluxe; No smoking; Credit cards; No handicapped access

This new Mediterranean villa is perched on a terraced hill with views reaching out to the ocean. The terraced garden of jacarandas, passion flowers, bananas, palms, cacti, and fruit trees was once a University of California teaching garden; it now offers the inn's guests fragrant and peaceful strolls as well as the opportunity to get their hands dirty and help cut or pinch! The interior of the peach-colored villa also offers a Mediterranean feel with pavers on the floor, French doors that open to the ocean, paintings by local artists, and a blue-and-peach color scheme. Each guest room has been designed to take advantage of the ocean and garden views and boasts a private bath, queen-size bed, and down comforters; balcony rooms are available. Guests enjoy breakfast in the sunny dining room with views of the Pacific and Mount Tamalpais. The full meal varies but may include such delicacies as heuvos rancheros, freshly baked sesame corn bread, and apple–ricotta-cheese pancakes. The inn's living room with inviting fireplaces is a popular gathering spot where guests enjoy chatting and reading. Casa del Mar is just two blocks from the beach; a hiking path through Mount Tamalpais State Park begins 50 feet from the inn.

Tomales Country Inn

25 Valley Street, P.O. Box 376, Tomales, CA 94971
Phone: (707) 878–9992
Key: Inn; 5 units; Moderate; No smoking; No credit cards; No handicapped access

This rustic Victorian b&b is surrounded by trees, gardens and lily ponds. The decor of the inn is an interesting mixture of unique collectibles and art. Guests may relax in the spacious social room with library, game table, and fireplace. The morning breakfast fare includes juice, melon, granola, and something freshly baked, such as muffins or scones.

CENTRAL CALIFORNIA

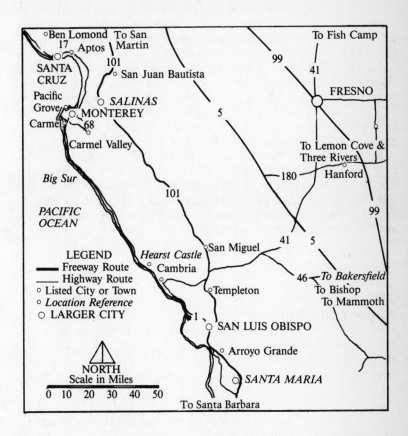

Ben Lomond To San
17 Aptos Martin
101
SANTA
CRUZ
San Juan Bautista
Pacific
Grove
SALINAS
Carmel MONTEREY
68
Carmel Valley

Big Sur

*PACIFIC
OCEAN*

101

To Fish Camp
99
41
FRESNO

To Lemon Cove &
Three Rivers
180 Hanford

99

LEGEND
━━ Freeway Route
── Highway Route
○ Listed City or Town
● *Location Reference*
◯ LARGER CITY

Hearst Castle
Cambria
San Miguel
41 5
46 — *To Bakersfield*
To Bishop
To Mammoth
Templeton

1
SAN LUIS OBISPO
Arroyo Grande
SANTA MARIA

NORTH
Scale in Miles
0 10 20 30 40 50

To Santa Barbara

Central Coast

California's Central Coast offers an array of small communities that dot the dramatic Pacific coast with unparalleled "Mediterranean" sunbathing beaches plus rich historical offerings. Original California missions can be found in several towns, such as San Juan Bautista, San Miguel, Carmel, and San Luis Obispo, and along with them stately examples of turn-of-the-century architecture, tree-lined streets, and coastal beauty. This region may be best known for the Hearst Castle in San Simeon, the state's most popular tourist attraction after Disneyland. But this region is becoming known for its grape-growing industry, as wineries and vineyards are beginning to compete with wine country as the state's "Little Napa." Travelers may stroll the boardwalk in Santa Cruz, observe the butterfly migration in Pacific Grove, and enjoy the quaint shops of Carmel, the "living Mission" and annual Mozart Festival in San Luis Obispo, and the unending, peaceful country drives through the rolling hills and wildflowers of the inland valleys.

Apple Lane Inn

6265 Soquel Drive, Aptos, CA 95003
Phone: (408) 475–6868
Key: Inn; 5 units; Moderate–Superior; No smoking; Credit cards; No handicapped access

This restored Victorian farmhouse was built in the 1870s among apple orchards and meadows. Before walking to the nearby beach about a mile away or visiting the local wineries, guests are invited to partake in a game of darts in the Cider Room. The five antique-decorated guest rooms offer both private and shared baths. The Blossom Room in mauves and white features a queen-size lace canopy bed and a spacious private bath with skylight and claw-foot tub. The farmhouse inn, set in two and a half acres of gardens, vineyards, and fields, serves a full country breakfast.

Bayview Hotel Bed & Breakfast Inn, Aptos

Bayview Hotel Bed & Breakfast Inn

8041 Soquel Drive, Aptos, CA 95003
Phone: (408) 688–8654
Key: Inn/Hotel; 14 units; Moderate–Superior; No smoking; Credit cards; No handicapped access

The 1878-built Victorian hotel with restaurant is a local architectural landmark. The three-story structure has been extensively restored with new paint, wall coverings, plumbing, and electrical systems, but the original marble fireplace and some furnishings still grace the rooms. At this writing the inn offers eight guest accommodations, but plans are underway to add six units in the currently unused third story of the inn by spring 1992. All guest rooms feature private baths, double beds, and antique furnishings; a two-room suite is also available. Breakfast at the Bayview is a continental fare of juice, fruit, pastries, müesli, yogurt, and cheese and is served in one of the restaurants dining rooms downstairs. The Veranda restaurant, located on the ground floor of the inn, serves dinner all week and lunch on weekdays. The popular bistro specializes in elegant "Americana" cuisine.

Aptos

Mangels House

570 Aptos Creek Road, P.O. Box 302, Aptos, CA 95001
Phone: (408) 688–7982
Key: Inn; 5 units; Moderate–Superior; Limited smoking; Credit cards; No handicapped access

This country Victorian house built in the 1880s is situated on four acres of garden and lawn and overlooks the State Redwood Forest, just 2/3 mile from the beach. The spacious rooms with high ceilings are decorated in a combination of antiques and painted pieces. A sitting room with library and piano is the locale of evening Dubonnet, cheese, and crackers by the large stone fireplace. The guest rooms, offering both shared and private baths, contain washbasins and individual touches such as wallpaper or stenciling and unusual art. The Mauve Room boasts its own marble fireplace. A full breakfast featuring a variety of egg dishes is included in the stay; guests may use the inn refrigerator for storing wine and picnic foods.

The Guest House

120 Hart Lane, Arroyo Grande, CA 93420
Phone: (805) 481–9304
Key: Home; 3 units; Inexpensive; Limited smoking; No credit cards; No handicapped access

This house, constructed in 1865 by a northeastern sea family, is located in the quaint Old Town area. It is decorated with New England heirlooms, antiques, oriental rugs, and oil paintings. The three guest rooms share two baths and boast fresh garden bouquets. The comfortable living room with a grand piano is the site of afternoon tea or wine. A full New England–style breakfast is served in the parlor, in the sun-room, or on the garden terrace surrounded by an abundance of colorful blooms.

Rose Victorian Inn

789 Valley Road, Arroyo Grande, CA 93420
Phone: (805) 481–5566
Key: Inn/Cottages; 7 units; Superior–Deluxe; No smoking; Credit cards; Handicapped access, 1 unit

This rose-colored, four-story inn complex built in 1885 consists of a main house and cottages that contain guest accommodations, as well as beautiful gardens with a rose arbor, gazebo, and koi ponds. The guest rooms, five in the house plus two cottages, offer king- or queen-size beds, nostalgic Victorian decor, and fresh roses from the garden. The inn's restaurant adjoins, serving gourmet dinners. A stay at the inn includes a full champagne breakfast served in the house's turn-of-the-century dining room and a five-course gourmet dinner at the restaurant. It has been rumored that the inn's special mascot is a "friendly" ghost from the past.

The Village Inn, Arroyo Grande

The Village Inn

407 El Camino Real, Arroyo Grande, CA 93420
Phone: (805) 489–5926
Key: Inn; 7 units; Moderate–Deluxe; No smoking; Credit cards; No handicapped access

Arroyo Grande

The new and the old were combined to create this recently built Victorian b&b with a western influence. The inn, near U.S. 101, has an exterior with clapboard siding and bay windows designed to capture a rural "village" feel; the interior of the b&b blends warm colors with antique furnishings and family heirlooms. The seven guest rooms, all with private baths and queen-size beds, are located upstairs and are furnished individually in a variety of color schemes with such special touches as window seats, skylights, wall coverings, and verandas. Soundproofing has been added. Guests may watch television in the living room, and the dining room with its wood-plank floor and antique oak furniture is the site of the full, gourmet breakfast each day; breakfast specialties include frittatas, quiches, and Swedish pancakes. Late-afternoon refreshments are also offered at the inn.

Chateau Des Fleurs

7995 Highway 9, Ben Lomond, CA 95005
Phone: (408) 336–8943
Key: Inn; 3 units; Moderate; No smoking; Credit cards; No handicapped access

This late-1870s Victorian mansion was once owned by the Bartlett family of pear fame; its pear trees still bear fruit for the morning breakfast. Guests may lounge on the front deck or in the gazebo and enjoy the garden with wishing well, flowers, fruit trees, and vegetables. The three spacious guest rooms, decorated in floral themes, feature private baths, iron and brass queen-size beds, ornate ceiling fans, and down comforters; the Rose Room boasts an in-room claw-foot tub on a raised platform. The Gallery common room with cozy, antique woodstove contains a library, stereo, television, piano, and organ. Breakfast, served in the formal dining room, includes homemade cinnamon rolls, muffins, coffee cake, fresh fruit, and a main course such as quiche, cheese blintzes, soufflés, omelettes, or Belgian waffles; French-blend coffee and juices are offered in the Gallery before breakfast. Guests enjoy sparkling cider, wine, eggnog, and cheese and crackers between 6:00 and 7:00 P.M.

Beach House

6360 Moonstone Beach Drive, Cambria, CA 93428
Phone: (805) 927–3136
Key: Home; 7 units; Moderate–Superior; No smoking; Credit cards;
No handicapped access

This private, three-story, A-frame house is situated on picturesque Moonstone Beach. The seven individually decorated guest rooms all boast private baths, antique oak furnishings, queen- or king-size beds, and breathtaking ocean views; two rooms feature fireplaces. Guests enjoy a sitting room on the ground floor as well as a second-floor common room that faces the ocean and has a large fireplace for chilly evenings as well as a large deck overlooking the ocean. The buffet-style breakfast with fresh fruit and muffins is served on the large dining-room table. Wine and cheese are offered each evening; telescopes and bicycles are available for guests' use.

The Blue Whale Inn

6736 Moonstone Beach Drive, Cambria, CA 93428
Phone: (805) 927–4647
Key: Inn; 6 units; Superior–Deluxe; No smoking; Credit cards; No
handicapped access

This newly built gray Cape Cod–style inn on the bluffs overlooks the Pacific Ocean and offers six individually designed minisuites. Each guest suite features a king- or queen-size canopy bed draped in French and English country fabrics that coordinate with the designer wall coverings. The luxurious accommodations with vaulted ceilings contain an armoire with television, a writing desk, and a telephone; further amenities include an oversized dressing room with small refrigerator, ceramic tiled bath, gas fireplace, picture window, and love seat. A complete country breakfast is served each morning in the dining room, which boasts three picture windows overlooking the ocean. The sitting room/library of the inn is the locale of afternoon wine and cheese and also offers picture-window views of the Pacific as well as a romantic woodstove, lots of reading material, and an entertainment center concealed in a country-French armoire. Guests enjoy a stroll along the paths of the inn's garden area, complete with benches and a waterfall pond.

The J. Patrick House, Cambria

The J. Patrick House

2990 Burton Drive, Cambria, CA 93428
Phone: (805) 927–3812
Key: Inn; 8 units; Moderate–Superior; No smoking; Credit cards; Handicapped access, 1 unit

This log home nestled in the pines is joined by an old-fashioned arbor and colorful garden to a private guest-room annex; together, they form this relaxing b&b retreat near the ocean. The log house contains an early American pine- and oak-furnished living room with a cheery fireplace, where guests gather for wine and cheese each evening, as well as a sunny dining room, where the breakfast of freshly ground coffee, home-baked cinnamon rolls and muffins, and fresh fruit with condiments is served. The guest rooms are individually decorated and reflect the same comfortable, traditional motif. All accommodations have private baths and cozy fireplaces. Warm, personal service is the hallmark of this b&b.

Olallieberry Inn

2476 Main Street, Cambria, CA 93428
Phone: (805) 927–3222
Key: Inn; 6 units; Moderate; No smoking; Credit cards; Handicapped access, 1 unit

The scrumptious dark-red berry that grows in the area is the namesake of this small historic inn at the far end of Cambria's East Village. The two-story, cream-colored Greek Revival–style home with delicate pinkish-red trim was built in 1873 and is registered with the Historic House Association of America. The six bedrooms of the home, decorated in tasteful late 1800s decor, are open to guests and boast specially selected linens and window and wall coverings. A hearty continental breakfast buffet is served in the white-wicker common room each morning; on weekends complimentary wine and appetizers are served in the front parlor. The inn is a short walk from charming shops and bistros.

Pickford House B&B

2555 MacLeod Way, Cambria, CA 93428
Phone: (805) 927–8619
Key: Inn; 8 units; Moderate; Limited smoking; Credit cards; Handicapped access, 1 unit

This recently built structure with a turn-of-the-century flavor offers interesting antiques, a spacious 1860s pub area, and views of the Santa Lucia Mountains. The guest rooms, all with televisions and private baths featuring claw-foot tubs and pull-chain toilets, are named after silent-movie stars, with the decor to match. Some rooms offer fireplaces with antique mantels. The full breakfast is served downstairs in the parlor, decorated with antiques and floral carpeting. Guests at the inn are given homemade cookies upon their departure.

The Cobblestone Inn

Junipero between Seventh & Eighth, P.O. Box 3185, Carmel, CA 93921
Phone: (408) 625–5222 / (800) AAA-INNS; **Fax:** (408) 625–0478
Key: Inn/Hotel; 24 units; Moderate–Deluxe; Limited smoking; Credit cards; No handicapped access

The Cobblestone Inn, Carmel

This country inn with an English country-garden atmosphere is just two blocks from the heart of Carmel's quaint shops and cafés. Guests cross a cobblestone courtyard to enter the living room and lounge with large stone fireplace; it is here that guests gather for tea, sherry, wine, and hors d'oeuvres. The two dozen guest rooms feature country antiques, romantic fireplaces, private baths, fresh fruit and flowers, soft quilts, wall-to-wall carpeting, and color television. Two suites are offered at the inn. A generous breakfast is served in the dining room or on the courtyard terrace, and picnic lunches may be ordered. As a special touch, the innkeepers will see that any shoes or golf clubs left outside a guest-room door are polished by the time guests open the door for their morning paper.

Cypress Inn

P.O. Box Y, Carmel, CA 93921
Phone: (408) 624-3871; **Fax:** (408) 624-8216
Key: Inn/Hotel; 33 units; Moderate–Deluxe; Smoking OK; Credit cards; No handicapped access

Originally opened in 1929, this landmark Spanish Mediterranean inn was carefully renovated in 1986. Located in the heart of Carmel Village, the inn features a spacious living room with fireplace and an intimate library overlooking a private garden/courtyard. A variety of rooms are offered to guests, most with oversized beds and all with private baths, telephones, and color cable televisions; some units boast sitting areas, wet bars, verandas, and ocean views. A continental breakfast is offered each morning; the inn boasts a full-service cocktail lounge. Owners' pets are welcome at Cypress Inn.

Happy Landing Inn

Monte Verde & Fifth streets, P.O. Box 2619, Carmel, CA 93921
Phone: (408) 624-7917
Key: Inn/Cottage; 7 units; Moderate–Superior; Limited smoking; Credit cards; No handicapped access

This 1925 Comstock-designed inn features guest rooms and a honeymoon cottage with antiques and cathedral ceilings. A ground-floor room opens onto a central garden with a pond and gazebo. Centrally located, the inn is just four blocks from the beach. The breakfast is served in the room each morning and features homemade breads and muffins, fresh fruit, and juice. A spacious lounge with cathedral ceilings and a stone fireplace offers daytime refreshments and relaxation.

Holiday House

Camino Real at Seventh Avenue, P.O. Box 782, Carmel, CA 93921
Phone: (408) 624-6267
Key: Inn; 6 units; Moderate; No smoking; No credit cards; No handicapped access

Carmel

Built in 1905, this quiet, residential-area inn has been hosting guests for more than fifty years. The brown-shingled house on a hillside with colorful gardens, fountain, and fish pond offers ocean views from the sun porch surrounded by pines. The individually decorated guest rooms offer such touches as slanted ceilings, ocean views, and brass beds; four rooms have private baths. A spacious living room with stone fireplace is the spot to relax, sip sherry, or enjoy the morning breakfast, which includes juice, cereals, fruit, sweet rolls and muffins, egg dishes, and beverages.

San Antonio House

P.O. Box 3683, Carmel, CA 93921
Phone: (408) 624–4334
Key: Inn; 4 units; Moderate–Superior; No smoking; Credit cards; No handicapped access

All four guest rooms at the inn have their own entrance, telephone, refrigerator, television, wood-burning fireplace, and private bath plus lots of antiques and paintings. The two-story turn-of-the-century house is surrounded by trees, gardens, lawns, and stone terraces and is close to shops, golfing, and the beach. Breakfast is served in the room, but guests may also dine in the courtyard. The expanded continental fare includes fresh fruit, juices, cereal, freshly baked pastries, and eggs.

Sandpiper Inn

2408 Bay View Avenue, Carmel, CA 93923
Phone: (408) 624–6433
Key: Inn; 15 units; Moderate–Superior; Limited smoking; Credit cards; No handicapped access

Offering a spectacular view of the ocean, the inn is within a pleasant walk of downtown. The guest rooms are decorated in antiques, and all have private baths. Accommodations include rooms with fireplaces, garden- or ocean-view rooms, and special honeymoon quarters. Breakfast is served at a large, formal dining-room table in the lounge, where television and the morning paper are also available.

Sea View Inn

P.O. Box 4138, Carmel, CA 93921
Phone: (408) 624–8778
Key: Inn; 8 units; Moderate; No smoking; Credit cards; No handicapped access

This 1906 three-story guest house is furnished with both antiques and contemporary pieces and has been redecorated throughout. Located just three blocks from the ocean and five blocks from town, it is situated centrally. Guest rooms, mostly with private bath, feature bay-window seats and large beds; one room features an intricate canopy bed with coordinated fabrics and wall covering. The homemade breakfast consists of fruit, juice, and muffins or coffee cake and is served fireside in the parlor, the site of afternoon sherry as well.

The Stonehouse Inn

Eighth below Monte Verde, P.O. Box 2517, Carmel, CA 93921
Phone: (408) 624–4569
Key: Inn; 6 units; Moderate–Superior; No smoking; Credit cards; No handicapped access

The turn-of-the-century home is most notable for its stone exterior, hand-shaped by Indians around 1906. The guest rooms, named after famous artist/guests from earlier days, feature airy colors, antiques, homemade quilts, fresh flowers, and fresh fruit and share two baths. The full breakfast is offered in the dining room or garden or by the large stone fireplace. Cheese and wine are offered each afternoon; guests enjoy cookies and port in the evening. Downtown is only two blocks away, and the beach is just three blocks from the inn.

Sundial Lodge

P.O. Box J, Carmel, CA 93921
Phone: (408) 624–8578
Key: Inn/Hotel; 19 units; Moderate–Deluxe; Limited smoking;
Credit cards; No handicapped access

This small hotel in the heart of town offers nineteen charming
rooms decorated with wicker, French country, or Victorian furnishings. All guest rooms offer private baths, touch-tone telephones, and
color television. Guests enter their rooms through the flower-filled
courtyard; most accommodations boast ocean or garden views. The
stay at Sundial includes a continental breakfast with homemade
muffins and a relaxing afternoon tea.

Vagabond's House

P.O. Box 2747, Carmel, CA 93921
Phone: (408) 624–7738
Key: Inn; 11 units; Moderate–Superior; Smoking OK; Credit cards;
Handicapped access, 2 units

This English Tudor country inn features wood-burning fireplaces
and refrigerators or kitchens in each antique-decorated guest room.
All rooms, some with "treetop" views, look out onto the flagstone
courtyard filled with oaks, ferns, flowers, and assorted hanging
plants. Each room has its own coffeepot, complete with fresh-
ground coffee, and a decanter of sherry. A continental breakfast is
served each morning in the room.

Robles Del Rio Lodge

200 Punta Del Monte, Carmel Valley, CA 93924
Phone: (408) 659–3705; **Fax:** (408) 659–5157
Key: Inn/Cottages; 31 units; Moderate–Superior; Smoking OK;
Credit cards; No handicapped access

This 1920s lodge was built originally as a private club and claims
to be the oldest lodge still operating in the valley. The rustic resort

sits on a mountaintop with panoramic views of sunny Carmel Valley. The thirty-one guest rooms and cottages range in decor from delicate Laura Ashley prints to board-and-batten country ambiance. Accommodations offer armoire-enclosed cable television; the cottages boast kitchenettes and fireplaces. A complimentary morning breakfast consisting of freshly baked muffins and breads, hard-boiled eggs, seasonal fruit, pastries, freshly squeezed juice, coffee, and herbal teas is served each morning around the large stone fireplace of the main-lodge living room. The Ridge Restaurant at the lodge serves French country–cuisine lunches and dinners to guests and the public every day except Monday.

The Valley Lodge

Carmel Valley & Ford roads, P.O. Box 93, Carmel Valley, CA 93924
Phone: (408) 659–2261 / (800) 641–4646; **Fax:** (408) 659–4558
Key: Inn/Cottages; 31 units; Moderate–Deluxe; Smoking OK; Credit cards; Handicapped access, 1 unit

This country inn with conference center is nestled in sunny Carmel Valley. Accommodations include garden/patio rooms, fireplace suites with wet bars and decks, and one- and two-bedroom cottages with fireplaces and kitchens. All guest rooms are individually decorated in a blend of antiques, reproductions, and comfortable country pieces and have open-beamed ceilings and rustic-looking woods. Fresh coffee and tea, color cable television, and flowers fresh from the garden are special touches for the guests' enjoyment. Guests may enjoy the pool, a hot spa, a sauna, a fitness center, and a game area. The inn is just a short walk from village shops and restaurants. A complimentary breakfast is served in the conference-center dining room or in the room. Groups of up to thirty may be accommodated in the conference facilities.

Del Monte Beach Inn

1110 Del Monte Avenue, Monterey, CA 93940
Phone: (408) 649–4410 / (800) 727–4410
Key: Inn/Hotel; 18 units; Inexpensive–Moderate; No smoking; Credit cards; No handicapped access

Monterey

This quaint European–style b&b hotel was built in the 1920s and has been restored throughout. The affordable inn offers rooms with mainly queen-size beds and such touches as colorful flower boxes, shutters, country curtains, calico wallpaper, and polished oak fixtures; guests enjoy bubble baths in the old-fashioned claw-foot tubs. Accommodations include a two-room suite as well as a full-service apartment with kitchen; all but two accommodations share baths. Each morning guests enjoy a breakfast of fresh rolls and muffins, fresh fruit, and juices in the downstairs parlor. The inn is located near the heart of Monterey, across the boulevard from the beach on Monterey Bay. Del Monte Beach is well equipped for families and offers student discounts.

The Jabberwock

598 Laine Street, Monterey, CA 93940
Phone: (408) 372–4777
Key: Inn; 7 units; Moderate–Deluxe; No smoking; No credit cards; No handicapped access

Goose-down pillows, romantic Victorian beds, eyelet-lace linens, and fresh flowers await guests who visit this converted convent that is only four blocks from Cannery Row and the Monterey Bay Aquarium and near the 17-mile drive. Guests enjoy the living-room sun porch that overlooks fern falls or the estate gardens, the site of evening hors d'oeuvres and aperitifs. The breakfasts, which are "razzleberry flabjous," are served fireside in the elegant dining room or in the room; the innkeepers "tuck" guests into bed with cookies and milk. The guest rooms feature a second-floor suite with an oversized king bed, a fireplace, private bath, dressing room, and spectacular views of the bay. The third floor of the inn, the Garrett Floor, boasts two guest rooms that share a sitting room and bath.

Old Monterey Inn

500 Martin Street, Monterey, CA 93940
Phone: (408) 375–8284
Key: Inn/Cottage; 10 units; Superior–Deluxe; No smoking; No credit cards; No handicapped access

Old Monterey Inn, Monterey

Surrounded by an acre of landscaped grounds with gardens and old oak trees, this 1920s English country home is within walking distance of the historic sites of Monterey. The living room tempts guests with a warming fireplace and a sampling of wines and cheeses. Rooms feature wicker and English antiques, skylights, fireplaces, and garden views; the Ashford Suite boasts a bedroom with king-size bed, a private bath, a dressing room, and a wisteria-draped sitting room with wood-burning fireplace, bay window, and antique pine furnishings. A separate cottage has stained glass and a bay-window seat. The full breakfast is served in the dining room or in the room.

The Spindrift Inn

652 Cannery Row, Monterey, CA 93940
Phone: (408) 646–8900 / (800) 841–1879; **Fax:** (408) 646–5342
Key: Inn/Hotel; 41 units; Superior–Deluxe; Smoking OK; Credit cards; Handicapped access, 2 units

Once referred to as the "old Chinese hotel" by author John Steinbeck, this hotel b&b has been totally rebuilt after years of being vacant. The tastefully appointed four-story inn has a New Orleans look and boasts colorful flower boxes. Its superb location is just one and one-half blocks from the aquarium, directly on the beach in Cannery Row. All forty-one guest rooms are distinctly decorated and furnished with canopies, imported fabrics, feather beds, oriental carpets, window seats, fireplaces, and comforters; some rooms have saunas. Guest rooms offer such extras as remote-control television in armoires, nightly turn-down service, refrigerators, and Swiss chocolates, and all rooms have private marble-and-brass baths with second telephone and hair dryers. The continental breakfast arrives with the morning newspaper on a silver tray and is enjoyed in the room. Afternoon tea is offered, and guests may relax on the roof garden with ocean vistas. Lunch and dinner room service is available at the hotel; bay-view meeting rooms may be reserved.

Centrella Hotel, Pacific Grove

Centrella Hotel

612 Central Avenue, P.O. Box 51157, Pacific Grove, CA 93950
Phone: (408) 372–3372; **Fax:** (408) 372–2036
Key: Inn/Hotel/Cottages; 26 units; Moderate–Deluxe; No smoking; Credit cards; Handicapped access, 1 unit

Located at the tip of the Monterey Peninsula, this century-old Victorian hotel invites guests to enjoy its brick walkways and sur-rounding gardens. The morning paper is delivered to each suite and cottage. All accommodations are appointed with hand-selected antiques and shared or private baths with claw-foot tubs. All suites feature skylights, wet bars, and color televisions, while cottages contain fireplaces, televisions, refrigerators, and wet bars. Both the complimentary breakfast and evening wine, sherry, and hors d'oeuvres are served buffet style before a cheery fire.

Gatehouse Inn, Pacific Grove

Gatehouse Inn

225 Central Avenue, Pacific Grove, CA 93950
Phone: (408) 649–8436
Key: Inn; 8 units; Moderate–Deluxe; Limited smoking; Credit cards; Handicapped access, 1 unit

Just one block from the ocean is this 1884 Victorian home, originally built as a seaside cottage. The lovingly restored inn features ocean views, period furnishings, and unique and colorful hand-printed wall coverings that are made with Victorian hand-mixed pigments. Each guest room offers a unique decor, from the Italian Room, with a 1900 Venetian chandelier and bath decorated in

Italian marble, to the Turkish Room, boasting a brass and inlaid mother-of-pearl bed and a wallpapered ceiling that grants the ambiance of being in a Moorish tent looking up at the midnight stars. The inn also offers two Art Deco–style Hollywood rooms that are reminiscent of the glamorous 1920s and 1930s. The morning fare is served in the guest kitchen and in the dining room and typically includes croissants, homemade muffins and cinnamon rolls, fresh fruit, granola, cereals, and quiche. Beverages are available any time plus afternoon tea, which includes sherry, wine, hors d'oeuvres, and chocolates. Guests at the Gatehouse enjoy Cannery Row attractions within walking distance, as well as a generous supply of books, games, newspapers, and magazines available at the inn.

The Gosby House, Pacific Grove

The Gosby House

643 Lighthouse Avenue, Pacific Grove, CA 93950
Phone: (408) 375-1287
Key: Inn; 22 units; Moderate–Superior; No smoking; Credit cards; No handicapped access

In the heart of historic Pacific Grove, this tastefully restored Queen Anne mansion with rounded corner tower and bay windows offers two parlors, one offering late-afternoon tea by the fire and one that hosts the generous buffet breakfast, which may be taken to the garden or to the room on a tray. The guest rooms feature polished natural woods, comforters, delicate wallpaper prints, ruffled curtains, armoires, fireplaces, and fresh fruit, and all but two accommodations have private baths with antique claw-foot tubs or modern tubs. Two suites offer kitchenettes. Hot cider, sherry, or tea are offered each evening.

Green Gables Inn, Pacific Grove

Green Gables Inn

104 Fifth Street, Pacific Grove, CA 93950
Phone: (408) 375–2095
Key: Inn; 11 units; Moderate–Superior; Limited smoking; Credit cards; Handicapped access, 1 unit

This half-timbered, step-gabled mansion on the edge of the Pacific Grove shoreline offers a panoramic view of Monterey Bay. The living room, with antiques and a stained-glass–adorned fireplace, is the locale of afternoon tea. Each morning a generous breakfast is served in the dining room or in the cozy living-room alcoves. The guest accommodations include upstairs rooms and guest rooms in the carriage house across the courtyard. Rooms feature soft colors, views, flowers, fruit, cozy quilts, and antiques. Suites at the inn have sitting rooms or areas with fireplaces, bedrooms, and private baths.

The House of Seven Gables Inn, Pacific Grove

The House of Seven Gables Inn

555 Ocean View Boulevard, Pacific Grove, CA 93950
Phone: (408) 372–4341
Key: Inn; 14 units; Moderate–Deluxe; No smoking; Credit cards; No handicapped access

Spectacular ocean views are enjoyed from each of the fourteen guest rooms at this 1886-built Victorian inn. Each guest room boasts a private bath, elegant European antiques, oriental rugs, chandeliers, and antique stained-glass windows. A generous full breakfast is served in the stately dining room with chandelier; high tea is offered each day at 4:00 P.M. The inn is conveniently located near all of the Monterey Peninsula attractions.

Old St. Angela Inn

321 Central Avenue, Pacific Grove, CA 93950
Phone: (408) 372–3246
Key: Inn; 8 units; Moderate–Superior; No smoking; Credit cards; No handicapped access

Just one-half block from the ocean and within walking distance of Cannery Row is this 1910-built country home. Converted to a rectory and then to a convent in 1928, the Cape Cod–style inn has returned to its origins with country pine furnishings, soft quilts, fresh flowers, and fine linens. Guests relax with afternoon wine, tea, or sherry by the living-room fireplace, and outside, enjoy the peaceful garden patio or a soak in the gazebo-enclosed Jacuzzi. Some rooms at the inn offer such amenities as private sitting areas, canopy beds, and handmade country pine furniture; accommodations include both private and shared baths. The Carriage House is a unique loft room with kitchenette and may accommodate up to four people. Breakfast is served in the glass-and-redwood solarium; guests help themselves to champagne, home-baked muffins and breads, fresh fruits, and more.

Pacific Grove Inn

581 Pine Avenue, Pacific Grove, CA 93950
Phone: (408) 375–2825
Key: Inn; 10 units; Moderate–Superior; No smoking; Credit cards; Handicapped access, 1 unit

This four-story Queen Anne–Victorian mansion was built in 1904. Situated just two blocks from Main Street and five blocks from the beach, the inn overlooks picturesque Monterey Bay. Rose gardens bloom around the inn, which has been completely renovated yet hosts its original woodwork and fretwork. Cherrywood antique furnishings and Belgian wool paisley carpets decorate throughout. The elegant guest rooms and suites boast private baths, brass beds, roman blinds, and George Washington Bates bedspreads, as well as enclosed televisions with remote control,

Pacific Grove Inn, Pacific Grove

heated towel racks, and gas-jet fireplaces; some rooms offer views of the bay. The complimentary continental breakfast consists of juice, fresh fruit, muffins, assorted breads, homemade granola, cereal, and yogurt.

Bed & Breakfast San Juan

315 the Alameda, P.O. Box 613, San Juan Bautista, CA 95045
Phone: (408) 623–4101
Key: Home; 5 units; Moderate; Limited smoking; No credit cards; Handicapped access, 1 unit

The 1858 Wilcox-Lang House, a well-established b&b home, is just two blocks from historic downtown San Juan Bautista. Guests here may stroll to the mission with its graceful arches, to California's second-most-visited State Historic Park, and to various boutiques and restaurants. The five guest rooms and the common room at the b&b feature period American furnishings; reservations are required in advance.

Heritage Inn, San Luis Obispo

Heritage Inn

978 Olive Street, San Luis Obispo, CA 93405
Phone: (805) 544–7440
Key: Inn; 9 units; Moderate; No smoking; Credit cards;
Handicapped access, 2 units

Within walking distance of historic downtown yet yielding creek-side and mountain views, this turn-of-the-century inn offers an ideal central location. Recently redecorated throughout, the inn is furnished in warm antiques; cheerful colors and fresh flowers abound; and each guest room hosts either a cozy window seat, fireplace, or walk-out terrace with views. Each room has its own vanity/sink area, and shared baths boast authentic claw-foot tubs, complete with bubble bath and pull-chain toilets. Guests also enjoy three accommodations with private baths. A large home-baked continental breakfast is served each morning in the fireside dining room, while wine and cheese are offered each evening in the parlor.

Country Rose Inn Bed & Breakfast, San Martin

Country Rose Inn Bed & Breakfast

455 Fitzgerald Avenue #E, San Martin, CA 95046
P.O. Box 1804, Gilroy, CA 95021
Phone: (408) 842–0441
Key: Inn; 5 units; Moderate–Superior; No smoking; Credit cards;
No handicapped access

This Dutch Colonial manor was originally built in the 1920s as
a ranch house nestled in a peach orchard. The farm dwelling has
been extensively remodeled as an inn and is still surrounded by
country scenery with views of the foothills and lots of ancient valley oaks, pine, and magnolia trees, ivy, and violets. The tranquil
b&b offers five guest accommodations, all with private baths. Each
guest room carries a rose motif, and special touches include some
window seats, wicker furnishings, Victorian wall coverings, a fireplace, and antiques. The romantic Rambling Rose Suite boasts a
paisley-covered king-size bed, a sitting room accessed through
French doors, and a double-sink bathroom with whirlpool tub. The
common areas of the inn are on the ground floor and offer pastoral
views of the grounds. Guests enjoy a baby grand piano in the salon,
a reading room, and walks through the gardens. The Breakfast
Room is part of the large country kitchen where guests gather for
the full home-cooked fare. In addition to juice and granola, the
menu may include orange French toast served with fruit, potato

custard with cream biscuits and fruit, mushroom-yogurt pie, lemon-shirred eggs, or spinach-ricotta pie, to name a sampling. Breakfast desserts range from breakfast apple pie to apricot shortcake.

The Babbling Brook Bed & Breakfast Inn, Santa Cruz

The Babbling Brook Bed & Breakfast Inn

1025 Laurel Street, Santa Cruz, CA 95060
Phone: (408) 427–2437
Key: Inn; 12 units; Moderate–Superior; No smoking; Credit cards; Handicapped access, 1 unit

Cascading waterfalls, a meandering creek, and an acre of gardens, pines, and redwoods surround this secluded inn built on the foundation of an 1870s tannery and an Ohlone Indian village. The dozen guest accommodations offer country French decor, private baths, telephones, televisions, fireplaces, private decks, and outside entrances; two rooms feature deep-soaking whirlpool tubs. The Countess Room has stained glass, a fireplace, library, and antiques. A country buffet breakfast and afternoon wine and cheese are included in the stay. The inn is within walking distance of the beach, wharf, shopping, and tennis.

Chateau Victorian

118 First Street, Santa Cruz, CA 95060
Phone: (408) 458–9458
Key: Inn; 7 units; Moderate–Superior; No smoking; Credit cards;
No handicapped access

This turn-of-the-century home was converted to a b&b in 1983 and is situated just a block from the beach near the boardwalk and wharf. The guest rooms all feature queen-size beds, private tiled baths, fireplaces, individually controlled heating systems, and Victorian decor; most accommodations overlook the gardens or the patio, and one room offers a view of the bay. An expanded continental breakfast of fruit juice, fruit, croissants, and muffins may be enjoyed in the dining room or in several areas surrounding the outside of the inn. Late-afternoon snacks and refreshments are also included in the stay at Chateau Victorian.

Cliff Crest

407 Cliff Street, Santa Cruz, CA 95060
Phone: (408) 427–2609
Key: Inn; 5 units; Moderate–Superior; No smoking; Credit cards;
No handicapped access

This 1887 estate is a historical landmark noted for its gardens and proximity to the ocean. Each guest room has its own bath, antique furnishings, and fresh flowers; the Belvedere and Rose rooms offer views of the Pacific. The smallest unit, the Pineapple Room, boasts a pineapple-carved four-poster bed and an 1887 stained-glass window, and the Empire Room offers a king-size four-poster bed and fireplace. The full breakfast features juice, fresh fruit, muffins, or coffee cake, and a main entree such as quiche or a frittata and is served in the room or in the downstairs solarium.

The Darling House, Santa Cruz

The Darling House

314 West Cliff Drive, Santa Cruz, CA 95060
Phone: (408) 458–1958
Key: Inn/Cottage; 8 units; Moderate–Deluxe; Limited smoking; Credit cards; No handicapped access

The sweeping verandas of this preserved Mission Revival home that was built in 1910 overlook the Pacific Ocean and Monterey Bay. The oceanside grounds of the residence are filled with citrus trees, roses, palms, and blossoms. The interior of the house has eight different inlaid hardwoods found on walls, floors, and doors as well as beveled glass, stenciled borders, and open-hearth fireplaces. The guest rooms and separate cottage are decorated in period pieces with Tiffany lamps, matching antique bedroom suites, and cozy down comforters and pillows. The cottage sleeps a family of four. Breakfast consists of goodies made from scratch and is served in the ocean-view dining room. Guests enjoy a hot tub/Jacuzzi located behind the inn, and the innkeepers can arrange horse-drawn carriage rides along the ocean.

Santa Cruz

Pleasure Point Inn Bed & Breakfast

2-3665 E. Cliff Drive, Santa Cruz, CA 95062
Phone: (408) 475–4657
Key: Home; 3 units; Moderate–Superior; No smoking; Credit cards;
No handicapped access

This tidy beachhouse with blue awnings and bright blooms
overlooks Monterey Bay and offers ocean views from most of its
rooms. The cozy home-style inn offers three guest rooms, each
with private bath and unique beach decor. The Pleasure Point
Suite boasts a sitting room with fireplace and breathtaking ocean
views from its private deck. Breakfast is served in the dining room,
at a more intimate table by the wine bar with views of the bay, or
on the deck, weather permitting; the morning fare includes juice,
fruit-filled croissants, cakes, and breads. Evening wine and hors
d'oeuvres are served in the comfortable common room. The inn is
within walking distance of shops and excellent surfing beaches.
Pleasure Point Inn charters a 40-foot cabin cruiser, which guests
may reserve for romantic sunset cruising, whale-watching, or fishing; advance reservations are usually necessary for these popular
outings.

Country House Inn

91 Main Street, Templeton, CA 93465
Phone: (805) 434–1598
Key: Inn; 6 units; Moderate; No smoking; Credit cards; No handi-
capped access

This designated historic site is located on Main Street in the
rustic town of Templeton, in the heart of the area's wine country.
The 1886-built Victorian offers guest rooms with either king- or
queen-size beds, private as well as shared baths, and antique furnishings. The main areas of the house feature two fireplaces for
relaxing or meeting with friends. A full breakfast is served in the
formal dining room and boasts home-baked breads and fresh fruit.
Guests at the inn may walk to the quaint shops of the western
town and enjoy the inn's surrounding lawns and flower gardens.

Central Valley

California's Central Valley offers a wide spectrum of scenery, from agricultural fields to snow-capped mountains, from deserts with creeks to nature's intriguing Devil's Postpile, and from Death Valley to Mount Whitney. Visitors delight in ghost towns, ski resorts, and unlimited recreation. The Central Valley is so wide that you cannot see from one side to the other, and it boasts one of the richest agricultural areas in the world, an area growing everything from dry crops, such as cotton, to intensive crops, such as table grapes, wines, fruits, nuts, and vegetables. The southern portions of the valley are known for their oil production. The area is notable for its extreme weather variations, which range from hot temperatures in the summer months to tule fog conditions and colder weather in the wintertime. Bishop lies on the edge of the Sierra Nevada in the Owens Valley. The valley is flanked by the spectacular rise of these mountains and also boasts desertlike conditions. It is noted for its winter skiing and the Mammoth Mountain and June Lake recreational offerings. The Owens Valley is not noted, however, for its agricultural production due to the diversion of its water supply to Los Angeles.

1898 Chalfant House

213 Academy, Bishop, CA 93514
Phone: (619) 872–1790
Key: Inn; 6 units; Inexpensive–Moderate; No smoking; Credit cards; No handicapped access

P. A. Chalfant, the editor and publisher of the valley's first newspaper, built this home in 1898. The beautifully restored house, in the center of the Western village–style town, offers tastefully furnished guest rooms, all with comfortable beds, antiques, handmade quilts and comforters, private baths, ceiling fans, and central air conditioning. The suite offers a private parlor and television. Guests may relax in the parlor with fireplace, the site of hot mulled cider or frosty orange drink and banana bread each afternoon and ice-cream sundaes in the evening. A full breakfast is served in the fireplace dining room and includes juice, fresh fruit, homemade jams and bread, and a special entree, such as Dutch baby with ham, maple pecan syrup, and hot fruit. The inn is within walking distance of shops, restaurants, the park, and a movie theater.

The Matlick House

1313 Rowan Lane, Bishop, CA 93514
Phone: (619) 873–3133
Key: Inn; 4 units; Moderate; No smoking; No credit cards; No handicapped access

This turn-of-the-century ranch house, originally owned by the apple orchard-ranching Matlick family, is nestled at the base of the valley between the Whites and the Sierra Nevada mountains. The two-story house with spacious first- and second-story porches is shaded by eighty-year-old elms and offers guests four suites, all with private baths, floral or country prints, handmade quilts, lace curtains, antiques, and ceiling fans. Several of the guest rooms boast views of the Sierras; Mabel's Suite enjoys a private exit to the second-story porch. Wine is served in the living room or on the veranda nightly, and a full country breakfast of freshly squeezed orange juice, biscuits, gravy, country fries, bacon, sausage, and eggs is served in the dining area. Picnic baskets are provided for a nominal fee at this b&b surrounded by quiet and fresh mountain air.

Karen's Bed & Breakfast Yosemite Inn

1144 Railroad Avenue, P.O. Box 8, Fish Camp, CA 93623
Phone: (209) 683–4550 / (800) 346–1443
Key: Inn; 3 units; Moderate; No smoking; No credit cards; No handicapped access

This blue contemporary-style country inn was built as a b&b in 1989. Situated at an elevation of 5,000 feet and nestled among towering pine, fir, and cedar trees, the inn is just 1 mile from Yosemite National Park. Guests enjoy an upstairs sitting area with cozy gas fireplace as well as a comfortable living room with woodstove. The formal dining room is the setting for the full country breakfast, often by candlelight. Guests are treated to an assortment of hot drinks, fruit, and juice as well as a main entree such as waffles, pancakes or eggs, potatoes, and coffee cakes. Afternoon refreshments of seasonal drinks and cookies or crackers and cheese are served. The three guest rooms of the inn all have private baths and carry a color

Karen's Bed & Breakfast Yosemite Inn, Fish Camp

theme of blue, peach, or rose. The light and airy accommodations offer queen beds or twin daybeds. Innkeepers are happy to assist the guest in planning any of the area's bountiful recreational offerings.

Yosemite Fish Camp Inn B&B

1164 Railroad Avenue, P.O. Box 25, Fish Camp, CA 93623
Phone: (209) 683–7426
Key: Home; 3 units; Inexpensive–Moderate; No smoking; Credit cards; No handicapped access

This two-story mountain home is surrounded by silver-tipped Christmas trees and meadows and overlooks a mountain pond and river. The three guest accommodations are located on the second story, and each room offers a view of the forest. The homey guest rooms are decorated uniquely in country style with antiques, oak and brass beds, and original Yosemite art pieces; the common sitting room hosts a cozy antique wood-burning stove. For breakfast, guests help themselves to coffee, tea, and juice on the table before being served the generous fare of fresh fruits and such home-cooked delicacies as fruit pancakes, French toast, homemade coffee cakes and muffins, and sausage and eggs. Guests enjoy tea, coffee, specially bottled wine, and other treats throughout the day. The inn is conveniently situated for winter skiing, golfing, horseback riding, and summer water sports and is close to the historic Yosemite Sugarpine Railroad.

The Irwin Street Inn

522 N. Irwin Street, Hanford, CA 93230
Phone: (209) 584–9286
Key: Inn/Hotel; 30 units; Moderate; Smoking OK; Credit cards; Handicapped access, 1 unit

This charming Victorian inn with popular restaurant is a few steps from Hanford's enchanting downtown area, rich in historic buildings and small-town activities. The Irwin Street Inn hosts a profusion of leaded-glass windows and antiques throughout its guest rooms and intimate restaurant, which serves breakfast and lunch daily and a five-course gourmet dinner on Friday and Saturday nights. Guest accommodations, scattered throughout the adjacent turn-of-the-century structures, all feature private baths and such detailing as oak-rimmed tubs, pull-chain toilets, four-poster beds, armoires, and oriental rugs. The breakfast of homemade goodies is offered in the main-house dining area, on the Victorian, brick-lined garden patio, or in the privacy of the guest room. Hanford is about one hour's drive from Sequoia National Park.

Lemon Cove Bed & Breakfast Inn

33038 Sierra Drive (Highway 198), Lemon Cove, CA 93244
Phone: (209) 597–2555
Key: Inn; 7 units; Inexpensive–Moderate; No smoking; Credit cards; No handicapped access

The scent of orange blossoms fills the air around this country b&b 23 miles from Sequoia National Park. The two-story English countryhouse is surrounded by acres of orange orchards, and, in season, guests may pick oranges for themselves. The country-Victorian-decorated guest rooms boast cozy comforters and antiques. Four upstairs rooms have private baths; two upstairs rooms share a bath. The Chantilly Lace Room offers a king-size bed, whirlpool tub, private bath, balcony, and fireplace. Guests enjoy a new television lounge downstairs as well as spectacular mountain views from the redwood deck with gazebo. The full breakfast includes a "chef's specialty," such as stuffed French toast with ham, fresh fruit, and syrup, along with juice and coffee, and is served in the dining room.

Snow Goose Bed & Breakfast Inn, Mammoth Lakes

Snow Goose Bed & Breakfast Inn

57 Forest Trail, P.O. Box 946, Mammoth Lakes, CA 93546
Phone: (619) 934–2660 / (800) 874–7368
Key: Inn; 18 units; Moderate–Deluxe; Limited Smoking; Credit cards; No handicapped access

This European-style country inn, painted blue with white trim, sports flower-filled window boxes and is surrounded by pine trees and aspens. The former lodge offers a comfortable living room decorated with French art and hosts a fireplace, a wide-screen television, and a cabinet full of games. The adjoining dining room is the site of the morning breakfast, served buffet style. The full fare may include such delectables as quiche, blueberry pancakes, filled pastry puffs, and frittatas served with fresh fruit, muffins, and breads. Beverages and hors d'oeuvres such as fresh vegetables and dip, fondue, and cheese balls are served each afternoon. The guest rooms at the inn are all individually decorated and include two-bedroom suites and kitchenettes; most rooms have queen-size beds and all rooms have private baths, color televisions, telephones, brass beds, and some antiques. The inn is close to shopping, horseback riding, hot-air ballooning, mountain-bike rentals, hiking, fishing, and lake recreation; honeymoon and snow-ski packages are available.

The Cort Cottage

P.O. Box 245, Three Rivers, CA 93271
Phone: (209) 561–4671
Key: Cottage; 1 unit; Moderate; No smoking; No credit cards; No handicapped access

Overlooking mountains and meadows of wildflowers is this b&b cottage nestled in a hillside near the main house. The contemporary wooden cottage, not far from the entrance to Sequoia National Park, was built in 1985 and offers a full kitchen and bath, a double bed, and comfortable sofa with double hide-a-bed. The b&b boasts a large half-circle window in the living room and a unique, spacious deck constructed from the bottom of a wine barrel. Coffee and tea are stocked in the kitchen of the cottage, and the gracious innkeepers deliver the morning breakfast of juice, fruit, muffins or fruit bread, and cereal as well as fresh eggs for the guest to cook as desired. Guests enjoy a hot tub for two, located directly under the Milky Way!

SOUTHERN CALIFORNIA

Known best as the home of Disneyland and the Hollywood stars, the "southland" also boasts spectacular swimming, surfing, and yachting from Santa Barbara to San Diego, mountain retreats, and desert playgrounds. Within this varietal expanse may be found serene country settings such as citrus-filled Ojai, the vineyard and horse-ranch areas of Los Olivos and Ballard, and the Danish community of Solvang. Artistic communities such as Laguna and Santa Barbara abound, as do several respected art museums, including the Norton Simon and Getty museums. The urban areas offer lots of people and cars as well as theater, fine restaurants, shopping, and history. A trip through downtown Los Angeles and Olvera Street will give a glimpse of the area's rich past, as do the many historic communities with original missions and adobes, such as San Juan Capistrano and San Diego (with zoo and animal park as well). Late-1880 California can be relived through the towns of Los Alamos and Julian. Recreation, history, beauty, and urban and rural settings all make up southern California, a bounty of travel choices.

SOUTHERN CALIFORNIA

9

Anaheim Country Inn

856 S. Walnut, Anaheim, CA 92802
Phone: (714) 778–0150 / (800) 755–7801
Key: Inn; 8 units; Inexpensive–Moderate; No smoking; Credit cards;
No handicapped access

This Princess Anne–style house with sweeping front porch and grounds filled with avocado trees and roses was built in 1910. Guests may relax in the quiet of this residential neighborhood—just minutes from Disneyland—on one of three porches; in the large Victorian parlor with beveled-glass windows, an 1890 pump organ, Victrola, and cozy fireplace; or in the quiet upstairs reading room. The eight guest rooms and their private and shared baths, located both upstairs and down, are decorated individually with iron, wicker, or poster beds and early 1900s furnishings. The Garden Room has an outside entrance to the garden with spa. The sunny dining room is the locale of the generous full breakfast; snacks are left in the refrigerator so that guests may help themselves.

Whispering Pines Bed & Breakfast

5850 Manzanita Avenue, P.O. Box 115, Angelus Oaks, CA 92305
Phone: (714) 794–2962
Key: Inn/Cottages; 14 units; Moderate–Superior; No smoking;
Credit cards; No handicapped access

This former rustic resort has been transformed into a unique bed & breakfast retreat with a fun 1930s feel. The quaint inn, nestled among the pines and oaks in the San Bernardino Mountains, offers nine guest rooms and five cottages surrounding a peaceful courtyard area with spacious redwood deck. Guest accommodations boast plush carpeting, polished knotty-pine walls covered with family photos, handicraft touches, 1930s-made quilts, and private baths. Most guest rooms contain queen-size beds, and some suites offer microwaves and refrigerators; the Hideaway Suite contains big floor pillows fronting a cozy Franklin stove. A full country breakfast is delivered to the room each morning and includes a variety of home-made muffins, breads, and granolas as well as fresh fruit and a specialty entree such as chili relleno with salsa and sour cream and country home fries. A bottle of complimentary wine or cider is presented to guests upon check-in; campfires are held at the inn each night offering informal entertainment, a mug of something hot to drink, and marshmallow roasting. Check with the inn for dinner and lunch offerings in the main house, as well as cookouts. Guests at Whispering Pines also receive a surprise treat each day in their rooms!

Garden House Inn

Third & Clarissa, P.O. Box 1881, Avalon, CA 90704
Phone: (310) 510–0356
Key: Inn; 9 units; Superior–Deluxe; No smoking; Credit cards; No handicapped access

This beautifully restored San Francisco–type townhouse was built in 1927 and is just a half block from the beach, shops, and cafés in Avalon. The white three-story house with green trim and patio offers an inviting entry with a sunny nook and an adjacent parlor with polished hardwood floors, an antique marble fireplace, and high-quality antique furnishings. The guest rooms, located upstairs, are all unique and feature televisions, designer wallpapers, some telephones, and early 1930s-style furnishings. A third-floor deck boasts unparalleled views of the sunrise over the harbor. Stays at this family-run inn include a generous buffet breakfast of cereals, pastries, fruits, and juice; evening sherry, taffy, and cookies; and late-afternoon hors d'oeuvres, wine, and Perrier.

Gull House

344 Whittley Avenue, P.O. Box 1381, Avalon, CA 90704
Phone: (310) 510–2547
Key: Home; 4 units; Superior; Smoking OK; No credit cards; No handicapped access

Located on beautiful Santa Catalina island just 65 miles from Los Angeles, this bed & breakfast offers two complete suites with a rear-yard pool, spa, and adjoining barbecue area. The contemporary 660-square-foot suites contain a private entrance, a spacious living room with fireplace, a bedroom, full bath, and "morning room" with table, chairs, and refrigerator. Gull House now offers two guest rooms with private bath, also decorated in contemporary furnishings. A continental breakfast is served each morning on the patio. The b&b closes November through March; advance reservations, with a two-night minimum stay, are required.

The Inn on Mt. Ada, Avalon

The Inn on Mt. Ada

398 Wrigley Road, P.O. Box 2560, Avalon, CA 90704
Phone: (310) 510–2030
Key: Inn; 6 units; Deluxe; No smoking; Credit cards; No handicapped access

The inn was built in 1921 as a summer home for the philanthropic owner of the island; in 1978 the home was given to the University of Southern California, which now leases the house for the purpose of maintaining a high-quality lodging establishment on the island. Located on five and one-half acres atop Mt. Ada, the old Georgian-Colonial house with shutters, moldings, and trim in grays, whites, and greens is surrounded by native trees and gardens and grants awesome views of the ocean. A traditionally furnished den, card lounge, and sun-room form the west wing of the first floor, while a spacious living room with vistas and an exquisite dining room make up the remaining common areas. The second floor of the mansion offers the four guest rooms and two suites of the inn. Such details as fireplaced sitting areas, walk-in closets, full bathrooms, and eclectic decor are found in these special accommodations. A full and hearty breakfast as well as lunch and dinner are included in the stay at this elite inn.

The Old Turner Inn

232 Catalina Avenue, P.O. Box 97, Avalon, CA 90704
Phone: (310) 510–2236
Key: Inn; 5 units; Moderate–Deluxe; No smoking; Credit cards; No handicapped access

This 1927 guest house has been given a new life as a cozy b&b with five guest rooms and suites. The quaintly decorated rooms feature antiques, brass beds, wallpaper, and private baths, and four accommodations offer romantic wood-burning fireplaces. The King and Queen suites have private sitting porches. Guests enjoy a living room and dining room with massive brick fireplace and country decor, as well as a glassed-in porch and colorful flower garden. Each morning a buffet breakfast featuring muffins and pastries, yogurt, fresh fruit, juice, and homemade granola is served on the antique buffet; wine, beverages, and light appetizers are served each late afternoon.

The Ballard Inn

2436 Baseline, Ballard, CA 93463
Phone: (805) 688–7770
Key: Inn; 15 units; Superior–Deluxe; No smoking; Credit cards; Handicapped access, 1 unit

This b&b inn, nestled in the historic town of Ballard within the lush Santa Ynez Valley, offers guests a blend of the old and new. The gabled inn, built in a nostalgic design with a multitude of fireplaces, offers four common rooms and fifteen guest rooms, each decorated in a theme consistent with the area's history yet containing the most modern conveniences. Three common rooms offer relaxation, wine, and a library, and the William Ballard dining room is the locale of breakfast. Guests also may dine on the veranda, and high tea is served each day at 5:00 P.M. Each guest room at the inn features a private bath and individual touches that include balconies, American antiques, quilts, antique-doll collections, Chumash Indian designs, and unique circular windows; several rooms have stone fireplaces. Business and group rates are available.

Gold Mountain Manor

1117 Anita, P.O. Box 2027, Big Bear City, CA 92314
Phone: (714) 585-6997
Key: Inn; 7 units; Moderate–Deluxe; No smoking; Credit cards; No handicapped access

This beautiful 7,000-square-foot mansion with bird's-eye-maple floors and beamed ceilings was built in the 1920s as a weekend lodge for wealthy gold miners. Now the log inn, on an acre of towering pine trees, has been meticulously restored and offers guests seven unique accommodations, six with fireplaces, one with a spa, and two with private access to the veranda, a pool table, and a player piano. The guest rooms include three with private and half baths and range from a rustic decor with stone-hearth fireplace and pine floors to the Clark Gable Room with an antique French walnut bed and the fireplace that honeymooned with Gable and Lombard. A homemade breakfast with such delights as crab quiche and baked cinnamon apples is served on the veranda or in the dining room; afternoon refreshments also are offered. The inn is one-half block from the National Forest.

Country Bay Inn

34862 Pacific Coast Highway, Capistrano Beach, CA 92624
Phone: (714) 496-6656; **Fax:** (714) 661-3045
Key: Inn/Hotel; 28 units; Inexpensive–Moderate; Smoking OK; Credit cards; No handicapped access

Ocean views, wood-burning fireplaces, and private patios and balconies accent the antique-furnished rooms in this 1930s inn/hotel. All guest rooms contain wet bar, television, and telephone;

most boast a refrigerator. Fireplace wood is provided in winter only. A complimentary breakfast of pastries, juice, and coffee or tea is served each morning. Free pickup from Amtrak may be arranged. Weekly rates are available in garden-view rooms.

Pelican Cove Inn, Carlsbad

Pelican Cove Inn

320 Walnut Avenue, Carlsbad, CA 92008
Phone: (619) 434–5995
Key: Inn; 8 units; Moderate–Superior; Smoking OK; Credit cards; Handicapped access, 1 unit

Located in the village, just 200 yards from the beach, is this contemporary Cape Cod–style inn painted a light gray with pastel-pink trim. Fronted by two large palms and bright blooms, the inn offers guests a sunny third-floor sun deck as well as guest rooms with private baths and entrances and romantic fireplaces; two new rooms boast Jacuzzi tubs. Each room is decorated with a pleasant mixture of contemporary and antique furnishings; feather beds, down comforters, and televisions are available. The generous continental breakfast is served in the guest parlor, on the garden patio, or on the sun porch. Extras at the inn include afternoon wine and use of beach chairs, towels, and picnic baskets.

Coronado Victorian House

1000 Eighth Street, Coronado, CA 92118
Phone: (619) 435–2200
Key: Inn; 5 units; Deluxe; No smoking; Credit cards; Handicapped access, 1 unit

This three-story 1894 Victorian home in the heart of Coronado has been meticulously renovated by its present owner, a task that took three years to complete. The historically designated blue-gray Victorian with white and burgundy trim, stained-glass doors and windows, and a generous supply of sun porches and balconies offers a unique bed & breakfast package: an elegant overnight accommodation, a gourmet health/ethnic-food breakfast, and dancing or exercise instruction in the first-floor dance studio! Dance teacher/innkeeper Bonni Marie Kinosian is the master of dance, as well as chef and hostess in her home filled with fine antiques and sunlit rooms. Guests enjoy a living room with the original carved wooden fireplace and antique checkerboard and a dining room that opens to a bilevel patio and sun porch. Guest rooms, all with private baths, include a two-bedroom suite with stained-glass windows, a wet bar, and original beamed ceilings. Special decorator touches in guest rooms include two pre–Civil War step-up sleigh beds and an antique quilt. The generous breakfast includes fresh fruits, juices, homemade rolls and baklava, health cereals, homemade yogurt, and such ethnic foods as rolled grape leaves and stuffed zucchini. Guests may choose from social ballroom, ballet, jazz, tap, Hawaiian, and belly dancing, as well as low-impact aerobics and stretching as a part of their b&b package; health and fitness walks are offered each morning.

Blue Lantern Inn

34343 Street of the Blue Lantern, Dana Point, CA 92629
Phone: (714) 661–1304; **Fax:** (714) 496–1483
Key: Inn/Hotel; 29 units; Superior–Deluxe; No smoking; Credit cards; Handicapped access, 1 unit

This 1990-built Cape Cod–style inn is a peaceful retreat on the south Orange County coast. The tan structure with neat white trim

Blue Lantern Inn, Dana Point

is marked by a gabled slate roof and cobblestone paths lined with bright blooms. The interior colors of the inn reflect the dramatic ocean scenery outside with hues of sea-foam green, lavender, periwinkle, and sand. The twenty-nine guest rooms feature luxury details including period furnishings, original art, print wallpapers, Jacuzzi tubs, televisions, terry robes, and refrigerators stocked with complimentary soft drinks. Guests stay warm and cozy in their quarters with romantic fireplaces and fluffy quilts. Balcony rooms are available. The morning breakfast fare is a full gourmet buffet in the dining room; complimentary beverages and cookies are available throughout the day. Afternoon tea is served from 4:30 to 6:30 P.M. The main level of the inn hosts a book-lined library, and an ocean-view dining room; the lower level of the Blue Lantern offers an exercise room and conference rooms for small groups. Bicycles are available for touring the scenic area; several restaurants are within walking distance.

Del Mar

Gull's Nest

12930 Via Esperia, Del Mar, CA 92014
Phone: (619) 259–4863
Key: Home; 2 units; Moderate; No smoking; No credit cards; No handicapped access

Nestled in a wooded residential area three blocks from Torrey Pines State Beach is this contemporary wooden home with two upper decks. Guests may choose from two rooms: one with queen-size bed, television, private bath, and private patio garden and the other a spacious studio with king-size bed, private bath, kitchen, and ocean views. The rustic hideaway pampers its guests with a full breakfast featuring freshly squeezed orange juice; wine or cold beverages are served on arrival. There is a cat in residence.

Rock Haus

410 Fifteenth Street, Del Mar, CA 92014
Phone: (619) 481–3764
Key: Inn; 10 units; Moderate–Superior; No smoking; Credit cards; No handicapped access

The early California bungalow-style house is situated in the heart of Del Mar Village, yet it boasts ocean views. Most of the ten guest rooms offer ocean views, and all have individual decor, with private- and shared-bath accommodations. The Huntsman's Room features a fireplace. Guests enjoy a continental fare each morning consisting of fresh fruit, muffins, breads, and juices and afternoon tea served in the cozy living room. Shops, restaurants, and the beach are a stroll away, and the innkeepers provide courtesy pickup service from Amtrak three blocks away.

Cedar Creek Inn

8020 Highway 79, Descanso, CA 92001
P.O. Box 1466, Alpine, CA 92001
Phone: (619) 445–9605
Key: Home; 2 units; Moderate; Limited smoking; No credit cards; No handicapped access

Part of the sprawling, historic Ellis Ranch on Sweetwater River, this mountain-cottage retreat is surrounded by three and three-quarters acres of trees and lawn. The single-story house offers guests patios and an exercise pool in its private, country setting forty-five minutes from San Diego. The two guest accommodations include the Cedar Creek Suite, a private studio apartment with deck, kitchen, and bath, as well as the Poolside Room, with private sitting area, kitchen, and bath. Both units have televisions and hide-a-beds. Rolls, coffee, and orange juice are served each morning in the kitchen of each unit.

Brookside Farm Bed & Breakfast Inn

1373 Marron Valley Road, Dulzura, CA 92017
Phone: (619) 468–3043
Key: Inn/Cottage; 10 units; Moderate; No smoking; Credit cards; Handicapped access, 2 units

This peaceful farmhouse with two cottages boasts a year-round stream, gigantic old oak trees, a European-style barn, a large garden, vineyard, and fruit trees, along with all the goats, chickens, and geese you would expect to find in this setting. Guests may enjoy a hot tub, hiking trails, or even the feeding of ranch animals. Each of the nine accommodations is decorated individually with antique tools or a Spanish decor. All accommodations have private baths; guests choose from six guest rooms in the house, two in the stone barn, and two cottages. This farm b&b doesn't disappoint at breakfast time, when all guests gather at 9:00 A.M. for farm-fresh omelettes and egg dishes, fruits, juices, and jams as well as homemade breads, muffins, and biscuits. The breakfast and gourmet dinners (offered on weekends and holidays for $15 per person) are prepared by the innkeeper/chef, Edd, who also offers a cooking school by arrangement. The terraces and garden at this farm b&b are available for small weddings.

Halbig's Hacienda

432 South Citrus Avenue, Escondido, CA 92027
Phone: (619) 745–1296
Key: Home; 3 units; Inexpensive; Smoking OK; No credit cards; Handicapped access, 3 units

Escondido

Nestled among fruit trees and gardens, with views of surrounding mountains, this adobe ranch–style home offers country atmosphere with proximity to restaurants, stores, the San Diego Wild Animal Park, and other north-county attractions. Three guest rooms with several antiques and shared baths are available to guests. Guests enjoy a television and a long veranda. Discounts are offered for extended stays. Pets and children are welcome.

Strawberry Creek Inn

26370 Highway 243, P.O. Box 1818, Idyllwild, CA 92349
Phone: (714) 659–3202
Key: Inn/Cottage; 10 units; Moderate–Superior; No smoking; Credit cards; Handicapped access, 1 unit

This homey wood-shingled inn with etched-glass windows and a deck under the towering pines offers a romantic mountain retreat. Guests enjoy a spacious living room with cozy fireplace and a glassed-in sun porch where the full breakfast is served. Guest rooms are located in the main house as well as around a sunny courtyard behind the inn and feature antiques and family mementos. Each courtyard room boasts a queen-size bed, private bath, small refrigerator, skylight, and fireplace; the Autumn Room features a Queen Anne–style four-poster bed and is decorated in fall colors. The rooms in the main house all have private baths. The inn's new Honeymoon Cottage features a king-size bed, whirlpool tub, fireplace, television and VCR, a fully equipped kitchen, and sunny glassed-in deck. Although the inn is located near the village, it is privately tucked among pines and old oaks for solitude and picturesque nature hikes.

Wilkum Inn

26770 Highway 243, P.O. Box 1115, Idyllwild, CA 92349
Phone: (714) 659–4087
Key: Inn; 5 units; Inexpensive–Moderate; No smoking; No credit cards; Handicapped access, 1 unit

This two-story shingled mountain retreat built around 1938 is situated on three quarters of an acre of lilacs, pines, and oaks. The nicely restored home's interiors boast warm knotty-pine paneling and Pennsylvania Dutch accents. A common room provides a large stone fireplace; guests breakfast in the dining room overlooking the patio. The five guest rooms are individually decorated with antiques, lace curtains, and collectibles. One upstairs room now includes a private bath while the other two upstairs rooms share a bath but boast in-room sinks; the downstairs Garden Room offers a private bath and French doors opening onto the yard. The inn also offers The Loft, a fully equipped private unit with kitchen and living room with fireplace but none of the b&b amenities. Guests enjoy a gourmet continental breakfast that includes four juices, fruit compote, and homemade breads, muffins, crepes, abelskivers, or Belgian waffles. Self-serve beverages are available all day, and popcorn or cheese and crackers are set out each evening.

Julian Hotel

2032 Main Street, P.O. Box 1856, Julian, CA 92036
Phone: (619) 765–0201
Key: Inn/Hotel/Cottage; 18 units; Moderate; Smoking OK; Credit cards; No handicapped access

The only hotel survivor of the area's mining-boom days, the hotel was constructed by freed slaves in 1897 and is listed in the National Register of Historic Places. The inn is completely furnished in authentic American antiques from the turn of the century (including some original hotel pieces such as the upright piano), and the lobby and some of the guest rooms have ceilings of both pressed tin and redwood car siding. Guest rooms have Victorian wallpapers, headboard canopies, and cozy comforters or quilts. The Honeymoon House is a one-bedroom cottage with wood-burning fireplace and lots of romantic lace. The complimentary full breakfast of eggs Florentine, fruit, nut bread, homemade granola, and juice is served in the dining room. Tea is served each evening in the parlor.

Pine Hills Lodge

2960 La Posada Way, Julian, CA 92036
Phone: (619) 765–1100
Key: Inn/Hotel/Cottages; 18 units; Inexpensive–Superior; Smoking OK; Credit cards; Handicapped access, 5 units

Julian

The rustic wooden lodge built in 1912 features a giant native-stone fireplace in the lobby, a country-style dining room, and an authentic Western bar. The guest accommodations include European-style rooms in the lodge with washbasins and claw-foot tubs down the hall and a dozen cottages with private baths, some with fireplaces and patios. A continental breakfast is served to guests every day except Sunday. A barbecue dinner-theater is offered on weekends.

Shadow Mountain Ranch

2771 Frisius Road, Box 791, Julian, CA 92036
Phone: (619) 765–0323
Key: Home; 6 units; Moderate; No smoking; No credit cards; Handicapped access, 1 unit

This ranch-style b&b was once an apple orchard and cattle ranch and is surrounded by meadows and pine-covered mountains. The individually decorated guest rooms include such features as wood-burning stoves, antiques, and Native American artifacts. One unusual guest accommodation is actually an "adult" tree house nestled in a century-old oak. Besides the full ranch breakfast, guests may enjoy the hot tub, hiking trails, or even the feeding of ranch animals. The evening brings a fireside glass of sherry or cup of warm vanilla milk. Guests also enjoy a lap pool, horseshoes, and badminton.

Carriage House

1322 Catalina Street, Laguna Beach, CA 92651
Phone: (714) 494–8945
Key: Inn; 6 units; Moderate–Superior; Smoking OK; No credit cards; No handicapped access

This Colonial inn in the artistic community of Laguna offers an array of room decors ranging from English and French country to a tropical Oriental theme. All guest quarters host large sitting rooms; and four suites contain complete kitchens. Guest-room French doors open onto a courtyard and fountain, where guests may enjoy the family-style breakfast. Guests are welcomed with a bottle of wine and fresh fruit in the suite. There is a two-night minimum stay on weekends; three-night minimum during holidays.

Casa Laguna Inn

2510 South Coast Highway, Laguna Beach, CA 92651
Phone: (714) 494–2996 / (800) 233–0449 (CA); **Fax:** (714) 494–5009
Key: Inn/Hotel/Cottage; 20 units; Moderate–Deluxe; Smoking OK; Credit cards; No handicapped access

This hillside California Mission–Spanish Revival inn with secluded gardens and meandering paths offers flower-filled patios with spectacular ocean views. Guests also enjoy the grounds' shady terrace, a tropical-bird aviary, a courtyard, a heated pool, and views from the bell tower at the restored 1930s villa that boasts hand-painted tile work and wrought-iron touches. The interior of the inn offers guests a library for relaxation and a pleasant mixture of contemporary and antique furnishings. The overnight accommodations include one private cottage, four suites, and fifteen guest rooms. All facilities offer private baths, individual decor, color cable television, and clock radios; many boast refrigerators, patios or balconies, and telephones. The inn serves a generous continental breakfast and afternoon refreshments of wine, hors d'oeuvres, and cheeses. The complimentary repasts are served in the library and may be enjoyed there, by the pool, or in the garden.

Eiler's Inn

741 South Coast Highway, Laguna Beach, CA 92651
Phone: (714) 494–3004
Key: Inn/Hotel; 12 units; Superior–Deluxe; Smoking OK; Credit cards; No handicapped access

Situated steps from the ocean in the heart of Laguna Beach is this European-style inn with French windows, lace curtains, and a courtyard with fountain, fish pond, and gardens. The guest rooms, built around the lush courtyard, are individually furnished in antiques and have private baths. One suite offers a kitchen, fireplace, and ocean view. Guests enjoy a library and living room downstairs as well as an ocean-view sun deck upstairs. The generous continental breakfast is served in the courtyard, as are evening wine and cheese. A classical guitarist is featured during the social period on weekends. Complimentary champagne, fresh flowers, and fruit baskets are placed in each guest room, and sun tea and coffee are available all day.

Hotel St. Maarten

696 South Coast Highway, Laguna Beach, CA 92651
Phone: (714) 494–1001 / (800) 228–5691; **Fax:** (714) 497–7107
Key: Inn/Hotel/Cottages; 55 units; Moderate–Deluxe; Smoking OK; Credit cards; No handicapped access

The hotel creates a tropical setting with a courtyard, balconies, and abundant hanging plants. Guest rooms and cottages at the hotel are individually furnished in some antiques, and suites offer their own Jacuzzis. A sauna, pool, and fine California-cuisine restaurant, Marigot, are located on the premises for all guests. The complimentary continental breakfast is served Monday through Friday only.

The Bed & Breakfast Inn at La Jolla

7753 Draper Avenue, La Jolla, CA 92037
Phone: (619) 456–2066
Key: Inn; 16 units; Moderate–Deluxe; Limited smoking; Credit cards; Handicapped access, 1 unit

This 1913 Irving Gill–built b&b is a part of the San Diego Historical Registry and was the John Philip Sousa family residence for several years in the 1920s. Cubist-style architecture describes the exterior of the inn, which is surrounded by the original gardens. The main house contains ten of the guest rooms; six are located in the annex. Guest rooms at the inn are elegantly and individually decorated in Laura Ashley or Ralph Lauren fabrics, and each room has either a queen-size bed or two twins. Fresh fruit, sherry, and flowers add a nice touch to each guest room. A light breakfast is served on fine china and linen on a tray in the room or in the garden, or the guest may join with others in the dining room. This b&b is located in the heart of La Jolla's cultural complex, just one and one-half blocks from the beach.

Bluebelle House, Lake Arrowhead

Bluebelle House

263 S. State Highway 173, P.O. Box 2177, Lake Arrowhead, CA 92352
Phone: (714) 336–3292
Key: Inn; 5 units; Moderate; No smoking; Credit cards; No handicapped access

A considerable amount of remodeling transformed this ship captain's home into a European-style bed & breakfast inn. The Alpine-style inn is just 2/10 mile from Lake Arrowhead Village and nearby private beaches that guests may enjoy. The country-English parlor of the inn boasts a large rock fireplace, European antiques, crystal, and fine art, along with an excellent library. Guests also relax on the deck and may play darts. Three of the five guest rooms are on the main floor and two share a bath; the Edelweiss Room is the largest accommodation and boasts a private bath and two queen-size beds. The two remaining rooms are upstairs and have private baths. The individually decorated rooms with queen-size beds, pretty sheets, and candy have varying themes. Breakfast is on the tree-shaded deck or in the dining room and is served with fine linen, silver, and crystal.

The Romantique Lakeview Lodge

28051 Highway 189, Lake Arrowhead, CA 92352
Phone: (714) 337–6633
Key: Inn; 9 units; Moderate–Deluxe; No smoking; Credit cards; Handicapped access, 1 unit

This hideaway amid a lush pine forest offers unobstructed views of Lake Arrowhead and privacy. The white Victorian-feel inn is furnished throughout with antiques and boasts oil paintings and gleaming brass and crystal touches, as well as fireplaces. The uniquely decorated guest rooms and suites feature king- and queen-size beds, romantic fireplaces, luxurious private baths, and VCRs and classic movies. Guests enjoy a continental breakfast, featuring "sinful" cinnamon rolls baked especially for the inn, on the lake-view patio. Located across the street from the village and lake, the lodge is within strolling distance of fine restaurants and shops.

San Diego Hideaway

8844 Alpine Avenue, La Mesa, CA 91941
Phone: (619) 460–2868
Key: Home; 2 units; Inexpensive; No smoking; No credit cards; No handicapped access

This ranch-style home on a hillside affords lovely views of nearby San Diego. The hospitable "hideaway" is situated in a residential area and is surrounded by trees, shrubs, and roses. Guests choose from two comfortable guest rooms, each with private bath and Victorian or Colonial decor; rooms are outfitted with a decanter of wine, fresh flowers, and fruit. A large upstairs living room with fireplace and player piano affords the same city views plus an adjoining porch; a downstairs family room offers television. Breakfast is served in either the sun-room or the formal dining room and includes an egg specialty, fresh fruits, and muffins. Late afternoon refreshments and hors d'oeuvres are also offered.

Union Hotel and Victorian Mansion

362 Bell Street, Los Alamos, CA 93440
Phone: (805) 344–2744
Key: Inn/Hotel; 16 units; Moderate–Deluxe; Smoking OK; Credit cards; No handicapped access

This restored 1880s hotel with 1864-built Victorian house annex is nestled in the heart of the antique-shop-filled town of Los Alamos. The grounds of the complex are reminiscent of a turn-of-the-century park, hosting a green reflection/swimming pool, a Jacuzzi in a gazebo, and old-fashioned benches and street lights; inside diversions include billiard and Ping-Pong rooms. Guests may choose from the highly unique accommodations in both buildings complete with hand-painted oil murals and appropriate costume-like robes to fit the mood; accommodations range from the Drive-in Movie Room, where guests sleep in a 1956 Cadillac convertible, to the Gypsy Room, with an authentic gypsy wagon as a bed and a sunken pool with waterfall as a bath. Bathrooms in the private-bath accommodations are cleverly hidden, as are the televisions. The stay at the inn includes a tour of town in a 1918 touring car (weather permitting), a full breakfast, and a multicourse family-style dinner. The b&b hosts guests on Friday, Saturday, and Sunday nights only.

Eastlake Inn

1442 Kellam Avenue, Los Angeles, CA 90026
Phone: (213) 250–1620
Key: Inn; 9 units; Moderate–Superior; No smoking; Credit cards; No handicapped access

Eastlake Inn, Los Angeles

This authentically restored 1887 inn on a downtown hilltop began as a grand duplex for two wealthy widows. The Eastlake-style b&b is in the middle of the city's first historic-preservation area and is surrounded by other fine Victorian restoration examples. The interiors are furnished in museum-quality antiques and feature red fir floors and stained glass. Two guest rooms share baths appointed with luxurious claw-foot tubs and chenille robes. All the guest rooms are decorated in interesting antiques, canopies, wicker, and beveled glass; a three-room honeymoon suite has a sun-room and a small library, and a one-room suite was the original dining room. The generous breakfast is served on fine china in the dining room or guest room or even in bed. Champagne and wine are offered on arrival, and snacks and refreshments are available on request. Special weekend packages at the inn include limousine tours for chocolate lovers, hot-air balloons, private gondola cruises, and box-seat baseball weekends (the inn is within walking distance of Dodger Stadium).

Salisbury House

2273 W. Twentieth Street, Los Angeles, CA 90018
Phone: (213) 737-7817 / (800) 373-1778
Key: Inn; 5 units; Moderate; No smoking; Credit cards; No handicapped access

Just minutes from downtown Los Angeles is this 1909 California Craftsman home-turned-inn that features original stained and leaded glass, wood-beamed ceilings, wood paneling, and antique-filled rooms. The inn, in a quiet residential area, offers five individual guest rooms with turn-of-the-century wall coverings, bay windows, comfortable furniture, and eyelet-and-lace touches as well as private and shared baths; all rooms boast refrigerators, and phones and televisions are available. The third floor Attic Suite comprises 600 square feet of area with a sitting room, private phone, televisions, claw-foot tub, pine floors, and gabled ceilings. A full breakfast with such delicacies as raspberry tea, house-blended coffee, quiche or apple puffed pancakes, and fresh fruit cobblers is served in the formal, wood-paneled dining room in buffet fashion.

Terrace Manor

1353 Alvarado Terrace, Los Angeles, CA 90006
Phone: (213) 381-1478
Key: Inn; 5 units; Moderate; No smoking; Credit cards; No handicapped access

This 1902-built National Historic Landmark home in downtown Los Angeles contains its original stained- and leaded-glass windows, polished hardwood floors, and rich paneled walls. The Tudor-Craftsman home, formerly owned by soap-opera stars and writers and featured in television movies and commercials, is filled with antiques and period furniture and has a hunter green, rose, and burgundy color scheme. The five guest rooms have private baths, some rare antiques, authentic wall coverings, and some brass and iron beds. The stay here includes a full breakfast with such delicacies as eggs Florentine and tarts and is served in the dining room or in the garden. As a special treat, the innkeepers are happy to make reservations for guests at the Magic Castle, a magicians' club that you cannot enter unless a member-magician invites you.

Malibu

Casa Larronde

22000 Pacific Coast Highway, P.O. Box 86, Malibu, CA 90265
Phone: (310) 456-9333
Key: Home; 1 unit; Moderate; No smoking; No credit cards; No handicapped access

A private beach and movie-star neighbors are attractive and unique ingredients of this home b&b in famous Malibu. The spacious two-story home offers a living room with ocean-view windows and a guest suite with fireplace, minikitchen, television, sitting area, beamed ceilings, ash paneling, and floor-to-ceiling ocean-view windows. The guest suite also boasts a 40-foot private deck with views of the bay and pier. The breakfast may be enjoyed on the deck, and complimentary champagne and hors d'oeuvres are offered in the evening. The b&b is closed during the summer and when the hosts are traveling.

Doryman's Inn

2102 W. Ocean Front, Newport Beach, CA 92663
Phone: (714) 675-7300
Key: Inn/Hotel; 10 units; Superior-Deluxe; Smoking OK; Credit cards; No handicapped access

This 1892-vintage hotel fronting the ocean has been totally renovated and decorated in carefully selected French country antique furnishings and wall coverings. Each individually decorated guest room boasts a fireplace and marble sunken bath, and two rooms have Jacuzzis. The continental breakfast is served in the parlor each morning. The inn restaurant furnishes dinner in the room or parlor upon request.

The Little Inn on the Bay

617 Lido Park Drive, Newport Beach, CA 92663
Phone: (714) 673-8800; **Fax:** (714) 673-1500
Key: Inn/Hotel; 30 units; Moderate-Deluxe; No smoking; Credit cards; No handicapped access

The Little Inn on the Bay, Newport Beach

This hotel b&b with marina has been renovated to a village-style hostelry a short stroll from the quaint shops of the Cannery and Lido Village. Pretty beaches are just a few blocks away. Each of the thirty guest rooms offers a view of the water and has soundproofing, air conditioning, and individual decor that reflects an 1800s New England feel in antique reproductions. The fourteen suites at the inn have wet bars, refrigerators, and microwave ovens, and all accommodations have private baths. A complimentary continental breakfast may be enjoyed in the room or on the scenic dock-side patio with views of boats and ducks. Daily complimentary services at the inn include a boat cruise of the bay from the inn's own dock, wine and hors d'oeuvres in the afternoon, a pedicab tour of Cannery Village, and an after-dinner snack. Guests also enjoy bicycles, board games, and a lending library at this hospitable b&b.

Portofino Beach Hotel

2306 West Oceanfront, Newport Beach, CA 92663
Phone: (714) 673–7030; **Fax:** (714) 723–4370
Key: Inn/Hotel; 15 units; Moderate–Deluxe; Smoking OK; Credit cards; No handicapped access

Newport Beach

Nestled on the sand in Newport Beach is this hotel with fifteen upstairs guest rooms. The luxuriously appointed accommodations, decorated uniquely in hues of dusty rose, cream, burgundy, and green, boast custom-made bedspreads, fresh flowers, nostalgic wall coverings and draperies, televisions, private baths, and telephones; some rooms feature spa-type tubs or minipatios. Two front rooms offer panoramic ocean views; five other rooms provide partial views of the ocean and Newport Pier. Guests enjoy an observation parlor with awe-inspiring sunset views over the Pacific. The complimentary morning fare of fruit, juice, and croissants is served in the downstairs Bar La Gritta lounge by a cozy fireplace; each afternoon cheese, crackers, and beverages are offered. The hotel provides beach chairs and towels for a day at the beach.

Hotel Nipton

72 Nipton Road, P.O. Box 357, Nipton, CA 92364
Phone: (619) 856–2335; **Fax:** (619) 856–2335
Key: Inn; 4 units; Inexpensive; Smoking OK; Credit cards; No handicapped access

This restored turn-of-the-century hotel is a part of the small desert town of Nipton, a former 1885 gold-mining camp. The community (population: 70) in the East Mojave National Scenic Area is also owned by the b&b innkeepers, who purchased the town for restoration in 1986. The carefully renovated hotel maintains the early 1900s desert flavor with foot-thick adobe walls, lobby with wood-burning stove, and historic photos of the town's earlier days. Guests are treated to panoramic views of the desert and mountains from the hotel's front porch surrounded by rock and cactus gardens. The four guest rooms, which share baths, are named after prominent individuals from the hotel's past; Room #3 is named after Clara Bow, who stayed in the 1930s. Modern conveniences at the inn include central air conditioning and heating and a Jacuzzi for stargazing. Guests are served a continental breakfast each morning; guests help themselves to apricot brandy anytime. A lounge next door serves sandwiches and beverages.

La Maida House

11159 La Maida Street, North Hollywood, CA 91601
Phone: (818) 769–3857
Key: Inn; 11 units; Moderate–Deluxe; No smoking; Credit cards;
No handicapped access

This 7,000-square-foot, 1920s villa in a quiet residential neighborhood is surrounded by flower gardens and fountains; guests also enjoy its gazebo, swimming pool, gym, grape-arbored patios, ponds with water lilies and goldfish, and a reflecting pool. The interiors of the old-world mansion are filled with antiques, oriental rugs, stained glass, and rich mahogany. The eleven guest rooms and suites at the inn feature private baths, some with claw-foot tubs or Jacuzzis; canopies; private patios or gardens; and valuable antiques or wicker furniture. Rooms also include private-line telephones and refrigerators. Early-morning coffee or tea and the newspaper are delivered to the room, and the continental breakfast is served between 8:00 and 9:00 A.M. Evening aperitifs are offered, and guests also may arrange for a pre-theater supper or a four-course dinner—all prepared by the inn's award-winning gourmet chef. The inn has a gift shop. The inn is just a few minutes' drive from the Hollywood Bowl, Universal Studios, and Beverly Hills.

Bushman Bed & Breakfast

1220 N. Montgomery Street, Ojai, CA 93023
Phone: (805) 646–4295
Key: Home; 4 units; Inexpensive; No smoking; No credit cards; No handicapped access

This 2,700-square-foot Spanish-style home is located on the edge of town among the oaks of the foothills with the mountains as a picturesque backdrop. The newly remodeled guest rooms, consisting of one double and three single accommodations, feature mahogany furnishings and a plantation-style decor. Guest rooms share baths. The living room offers fine books and a fireplace. A side patio with a fountain and the sounds of birds chirping is a restful choice for the morning breakfast, which includes apple-raisin bran muffins and sliced oranges or fresh orange juice from the family orchard.

Ojai

Casa de la Luna Bed & Breakfast

710 S. La Luna Avenue, Ojai, CA 93023
Phone: (805) 646–4528
Key: Home; 7 units; Moderate; No smoking; No credit cards;
Handicapped access, 1 unit

This elegant, 5,000-square-foot, Spanish-style hacienda offers
seven private guest accommodations surrounded by seven acres of
oaks and the locally well-known Gardens of Perpetual Spring.
Guests are invited to tour the entire tranquil estate and view both
the exotic plant nursery, with its more than 1,000 plants, and gardens with meandering pathways through colorful blooms. The
overnight accommodations include The Estate Suite with fireplace,
king-size bed, and private bath. Guests "choose" their own full
gourmet breakfast from a generous checklist; the morning fare is
served in the large, formal dining room. Guests are encouraged to
enjoy the living room of the house with its carved wooden mantel
and fireplace and etched-glass windows, the extensive library with
antique desk, and a relaxing atrium. The innkeepers' art is on display throughout the house; many pieces are for sale.

Casa Cody

175 S. Cahuilla Road, Palm Springs, CA 92262
Phone: (619) 320–9346
Key: Inn; 17 units; Inexpensive–Deluxe; Smoking OK; Credit cards;
Handicapped access, 10 units

The second-oldest operating hotel in Palm Springs, Casa Cody
was founded in the 1920s by Hollywood pioneer Harriet Cody. The
Santa Fe–style suites and villas have been completely refurbished in
tasteful decor and art and offer such amenities as fully equipped
kitchens and wood-burning fireplaces in many of the units. Ten
suites, with one or two bedrooms, are nestled around an inviting
pool area; a new wing, the Apache, offers seven additional guest
rooms and suites. In addition to the pool, guests may enjoy a
secluded Jacuzzi and Saturday-afternoon wine and cheese poolside.
The complimentary continental breakfast is served casually at one
of the inn's two pools. Casa Cody is a short walk from downtown
shops, fine restaurants, and the Desert Museum and is convenient
to hiking trails, tennis, and golf.

Villa Royale Bed & Breakfast Inn

1620 Indian Trail, Palm Springs, CA 92264
Phone: (619) 327–2314; **Fax:** (619) 322–4151
Key: Inn; 34 units; Moderate–Deluxe; Smoking OK; Credit cards;
Handicapped access, 2 units

This "international" country inn on three and one-half landscaped acres with wandering brick paths, streams, and gardens offers
a unique b&b escape to those wanting a taste of European elegance.
Each of the thirty-four suites and guest rooms is decorated uniquely
in antique furnishings, colors, and art imported and selected personally by the gracious innkeepers from a different European country,
along with such special handicraft touches as custom-designed
quilts, woven hangings, carvings, sculptures, and pillows. The
deluxe accommodations boast fully equipped kitchens or refrigerators, phones, color cable televisions carefully concealed, oversized
beds, many wood-burning fireplaces, coordinated wall coverings,
and private patios landscaped with plants from the "theme" country; a few units boast private spas, and three villas host private
pools. The units are grouped around three gracious courtyards
framed by bougainvillea and shade trees. Guests enjoy the tranquil
"classical music" courtyard, an outdoor living room with fireplace,
a new water garden with waterfall, two swimming pools, a Jacuzzi, a
rooftop sun deck, a film library, and bicycles. The breakfast of fresh
juice, fruit, and home-baked muffins is served each morning on the
arched pool-side patio or on the sun patio; the morning newspaper is
left at each door. Gourmet international lunches and dinners are
offered; a bar is open to guests.

Donnymac Inn

119 N. Meridith, Pasadena, CA 91106
Phone: (818) 440–0066
Key: Inn; 4 units; Moderate; No smoking; No credit cards; No
handicapped access

Newly restored to its 1912 glory is this two-story inn with
freshly landscaped gardens. Guest rooms boast fresh flowers, fruit,
and wine for sipping. The breakfast fare may be enjoyed in the room,
on the mountain-view Garden Balcony, or in the gazebo overlooking

Donnymac Inn, Pasadena

the gardens. Special offerings at the inn include a gazebo-housed spa, picnic baskets, and pickup service for air, train, and bus travelers. A complimentary bottle of champagne is offered for birthdays, anniversaries, and honeymoons.

Christmas House Bed & Breakfast Inn

9240 Archibald Avenue, Rancho Cucamonga, CA 91730
Phone: (714) 980–6450
Key: Inn; 7 units; Inexpensive–Superior; No smoking; Credit cards; No handicapped access

Turn-of-the-century gala yuletide gatherings amidst intricate wood carvings and a profusion of red-and-green stained-glass windows inspired the name of this perfectly restored Queen Anne–Victorian that stands as a historical landmark. The interior of the house boasts period furnishings, seven fireplaces, and rich redwood and mahogany throughout; guests are welcome to enjoy the entire house. Guests also enjoy a sweeping veranda and one acre of gardens. The guest rooms are uniquely decorated in antiques and include shared and private baths, each outfitted with thick terry robes. A suite features French doors leading to a private garden and has a Jacuzzi. The inn serves a generous continental breakfast weekdays and a full fare on weekends; the meal is served elegantly with antique china, white linens, and crystal. Guests are served afternoon

Christmas House Bed & Breakfast Inn, Rancho Cucamonga

cream tea on the weekends, and the innkeepers turn back beds and leave chocolate-flower arrangements on pillows each evening. During the month of December, the house is decorated extravagantly in Victorian Christmas splendor, and the old-fashioned festivities include caroling, a wassail bowl, and figgy pudding. The inn becomes a "dead" & breakfast several times a year when it hosts overnight murder mysteries.

Casa Tropicana B&B Inn

610 Avenida Victoria, San Clemente, CA 92672
Phone: (714) 492–1234; **Fax:** (714) 498–0630
Key: Inn; 9 units; Superior–Deluxe; No smoking; Credit cards; Handicapped access, 1 unit

This recently built five-story Spanish-style inn across from the beach and pier offers deluxe b&b accommodations on the second and third floors. The first floor of the building contains a restaurant. The deluxe rooms carry different tropical themes, such as Key Largo, and all feature fireplaces, color televisions, refrigerators, ice makers, champagne, and Jacuzzi tubs; some boast wet bars. Guests enjoy a full complimentary breakfast chosen from an extensive menu of Spanish and American food served on the deck or in the room. Decks located on guest-room floors offer panoramic views of the ocean.

Britt House, San Diego

Britt House

406 Maple, San Diego, CA 92103
Phone: (619) 234–2926
Key: Inn/Cottage; 10 units; Moderate; Limited smoking; Credit cards; No handicapped access

This carefully restored Queen Anne–Victorian is a pleasant mixture of period furnishings, collectibles, and cozy touches such as stuffed animals and in-room cookies and fruit. Claw-foot tubs grace one of the shared baths. The separate cottage contains a kitchen. Daily homemade yeast breads and egg dishes are a part of the full breakfast. A formal afternoon tea with Irish tea and a variety of sweet and hearty delectables is served in the parlor with its 12-foot-high ceilings, oak manteled fireplace, and elaborate fretwork. Two-story stained-glass windows grace the foyer of this beautifully restored inn.

The Cottage

P.O. Box 3292, San Diego, CA 92163
Phone: (619) 299–1564
Key: Home/Cottage; 2 units; Inexpensive–Moderate; No smoking;
Credit cards; No handicapped access

Situated in an older residential and rural canyon area of the city
is this Victorian-furnished guest house and private guest room. The
cottage offers a full kitchen, bathroom, wood-burning stove, and oak
pump organ. The Garden Room, located in the innkeeper's home,
has a private entrance, private bath, and king-size bed. Guests are
served a freshly baked continental breakfast each morning.

Heritage Park Bed & Breakfast Inn, San Diego

Heritage Park Bed & Breakfast Inn

2470 Heritage Park Row, San Diego, CA 92110
Phone: (619) 295–7088
Key: Inn; 9 units; Moderate–Superior; No smoking; Credit cards;
Handicapped access, 1 unit

San Diego

This Queen Anne–Victorian home with a two-story corner tower and encircling veranda sits on San Diego's historical park in the company of other classic structures and is fronted by cobblestone walkways. Totally restored to its original floor plan, this inn offers vintage movies each evening in the antique-filled parlor. Accommodations with private and shared baths are uniquely decorated in period antiques and have Victorian wall coverings or stenciling, polished wooden floors, oriental rugs, and handmade quilts. A full gourmet breakfast may be enjoyed in the room or on the sunny veranda. A special five-course candlelight dinner may be arranged in advance. Special packages are available.

Keating House Inn

2331 Second Avenue, San Diego, CA 92101
Phone: (619) 239–8585
Key: Inn/Cottage; 8 units; Moderate; Limited smoking; Credit cards; Handicapped access, 2 units

This historic 1888-built Queen Anne–Victorian landmark on Bankers Hill above the bay is just four blocks from the Balboa Park attractions. Pleasant, sunny gardens and shaded patios provide relaxation around the restored home with stained-glass windows, two-story bay windows, gabled roofs, and tower. The four upstairs guest rooms, comfortably decorated in country antiques and plants, share two baths; two rooms share a balcony. Two new guest rooms on the main floor share a bath. Guests may also stay in the inn's two-bedroom cottage, rented separately or as one unit. The cottage accommodations have private baths, and cottage guests eat breakfast in the house family style. Guests may enjoy the parlor and sunny garden and porch. The dining room or outside patio, weather permitting, are the sites of the morning breakfast of fresh fruit compote, freshly baked breads, assorted rolls, and juice. Extras at the inn include evening sherry and wine, fresh flowers, and the morning paper delivered to the room.

Surf Manor and Cottages

P.O. Box 7695, San Diego, CA 92167
Phone: (619) 225–9765
Key: Cottages; 7 units; Moderate; No smoking; No credit cards; No handicapped access

This "two part" b&b offering, available September through June, consists of Surf Manor, directly on the oceanfront with wide, sandy beach and near the Ocean Beach Fishing Pier, and The Cottages, consisting of four original beach cottages within a block of South Mission Beach and boasting a small private garden. Each cozy three- or four-room suite, decorated in assorted antiques and country-spring wallpapers and fabrics, grants privacy with its own living room, bedroom, bath, kitchen, color television, and parking place. Each refrigerator is stocked with the ingredients for a continental or full English breakfast, as requested. Weekly rates are available in July and August.

The Grand Cottages

809 S. Grand Avenue, San Pedro, CA 90731
Phone: (310) 548–1240; **Fax:** (310) 514–2279
Key: Cottages; 4 units; Superior; No smoking; Credit cards; No handicapped access

Nestled in a quiet neighborhood near downtown San Pedro is this intimate group of cottages that served as a location site for the movie *Swing Shift*, starring Goldie Hawn and Kurt Russell. The four 1920s-built cottages, which border a center walkway, have been restored and decorated in 1920s, '30s, and '40s theme, with soft pastels and period furniture. Each cottage features a Murphy bed that pulls out from the wall, a dining nook, a fireplace or antique Wedgwood stove, a private patio, a master bedroom with new queen-size bed, a walk-in closet, and a bathroom with tub and shower. As a nostalgic bonus, guests will find a VCR with a cassette of *Swing Shift* in each suite. The cottages are located next to The Grand House, a popular folk-art shop and restaurant with picturesque garden and fountain. The complimentary gourmet breakfast is offered in the cottage or on the Grand House patio, weather permitting. The stay also includes a snack of champagne, cheese and crackers, and a fruit platter.

The Arlington Inn

1136 Del la Vina Street, Santa Barbara, CA 93101
Phone: (805) 965–6532; **Fax:** (805) 965–3840
Key: Inn/Hotel; 44 units; Moderate; Smoking OK; Credit cards; No handicapped access

Conveniently located downtown near theaters, shops, and restaurants, this four-building hotel consists of both the old and new. The main house was built in 1880. A majority of guest-room offerings are minisuites complemented by such amenities as kitchens and gardens. A full English country breakfast featuring freshly squeezed orange juice, a variety of homemade muffins and pastries, and a specialty such as Garden Scramble is served, and an evening wine-and-cheese tasting is presented at 5:00 P.M. Corporate rates and long-term accommodations are available.

The Bath Street Inn

1720 Bath Street, Santa Barbara, CA 93101
Phone: (805) 682–9680 / (800) 549–2284 (CA) / (800) 788–2284
Key: Inn; 7 units; Moderate–Superior; No smoking; Credit cards; No handicapped access

This restored 1885 Queen Anne–Victorian inn, situated in a tree-lined residential area downtown, provides guests with a unique common-lounge area on the gabled third floor. Sunny patio breakfast dining is enjoyed in the rear gardens. The inn offers complimentary bicycles and afternoon refreshments of lemonade, cheese, and crackers. Guest rooms with mountain views at the inn feature private baths, polished hardwood floors, traditional wallpapers, antiques, and fresh flowers. A library and television room have been added for guests' enjoyment, as has a summerhouse for outdoor socializing.

Bayberry Inn

111 West Valerio Street, Santa Barbara, CA 93101
Phone: (805) 682–3199; **Fax:** (805) 962–0103
Key: Inn; 8 units; Moderate–Superior; No smoking; Credit cards;
No handicapped access

Built as a French ambassador's residence in 1886, the inn has a
distinctive shingled exterior with blue-and-white trim and shutters.
The inn features glorious flower arrangements, five cozy fireplaces
(four within guest rooms), a sun deck, and interesting antiques from
around the world. Guest rooms feature imported canopy beds and
have sitting areas and romantic turn-of-the-century decor; one guest
room even offers a Jacuzzi. Refreshments and hors d'oeuvres are
served in the evening, and a full gourmet breakfast is graciously
served on fine china and silver.

Blue Quail Inn and Cottages

1908 Bath Street, Santa Barbara, CA 93101
Phone: (805) 687–2300 / (800) 676–1622
Key: Inn/Cottages; 9 units; Moderate–Superior; No smoking; Credit
cards; No handicapped access

Antiques and a country motif decorate the individual rooms and
suites of this redwood-frame inn and its four cottages. The cottages
feature their own living room and bath, and all suites have their
own parlor. Bicycles and picnic lunches are available with prior
notice. In addition to the complimentary breakfast of freshly baked
popovers and muffins, guests enjoy cold lemonade or spiced apple
cider in the evening.

The Cheshire Cat

36 W. Valerio Street, Santa Barbara, CA 93101
Phone: (805) 569–1610; **Fax:** (805) 682–1876
Key: Inn; 11 units; Moderate–Deluxe; No smoking; No credit cards;
No handicapped access

Santa Barbara

Two vintage homes have been lovingly restored to create a "fairy-tale" b&b with delicate Laura Ashley wall coverings and fabrics, high ceilings, bay windows, and lots of private nooks. The inn offers eleven guest rooms, all with private baths, English antiques, and king- or queen-size brass beds, and some rooms feature a fireplace, patio, or spa. Flowers, chocolates, and liqueurs are placed in each room. Names of the guest rooms are taken from *Alice's Adventures in Wonderland*, and especially notable is Alice's own suite. Breakfast is served in the dining room on chilly days and on the patio in warm weather; wine and cheese are offered on Saturday evenings. A relaxing courtyard patio is nestled between the two homes of the inn, and a spa is built into the private gazebo.

The Glenborough Inn, Santa Barbara

The Glenborough Inn

1327 Bath Street, Santa Barbara, CA 93101
Phone: (805) 966–0589; **Fax:** (805) 564–7110
Key: Inn/Cottage; 9 units; Moderate–Superior; No smoking; Credit cards; No handicapped access

This 1906 Craftsman house and the 1880s summer cottage kitty-corner across the street provide the nine guest accommodations at the inn. The main house offers a cozy parlor with wood-burning stove, comfortable antiques, oak floors with oriental rugs, guest refrigerator, and games and reading material. Four upstairs rooms share a bath and feature nostalgic, turn-of-the-century decor; the main house offers a private garden suite with fireplace, sitting room, private entrance and deck, and patio with fountain. The cottage offers two spacious suites with canopies, fireplaces, private entrances, and private baths as well as two guest rooms with private baths and pretty antiques. Guests are treated to a full gourmet breakfast prepared from scratch and served in the room or in the gardens. A fully enclosed outdoor hot tub may be enjoyed in total privacy, and hot and cold beverages, cookies, and homemade hors d'oeuvres are offered either fireside or in the gardens each evening. Bicycles are available.

Long's Sea View B&B

317 Piedmont Road, Santa Barbara, CA 93105
Phone: (805) 687–2947
Key: Home; 1 unit; Moderate; No smoking; No credit cards; No handicapped access

This home b&b, located near Santa Barbara attractions, offers a rural atmosphere within the city. A full breakfast featuring tree-ripened orange juice in season is served on a 45-foot-long patio that affords views of the ocean, the Channel Islands, and the family orchard. The large, airy guest room has a king-size bed, antique furnishings, and a private bath and entrance; a third person may be accommodated in the adjoining den. Wine is served on arrival and guests may enjoy the patio and gardens.

Ocean View House

P.O. Box 20065, Santa Barbara, CA 93102
Phone: (805) 966–6659
Key: Home; 1–2 units; Inexpensive; No smoking; No credit cards; No handicapped access

This private home, located in a quiet suburban neighborhood, is within walking distance of the ocean. The guest room with antiques adjoins a private bath and paneled den with television. Guests may breakfast on the backyard patio with ocean views. An extended continental fare is served on china. The complimentary wine and sherry in the room may be enjoyed on the patio while watching the ships cross the ocean. Well equipped for children, the fenced yard is grassy and sports a playhouse complete with toys. A two-night-minimum stay is required. Pets are allowed on approval.

The Old Yacht Club Inn

431 Corona del Mar, Santa Barbara, CA 93103
Phone: (805) 962–1277/962–3989 / (800) 549–1676 (CA) / (800) 676–1676
Key: Inn; 9 units; Moderate–Superior; No smoking; Credit cards; No handicapped access

Just one-half block from the beach is Santa Barbara's first b&b, composed now of two old residences that sit side by side. The original b&b structure was the city's yacht club in the 1920s, and the 1925-built home next door became an inn expansion in 1983. Together the homes, comfortably decorated in antiques and colorful fabrics, offer nine guest rooms filled with homey touches, decanters of sherry, and oriental rugs; most rooms offer sitting areas and private entries, and all accommodations have private baths. Guests may sip sherry by the parlor fire or on the porch, and the inn is well-known for its gourmet breakfasts featuring omelettes, quiches, frittatas, or French toast. Candlelight dinners may be arranged at the inn, and guests are able to use the inn's bicycles, beach towels, and beach chairs. The inn provides golfing privileges at a nearby country club.

The Olive House

1604 Olive Street, Santa Barbara, CA 93101
Phone: (805) 962–4902
Key: Inn; 6 units; Moderate–Superior; No smoking; Credit cards; Handicapped access, 2 units

This 1904 California Craftsman home was saved from destruction in 1980, moved to its present site, and lovingly restored to its original beauty. Bay windows and window seats, stained and leaded glass, redwood-paneled wainscots, and coffered ceilings grace the interior of the inn, which is decorated eclectically in a blend of comfortable seating alongside selected antiques. The guest rooms offer private baths, queen- or king-size beds, and some decks and/or views of the ocean and city. Newspapers and coffee greet early risers; the extended continental fare is served in the spacious, sunny dining room equipped with a studio grand piano for guests' use. Refreshments are served in the living room with fireplace in the late afternoon. The inn is located in a quiet residential area near the Mission and is a short walk from State Street shops and entertainment.

The Parsonage

1600 Olive Street, Santa Barbara, CA 93101
Phone: (805) 962–9336
Key: Inn; 6 units; Moderate–Superior; Limited smoking; Credit cards; No handicapped access

This Queen Anne–Victorian house was built as a parsonage for the Trinity Episcopal Church in 1892. Located in the upper east residential area, it is near downtown attractions. A private solarium in the master suite offers views of the city and Channel Islands. Oriental rugs, antiques, and bird's-eye-redwood woodwork enhance the former rectory interiors. The special Honeymoon Suite boasts a bedroom, solarium, and private bath along with a king-size canopy bed, stained-glass windows, and outstanding views. Breakfast is served outside on the spacious sundeck with gazebo.

Simpson House Inn

121 E. Arrellaga, Santa Barbara, CA 93101
Phone: (805) 963–7067 / (800) 676–1280
Key: Inn; 6 units; Moderate–Superior; No smoking; Credit cards; Handicapped access, 1 unit

This 1874-built b&b, honored with a "Structure of Merit" award, is nestled on a secluded acre of grounds with tall hedges, English gardens, curving paths, lawns, and mature shade trees and is within walking distance of town. The restored inn, appointed throughout with tasteful antiques, includes a spacious sitting room with library and fireplace and an adjoining formal dining room. French doors lead

Simpson House Inn, Santa Barbara

to a garden veranda with white wicker seating. The six guest rooms, several named for the original Simpson family owners, offer special features such as English laces, oriental rugs, antiques, and queen- or king-size beds; all units boast private baths. The Robert and Julia Simpson Room features a private sitting area and French doors that open onto a spacious garden deck, and the Parlor Room boasts a bay window, and small library. The full morning meal is served on the veranda, the brick patio, the private decks, or in the dining room and consists of such specialties as Apple French Toast and Simpson House Savory Eggs. The inn offers evening wine and hors d'oeuvres as well as afternoon tea on request.

The Tiffany Inn

1323 De la Vina Street, Santa Barbara, CA 93101
Phone: (805) 963–2283
Key: Inn; 7 units; Moderate–Deluxe; No smoking; Credit cards; No handicapped access

This 1898 Victorian home has been completely restored with its diamond-paned windows, wood staircase, and authentic bath intact. Guests enjoy an old-fashioned garden with wicker furniture and a lattice-covered porch as well as evening wine and cheese before a parlor fire. Guest rooms with turn-of-the-century furnishings, queen-size beds, and several fireplaces offer both shared and private baths. A honeymoon suite is also available with Jacuzzi tub for two, as is a third-floor penthouse suite with private balcony, refrigerator, sitting room, and Jacuzzi bath; guests in the suites enjoy breakfast in the room. The fully homemade breakfast, which includes quiche, French toast, muffins, and breads, is served each morning in the dining room or on the old-fashioned porch.

The Upham Hotel & Garden Cottages

1404 De la Vina Street, Santa Barbara, CA 93101
Phone: (805) 962–0058 / (800) 727–0876; **Fax:** (805) 963–2825
Key: Inn/Hotel/Cottages; 49 units; Moderate–Deluxe; Smoking OK; Credit cards; No handicapped access

Claiming to be the "oldest continuously operating hostelry in southern California," this restored 1871 Victorian and its adjoining cottages are nestled on a garden-filled acre in downtown Santa Barbara. The individually decorated rooms offer period furnishings and antiques and cozy comforters; some accommodations have fireplaces, and many boast private porches or patios. Guests enjoy wine and cheese around the lobby fireplace in late afternoon; a complimentary continental breakfast is offered each morning in the lobby or on the garden veranda. The breakfast includes freshly brewed coffee and tea, juices, seasonal fruits, cereals, and a variety of muffins, breads, and pastries; the morning newspaper is also complimentary. The inn offers banquet and conference facilities.

Villa Rosa

15 Chapala Street, Santa Barbara, CA 93101
Phone: (805) 966–0851; **Fax:** (805) 962–7159
Key: Inn/Hotel; 18 units; Moderate–Deluxe; Smoking OK; Credit cards; No handicapped access

Claiming "eighteen rooms just eighty-four steps from the beach," this hotel-type b&b is a contemporary rendition with rough-hewn beams, plantation shutters, and louvered doors. A lounge adjoins the pool and spa in the garden courtyard. Included are a continental breakfast and complimentary port and sherry offered in the lobby each evening. Guests are also treated to afternoon wine and cheese. Light and airy guest rooms and suites, all with private baths, boast pastel color schemes and a combination of contemporary and Spanish Colonial furnishings.

Channel Road Inn, Santa Monica

Channel Road Inn

219 W. Channel Road, Santa Monica, CA 90402
Phone: (310) 459–1920; **Fax:** (310) 454–9920
Key: Inn; 14 units; Moderate–Deluxe; No smoking; Credit cards; Handicapped access, 1 unit

Claiming to be the oldest residence in the city, this structure was built in 1910 and moved to its present site at the mouth of Santa Monica Canyon several years ago. The three-story Colonial Revival inn has been renovated and decorated to reflect a fine Santa Monica home in the 1920s with pastel-pink upholstered furnishings, lavender Chinese rug, oak floors, birch woodwork and a stately fireplace. Guests enjoy a sunny library with white wicker and green chintz furnishings. The fourteen guest rooms and suites, all with private baths, are individually decorated and some rooms boast four-poster beds, lace bed coverings, and Amish quilts. Bathrooms are stocked with bathrobes and bubble bath, and all accommodations offer telephones, armoire-tucked televisions and refrigerators, fresh fruit and flowers, and evening turn-down service with berries and a tray of home-baked cookies. Served in the sun-filled breakfast room or in the guest room, breakfast includes juice, homemade muffins and breads, fresh fruit, and a hot dish such as egg soufflé or baked bread pudding. Complimentary wine and cheese are served each afternoon. The inn also offers guests a hillside spa and bicycles for biking to the beach one block away, as well as small conference facilities.

The Seal Beach Inn and Gardens

212 Fifth Street, Seal Beach, CA 90740
Phone: (310) 493-2416; **Fax:** (310) 799-0483
Key: Inn/Hotel; 23 units; Moderate–Deluxe; No smoking; Credit cards; Handicapped access, 1 unit

This romantic, classic country inn with lush, colorful gardens sits in the charming village of Seal Beach. In a quiet residential neighborhood one block from the beach, the old-world b&b with blue canopies, window boxes, shutters, and brick courtyard offers twenty-three guest rooms, no two alike. Most guest rooms have kitchens and sitting areas, and all have private baths, antiques, televisions, and telephones. Guests enjoy a library with tiled fireplace, brass chandeliers, an ornate antique tin ceiling, lace curtains, and vintage furnishings. The generous morning fare is served in the tearoom, by the pool, or in the gardens that are dotted with interesting art and remain abloom year-round. Special packages are available.

Storybook Inn

28717 Highway 18, P.O. Box 362, Skyforest, CA 92385
Phone: (714) 336-1483
Key: Inn/Cottage; 10 units; Moderate–Deluxe; No smoking; Credit cards; No handicapped access

Skyforest

This 9,000-square-foot three-story mansion was built in the 1940s as an entertainment home. Situated 2 miles from Lake Arrowhead, the inn has views for 100 miles. Accommodations include nine rooms decorated in antiques in the mansion, plus an adjoining two-bedroom cabin with fireplace, loft room, deck for barbecues or sunbathing, and full kitchen. Guest rooms are decorated in various themes, such as the Gone with the Wind room; all accommodations come with elaborate flower bouquets, and guests receive the morning paper in their rooms. The full breakfast varies around the themes of the holidays and may be enjoyed in bed, in the dining area, or in the solarium. The inn also offers a social hour with hot and cold hors d'oeuvres. The 2,500-square-foot lobby features plush carpeting, two massive brick fireplaces, and mahogany paneling. A gazebo and a conference room with wet bar and antiques are available for weddings.

Cottonwood Meadow

2601 Baseline Avenue, Solvang, CA 93463
Phone: (805) 688–2602
Key: Home; 3 units; Moderate; No smoking; No credit cards; No handicapped access

This ranch-style b&b is situated on five country acres near the Danish community of Solvang and boasts horses, sheep, chickens, and more than 300 assorted trees. The spacious, two-story cedar house offers three bedrooms for guests: two rooms upstairs that share a bath and a large suite downstairs. The breakfast of Danish pastries, blueberry muffins, two types of fresh fruit, and juice is served in the formal dining room or on the outside deck. Guests enjoy the sunken conversation pit in the living room decorated with antiques and Navajo rugs.

Petersen Village Inn

1576 Mission Drive, Solvang, CA 93463
Phone: (805) 688–3121 / (800) 321–8985
Key: Inn/Hotel; 40 units; Moderate–Deluxe; Limited smoking; Credit cards; Handicapped access, 1 unit

Petersen Village Inn, Solvang

This Danish-style hotel is a part of a "village" in the heart of Solvang. The b&b rooms are scattered throughout the "village" on the second floor of many of the dozen village buildings and offer views of the quaint Danish streets, shops, and courtyard. Each hotel minisuite is decorated individually, and many have wallpapers, authentic canopy beds, sitting areas with couches, down pillows, and balconies. A complimentary breakfast of hard rolls, pastry, coffee, and juice is served in the Petersen Square courtyard bakery each morning, and guests may enjoy wine and cheese in the wine bar each evening. This family-owned hotel offers a European touch and personal services as well as large hotel amenities such as dining and conference facilities.

Inn on Summer Hill

2520 Lillie Avenue, Summerland, CA 93067
Phone: (805) 969–9998 / (800) 999–8999; **Fax:** (805) 969–9998
Key: Inn; 16 units; Moderate–Deluxe; No smoking; Credit cards; Handicapped access, 1 unit

This California Craftsman–style inn, built in 1990, has been designed with arbors, balconies, and river-rock columns and walkways. English flower gardens and local tropical vegetation are lush; the pansy is the inn's signature flower, used extensively throughout the gardens. The interior of the b&b is a romantic delight, filled with an enjoyable extravagance of prints, colors, and keepsakes in an elegant European-country decor. Each of the sixteen suites offers

Inn on Summer Hill, Summerland

a totally different style of furnishings, but each accommodation boasts fresh flowers, down comforters, quilts, chaise, loveseat, chairs, refrigerator, and armoire filled with VCR, television, and stereo. The private baths include hair dryers, telephones, hand-painted porcelain laundry hampers, and thick terry robes. The canopy beds of the inn are draped in varying floral, striped, and gingham fabrics; in some rooms the beds are so high that pine stepping stools are provided. Every room has French doors leading to a patio or balcony view of the sea at this inn near the exclusive community of Montecito. Breakfast, served in bed or on the patio, consists of fresh fruits, juice, choices of breakfast breads, and a special hot entree such as Belgian waffles. Guests also enjoy afternoon wine, cheese, and fruit, as well as evening desserts, served in the fireside country dining room.

Loma Vista Bed and Breakfast

33350 La Serena Way, Temecula, CA 92390
Phone: (714) 676–7047
Key: Inn; 6 units; Moderate–Superior; No smoking; Credit cards; No handicapped access

Surrounded by area wineries on a private hilltop is this Mission-style bed & breakfast offering panoramic views of lush citrus groves, flowing vineyards, and mountains. Guests may choose from six guest rooms, all with air conditioning and private baths; the Champagne Room features a king-size bed and Art Deco decor, and the Chardonnay Room is appointed throughout with oak, an old-style pull-chain toilet, and private patio. The Sauvignon Blanc Room is decorated in light desert hues and boasts a private patio overlooking the entire Temecula Valley. The stay at Loma Vista includes a gourmet champagne breakfast as well as medal-winning Temecula wine and hors d'oeuvres served on the view patio each evening.

The Venice Beach House

No. 15, Thirtieth Avenue, Venice, CA 90291
Phone: (310) 823–1966
Key: Inn; 9 units; Moderate–Superior; No smoking; Credit cards; No handicapped access

The 1911 historic-landmark building offers guest rooms and suites, some with balconies, sitting rooms, whirlpool tubs, or side-by-side claw-foot tubs. All the charming guest accommodations feature antiques and antique quilts; one accommodation boasts a fireplace. The generous continental breakfast is served in bed, in the parlor, or on the veranda with ocean views. In the evening, guests share refreshments in front of a cozy fire or on the veranda watching the summer sun set.

Bella Maggiore Inn

67 S. California Street, Ventura, CA 93001
Phone: (805) 652–0277 / (800) 523–8479 (CA)
Key: Inn; 28 units; Moderate–Deluxe; Smoking OK; Credit cards; No handicapped access

As a part of the Ventura Historic Walking Tour, this b&b stands out with its classical Italian facade of stone and umbrella awnings. The downstairs area of the inn, its lobby, features antiques, a baby grand piano, and fresh flowers from the garden. Guests may enjoy the full breakfast here as well as afternoon refreshments and appetizers. The picturesque patio courtyard with Roman fountain is surrounded by flowers and greenery and is a breakfast locale as well. The guest rooms at the inn feature private baths, ceiling fans, shutters, fresh flowers, candy, Italian Capuan beds, and a variety of color schemes. The inn has recently added a new wing, which features three-room suites with fireplaces, wet bars, microwave ovens, refrigerators, skylights, Jacuzzi spas, and elegant decor. Some guest rooms open onto the patio or sun deck at this European-style inn just blocks from the beach.

La Mer, Ventura

La Mer

411 Poli Street, Ventura, CA 93001
Phone: (805) 643–3600
Key: Inn; 5 units; Moderate–Deluxe; No smoking; Credit cards; No handicapped access

This 1890-built Cape Cod–style b&b is nestled on a hillside a few blocks from town and grants inspiring views of the ocean. The distinctive guest rooms, all with private baths, are each a European adventure with such offerings as the Madame Pompadour Room with bay window, balcony, and woodstove; the Austrian Wienerwald with sunken tub; and the Flemish Peter Paul Rubens with an ocean-view veranda. The guest rooms feature antiques, cozy European comforters, and complimentary wine; all but one room have private entrances. A breakfast buffet featuring apple strudel or homemade cake is served in the Bavarian-style dining room from 8:00 to 9:30 A.M. each morning; the inn also serves wine, champagne, sparkling apple cider, or Austrian beer. Guests at this old-world b&b have use of a turn-of-the-century lounge. The inn also offers therapeutic massages by appointment, as well as antique horse-and-carriage rides to the country (with gourmet picnic baskets) or on wine-tasting excursions. Midweek packages are available.

Hendrick Inn

2124 E. Merced Avenue, West Covina, CA 91791
Phone: (818) 919–2125
Key: Home; 4 units; Inexpensive; Smoking OK; No credit cards; No handicapped access

Once photographed both inside and out by *Life* magazine, this rambling home has been a b&b since 1980. Guests from all over the world have come to enjoy a beautiful deck area with swimming pool, a Jacuzzi, and two living rooms with fireplaces. Guest accommodations at this reasonable retreat include a master suite with king-size bed and private bath (available for stays of three nights or longer); a rainbow-decorated guest room with double bed and shared bath; and two guest rooms with three twin-size beds and shared baths. The stay includes a full breakfast, which varies each day; other meals are available upon arrangement. The home b&b is twenty-five minutes from Disneyland and an hour from Los Angeles International Airport.

Reservation and/or Referral Agencies and B&B Associations in California

A majority of the following reservation and/or referral agencies and associations request that a self-addressed, stamped envelope accompany any requests for information.

Reservation and/or Referral Agencies:

Accommodation Referral
  Reservations
P.O. Box 59
St. Helena, CA 94574
(707) 963–8466 / 963–VINO
Fax: (707) 963–1762
Serving: Napa County

Accommodations in Santa
  Barbara
3344 State Street
Santa Barbara, CA 93105
(805) 687–9191 / (800) 292–2222
Fax: (805) 569–0726
*Serving: Santa Barbara and
  Ventura counties*

American Family Inn/Bed &
  Breakfast San Francisco
P.O. Box 349
San Francisco, CA 94101
(415) 931–3083 / (800) 452–8249
Fax: (415) 921–2273
*Serving: San Francisco,
  Carmel/Monterey, Marin
  County, Wine Country*

American Historic Homes Bed
  & Breakfast
P.O. Box 336
Dana Point, CA 92629
(714) 496–6953
Fax: (714) 499–4022
*Serving: California, United
  States*

Bed & Breakfast Exchange
1458 Lincoln Avenue #3
Calistoga, CA 94515
(707) 942–5900 / (800) 464–2924
*Serving: Napa and Sonoma
  counties, San Francisco,
  northern coast*

Bed & Breakfast Exchange of
  Marin
45 Entrata Avenue
San Anselmo, CA 94960
(415) 485–1971
Serving: Marin County

Bed & Breakfast Homestay
P.O. Box 326
Cambria, CA 93428
(805) 927–4613
*Serving: Cambria and
  the Central Coast*

Bed & Breakfast International
  Reservations
P.O. Box 282910
San Francisco, CA 94128-2910
(415) 696–1690 / (800) 872–4500
  (reservations)
Fax: (415) 696–1699
*Serving: California, southern
  Nevada*

Appendix

Bed & Breakfast of Los
  Angeles
32074 Waterside Lane
Westlake, CA 91361
(818) 889–8870
*Serving: Ventura, Los Angeles,
  and Orange counties and
  the limited coast from San
  Diego to San Francisco*

Bed & Breakfast of Southern
  California
1943 Sunny Crest Drive, Suite
  #304
Fullerton, CA 92635
(714) 738–8361 / (800) 336–4143
Serving: southern California

California Houseguests
  International
18653 Ventura Blvd. #190
Tarzana, CA 91356
(818) 344–7878
*Serving: California, selected
  U.S. states, and foreign
  countries*

Christian B&B of America
P.O. Box 336
Dana Point, CA 92629
(714) 496–6953
*Serving: California, United
  States*

Country Inns Lodging
  Information
615 N. Main Street
Fort Bragg, CA 95437
(707) 964–0640
Serving: Mendocino coast

El Camino Real Bed &
  Breakfast
P.O. Box 7155
Northridge, CA 91327-7155
(818) 363–6753
*Serving: southern California,
  Utah, and Idaho*

Eye Openers Bed & Breakfast
  Reservations
P.O. Box 694
Altadena, CA 91003
(213) 684–4428 / (818) 797–2055
Fax: (818) 798–3640
Serving: California

Hospitality Plus
P.O. Box 388
San Juan Capistrano, CA
  92693
(714) 496–6953
Serving: California

Inns of Point Reyes
P.O. Box 145
Inverness, CA 94937
(415) 663–1420 / (415) 485–2649
Serving: west Marin County

Laguna Beach B&B
33261 Mesa Vista
Dana Point, CA 92629
(714) 496–6953
*Serving: Laguna Beach, Newport
Beach, and San Clemente*

Meagan's Friends Bed &
  Breakfast Reservations
1776 Royal Way
San Luis Obispo, CA 93405
(805) 544–4406
Fax: (805) 546–8642
*Serving: San Luis Obispo
  and Santa Barbara counties
  and U.S. referrals*

Napa Valley's Finest Lodgings
(707) 224–4667
*Serving: Napa Valley and
Sonoma and Monterey counties*

The Quince Street Trolley
  B&B Accommodations
P.O. Box 7654
San Diego, CA 92167
(619) 422–7009 / (619) 226–8454
Serving: San Diego County

Rent A Room Bed & Breakfast
11531 Varna Street
Garden Grove, CA 92640
(714) 638–1406
*Serving: region from Los
  Angeles to San Diego*

Wine Country Bed & Breakfast
P.O. Box 3211
Santa Rosa, CA 95403
(707) 578–1661
Serving: Wine Country

Wine Country Reservations
P.O. Box 5059
Napa, CA 94581-0059
(707) 257–7757
Fax: (707) 257–7844
*Serving: Napa Valley
  and portions of Sonoma
  County*

Appendix

Associations

Bed & Breakfast Association
of Napa Valley
P.O. Box 5059
Napa, CA 94581-0059
(707) 257-7757
Fax: (707) 257-7844
Serving: Napa Valley

Bed & Breakfast Innkeepers of
Humboldt County
P.O. Box KS-40
Ferndale, CA 95536
(707) 786-4000
Serving: Humboldt County

Bed & Breakfast Innkeepers of
Northern California
(800) 284-INNS
Serving: northern California

Bed & Breakfast Innkeepers of
Santa Cruz
P.O. Box 464
Santa Cruz, CA 95061
(408) 425-8212
Serving: Santa Cruz County

Bed & Breakfast Innkeepers of
Southern California
P.O. Box 15425
Los Angeles, CA 90015-0385
*Serving: region from Cambria
to San Diego*

Eureka Bed & Breakfast
Association
P.O. Box 207
Eureka, CA 95502
Serving: Eureka

Gold Country Inns of Tuolumne
County
P.O. Box 462
Sonora, CA 95370
(209) 533-3445
Serving: Tuolumne County

Sacramento Innkeepers'
Association
2120 "G" Street
Sacramento, CA 95816
(916) 441-5007
Serving: Sacramento

Santa Barbara Bed & Breakfast
Innkeepers Guild
P.O. Box 90734
Santa Barbara, CA 93190
(805) 963-8191 / (800) 776-9176
Serving: Santa Barbara

Wine Country Inns of Sonoma
County
P.O. Box 51
Geyserville, CA 95441
(707) 433-INNS
*Serving: Sonoma County,
Wine Country*

Yosemite Bed & Breakfasts of
Mariposa County
P.O. Box 1100
Mariposa, CA 95338
*Serving: Yosemite Park,
Mariposa County (Gold
Country)*

INDEX

Index

Index

Index

Index

Index

Index

Index

About the Author

Also the author of *Bed & Breakfast in the Caribbean* and *Southern California: Off the Beaten Path*, Ms. Strong, along with husband Rob, created and ran a nine-guest-room, turn-of-the-century b&b inn in central California. Ms. Strong originally began work on this publication at the request of inn guests who were constantly inquiring about a book that would include descriptions of all the state's offerings. This fifth, thoroughly updated, and expanded edition of *Bed & Breakfast in California* follows highly successful previous editions and offers more than 400 bed & breakfast establishments throughout California. Kathy hopes the book will not only better serve the experienced b&b fans but convince the timid first-timers to give this delightful kind of accommodation a try.